Tarkeshwar Barua, Kamal Kant Hiran, Ritesh Kumar Jain, Ruchi Doshi
Machine Learning with Python

Also of Interest

Mobile Applications Development.
With Python in Kivy Framework
Tarkeshwar Barua, Ruchi Doshi, Kamal Kant Hiran, 2021
ISBN 978-3-11-068938-9, e-ISBN (PDF) 978-3-11-068948-8

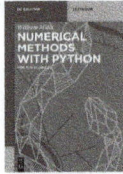

Numerical Methods with Python.
for the Sciences
William Miles, 2023
ISBN 978-3-11-077645-4, e-ISBN (PDF) 978-3-11-077664-5

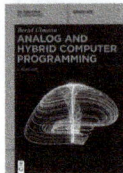

Analog and Hybrid Computer Programming
Bernd Ulmann, 2023
ISBN 978-3-11-078759-7, e-ISBN (PDF) 978-3-11-078773-3

Analog Computing
Bernd Ulmann, 2022
ISBN 978-3-11-078761-0, e-ISBN (PDF) 978-3-11-078774-0

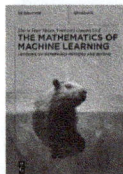

The Mathematics of Machine Learning.
Lectures on Supervised Methods and Beyond
Maria Han Veiga, François Gaston Ged, 2024
ISBN 978-3-11-128847-5, e-ISBN (PDF) 978-3-11-128899-4

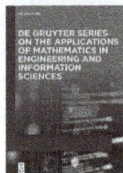

De Gruyter Series on the Applications of Mathematics in Engineering and
Information Sciences
Edited by Mangey Ram
ISSN 2626-5427, e-ISSN 2626-5435

Tarkeshwar Barua, Kamal Kant Hiran,
Ritesh Kumar Jain, Ruchi Doshi

Machine Learning with Python

—

DE GRUYTER

Authors

Tarkeshwar Barua
Professor of Computer Application
Chandigarh Group of colleges
Punjab, India
tbarua1@gmail.com

Ritesh Kumar Jain
Geetanjali Institute of Technical Studies
Udaipur
India
riteshkrjain@gmail.com

Kamal Kant Hiran
Department of CSE
Sir Padampat Singhania University
Udaipur, India
kamal.hiran@spsu.ac.in

Ruchi Doshi
Founder & CEO
RESAISHALA Technocrats Pvt. Ltd.
Udaipur, Rajasthan, India
doshiruchi18@gmail.com

ISBN 978-3-11-069716-2
e-ISBN (PDF) 978-3-11-069718-6
e-ISBN (EPUB) 978-3-11-069725-4

Library of Congress Control Number: 2024934747

Bibliographic information published by the Deutsche Nationalbibliothek
The Deutsche Nationalbibliothek lists this publication in the Deutsche Nationalbibliografie;
detailed bibliographic data are available on the Internet at http://dnb.dnb.de.

© 2024 Walter de Gruyter GmbH, Berlin/Boston
Cover image: style-photography/iStock/Getty Images Plus
Typesetting: Integra Software Services Pvt. Ltd.

www.degruyter.com

Contents

Chapter 3
Data Preprocessing in Python —— 90

Chapter 7
Neural Networks and Deep Learning —— 360

Chapter 1
Introduction to Machine Learning

1.1 What Is Machine Learning?

Machine learning (ML) is a discipline within the field of artificial intelligence (AI) that concentrates on the creation of algorithms and models, allowing computer systems to acquire knowledge and make forecasts or choices without the need for explicit programming. The primary objective of ML is to empower computers to autonomously learn and enhance their performance based on experience or data.

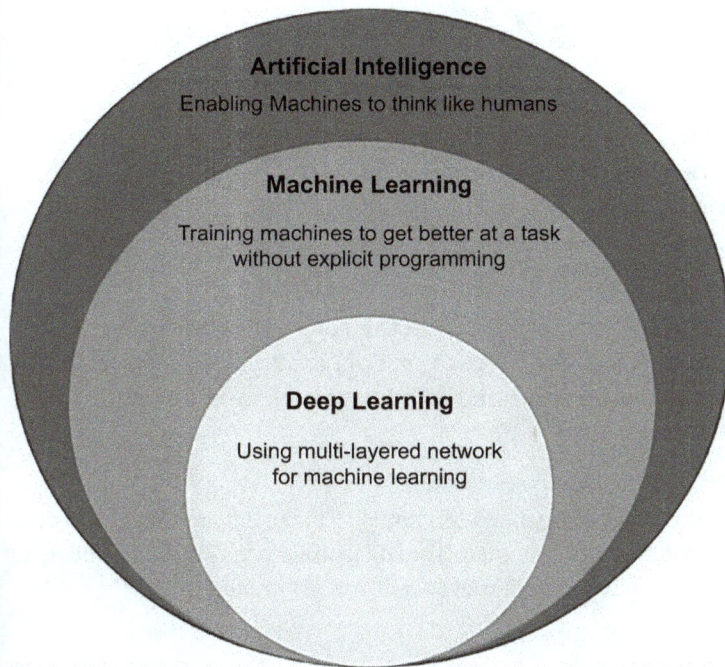

Fig. 1.1: AI, ML, and deep learning.

1.1.1 Definition of Machine Learning

Different experts and sources may provide slightly varied definitions of ML, reflecting different perspectives on the field. Here are a few diverse definitions given by various authorities:

https://doi.org/10.1515/9783110697186-001

Arthur Samuel (1959)
"Machine learning is a field of study that gives computers the ability to learn without being explicitly programmed."

Tom Mitchell (1997)
"A computer program is said to learn from experience E with respect to some class of tasks T and performance measure P, if its performance at tasks in T, as measured by P, improves with experience E."

Andrew Ng (Cofounder of Coursera, Stanford University)
"Machine learning is the science of getting computers to act without being explicitly programmed."

Pedro Domingos (Author of *The Master Algorithm*)
"Machine learning is the automation of discovery, and it is responsible for making our smartphones work, helping doctors diagnose diseases, beating humans at board games, and much more."

Ian Goodfellow and Yoshua Bengio (Authors of *Deep Learning*)
"Machine learning is the field of study that gives computers the ability to learn without being explicitly programmed. It is a type of artificial intelligence that provides systems with the ability to automatically learn and improve from experience."

Microsoft Azure Machine Learning Documentation
"Machine learning is the process of using algorithms to make a computer make decisions without being explicitly programmed. The algorithms use statistical models to enable a computer to carry out tasks without specific programming."

1.1.2 Historical Background

The historical progression of ML encompasses multiple decades, and its advancement is characterized by significant milestones and contributions. Provided below is a concise summary of the historical context of ML.

1950s – Early Concepts
The establishment of ML can be traced back to the 1950s when renowned figures like Alan Turing made significant contributions. Turing introduced the concept of ma-

chines capable of acquiring knowledge through experience, which subsequently paved the way for future advancements in this field.

1956 – Dartmouth Conference

The phrase "artificial intelligence" (AI) was introduced during the Dartmouth Conference in 1956. This conference established the foundation for the development of AI and ML as multidisciplinary areas of study.

1960s – Decision Trees and Nearest Neighbors

The development of decision tree algorithms and the introduction of nearest neighbors algorithms occurred during the 1960s, thereby making notable contributions to the early techniques of pattern recognition.

1970s – Backpropagation and Rule-Based Systems

The algorithm for training artificial neural networks, known as backpropagation, was first introduced in the 1970s. Similarly, rule-based systems, which emphasize the explicit programming of decision rules, also experienced a surge in popularity during this era.

1980s – Expert Systems

Expert systems, which employed rule-based logic to imitate human decision-making, attained prominence during the 1980s. Nevertheless, because of their incapacity to effectively manage uncertainty and readily adapt to novel information, there was a redirection of attention.

1990s – Support Vector Machines and Boosting

The 1990s witnessed the emergence of support vector machines (SVMs) to classify tasks and boost algorithms for enhancing the efficacy of feeble learners.

Late 1990s – Rise of Data Mining

The late 1990s witnessed an upsurge in fascination with data mining, a field closely associated with ML, which concentrated on extracting knowledge from data, owing to the increased availability of large datasets.

2000s – Ensemble Learning and Deep Learning

The 2000s witnessed a surge in the popularity of ensemble learning techniques, which amalgamate numerous models to augment performance. In parallel, the emergence of deep learning, a branch of ML that concentrates on neural networks with multiple layers, was propelled by the advancement in computational power.

2010s – Deep Learning Dominance

The decade of the 2010s observed the prevalence of deep learning in diverse domains, attaining significant advancements in the realms of image and speech identification, natural language comprehension, and beyond. The progress made in technological infrastructure, particularly the utilization of graphics processing units (GPUs), proved to be pivotal in the triumph of deep learning.

Present – Continued Advancements

ML is experiencing rapid evolution, characterized by continuous research and development in various domains such as reinforcement learning, transfer learning, and explainable AI. The application of this field extends across diverse sectors including healthcare, finance, and autonomous systems.

The historical context of ML showcases a progression from initial conceptualizations to the present era of sophisticated algorithms and widespread practical implementations. The advancement in computational capabilities, the availability of extensive datasets, and interdisciplinary collaborations have collectively acted as driving forces for the advancement of this field.

1.1.3 Types of Machine Learning

ML, a branch of AI, enables computers to acquire knowledge and reach conclusions without the need for explicit instructions. This revolutionary discipline encompasses different methodologies, each designed to address specific learning situations. The main forms of ML comprise supervised learning, unsupervised learning, and reinforcement learning, each providing distinct approaches and applications for solving various problems. Now, let us delve into an investigation of these foundational classifications.

1.1.3.1 Supervised Learning

In supervised learning, the algorithm undergoes training on a dataset that has been labeled, wherein the input data is matched with corresponding output labels. The objective is for the algorithm to acquire knowledge of a mapping from the input to the output, such that when faced with new, unseen input data, it can make accurate predictions about the corresponding output.

No training data
required

Machine learns
from training
data

Unsupervised
Learning

Supervised
Learning

Types of Machine
Learning

Reinforcement
Learning

Machine learns
on its own

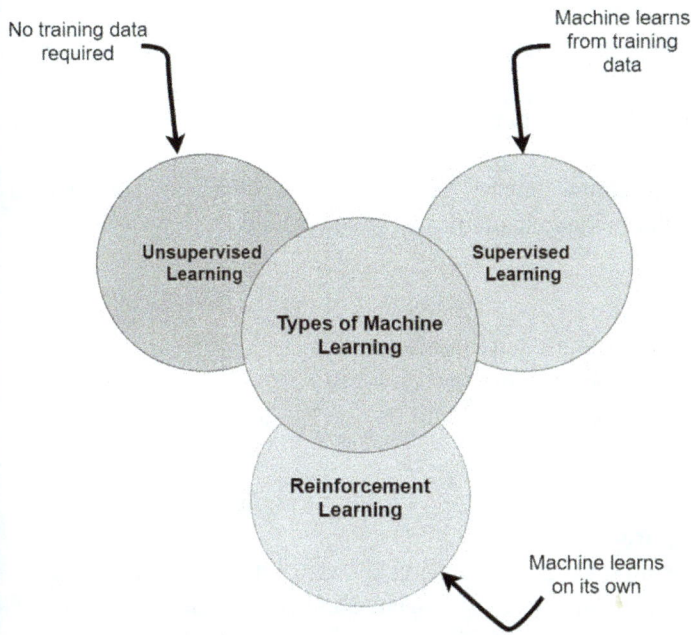

Fig 1.2: Types of machine learning.

Key Characteristics

Training data: The dataset used for training purposes comprises pairs of inputs and corresponding outputs, with each input having its correct output provided.
Learning objective: The algorithm aims to learn the relationship or mapping between inputs and outputs.
Examples: Common applications include image classification, spam filtering, and regression problems.

Example Scenario

Task: Predicting whether an email is spam or not.
Training data: Emails categorized as spam or nonspam.
Learning objective: The algorithm acquires knowledge to categorize new emails by recognizing recurring patterns from the data it has been trained on.

1.1.3.2 Unsupervised Learning

Unsupervised learning pertains to the handling of unlabeled data, whereby the algorithm is presented with data sans explicit instructions regarding its utilization. The system endeavors to ascertain patterns, relationships, or structures inherent within the data.

Key Characteristics

Training data: The dataset is unlabeled, meaning there are no predefined output labels.

Learning objective: Uncover concealed patterns or interconnections among the data.

Examples: Clustering, dimensionality reduction, and association rule learning are prevalent tasks within the field of unsupervised learning.

Example Scenario

Task: Grouping similar customer purchase behaviors.

Training data: Purchase data without specific labels.

Learning objective: The algorithm identifies natural groupings or clusters of similar purchase patterns.

1.1.3.3 Reinforcement Learning

Reinforcement learning entails an agent acquiring knowledge to reach conclusions by executing actions within a given setting. The agent obtains input in the form of rewards or penalties, enabling it to acquire skills to enhance its conduct and accomplish a particular aim.

Key Characteristics

Environment: The agent interacts with an environment and takes actions to achieve goals.

Feedback: The agent is provided with feedback through the dispensation of rewards or punishments contingent upon its enacted actions.

Learning objective: Learn a policy that maps states to actions to maximize cumulative rewards.

Examples: Game playing, such as the case with AlphaGo, robotic control, and the development of autonomous systems.

Example Scenario

Task: Teaching a computer program to play a game.

Environment: The game environment.

Learning objective: The agent learns a strategy (policy) to take actions that maximize the game score over time.

The three aforementioned ML classifications exhibit distinct methodologies for addressing problems according to the characteristics of the data at hand and the objectives of the learning process. Every classification possesses its own set of practical applications and is well-matched for specific scenarios.

1.1.4 Applications of Machine Learning

ML has penetrated multiple sectors, fundamentally transforming the method by which tasks are executed and choices are made. The uses of ML are varied and potent, encompassing fields such as healthcare, finance, marketing, and more. The ensuing paragraphs offer comprehensive analysis of a few principal applications.

Healthcare

Disease diagnosis: ML aids in diagnosing diseases by analyzing medical images (e.g., X-rays and MRIs) and identifying patterns indicative of specific conditions.
Predictive analytics: Predictive models are employed to forecast the occurrence of disease outbreaks, the likelihood of patient readmissions, and the estimation of individual health risks, thus enabling proactive healthcare interventions.

Finance

Fraud detection: ML algorithms scrutinize transaction data to discern atypical patterns and ascertain potentially deceitful activities in real time.
Algorithmic trading: Predictive models utilize their analytical capabilities to examine market trends and historical data, enhancing the process of making informed decisions within the realm of algorithmic trading and thereby optimizing investment strategies.

Marketing and E-Commerce

Recommendation systems: ML powers personalized recommendation engines in e-commerce platforms and streaming services, enhancing user experience by suggesting relevant products or content.
Customer segmentation: Clustering algorithms enable the segmentation of customers according to their behavior, thus providing businesses with the opportunity to customize marketing strategies for distinct customer groups.

Natural Language Processing (NLP)

Chatbots and virtual assistants: NLP facilitates the creation of conversational agents that possess the capability to comprehend and provide feedback to human language, thereby augmenting customer assistance and user engagements.
Language translation: ML enables the instantaneous translation of languages, thus dismantling linguistic obstacles and promoting worldwide communication.

Autonomous Vehicles

Object detection and recognition: ML algorithms are utilized to analyze sensor data to identify and categorize various entities such as objects, pedestrians, and obstacles. These algorithms play a crucial role in the decision-making process within autonomous vehicles.

Path planning: Reinforcement learning is applied for path planning, enabling vehicles to navigate complex environments and make dynamic decisions.

Image and Speech Recognition

Facial recognition: ML is employed for facial recognition in security systems, unlocking devices, and identity verification.

Speech-to-text and text-to-speech: NLP models convert spoken language into written text and vice versa, facilitating voice commands and accessibility features.

Manufacturing and Industry

Predictive maintenance: ML is capable of making predictions about equipment failures and maintenance requirements by examining sensor data, leading to a decrease in downtime and an enhancement in operational efficiency.

Quality control: Computer vision systems inspect and identify defects in manufactured products, ensuring quality standards are met.

Education

Personalized learning: ML models adapt educational content based on individual student progress, tailoring the learning experience to meet specific needs.

Student performance prediction: Predictive analytics identifies students at risk of academic challenges, allowing for timely intervention and support.

The aforementioned applications serve as prime examples of the multifaceted nature and profound capabilities of ML in diverse domains, fostering ingenuity and effectiveness in resolving intricate issues. As the progression of technology persists, the breadth of ML applications is projected to broaden, subsequently reforming sectors and enhancing daily existence.

1.1.5 Challenges in Machine Learning

Although ML has made notable progress, it also faces various obstacles that affect its progress, implementation, and efficacy. Resolving these obstacles is imperative for furthering the field and guaranteeing morally sound, resilient, and comprehensible ML systems. Presented below are the principal challenges encountered in ML.

Data Quality and Quantity

Challenge: ML models heavily depend on training data that is of high quality and sufficient in quantity. Inaccurate or biased predictions can result from datasets that are incomplete, biased, or contain noise.

Mitigation: Rigorous data preprocessing, augmentation, and ensuring diverse and representative datasets can help alleviate these challenges.

Bias and Fairness

Challenge: Models can inherit biases present in training data, perpetuating unfair and discriminatory outcomes. Ensuring fairness in predictions across different demographic groups is a critical concern.

Mitigation: Implementing fairness-aware algorithms, auditing models for biases, and promoting diversity in the data collection process are strategies to address bias.

Interpretability and Explainability

Challenge: Many ML models, particularly deep neural networks, are regarded as "opaque systems," posing difficulties in comprehending and deciphering their decision-making mechanisms.

Mitigation: Developing interpretable models, using model-agnostic interpretability tools, and incorporating explainability techniques can enhance transparency.

Overfitting and Underfitting

Challenge: Models may become too complex (overfitting) and memorize training data, leading to poor generalization. Conversely, overly simplistic models (underfitting) may fail to capture underlying patterns.

Mitigation: By utilizing methodologies such as regularization, cross-validation, and ensemble techniques, one can achieve a harmonious equilibrium between the issues of overfitting and underfitting.

Lack of Standardization

Challenge: The absence of standardized evaluation metrics, datasets, and model architectures can impede reproducibility and hinder fair comparisons between different models.

Mitigation: Encouraging open science practices, sharing benchmarks, and adopting standardized evaluation protocols contribute to increased transparency and collaboration.

Computational Complexity and Resource Requirements

Challenge: Training and deploying complex models, particularly deep learning models, can demand significant computational resources, limiting accessibility for smaller organizations or researchers.

Mitigation: Optimization techniques, model compression, and the use of specialized hardware can help manage computational demands.

Ethical Considerations

Challenge: Ethical concerns arise from biased models, potential misuse of AI, and the ethical implications of automated decision-making in critical areas such as healthcare and criminal justice.

Mitigation: Incorporating ethical considerations in model development, promoting diversity and inclusivity, and adhering to ethical guidelines and standards are essential.

Adversarial Attacks

Challenge: Adversarial attacks involve manipulating input data to mislead ML models, compromising their performance and reliability.

Mitigation: Developing robust models, incorporating adversarial training, and regularly updating models to counter emerging attack strategies are strategies to address this challenge.

Continuous Learning

Challenge: Many ML models are designed for static datasets, and adapting to evolving data over time (concept drift) is a challenge.

Mitigation: Implementing online learning approaches, retraining models periodically, and staying vigilant to changes in data distributions help address continuous learning challenges.

Privacy Concerns

Challenge: Handling sensitive information in training data raises privacy concerns, especially in healthcare and finance applications.

Mitigation: Adopting privacy-preserving techniques, such as federated learning and differential privacy, helps protect individual privacy while still allowing model training.

Addressing these challenges requires collaboration across the ML community, ongoing research, and a commitment to ethical and responsible AI development. As the field evolves, finding effective solutions to these challenges will be pivotal for the widespread and responsible deployment of ML systems.

1.2 Python in the Machine Learning Landscape

Python has emerged as the predominant programming language in the realm of ML due to its versatility, ease of utilization, and the existence of a wide range of libraries and frameworks. Its straightforward syntax and high degree of readability make it accessible to both novice and experienced programmers. Python's extensive support for data manipulation, statistical analysis, and ML libraries, such as Scikit-learn, TensorFlow, and PyTorch, has played a significant role in its widespread adoption.

Beyond its powerful libraries, Python boasts an energetic and engaged community that actively contributes to the development and enhancement of ML tools. The language's integration capabilities and compatibility with other technologies make it a favored choice for constructing comprehensive ML pipelines. Furthermore, its popularity is further underscored by its application across various industries, ranging from data science and finance to healthcare and autonomous systems. As Python continues to evolve, its position within the ML landscape remains crucial, providing a strong foundation for researchers, data scientists, and developers to drive innovation and progress in the field.

1.2.1 Why Python for Machine Learning?

Python has become the preferred programming language for ML due to various compelling factors. The efficient development is facilitated by its simple and easy-to-understand syntax, which makes it accessible for both novices and experienced developers. Python's extensive ecosystem incorporates powerful libraries like Scikit-learn, TensorFlow, and PyTorch, providing robust tools for a wide range of tasks, from data preprocessing to complex deep learning models.

The language's versatility is demonstrated by its ability to seamlessly integrate with other technologies, enabling smooth incorporation into different data science workflows and frameworks. Python's strong community support plays a crucial role, ensuring a vast array of resources, tutorials, and forums for problem-solving. Its popularity extends beyond the realm of ML, fostering collaborations across different disciplines. The open-source nature of Python and its compatibility with various platforms contribute to its widespread adoption in research, industry, and academia. Consequently, Python's user-friendly nature, extensive libraries, and community support collectively establish it as the preferred language for practitioners and researchers navigating the diverse field of ML.

1.2.2 Popular Python Libraries for ML

In the realm of ML, Python is synonymous with a rich ecosystem of libraries that empower developers and researchers to build and deploy sophisticated models. Here are three standout libraries that have played pivotal roles in shaping the landscape of ML:

Fig 1.3: Popular Python libraries and tools for ML.

1.2.2.1 Scikit-learn
The ML library, Scikit-learn, is renowned for its adaptability and user-centric design, offering an assortment of uncomplicated and effective resources for the examination and construction of data. It encompasses an extensive range of algorithms that cater to classification, regression, clustering, and dimensionality reduction tasks.

1.2.2.2 TensorFlow
Developed by Google, TensorFlow is an immensely robust open-source library that demonstrates exceptional performance in the realm of deep learning applications. Its remarkable adaptability and capacity for expansion render it well-suited for individuals ranging from novices to seasoned professionals. TensorFlow provides extensive support for the creation and implementation of intricate neural network frameworks.

1.2.2.3 PyTorch
PyTorch is a dynamic and popular deep learning library known for its imperative programming style. Favored by researchers and developers alike, PyTorch facilitates building dynamic computational graphs, offering flexibility and ease in experimenting with various neural network architectures.

These libraries serve as pillars in the Python ML ecosystem, each contributing unique strengths and functionalities. Their widespread adoption underscores their significance in the development and advancement of ML applications.

1.2.3 Python vs Other Programming Languages in ML

Python has become the prevailing programming language in the realm of ML; however, it is crucial to evaluate it alongside other languages that are frequently employed in this particular domain.

Tab. 1.1: Comparison between Python vs Other Programming Languages.

Aspect	Python	R	Java	C++
Versatility	✔ Comprehensive ecosystem	✘ Limited in broader software dev	✔ Suitable for enterprise integration	✘ Steeper learning curve
Readability	✔ Readable syntax	✘ Steeper learning curve	✘ Verbosity	✘ Verbosity
Community Support	✔ Large and active community	✘ Smaller community	✔ Strong support for enterprise	✘ Smaller community
Statistical Focus	✘ Less emphasis on statistics	✔ Strong statistical capabilities	✘ Limited statistical focus	✘ Limited statistical focus
Data Visualization	✘ Moderate capabilities	✔ Strong visualization capabilities	✘ Limited capabilities	✘ Limited capabilities
Performance	✘ Generally lower performance	✘ Generally lower performance	✔ Better performance in certain cases	✔ Efficient and high performance
Learning Curve	✔ Beginner-friendly	✘ Steeper learning curve	✘ Moderate learning curve	✘ Steeper learning curve
Enterprise Integration	✘ Generalpurpose limitations	✘ Generalpurpose limitations	✔ Robust, suitable for integration	✘ Generalpurpose limitations
Low-Level Control	✘ Limited low-level control	✘ Limited low-level control	✘ Limited low-level control	✔ Provides low-level control

It is of vital significance to take into account that the selection of programming language frequently relies on the precise demands of the ML venture, the developer's acquaintance with the language, and considerations of effectiveness. Every language possesses its own merits and is appropriately equipped for specific situations.

1.2.4 Community and Resources for Python ML

The Python community for ML is a lively and cooperative ecosystem that has a crucial function in the progress, dissemination, and enhancement of ML endeavors. Presented here is a summary of the community and the ample resources that are accessible for Python in the field of ML.

Open-Source Collaboration

Collaborative development: The Python ML community thrives on open-source collaboration, with developers worldwide contributing to libraries, frameworks, and tools. This collective effort leads to continuous improvements, bug fixes, and the evolution of the ecosystem.

Online Forums and Discussion Groups

Stack overflow: Python developers actively engage in discussions on platforms like Stack Overflow, seeking and providing help on a wide range of ML topics.
Reddit (r/MachineLearning): The ML subreddit on Reddit serves as a hub for discussions, sharing research papers, and seeking advice from the community.

Conferences and Meetups

PyCon: Python conferences, such as PyCon, often feature dedicated tracks and sessions for ML, providing a platform for networking, knowledge sharing, and collaboration.
Local meetups: Python and ML enthusiasts frequently organize local meetups, fostering community building and face-to-face interactions.

Educational Platforms

Coursera, edX, and Udacity: These platforms offer a plethora of ML courses and specializations in Python, providing learners with comprehensive resources and hands-on projects.
Kaggle: Kaggle serves as both a competition platform and a learning resource, allowing users to explore datasets, compete, and collaborate on ML projects.

Documentation and Tutorials

Official documentation: Libraries like Scikit-learn, TensorFlow, and PyTorch have extensive and well-maintained documentation, offering comprehensive guides, tutorials, and examples.

Online blogs and websites: Numerous blogs and websites, such as Towards Data Science and Analytics Vidhya, provide in-depth tutorials, case studies, and best practices for ML in Python.

Version Control and Collaboration

GitHub: The Python ML community heavily utilizes GitHub for version control, collaborative development, and sharing of code repositories. This platform facilitates collaboration on open-source projects and promotes code transparency.

Social Media Engagement

Twitter: Many researchers, practitioners, and organizations share insights, research papers, and updates related to Python in ML on Twitter, fostering real-time communication and awareness.

LinkedIn groups: Groups on LinkedIn that are centered around ML offer a platform for professionals to exchange experiences, job prospects, and valuable material.

Mailing Lists and Newsletters

Scikit-learn mailing list: The Scikit-learn community maintains a mailing list for discussions, announcements, and community updates.

Weekly newsletters: Newsletters like "Pycoders Weekly" curate the latest Python and ML news, articles, and resources, keeping the community informed.

The collaborative and inclusive nature of the Python ML community, coupled with the abundance of educational resources and platforms, makes it an ideal environment for developers, researchers, and learners to thrive and contribute to the evolving landscape of ML in Python.

1.3 Setting Up Your Python Environment

Embarking on ML projects requires a well-configured Python environment. Establishing the right foundation ensures smooth development, efficient collaboration, and reproducibility. Here's a concise guide to setting up your Python environment for ML success.

1.3.1 Installing Python

Installing Python is the foundational step for any ML endeavor. Follow these steps for a seamless installation:

Download Python

Visit the Python website's official domain, https://www.python.org/downloads/, to obtain the most recent edition that is compatible with your designated operating system.

Run the Installer

Perform the execution of the installer that has been downloaded. While the installation process is taking place, it is essential to verify and select the option labeled "Add Python to PATH." By doing so, Python will be conveniently accessible through the command line interface.

Verify Installation

Launch a command prompt on Windows or a terminal on macOS/Linux and enter the command "python –version" or "python –V." The installed version of Python will be displayed, thereby confirming the successful completion of the installation.

```
$ python --version
Python 3.8.12
```

Fig 1.4: Python version.

This example demonstrates checking the Python version, with the result indicating that Python 3.8.12 is installed. Now, with Python installed, you're ready to proceed to the next steps of setting up your ML environment.

1.3.2 Virtual Environments and Why They're Important

In Python, virtual environments are crucial for managing project dependencies and isolating different projects from each other. Here's why virtual environments are essential and how to use them.

Dependency Isolation

Virtual environments create isolated spaces for Python projects. Each environment has its own set of installed packages, preventing conflicts between project dependencies.

Version Control

By enclosing the dependencies of a project within a virtual environment, one can exercise authority over the versions of libraries employed for a particular project. This guarantees the preservation of project reproducibility throughout its lifespan.

Clean Development Environment
Virtual environments keep your system's global Python environment clean. You can experiment with different versions of libraries and frameworks without affecting other projects or the system-wide Python installation.

Easy Replication
Virtual environments make it easy to replicate the development environment on another machine. By sharing the requirements.txt or environment.yml file, others can recreate the exact environment used for a project.

Installation and Activation
Create virtual environments by utilizing the venv module or employing external utilities such as virtualenv or Conda. Employ commands like "source venv/bin/activate" (for Linux/macOS) or "venv\Scripts\activate" (for Windows) to activate the environment.
Example (command line):

```
# Create a virtual environment named 'myenv'
$ python -m venv myenv

# Activate the virtual environment
$ source myenv/bin/activate    # On Linux/macOS
$ myenv\Scripts\activate       # On Windows
```

Fig. 1.5: Python environment.

Once activated, the terminal prompt changes to indicate the active virtual environment, ensuring that any installed packages are specific to the project tied to that environment.
Understanding and leveraging virtual environments is a best practice in Python development, especially in the context of ML projects, where dependencies can be project-specific and evolve over time.

1.3.3 Essential Python Libraries for ML

Several crucial Python libraries play a crucial role in the advancement of ML by offering a range of useful tools for tasks such as data manipulation, statistical analysis, and the construction of ML models. The subsequent section delves deeply into these indispensable libraries.

NumPy

Description: NumPy represents an essential library for performing numerical computations using the Python programming language. It offers comprehensive assistance for handling extensive, multidimensional arrays and matrices, while also offering efficient mathematical operations to manipulate these arrays effectively.

Importance: NumPy serves as the foundational framework for the manipulation of data and the execution of numerical operations in the field of ML. It constitutes the fundamental building block for numerous other libraries within the wider ecosystem.

Pandas

Description: The Pandas library is a flexible tool for manipulating data, providing various data structures, such as DataFrames, which are particularly well-suited for managing structured data. It offers an array of tools for data cleaning, exploration, and analysis.

Importance: Pandas streamlines the process of data preprocessing, thereby facilitating the optimization of data for ML models. Its proficiency lies in its capacity to effectively handle tabular and time-series data.

Matplotlib:

Description: Matplotlib is an extensive plotting library for generating Python-based visualizations, encompassing 2D static, animated, and interactive representations. It offers a versatile framework to construct diverse plots and charts.

Importance: Visualization is crucial for understanding data patterns. Matplotlib facilitates the creation of informative plots, aiding in data exploration and communication.

Scikit-learn

Description: Scikit-learn, an enduring ML library, furnishes uncomplicated and effective instruments to extract valuable information and scrutinize data. The library encompasses a diverse range of algorithms for classification, regression, clustering, and beyond.

Importance: Scikit-learn serves as a primary resource for deploying ML models. With its standardized application programming interface (API) and comprehensive documentation, it provides accessibility to individuals at all levels of expertise.

TensorFlow

Description: TensorFlow, an open-source ML library, was created by Google and is capable of supporting both deep learning and traditional ML. This library simplifies the process of developing and training intricate neural network models.

Importance: TensorFlow is extensively employed for deep learning implementations, encompassing the domains of image and speech identification, natural language processing, and other related areas. Its adaptability and scalability render it appropriate for a diverse range of undertakings.

PyTorch

Description: PyTorch, renowned for its adaptability and user-friendly interface, is a dynamic and open-source deep learning framework. It offers a dynamic computational graph, rendering it well-suited for research and experimentation.
Importance: PyTorch is widely embraced by researchers due to its user-friendly architecture and flexible computational abilities, rendering it extensively employed within both academic and industrial domains to construct state-of-the-art deep learning models.

Keras

Description: Keras, a Python-based high-level neural networks API, is designed to operate on TensorFlow, Theano, or Microsoft Cognitive Toolkit. It offers a user-friendly platform for constructing and exploring neural networks.
Importance: Keras simplifies the development of neural network architectures and is often the choice for quick prototyping and experimentation. It abstracts low-level details, allowing developers to focus on model design.

These essential Python libraries collectively form a robust ecosystem for ML development. Understanding their functionalities and integrating them into projects enables efficient data handling, model building, and visualization.

1.3.4 Using Package Managers: Pip and Conda

Package managers are essential tools for managing Python libraries and dependencies. Two widely used package managers in the Python ecosystem are pip and conda. Here's an overview of how to use them.

pip

Description: pip serves as the primary package manager for the Python programming language. It streamlines the procedure of installation, enhancement, and administration of Python packages.
Installation: If one is utilizing Python 3.4 or a more recent version, it is probable that the pip package manager is already present. To enhance the pip package manager to the most recent iteration, execute the following command:

```
$ python -m pip install -upgrade pip
```
Installing a package:
```
$ pip install package_name
```
Example (installing NumPy):
```
$ pip install numpy
```

Description: conda is a cross-platform package manager and environment management system. It is particularly powerful for managing packages with complex dependencies.

Installation: Install conda by downloading and installing Anaconda or Miniconda.

Creating a virtual environment
```
$ conda create -name myenv
```
Activating the virtual environment:
```
$ conda activate myenv
```
Installing a package:
```
(myenv) $ conda install package_name
```
Example (installing NumPy):
```
(myenv) $ conda install numpy
```
Deactivating the virtual environment:
```
(myenv) $ conda deactivate
```
Removing a virtual environment:
```
$ conda env remove -name myenv
```

Using pip and conda appropriately is crucial for managing dependencies in your Python environment. Choose the one that best fits your project requirements and ecosystem compatibility. It's common to use pip for general Python packages and conda for packages with non-Python dependencies or in data science environments.

1.3.5 Setting Up Jupyter Notebook

The Jupyter Notebook, which is extensively utilized for interactive data analysis, exploration, and ML development, possesses significant capabilities. A comprehensive tutorial outlining the process of setting up Jupyter Notebook in your Python environment is presented here.

Installation
- Ensure that your Python environment is activated (either globally or within a virtual environment).
- Use **pip** to install Jupyter Notebook:
  ```
  $ pip install jupyter
  ```

Starting Jupyter Notebook
- To initiate the Jupyter Notebook server, execute the provided command in your terminal or command prompt.
  ```
  $ jupyter notebook
  ```

This action will initiate the launch of a fresh tab in the web browser, thereby revealing the Jupyter Notebook dashboard.

Creating a New Notebook
- In the Jupyter Notebook dashboard, one should proceed by selecting the "New" button and subsequently opting for the "Python" option to generate a fresh Python notebook.

Using Jupyter Notebooks
- Jupyter Notebooks are composed of cells that can contain either code or markdown (text). The execution of a cell can be initiated by selecting it and clicking the "Run" button or by utilizing the appropriate keyboard shortcut, typically Shift + Enter.
- To incorporate an additional cell, one may employ the "+" icon located in the toolbar or alternatively press the B key on the keyboard to introduce a cell beneath the presently chosen cell.

Installing Additional Kernels
- Jupyter facilitates the utilization of diverse programming languages by means of distinct kernels. If one desires to employ a virtual environment other than the standard Python environment, it is possible to procure a kernel for said environment. By installing the ipykernel package, it becomes feasible to generate a fresh kernel.
  ```
  $ pip install ipykernel
  $ python -m ipykernel install -user -name=myenv -display-name="My Environment"
  ```

Now, in your Jupyter Notebook, you can choose "My Environment" as a kernel.

Exporting Notebooks
- You can export your Jupyter Notebooks to various formats, including HTML, PDF, and Markdown. Use the "File" menu to access the "Download as" option and choose your preferred format.

Closing Jupyter Notebook
- To stop the Jupyter Notebook server, go back to the terminal where it's running and press Ctrl + C. Confirm with Y and press Enter.

Establishing Jupyter Notebook offers an interactive and perceptible milieu for crafting ML models, illustrating data, and recording your endeavors. It harmoniously incorporates the Python framework, rendering it a multifaceted instrument for data scientists and programmers alike.

1.3.6 Best Practices for Managing ML Projects in Python

Managing ML projects in Python involves more than just writing code. Adopting best practices ensures project organization, reproducibility, and collaboration. Here's a detailed guide.

Project Structure
- Organize your project with a clear directory structure. Commonly used structures include separating data, code, and documentation into distinct directories.

```
my_project/
├── data/
├── src/
│    ├── __init__.py
│    ├── data_processing.py
│    └── model_training.py
├── notebooks/
├── README.md
└── requirements.txt
```

Version Control with Git
- Use Git for version control. Initialize a Git repository at the project's root and commit regularly. Host your code on platforms like GitHub or GitLab for collaboration and backup.

```
$ git init
$ git add .
$ git commit -m "Initial commit"
```

Virtual Environments

– Always use virtual environments to isolate project dependencies. Include a **requirements.txt** or **environment.yml** file to document and recreate the environment.

```
$ python -m venv venv
$ source venv/bin/activate
(venv) $ pip install -r requirements.txt
```

Documentation

– Ensure thorough documentation is maintained. Clarify the functionality of the code through the utilization of README files, docstrings, and comments. Provide instructions on configuring the environment and executing the project.

Automated Testing

– Implement unit tests to ensure code correctness. Tools like pytest can be used for automated testing. Run tests regularly to catch potential issues early.

```
(venv) $ pip install pytest
(venv) $ pytest tests/
```

Continuous Integration (CI)

– Establish a continuous integration (CI) framework, such as GitHub Actions or Travis CI, to execute tests and verifications automatically upon the submission of modifications to the repository. This guarantees the perpetual functionality of the codebase.

```
# Example GitHub Actions workflow
name: CI
on: [push, pull_request]
jobs:
  test:
    runs-on: ubuntu-latest
    steps:
      - name: Set up Python
        uses: actions/setup-python@v2
        with:
          python-version: 3.8
      - name: Install dependencies
```

```
run: |
    python -m venv venv
    source venv/bin/activate
    pip install -r requirements.txt
- name: Run tests
  run: |
      pytest tests/
```

Logging and Monitoring
- Implement proper logging in your code to capture important information and errors. Utilize logging libraries (e.g., logging in Python) to manage logs. For ML models, monitor model performance and drift over time.

Reproducibility
- Document the steps to reproduce your experiments. Include information on data sources, preprocessing steps, and model hyperparameters. This ensures that others can reproduce your results.

Code Reviews
- Incorporate code review practices. Peer reviews help catch bugs, improve code quality, and ensure that the project adheres to coding standards.

Environment Variables
- Employ environment variables to safeguard sensitive data, such as API keys or database credentials. It is inadvisable to embed these values directly within your code.

Scaling and Deployment
- If applicable, plan for scaling your ML models. Consider containerization (e.g., Docker) for deployment, and design your models to handle production-level loads.

Collaboration Platforms
- Leverage collaboration platforms like Jupyter Notebooks or Google Colab for interactive development and sharing insights.

By incorporating these best practices, you establish a solid foundation for managing ML projects in Python. This promotes collaboration and maintainability, and ensures the reproducibility of your work.

Summary

– ML is a constituent part of AI, which enables computers to acquire knowledge and render judgments through experiential learning without the need for explicit programming.
– Developed from foundational concepts in the 1950s, ML has progressed through key milestones, including expert systems, SVMs, and the dominance of deep learning in the 2010s.
– Supervised learning entails instructing an algorithm using annotated data, wherein the system is directed to comprehend the correlation between inputs and outputs through input-output pairs. Image classification and spam filtering are among the widely recognized applications of this approach.
– Unsupervised learning pertains to the handling of data that lacks labels, thereby compelling the algorithm to unveil patterns or correlations present within the data in the absence of pre-established output labels. The encompassed tasks encompass clustering and dimensionality reduction, which encompass the grouping of analogous customer purchase behaviors.
– Reinforcement learning is centered around the acquisition of decision-making skills by an agent through its active engagement with an environment, wherein it acquires feedback in the form of rewards or penalties. This approach finds application in various domains such as game playing (for instance, AlphaGo) and robotic control, with the ultimate aim of learning a strategy to optimize cumulative rewards within a given environment.
– ML is widely applied across industries, transforming healthcare with disease diagnosis and predictive analytics, enhancing finance through fraud detection and algorithmic trading, improving marketing with recommendation systems, and contributing to autonomous vehicles, image recognition, education, and more.
– Key challenges include ensuring data quality and mitigating biases, addressing interpretability issues in complex models, balancing overfitting and underfitting, promoting standardization for fair comparisons, managing computational complexity, navigating ethical considerations, countering adversarial attacks, adapting to continuous learning, and addressing privacy concerns in handling sensitive information.
– Python's versatility, readability, and extensive library support, including Scikit-learn, TensorFlow, and PyTorch, have made it the dominant programming language in the ML landscape. Its active community and integration capabilities contribute to its widespread adoption across industries.
– The foundational Python libraries for ML development encompass NumPy and Pandas, which are employed for data manipulation, Matplotlib, which is utilized for visualization, Scikit-learn, which is employed for ML algorithms, TensorFlow and PyTorch, which are utilized for deep learning, and Keras, which is employed for high-level neural network APIs.

– Utilize pip and conda for managing Python libraries and dependencies based on project requirements.
– Set up Jupyter Notebook for interactive data analysis and ML development, allowing seamless integration with Python libraries.

Exercise (MCQs)

1. **What is machine learning?**
   a) Explicit programming
   b) AI subset
   c) Data manipulation
   d) Virtual environments

2. **What is supervised learning primarily based on?**
   a) Unlabeled data   b) Reinforcement   c) Labeled dataset   d) Clustering

3. **Which library is known for its imperative programming style in deep learning?**
   a) Scikit-learn   b) TensorFlow   c) PyTorch   d) Keras

4. **What is the role of virtual environments in Python?**
   a) Handling data
   b) Managing machine learning models
   c) Isolating project dependencies
   d) Running Jupyter Notebook

5. **Which Python library is essential for numerical computing and supports large arrays?**
   a) Matplotlib   b) TensorFlow   c) Pandas   d) NumPy

6. **What is conda primarily used for in Python development?**
   a) Version control
   b) Package management and environment management
   c) Data visualization
   d) Deep learning

7. **Which tool is widely used for version control in Python projects?**
   a) Pip   b) Jupyter Notebook   c) Git   d) Conda

8. **What is Jupyter Notebook commonly used for in machine learning?**
   a) Running Python scripts
   b) Managing virtual environments
   c) Interactive data analysis and development
   d) Version control

9. **What is an example of a continuous integration (CI) system?**
    a) PyTorch   b) Jupyter Notebook   c) Travis CI   d) Scikit-learn

10. **Why is proper logging important in machine learning code?**
    a) To write documentation
    b) To capture errors and important information
    c) To create visualizations
    d) To implement unit tests

Answers

1. b) AI subset
2. c) Labeled dataset
3. c) PyTorch
4. c) Isolating project dependencies
5. d) NumPy
6. b) Package management and environment management
7. c) Git
8. c) Interactive data analysis and development
9. c) Travis CI
10. b) To capture errors and important information

Fill in the Blanks

1. Machine learning, a subset of artificial intelligence, enables computers to learn and make decisions without being _____ programmed.
2. In supervised learning, the algorithm is trained on a _____ dataset, where the input data is paired with corresponding output labels.
3. Unsupervised learning deals with _____ data, where the algorithm is given data without explicit instructions on what to do with it.
4. Reinforcement learning involves an agent learning to make decisions by taking actions in an _____.
5. Machine learning has diverse applications across various industries, including healthcare, finance, marketing, and more, revolutionizing the way tasks are performed and decisions are made. These applications exemplify the versatility and transformative potential of machine learning across various sectors, driving innovation and efficiency in solving _____ problems.
6. Python has become the dominant programming language in the machine learning landscape due to its _____, ease of use, and a rich ecosystem of libraries and frameworks.

7. Scikit-learn, TensorFlow, and PyTorch are examples of _____ libraries in the Python machine learning ecosystem.
8. Virtual environments in Python are crucial for managing project dependencies and isolating different projects from each other. They create isolated spaces for Python projects, preventing conflicts between _____.
9. _____ is the default package manager for Python, simplifying the process of installing, upgrading, and managing Python packages.
10. Jupyter Notebook is a powerful tool widely used for interactive data analysis, exploration, and machine learning development. It provides an interactive and visual environment for developing machine learning models, visualizing data, and documenting your work. It seamlessly integrates with the Python _____, making it a versatile tool for data scientists and developers alike.

Answers

1. explicitly
2. labeled
3. unlabeled
4. environment
5. complex
6. versatility
7. machine learning
8. project dependencies
9. pip
10. ecosystem

Descriptive Questions

1. Explain the fundamental types of machine learning discussed in the overview, highlighting their key characteristics and providing examples for each.
2. Discuss the transformative applications of machine learning across various industries, providing detailed insights into specific use cases in healthcare, finance, marketing, and autonomous systems.
3. Why has Python become the dominant programming language in the machine learning landscape? Provide a comprehensive explanation, touching on its features, ecosystem, and community support.
4. Explore the significance of virtual environments in Python for machine learning projects. Explain how they contribute to dependency isolation, version control, and maintaining a clean development environment.

5. Elaborate on the essential Python libraries for machine learning, such as NumPy, Pandas, Matplotlib, Scikit-learn, TensorFlow, PyTorch, and Keras. Describe the role and importance of each library in the machine learning ecosystem.
6. Compare and contrast the use of pip and conda as package managers in Python, emphasizing their features and best use cases.
7. Provide a step-by-step guide on setting up Jupyter Notebook in a Python environment, including installation, starting the notebook, creating a new notebook, and installing additional kernels.
8. Discuss the best practices for managing machine learning projects in Python, covering aspects like project structure, version control with Git, documentation, automated testing, and continuous integration.
9. Explain the importance of proper logging and monitoring in machine learning projects, emphasizing their role in capturing information and errors, especially for ML models' performance and drift over time.
10. How can reproducibility be ensured in machine learning experiments? Discuss the steps to document and reproduce experiments, including details on data sources, preprocessing, and model hyperparameters.

Chapter 2
Basics of Python Programming

2.1 Why Python?

Python, a widely used general-purpose interpreted programming language, has gained immense popularity. It boasts a dynamic type system, automatic memory management, and supports multiple programming paradigms such as imperative, functional, and procedural. Python enables the creation of automated solutions for various tasks. Currently, major IT companies including Google, Microsoft, and Apple rely on Python as their primary programming language. Notably, Python stands out as the easiest programming language to learn within a short period of time. It empowers developers to build a wide range of applications, such as desktop, web, and mobile, with minimal coding effort, thanks to the abundance of frameworks and libraries available.

Furthermore, Python is free and open source, with comprehensive documentation accessible online. Python primarily emphasizes business logic over basic programming concepts. Although Python is available in various versions, we will primarily focus on version 3.7, with the upcoming release of Python 3.8 in October 2019, which will introduce new features and address performance-related issues. Python possesses the traits of being dynamically typed, automatically garbage-collected, and having memory management capabilities, while supporting multiple programming paradigms including procedural, object-oriented, and functional. It is an agile language that allows for rapid development of customized solutions in a short span of time. Additionally, Python facilitates modular application development, enabling developers to join modules together seamlessly before the final release.

2.1.1 Drawbacks of Python

All programming languages possess both advantages and disadvantages. Python, too, exhibits certain disadvantages, some of which are outlined below.

- In comparison to other programming languages like C, C++, and Java, Python's program execution is considerably slower. Java, being the fastest language, owes its speed to the Java Virtual Machine (JVM) and Just-In-Time (JIT) compiler. For more detailed information, please refer to YouTube videos.
- The generation of intricate graphics places a heavy computational burden, resulting in a degradation of graphics quality.
- In the absence of Cython, code execution suffers from sluggishness. Cython allows for code compilation at the C level, leveraging C compiler optimizations.

https://doi.org/10.1515/9783110697186-002

–   Improved performance necessitates the utilization of GPU or Cython.
–   To avoid resource wastage, the application's speed can be constrained.

2.1.2 History of Python

Python language, which was created by Guido van Rossum in 1991, is not named after the type of snake, but rather after a British Comedy group called "Monty Python's Flying Circus." Guido van Rossum, being a big fan of the group and their quirky humor, named the language in their honor. In the year 2000, Python 2.0 was released with new features such as comprehensions, cycle detecting garbage collection, and Unicode support, 10 years after the initial release of Python 1.0. Python programs often pay tribute to the group by incorporating their jokes and famous quotes into the code.

Python is available in two major versions: Python 3.x and Python 2.x. Python 2.x, which is considered a legacy version, will be supported until 2020, while Python 3.x is the more frequently updated and popular version. Some features from Python 3 can be imported into Python 2.x using the "_future_" module. Python 3.0, released in 2008, was a major release that lacked backward compatibility, meaning that code written in Python 2.x could not run on the Python 3.x series.

However, this issue was addressed in Python 2.7, as a large amount of code had already been written in the Python 2.x series. Initially, support for Python 2.7 was set to end in 2015, but it has since been extended to 2020. Guido van Rossum took on the responsibility of leading the Python project until July 2018, when he passed on the role to a five-person steering council. This council will now be responsible for releasing future versions of Python.

2.1.3 Major Features of Python

–   Reading and comprehension are facilitated due to the presence of tabular space rather than curly braces, making it effortless to learn.
–   Using the English language facilitates the coding of Python programs, rendering the process significantly easier.
–   The Python programming language is built upon an interpreted language, which greatly reduces the time required to execute our applications.
–   Procedural programming, object-oriented programming, and functional programming are all supported by Python through the Thread module, allowing for the use of Multi Threading.
–   Parsing Python, Android, and iOS templates facilitates the generation of dynamic pages for clients.

–   Interactive language, python code does not perform any conversion of human-readable code into executable code. This characteristic renders python highly interactive as it allows for real-time modifications.
–   The KIVY framework provides support for Python, Android, and iOS.
–   Same code can be executed on all available platforms due to platform independence.

2.1.4 Market Demand

There are numerous programming languages currently utilized for application development in the market. However, I would like to present some facts sourced from various internet platforms. These facts encompass primary introductory languages, sector-wise demand, salary considerations, and market share.

Fig. 2.1 depicts the global market demand trends for various programming languages over the last decade. The graph illustrates the oscillations in the requirement of languages such as Python, Java, C++, and JavaScript, etc., across different industries and regions. Fig. 2.2 presents a comparative analysis of average annual salaries earned by professionals with these programming language skills. Data is collected from broad surveys that are conducted across major tech hubs worldwide to provide insight into remuneration levels for each language. Furthermore, Fig. 2.3 demonstrates the relative popularity of these programming languages as measured by online search trends, enrollment in coding courses and adoption rates in software development projects among others. This popularity index gives a complete view of the dynamic landscape of programming languages which helps in identifying new trends and possible future shifts in demand.

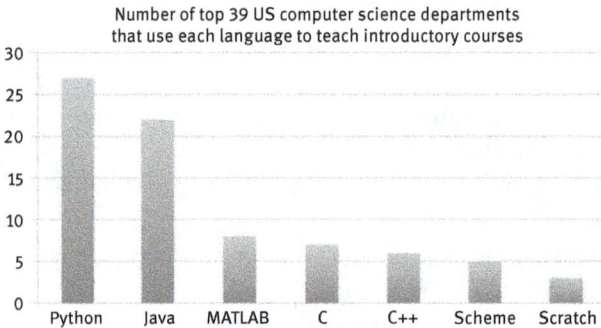

Fig. 2.1: Market demand of programming language.
Source: https://doi.org/10.1515/9783110689488 (Page-8)

2016 Average Developer Salary in the U.S.

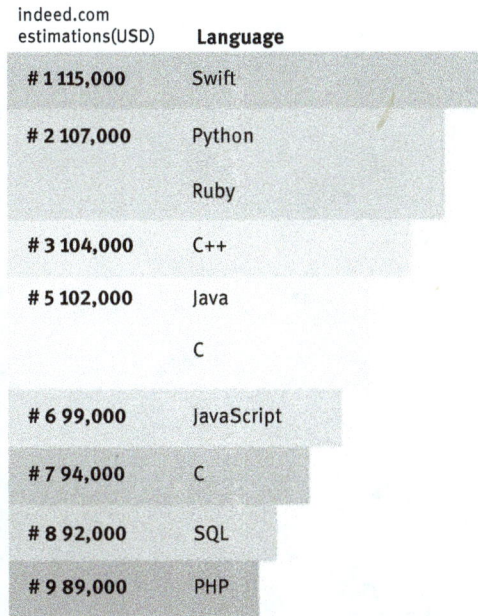

indeed.com estimations(USD)	Language
# 1 115,000	Swift
# 2 107,000	Python
	Ruby
# 3 104,000	C++
# 5 102,000	Java
	C
# 6 99,000	JavaScript
# 7 94,000	C
# 8 92,000	SQL
# 9 89,000	PHP

Fig. 2.2: Language-wise average salary.

2.1.5 Why Python in Mobile App Development?

In today's world, mobile devices have become an integral part of our daily lives, making it nearly impossible for individuals to function without their smartphones. These devices have greatly simplified our lives. Recognizing this, many software companies have shifted their focus to mobile app development. However, developing mobile apps presents a number of challenges due to the existence of various mobile phone platforms such as Android, iOS, Windows, etc., each with its own unique software requirements. Consequently, programmers are required to write code natively for each platform, a time-consuming task. To mitigate this issue, a cross-platform approach is recommended. Python, with its ease of use and extensive library support, simplifies the process of app development.

The importance of Python can be seen in the figure below, which highlights the market demand in various sectors. Python is renowned for its simplicity and versatility, as it can be learned and utilized on multiple platforms. It offers robust integration capabilities with various technologies, leading to increased programming productivity throughout the development life cycle. Python is particularly well-suited for large and

Worldwide, Nov 2016 compared to a year ago:

Rank	Change	Language	Share	Trend
1		Java	23.4%	−0.5%
2		Python	13.7%	+2.4%
3		PHP	9.8%	−0.9%
4		C#	8.4%	−0.4%
5	↑↑	Javascript	7.6%	+0.6%
6	↓	C++	7.1%	−0.7%
7	↓	C	7.0%	−0.5%
8		Objective-C	4.7%	−0.5%
9	↑	R	3.2%	+0.5%
10	↓	Swift	3.2%	+0.3%
11		Matlab	2.6%	−0.1%
12		Ruby	2.0%	−0.3%
13	↑	VBA	1.5%	+0.1%
14	↓	Visual Basic	1.4%	−0.5%

Fig. 2.3: Language-wise popularity.

complex projects with evolving requirements. Furthermore, it is currently the fastest growing programming language and is compatible with millions of phones across diverse industries. Additionally, Python code is highly readable. Table 2.1 shows the various python versions released from Python 1.0 to Python 3.12.

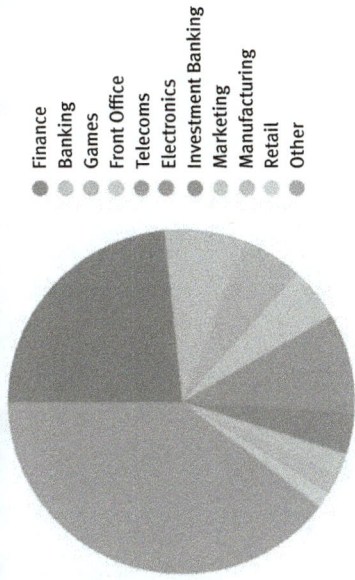

Finance
Banking
Games
Front Office
Telecoms
Electronics
Investment Banking
Marketing
Manufacturing
Retail
Other

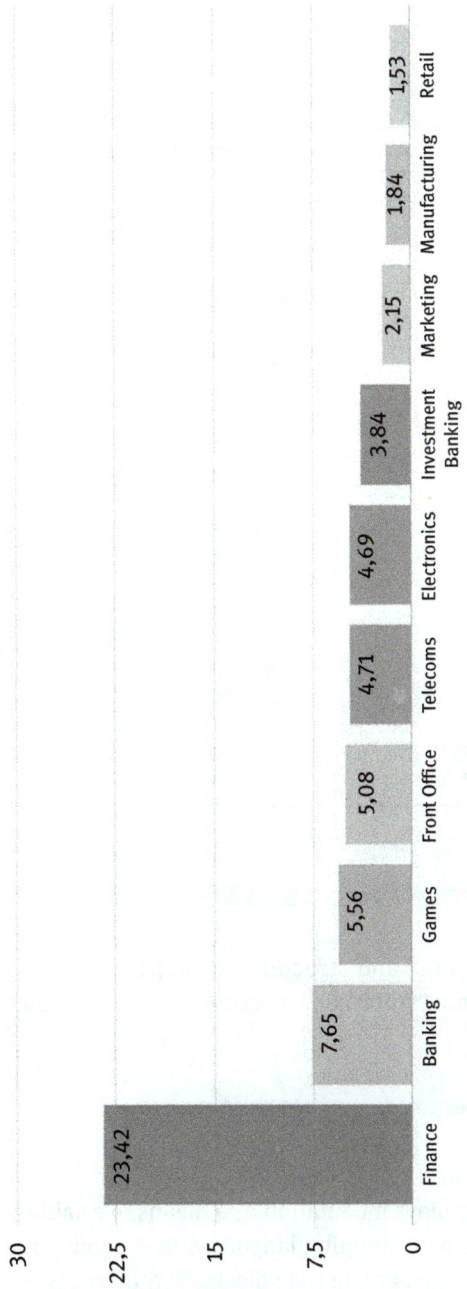

Finance	Banking	Games	Front Office	Telecoms	Electronics	Investment Banking	Marketing	Manufacturing	Retail
23,42	7,65	5,56	5,08	4,71	4,69	3,84	2,15	1,84	1,53

30

22,5

15

7,5

0

Fig. 2.4: Industry sector-wise market demand.

2.1.6 Python Versions

Tab. 2.1: Python versions.

Version	Release date
Python 1.0	1991
Python 2.0	Oct 2000
Python 2.1	April 2001
Python 2.2	Dec 2001
Python 2.3	July 2003
Python 2.4	Nov 2004
Python 2.5	Sep 2006
Python 2.6	Oct 2008
Python 2.7	July 2010
Python 3.0	Dec 2008
Python 3.1	June 2009
Python 3.2	Feb 2011
Python 3.3	Sep 2012
Python 3.4	March 2014
Python 3.5	Sep 2015
Python 3.6	Dec 2016
Python 3.7	June 2018
Python 3.8	Oct 2019
Python 3.9	Oct 2020
Python 3.10	Oct 2021
Python 3.11	Oct 2022
Python 3.12	Oct 2023

2.2 Python Syntax and Structure

Python syntax and structure encompass the rules and organization principles that govern how Python code is written and structured.

2.2.1 Indentation and Whitespace

Indentation

Python employs indentation as a means to establish code blocks. In contrast to numerous other programming languages that employ braces {} or keywords such as begin and end to demarcate code blocks, Python relies on uniform indentation. This particular characteristic distinguishes Python and is indispensable for the legibility and organization of the code.

```
def welcome(name):
  if name == "Ritesh":
    print("Hello, Ritesh!")
  else:
    print("Hello, stranger!")

# Call the function
welcome("Bob")
```

The example provided above illustrates how the scope of the if-else block is determined by the indentation, specifically the whitespace that precedes the print statements and else statement. Typically, this indentation consists of four spaces, although it is also possible to use a tab. It is crucial to maintain consistency in the chosen indentation style across the entire codebase.

Whitespace

Whitespace, including spaces and tabs, is used for separation and clarity in Python code. However, excessive or inconsistent use of whitespace can lead to syntax errors.

```
# Good use of whitespace for readability
total = 5 + 3 * 2

# Avoid excessive whitespace
total = 5 + 3 * 2
```

In the illustration, the initial utilization of whitespace is evident and augments legibility. The subsequent utilization, characterized by an excessive number of spaces, is technically accurate but may impede the comprehension of the code. It is generally advisable to adhere to PEP 8, the Python code style guide, which furnishes guidelines for the arrangement of code, encompassing the utilization of whitespace.

2.2.2 Comments and Documentation

Comments

Comments in Python are used to explain code and make it more understandable. They are not executed and are preceded by the # symbol.

```
# This is a single-line comment

def add_numbers(a, b):
```

```
# This function adds two numbers
return a + b
```

Comments are essential for documenting code, explaining complex parts, or leaving notes for other developers. However, it's crucial not to overuse comments or state the obvious, as the code should be self-explanatory whenever possible.

Documentation

Documentation refers to more extensive explanations of code, often provided in docstrings. Docstrings are triple-quoted strings that document a module, function, class, or method.

```
def multiply(a, b):
    """

    Multiply two numbers.

    Parameters:
    - a (int): The first number.
    - b (int): The second number.

    Returns:
    int: The result of multiplying a and b.
    """

    return a * b
```

The docstring in this given example offers comprehensive details regarding the function, which encompasses its objective, parameters, and the value it returns. The significance of having appropriate documentation cannot be overstated, as it plays a vital role in aiding fellow developers in comprehending the utilization of your code, while also facilitating the seamless operation of tools such as automatic documentation generators.

2.3 Data Types and Variables

Python is a language that is dynamically typed, which implies that there is no requirement to explicitly declare the data type of a variable. Nevertheless, comprehending data types is of utmost importance for proficient programming.

2.3.1 Primitive Data Types

Primitive data types serve as the fundamental constituents for constructing intricate data structures. Within the domain of Python, prevalent primitive data types encompass:

int (Integer): Represents whole numbers.
float (Float): Represents decimal numbers.
str (String): Represents textual data.
bool (Boolean): Represents True or False values.
NoneType: Represents the absence of a value.

```
# Integer
age = 25

# Float
height = 5.8

# String
name = "John"

# Boolean
is_student = True

# NoneType
no_value = None
```

Understanding these primitive data types is foundational for working with variables in Python.

2.3.2 Lists and Tuples

Lists
In the realm of the Python programming language, a list proves to be a highly adaptable and dynamic data structure that assumes a critical role in the arrangement and manipulation of groups of elements. Lists possess the ability to be modified, follow a specific order, and accommodate elements of diverse data types. This particular chapter delves into the complex nuances of lists, elucidating their formation, manipulation, and assorted operations through extensive illustrations.

Creating Lists

Defining a sequence of elements enclosed within square brackets [] is a fundamental operation in Python, known as creating lists. Lists, being mutable, have the ability to store elements of different data types and allow for modification of their content after their initial creation.

– **Basic list creation:**
To create a list, one encapsulates elements within square brackets, separated by commas.

```
fruits = ["apple", "banana", "orange"]
```

– **List with mixed data types:**
Python lists are capable of accommodating elements of various data types, thereby offering a high degree of flexibility.

```
mixed_list = [1, "apple", 3.14, True]
```

– **Empty list:**
An empty list is created without any elements, useful for dynamic population.

```
empty_list = []
```

– **Using the list() constructor:**
The list can be created from an iterable, such as a string, tuple, or another list, by utilizing the constructor list().

```
word_list = list("Python")

# Output: ['P', 'y', 't', 'h', 'o', 'n']
```

Nested Lists

Lists can be nested, allowing the creation of multidimensional structures.

```
matrix = [[1, 2, 3], [4, 5, 6], [7, 8, 9]]
```

Here, matrix is a 2D list representing a matrix.

Accessing Elements

Retrieving particular values from Python lists involves the act of accessing elements based on their respective index. The indexing of lists in Python follows a zero-based approach, whereby the initial element possesses an index of 0, the subsequent element possesses an index of 1, and so forth.

– **Basic indexing:**
Index notation is used to access elements within a list, wherein the indexing begins from 0.

```
fruits = ["apple", "banana", "orange"]
first_fruit = fruits[0]

# Output: apple
```

– **Negative indexing:**
Negative indexing is a functionality in lists that enables us to retrieve elements from the list's end, which offers a practical approach to navigating elements in a backward manner. The final element is assigned an index of – 1, while the penultimate element is assigned an index of – 2, and so forth.

```
fruits = ["apple", "banana", "orange", "kiwi", "grape"]

# Accessing elements using negative indexing
last_fruit = fruits[-1]    # Equivalent to fruits[4]
second_last = fruits[-2]  # Equivalent to fruits[3]

print(last_fruit)        # Output: grape
print(second_last)       # Output: kiwi
```

List Slicing
List slicing enables the creation of a novel list through the extraction of a subset of elements from a preexisting list. The slicing syntax, **list[start:stop:step]**, entails the utilization of the start index as the point of origin, the stop index as the point of termination, and the step size as the interval between elements.

```
numbers = [1, 2, 3, 4, 5, 6, 7, 8, 9]

# Basic slicing
subset1 = numbers[2:6]       # Elements from index 2 to 5
print(subset1)               # Output: [3, 4, 5, 6]
# Slicing with step
```

```
subset2 = numbers[1:8:2]    # Elements from index 1 to 7, every 2nd element
print(subset2)              # Output: [2, 4, 6, 8]

# Slicing with negative indices
subset3 = numbers[-5:-2]    # Elements from index -5 to -3
print(subset3)              # Output: [5, 6, 7]
```

In the above example, subset1 extracts elements from index 2 to 5, subset2 includes elements from index 1 to 7 with a step of 2, and subset3 selects elements using negative indices.

Modifying Elements

Modifying elements in Python lists is a crucial aspect of working with mutable data structures. Lists allow us to change the values of existing elements at specific indices.

– Basic modification:

To alter an element within a list, one employs its index and designates a fresh value to said index.

```
fruits = ["apple", "banana", "orange"]
fruits[1] = "kiwi"

# Output: ["apple", "kiwi", "orange"]
```

– Modifying multiple elements:

The slicing used to modify multiple elements, assigning a new list to the specified range of indices.

```
numbers = [1, 2, 3, 4, 5]
numbers[1:4] = [10, 20, 30]

# Output: [1, 10, 20, 30, 5]
```

– Modifying with negative indexing:

Negative indexing can be used for modification, similar to positive indexing.

```
fruits = ["apple", "kiwi", "orange"]
fruits[-1] = "grape"
# Output: ["apple", "kiwi", "grape"]
```

Adding Elements

Adding elements to Python lists is a fundamental operation that allows you to dynamically expand the size of the list. There are several methods to add elements to a list, each serving different purposes.

– **Using append() method:**
Methods such as append() can be employed to incorporate elements, thereby enabling the list to grow dynamically. The addition of an element to the end of the list is facilitated by the append() method.

```
fruits = ["apple", "banana", "orange"]
fruits.append("grape")

# Output: ["apple", "banana", "orange", "grape"]
```

– **Using insert() method:**
The method of insert() enables the addition of an element at a particular index.

```
fruits = ["apple", "banana", "orange"]
fruits.insert(1, "kiwi")

# Output: ["apple", "kiwi", "banana", "orange"]
```

– **Using extend() method or + = operator:**
The extend() method appends elements from an iterable, such as another list, to the list's end. The + = operator accomplishes the identical outcome.

```
fruits = ["apple", "banana", "orange"]
new_fruits = ["grape", "kiwi"]
fruits.extend(new_fruits)

# Output: ["apple", "banana", "orange", "grape", "kiwi"]
```

In this instance, the elements derived from the new_fruits list are appended to the concluding segment of the fruits list.

– **Using + = operator for single element:**
The + = operator has the capability to add a sole element to the list's termination point.

```
fruits = ["apple", "banana", "orange"]
fruits += ["grape"]
```

```
# Output: ["apple", "banana", "orange", "grape"]
```

In this particular context, the element denoted as "grape" is appended to the fruits list through the utilization of the + = operator.

Removing Elements

Removing elements from Python lists is a fundamental operation for the purpose of preserving and adjusting lists. Diverse methods can be employed based on the particular need.

– **Using remove() method:**
The remove() function is responsible for eliminating the initial instance of a predetermined element from the list.

```
fruits = ["apple", "banana", "orange", "banana"]
fruits.remove("banana")
```

```
# Output: ["apple", "orange", "banana"]
```

In this particular instance, the initial instance of the term "banana" is eliminated from the enumeration of fruits.

– **Using pop() method:**
The removal and retrieval of an element at a specified index is facilitated by the pop() method. In the event that no index is specified, the method proceeds to remove and return the last element.

```
fruits = ["apple", "banana", "orange"]
removed_fruit = fruits.pop(1)
```

```
# Output: removed_fruit = "banana", fruits = ["apple", "orange"]
```

Here, the element at index 1 ("banana") is removed and assigned to the variable removed_fruit.

– **Using del statement:**
The del statement can be used to remove elements by index or delete the entire list.

```
fruits = ["apple", "banana", "orange"]
del fruits[1]
```

```
# Output: ["apple", "orange"]
```

In this example, the element at index 1 ("banana") is removed using the del statement.

– **Using clear() method:**
The clear() method eliminates all elements from the list, resulting in an empty state.

```
fruits = ["apple", "banana", "orange"]
fruits.clear()
```

```
# Output: []
```

Length of a List
The len() function enables the calculation of the quantity of elements present in a given list.

```
num_elements = len(numbers)
```

```
# Output: 5
```

Nesting Lists
Creating lists within lists in the Python programming language entails the creation of a list where the constituent elements are also lists. This particular technique facilitates the generation of intricate data structures, including but not limited to matrices or lists that contain other lists. It is important to note that each individual element within the outer list has the potential to be a list in its own right.

```
nested_list = [[1, 2, 3], ["a", "b", "c"]]
print(nested_list[0][1])
```

```
# Output: 2
```

Tuples
A Python tuple is a compilation of ordered and unchangeable components. Following its creation, the components of a tuple remain unmodifiable, unappendable, and un-removable. Tuples are established through the use of parentheses () and have the abil-

ity to hold components of varying data types. Presented here is a comprehensive elucidation of tuple operations, accompanied by examples and intricate particulars.

Creating Tuples

Creating tuples in Python is a simple procedure that entails the utilization of parentheses (). Tuples have the capability to incorporate elements of diverse data types, and once they are formed, their values cannot be altered. Various approaches exist to generate tuples:

– Using parentheses:
The creation of a tuple is typically accomplished through the act of enclosing elements within parentheses, which is considered to be the most prevalent method.

```
fruits_tuple = ("apple", "banana", "orange")
```

In this example, fruits_tuple is a tuple containing three string elements.

– Without parentheses:
Tuples can also be created without explicit parentheses. The commas alone are sufficient to define a tuple.

```
numbers_tuple = 1, 2, 3
```

In this case, numbers_tuple is a tuple containing three integer elements.

– Mixed data types:
Tuples have the capability to encompass elements originating from diverse data types.

```
mixed_tuple = (1, "apple", 3.14, True)
```

Here, mixed_tuple is a tuple with an integer, a string, a float, and a boolean.

– Creating an empty tuple:
An empty tuple can be created using an empty pair of parentheses.

```
empty_tuple = ()
```

empty_tuple is a tuple with no elements.

– Single-element tuple:
A tuple containing only one element necessitates the inclusion of a trailing comma to differentiate it from a typical value enclosed in parentheses.

```
single_element_tuple = ("apple",)
```

Here, single_element_tuple is a tuple with a single string element.

Accessing Elements

Accessing elements in a tuple is similar to accessing elements in other sequences in Python, such as lists or strings. Tuples use zero-based indexing, and individual elements can be retrieved using square brackets [].

– **Basic indexing:**
To access an element in a tuple, specify its index within square brackets.

```
fruits_tuple = ("apple", "banana", "orange")
first_fruit = fruits_tuple[0]
```

```
# Output: "apple"
```

In this example, first_fruit is assigned the value at index 0, which is "apple."

– **Negative indexing:**
Negative indexing enables the retrieval of elements from the termination of the tuple.

```
last_fruit = fruits_tuple[-1]
```

```
# Output: "orange"
```

Here, last_fruit is assigned the value of the last element using negative indexing.

– **Slicing:**
Tuple slicing allows you to create a new tuple by extracting a subset of elements.

```
numbers_tuple = (1, 2, 3, 4, 5)
subset = numbers_tuple[1:4]
```

```
# Output: (2, 3, 4)
```

In this example, subset includes elements from index 1 to 3.

– **Omitting indices:**
If the start or stop index is not provided when slicing a tuple, the default behavior is to use the beginning or end of the tuple, respectively.

```
subset_start = numbers_tuple[:3] # Equivalent to numbers_tuple[0:3]
```

```
subset_end = numbers_tuple[2:] # Equivalent to numbers_tuple[2:len
(numbers_tuple)]
```

Immutable Nature

The characteristic that sets tuples in Python apart from other data structures, like lists, is their immutable nature. Immutability implies that, once a tuple is created, its elements cannot be altered, adjusted, appended, or erased.

```
tuple2[1] = "kiwi" # Raises TypeError
```

- **Element modification is not allowed:**
    - Once a tuple is created, cannot change the value of its elements.
    - Modifying a tuple will lead to the occurrence of a TypeError.

```
fruits_tuple = ("apple", "banana", "orange")
fruits_tuple[1] = "kiwi" # Raises TypeError
```

- **Adding and removing elements is prohibited:**
    - Tuples do not support operations like append() or remove() that modify the tuple in-place.
    - We cannot add or remove elements from an existing tuple.

```
fruits_tuple.append("grape") # Raises AttributeError
```

- **Immutable through iterations:**
    - The immutability of tuples extends to all elements contained within the tuple.
    - If a tuple contains mutable objects (e.g., lists), the tuple itself remains immutable, but the objects inside it can be modified.

```
nested_tuple = ([1, 2, 3], "apple")
```

```
nested_tuple[0][1] = 10 # Valid, as the list inside the tuple is mutable
```

Tuple Unpacking

Tuple unpacking is a functionality present in the Python programming language, which facilitates the assignment of values from a tuple to separate variables within a single line of code. This characteristic offers a practical and efficient approach to extracting elements from a tuple and assigning them to variables, thereby eliminating the need for multiple assignment statements.

– Basic tuple unpacking

```
# Creating a tuple
coordinates = (3, 7)

# Tuple unpacking
x, y = coordinates

# Variables x and y now hold the values 3 and 7, respectively
```

In this illustration, the values of the coordinates tuple are decomposed into the variables x and y. It is essential that the count of variables on the left side of the assignment corresponds to the count of elements in the tuple.

– Unpacking in functions:

Tuple unpacking is often used in function returns to conveniently capture multiple values.

```
def get_coordinates():
 return 5, 10

# Calling the function and unpacking the result
x, y = get_coordinates()
# x is now 5, y is now 10
```

Here, the function get_coordinates returns a tuple, and the values are unpacked into variables x and y when calling the function.

– Extended unpacking:

In Python, we can use the * operator to capture remaining elements when unpacking.

```
# Creating a tuple
numbers = (1, 2, 3, 4, 5)

# Unpacking with extended unpacking
first, *rest, last = numbers

# first is 1, rest is [2, 3, 4], last is 5
```

In this example, the *rest syntax captures all elements between the first and last elements in the tuple.

– Ignoring elements:
We can use an underscore _ to ignore specific elements during unpacking.

```python
# Creating a tuple
point = (8, 3, 5)

# Unpacking and ignoring the middle value
x, _, z = point

# x is 8, z is 5
```

Here, the underscore _ is used to ignore the second element in the tuple.

2.3.3 Dictionaries and Sets

Dictionaries
A Python dictionary is a nonsequential aggregation of key-value pairs, where every key must be exclusive. In alternative programming languages, dictionaries are referred to as associative arrays or hash maps. They are established by employing curly braces {} and encompass keys along with their corresponding values.

Creating a Dictionary
Defining a collection of key-value pairs using curly braces {} is a fundamental step in the creation of a dictionary in Python. It is of utmost importance that each key within the dictionary is distinct, as the keys are intrinsically linked to their corresponding values. Dictionaries present a versatile and effective means of organizing and retrieving data by means of keys.

– Basic dictionary creation:

```python
# Creating a dictionary of student information
student = {
    "name": "John Doe",
    "age": 20,
    "grade": "A",
    "courses": ["Math", "Physics", "English"]
}
```

In this particular instance, a dictionary, by the name of "student," is established, consisting of four pairs of keys and values. These keys, indeed, are strings – specifically "name," "age," "grade," and "courses" – while the values can take on various data types. These data types encompass strings, integers, lists, and, intriguingly, even other dictionaries.

– **Creating an empty dictionary:**
An empty dictionary may be generated through the utilization of vacant curly braces {}.

```python
# Creating an empty dictionary
empty_dict = {}
```

– **Dictionary with mixed data types:**
Dictionaries have the capability to store values that belong to various data types.

```python
# Creating a dictionary with mixed data types
mixed_dict = {
    "name": "Alice",
    "age": 25,
    "is_student": False,
    "grades": {"Math": "A", "English": "B"}
}
```
Here, the "grades" key is associated with another dictionary containing subject grades.

– **Using the dict() constructor:**
We may also construct a dictionary by utilizing the dict() constructor and providing key-value pairs as arguments.

```python
# Creating a dictionary using dict() constructor
fruit_dict = dict(apple=3, banana=5, orange=2)
```

Accessing Elements in Dictionary
Accessing elements in a dictionary in Python involves retrieving the values associated with specific keys. Dictionaries use keys to uniquely identify and access their corresponding values.

– **Basic accessing:**

```python
# Creating a dictionary of student information
student = {
    "name": "John Doe",
    "age": 20,
    "grade": "A",
```

```
    "courses": ["Math", "Physics", "English"]
}

# Accessing elements using keys
student_name = student["name"]
student_age = student["age"]
```

In this example, the values associated with the keys "name" and "age" are accessed and assigned to variables.

– Default value with get():
The get() method enables the specification of a default value that will be returned in the event that the key is not discovered.

```
# Providing a default value with get()
instructor = student.get("instructor", "Not specified")

# If "instructor" key exists, instructor will contain its value;
otherwise, it will be "Not specified"
```

– Handling key errors:
If one attempts to retrieve a key that is not present in the dictionary, it will lead to the occurrence of a KeyError. To prevent this from happening, one can utilize the get() method, which will yield a value of None if the specified key is not found.

```
# Using get() to handle key errors
grade = student.get("grade")

# If "grade" key exists, grade will contain its value; otherwise, it
will be None
```

– Checking key existence:
We are able to utilize the "in" keyword to verify the existence of a specific key within the dictionary prior to accessing it.

```
# Checking if a key exists
if "courses" in student:
  student_courses = student["courses"]
else:
  student_courses = []
```

– Using keys(), values(), and items() methods:
The methods keys(), values(), and items() provide the means to retrieve keys, values, and key-value pairs, correspondingly.

```
# Accessing keys, values, and items
all_keys = student.keys()
all_values = student.values()
all_items = student.items()
```

Modifying and Adding Elements in Dictionary
Modifying and adding elements in a dictionary in Python are common operations that allow us to update the content of the dictionary.

– Modifying existing elements:

```
# Creating a dictionary of student information
student = {
  "name": "John Doe",
  "age": 20,
  "grade": "A",
  "courses": ["Math", "Physics", "English"]
}
# Modifying the value associated with the "age" key
student["age"] = 21
```

In this instance, the numerical value linked to the designated identifier "age" has been altered from 20 to 21.

– Adding new elements:

```
# Creating a dictionary of student information
student = {
  "name": "John Doe",
  "age": 20,
  "grade": "A",
  "courses": ["Math", "Physics", "English"]
}
# Adding a new key-value pair for the "gender" information
student["gender"] = "Male"
```

Here, a novel key-value pair consisting of the key "gender" and the value "Male" is appended to the dictionary.

– **Modifying or adding multiple elements:**
The update() method allows for the simultaneous modification or addition of multiple elements.

```
# Creating a dictionary of student information
student = {
    "name": "John Doe",
    "age": 20,
    "grade": "A",
    "courses": ["Math", "Physics", "English"]
}
```

```
# Modifying and adding multiple elements
student.update({"age": 21, "gender": "Male", "city": "New York"})
```

The update() method is employed in this particular instance to alter the value linked to the "age" key, introduce a fresh key-value pair for the attribute of "gender," and append yet another new key-value pair for the attribute of "city."

Removing Elements from Dictionary
Deleting specific key-value pairs is a frequent task in Python when working with dictionaries. This can be accomplished by employing various approaches.

– **Using del statement:**
The del statement provides the functionality to eliminate a particular key and its corresponding value from a dictionary.

```
# Creating a dictionary of student information
student = {
    "name": "John Doe",
    "age": 20,
    "grade": "A",
    "courses": ["Math", "Physics", "English"]
}
```

```
# Removing the "grade" key and its value
del student["grade"]
```

In this particular instance, the dictionary's key "grade" and its corresponding value are extracted from the dictionary by employing the del statement.

Using pop() method:
The pop() function effectively eliminates a designated key and subsequently produces the value associated with it. Moreover, this particular function also offers the ability to supply a predetermined value in the event that the key in question cannot be located.

```
# Creating a dictionary of student information
student = {
    "name": "John Doe",
    "age": 20,
    "grade": "A",
    "courses": ["Math", "Physics", "English"]
}

# Removing and retrieving the value associated with the "courses" key
courses = student.pop("courses")
```

The "courses" key and its corresponding value are extracted from the dictionary, and the value is subsequently assigned to the variable courses.

– Using popitem() method:
The popitem() function is utilized to eliminate and retrieve the final key-value pair found within the dictionary. It is crucial to acknowledge that the arrangement in which the data was introduced remains unaltered beginning from Python 3.7.

```
# Creating a dictionary of student information
student = {
    "name": "John Doe",
    "age": 20,
    "grade": "A",
    "courses": ["Math", "Physics", "English"]
}

# Removing and retrieving the last key-value pair
last_item = student.popitem()
```

In this instance, the final key-value pair within the dictionary is eliminated and designated to the variable last_item.

– Using clear() method:
The clear() function eliminates all pairs of keys and values from the dictionary, resulting in an empty state.

```
# Creating a dictionary of student information
student = {
    "name": "John Doe",
    "age": 20,
    "grade": "A",
    "courses": ["Math", "Physics", "English"]
}
```

```
# Clearing all elements from the dictionary
student.clear()
```

After calling clear(), the dictionary is empty.

Sets

A Python set is an unordered assemblage of distinct elements. Sets are established by employing curly brackets {} and are advantageous for multiple operations such as verifying membership, discovering intersections, unions, and disparities amidst sets.

Creating a Set

Defining an unordered collection of unique elements is the process of creating a set in Python. The sets are denoted by curly braces {} and can be formed by using existing iterables such as lists or by explicitly stating the elements.

– **Basic set creation:**

```
# Creating a set with explicit elements
fruits_set = {"apple", "banana", "orange"}
```

```
# Creating an empty set
empty_set = set()
```

In the initial instance, a collection denoted as fruits_set is established, consisting of three components: "apple," "banana," and "orange." In the subsequent example, an unfilled collection referred to as empty_set is generated by employing the set() constructor.

– **Creating a set from an iterable:**

```
# Creating a set from a list
colors_list = ["red", "green", "blue", "red"]
```

```
colors_set = set(colors_list)
```

The set() constructor is employed in this instance to generate a set called colors_set from a list known as colors_list. It should be noted that sets inherently eliminate any duplicate elements, thereby resulting in a set that exclusively consists of distinct elements.

Adding Elements in Set

The process of including items in a set in Python is accomplished through the utilization of the add() function for the addition of a singular element and the update() function for the inclusion of multiple elements.

– Adding a single element:
To include an individual element in a set, the add() method can be utilized.

```
# Creating a set
fruits_set = {"apple", "banana", "orange"}

# Adding a single element
fruits_set.add("kiwi")
```

In this particular instance, the inclusion of the element "kiwi" within the fruits_set is achieved through the utilization of the add() method.

– Adding multiple elements:
To incorporate multiple elements into a set, one can employ the update() function by supplying an iterable object, such as a list or another set.

```
# Creating a set
fruits_set = {"apple", "banana", "orange"}

# Adding multiple elements
fruits_set.update(["grape", "pineapple"])
```

The fruits_set incorporates the elements "grape" and "pineapple" through the utilization of the update() method.

Removing Elements from Set

Removing elements from a set in Python necessitates the utilization of techniques such as remove(), discard(), and pop(). These techniques offer various approaches to eliminating elements from sets.

– Using remove() method:
The remove() function is utilized to eliminate a particular element from the set. In the event that the element does not exist, it will raise a KeyError.

```
# Creating a set
fruits_set = {"apple", "banana", "orange"}

# Removing a specific element
fruits_set.remove("banana")
```

In this example, the element "banana" is removed from the fruits_set.

– Using discard() method:
The discard() method eliminates a particular element from the set. In case the element is absent, no action is taken and no error is raised.

```
# Creating a set
fruits_set = {"apple", "banana", "orange"}

# Discarding an element
fruits_set.discard("kiwi")
```

Here, the element "kiwi" is discarded from the fruits_set, but if "kiwi" were not present, it would not raise an error.

– Using pop() method:
The pop() function is responsible for eliminating and returning an indiscriminate component from the collection. In the event that the collection is devoid of any elements, it will generate a KeyError.

```
# Creating a set
fruits_set = {"apple", "banana", "orange"}

# Pop an arbitrary element
popped_element = fruits_set.pop()
```

In this instance, a random element is removed from the fruits_set, and its value is subsequently assigned to the variable popped_element.

– Clearing the entire set:
The clear() method eradicates all elements from the set, resulting in an empty set.

```
# Creating a set
fruits_set = {"apple", "banana", "orange"}

# Clearing all elements from the set
fruits_set.clear()
```

After calling clear(), the fruits_set becomes an empty set.

Set Operations

Sets in Python support various operations that enable us to perform common set-related tasks. Below are the fundamental set operations:

– **Union (|) – combining sets:**
The amalgamation of two sets encompasses all distinct elements from both sets.

```
set1 = {1, 2, 3}
set2 = {3, 4, 5}

union_set = set1 | set2
# or using method: union_set = set1.union(set2)

# Output: {1, 2, 3, 4, 5}
```

– **Intersection (&) – common elements:**
The intersection of two sets comprises elements that are shared by both sets.

```
set1 = {1, 2, 3}
set2 = {3, 4, 5}

intersection_set = set1 & set2
# or using method: intersection_set = set1.intersection(set2)

# Output: {3}
```

– **Difference (-) – elements in the first set but not in the second:**
The dissimilarity between two sets comprises of elements that exist in the initial set but do not belong to the subsequent set.

```
set1 = {1, 2, 3}
set2 = {3, 4, 5}
```

```
difference_set = set1 - set2
# or using method: difference_set = set1.difference(set2)

# Output: {1, 2}
```

– Symmetric difference (^) – elements in either set, but not both:
The set obtained by taking the symmetric difference of two sets is composed of elements that belong to either of the sets, but not to both sets simultaneously.

```
set1 = {1, 2, 3}
set2 = {3, 4, 5}

symmetric_difference_set = set1 ^ set2
# or using method: symmetric_difference_set = set1.symmetric_difference
(set2)

# Output: {1, 2, 4, 5}
```

2.4 Control Structures

Control statements in Python are utilized to regulate the progression of execution within a program. They afford us the ability to render decisions, iterate through a code block, or bypass specific sections of code contingent upon predetermined conditions. The key control statements in Python encompass the following:
– Conditional statements
– Loops

2.4.1 Conditional Statements

Conditional statements in programming are constructs that facilitate the execution of diverse code blocks predicated on specified conditions. These constructs empower a program to exercise discernment, select between disparate actions, and govern the progression of execution. Conditional statements are paramount for composing dynamic and adaptable code.

Conditional statements play a fundamental role in designing algorithms, handling user inputs, and responding to various scenarios within a program. They contribute to the logical structure and decision-making capabilities of computer programs.

The fundamental concept entails evaluating the veracity or falsity of a particular condition, and subsequently, implementing distinct sections of code in accordance with the outcome.

– if statement:

The if statement is employed to execute a block of code on the condition that a specified condition holds true.

Syntax

```
if condition:
 # code to be executed if the condition is true

x = 10
if x > 5:
   print("x is greater than 5")
```

The print statement will be executed solely if the condition $x > 5$ is verified, as illustrated in this example.

– if-else statement:

The if-else statement grants the capability to execute a specific block of code when a given condition is found to be true, and alternatively, to execute a distinct block of code when the condition is found to be false.

```
if condition:
 # code to be executed if the condition is true
else:
 # code to be executed if the condition is false

x = 3

if x % 2 == 0:
   print("x is even")
else:
   print("x is odd")
```

In this instance, the program shall output whether x is classified as even or odd contingent upon the condition.

– if-elif-else statement:

The if-elif-else statement is an expansion of the if-else statement, enabling the examination of multiple conditions in a sequential manner.

```
if condition1:
   # code to be executed if condition1 is true
```

```
elif condition2:
  # code to be executed if condition2 is true
else:
  # code to be executed if none of the conditions are true

x = 0

if x > 0:
  print("x is positive")
elif x < 0:
  print("x is negative")
else:
  print("x is zero")
```

The program in this illustration verifies the positivity, negativity, or neutrality of x, and proceeds to display the associated notification.

2.4.2 Loops

Looping statements in programming enable the execution of a designated block of code multiple times depending on a specified condition. They play a crucial role in automating redundant tasks, iterating through data collections, and performing operations until a specific condition is satisfied. Python offers two main types of looping statements: for loops and while loops.

– for loop:
The for loop is employed to iterate through a sequence, be it a list, tuple, string, or range, or any other iterable objects. This loop carries out a set of instructions for every element present in the sequence.

Syntax

```
for variable in iterable:
  # code to be executed for each iteration

fruits = ["apple", "banana", "orange"]
for fruit in fruits:
  print(fruit)
```

In this example, the for loop iterates over the list of fruits, and the code inside the loop prints each fruit.

– while loop:

The while loop persists in executing a block of code for as long as a specified condition remains true. It iterates the execution until the condition becomes false.

Syntax

```
while condition:
  # code to be executed as long as the condition is true

count = 0
while count < 5:
  print(count)
  count += 1
```

The while loop, in this particular case, outputs the count value and increases it by 1 during each iteration, provided that the count is below 5.

2.5 Functions and Modules

Functions and modules are essential principles in Python that endorse the organization, legibility, and reusability of code. Functions encapsulate the logic of code, while modules and packages furnish a structured approach to arranging and aggregating correlated functionality.

Functions in Python enable us to encapsulate and reuse code, enhancing the legibility and maintainability of our programs.

Modules and packages aid in the organization of code into manageable units, thereby facilitating code reuse and maintenance.

2.5.1 Defining Functions

In Python, a function is a reusable block of code that is created to execute a particular task. Functions play a crucial role in the organization of code, enhancement of readability, and encouragement of code reuse.

When defining a function in Python, the def keyword is utilized, followed by the function name, a set of parentheses that may contain optional parameters, and a colon. The function body is indented and has the potential to incorporate a return statement, which specifies the output of the function.

Syntax

```
def function_name(parameters):
  # code to be executed
  return result # optional
```

Example 1: Simple addition function:

```
def add_numbers(a, b):
  sum_result = a + b
  return sum_result

# Calling the function
result = add_numbers(5, 3)
print(result) # Output: 8
```

The add_numbers function in this illustrative case accepts two parameters, namely a and b, performs the summation operation on them, and subsequently provides the outcome as the returned value.

Example 2: Greeting function:

```
def greet(name):
  greeting_message = f"Hello, {name}!"
  return greeting_message

# Calling the function
message = greet("Alice")
print(message) # Output: Hello, Alice!
```

Here, the greet function takes a name parameter and returns a personalized greeting message.

Example 3: Square function with default parameter:

```
def square_number(number, power=2):
  result = number ** power
  return result

# Calling the function
```

```
square_result = square_number(4)
print(square_result) # Output: 16

# Calling the function with a different power
cube_result = square_number(4, 3)
print(cube_result) # Output: 64
```

The square_number function in this particular example is designed to compute the square of a given number as its default behavior, although it is also possible to configure it to calculate the cube or any other desired power.

2.5.2 Lambda Functions

Lambda functions, which are also referred to as "anonymous functions," are characterized by their brevity and frequent utilization in performing small, uncomplicated tasks. These functions are established through the employment of the lambda keyword and have the ability to accept an arbitrary quantity of arguments; however, they are limited to solely possessing a solitary expression. The implementation of lambda functions proves to be especially advantageous when dealing with temporary operations that can be conveyed as arguments to higher-order functions.

Lambda functions are especially useful when a small, one-off function is needed and defining a full function using **def** seems too verbose. They are commonly used in situations where functions are treated as first-class citizens, such as when passing functions as arguments to higher-order functions.

Syntax

```
lambda arguments: expression
```

The lambda keyword is succeeded by a series of parameters, a colon, and an expression. The outcome of the expression constitutes the output value of the lambda function.

Example 1: Adding two numbers

```python
add_numbers = lambda x, y: x + y

result = add_numbers(5, 3)
print(result) # Output: 8
```

A lambda function add_numbers is defined in this instance to compute the sum of two numbers. Following this, the lambda function is invoked with the arguments 5 and 3, and the outcome is subsequently displayed.

Example 2: Squaring a number

```python
square = lambda x: x ** 2
result = square(4)
print(result) # Output: 16
```

A lambda function, named square, is defined to compute the square of a given number. Subsequently, the lambda function is invoked with the input argument 4, and the outcome is displayed.

Example 3: Checking if a number is even

```python
is_even = lambda x: x % 2 == 0
result = is_even(7)
print(result) # Output: False
```

In this given instance, a lambda function named is_even is established to verify whether a given number is divisible by two without a remainder. Consequently, the lambda function is subsequently invoked with the parameter 7, and the resulting outcome is subsequently displayed.

2.5.3 Modules and Packages

The fundamental concepts in Python that enhance code organization, readability, and reusability are modules and packages. Modules enable the encapsulation of related code into distinct files, while packages offer a means to structure these modules within a hierarchical directory.

Modules

A Python module is a file that consists of Python definitions, statements, and functions. This enables the organization of related code into distinct files, thereby enhancing the modularity and maintainability of the code. The utilization of functions, classes, and variables defined in a module is achieved by importing it into other Python scripts.

Syntax to create a module (my_module.py)

```
# my_module.py

def add(a, b):
   return a + b

def subtract(a, b):
   return a - b
```

Using the module in another script (main_program.py)

```
# main_program.py

import my_module

result = my_module.add(5, 3)
print(result) # Output: 8
```

In this particular instance, the module, my_module, encompasses functions for addition and subtraction. The importation of this module into the main_program.py file allows for the utilization of the add function.

Packages

A package is a method of organizing associated modules within a unified directory structure. It serves the purpose of preventing naming conflicts among distinct modules. In essence, a package constitutes a directory that encompasses multiple Python files, also known as "modules." For a directory to be regarded as a package, it is imperative that it includes a designated file labeled __init__.py.

Package Structure

```
my_package/
|-- __init__.py
|-- module1.py
|-- module2.py
```

Using modules from a package (main_program.py)

```
# main_program.py

from my_package import module1

result = module1.square(4)
print(result) # Output: 16
```

In this example, my_package is a package, and module1 is a module within that package. The square function from module1 is used in main_program.py.

2.6 Working with Files

The ability to read from and write to files is a crucial aspect of data storage, retrieval, and manipulation in any programming language. In Python, file operations are made simple with the aid of built-in functions and methods. Opening, reading, and writing to files allows for persistent data storage and the exchange of information between programs.

Dealing with files in Python is essential for managing data persistence and external data sources. It offers a means of interacting with data stored on disk, enabling the integration of Python programs with external data and facilitating efficient data management.

2.6.1 File I/O

File I/O in Python pertains to the procedures encompassing the act of both retrieving data from and storing data into files. Python furnishes an assortment of pre-existing functions and methods for file I/O, affording you the capability to engage with files on your operating system. The fundamental constituents of file I/O encompass the act of initiating file access, acquiring data from files, inscribing data into files, and ultimately terminating file access.

Opening a File

The Python open() function is an inherent function used to initiate the process of opening files. This function is an essential component of file management within the Python programming language, facilitating a multitude of file-related tasks such as reading, writing, and appending. As a result of executing the open() function, a file object is returned, which in turn grants access to a range of methods for the manipulation of files.

Syntax

```
file = open("filename.txt", "mode")
```

- file: Specifies the file path or name.
- mode: Specifies the mode of operation (optional; default is 'r' for read).

Modes

- 'r': The file is opened for reading.
- 'w': The file is opened for writing. If the file already exists, it is truncated.
- 'a': The file is opened for writing, but new data is appended to the end if the file already exists.
- 'b': 'b' is appended to the mode for binary files (e.g., 'rb' or 'wb').
- 'x': Fails if the file already exists.
- 't': 't' is appended to the mode for text files (e.g., 'rt' or 'wt').

```
# Opening a file in read mode
file = open("example.txt", "r")
```

Using "with" Statement

The with statement is employed in conjunction with file operations for the purpose of guaranteeing proper closure of the file following the completion of said operations.

```
with open("example.txt", "r") as file:
    content = file.read()
    # perform operations with content

# file is automatically closed outside the "with" block
```

Reading from a File

Reading from a file in Python involves opening the file in a specific mode, reading its content, and then closing the file. Python provides various methods for reading different amounts of data from a file.

– Opening a file for reading:

Use the open() function to initiate the process of accessing a file in read mode ('r'). Alternatively, it is possible to explicitly specify 'rt' in order to denote text mode.

```python
with open("example.txt", "r") as file:
 # File operations go here
```

– Reading the entire content:

The read() function retrieves the complete content of the file and presents it as a unified string.

```python
with open("example.txt", "r") as file:
  content = file.read()
  print(content)
```

– Reading line by line:

The readline() function is responsible for reading a solitary line from the document whenever it is invoked. This feature proves to be advantageous while handling voluminous files.

```python
with open("example.txt", "r") as file:
  line = file.readline()
    while line:
    print(line.strip()) # strip() removes newline characters
      line = file.readline()
```

– Reading all lines into a list:

The method called readlines() is responsible for reading and retrieving all lines from the file, after which it will present them in the form of a list.

```python
with open("example.txt", "r") as file:
  lines = file.readlines()
  for line in lines:
   print(line.strip())
```

– Iterating over lines using a for loop:
We can additionally iterate directly over the file object, whereby lines are automatically read.

```
with open("example.txt", "r") as file:
  for line in file:
    print(line.strip())
```

Writing to a File

To perform file writing operations in Python, it is necessary to first open the file using a designated mode, subsequently write the desired data into it, and finally close the file. In the Python programming language, there exist multiple methods that facilitate the process of writing data to a file.

– Opening a file for writing:
The open() function is utilized to initiate the opening of a file in the write mode ('w'). In the event that the file has already been created, opening it in write mode will result in the removal of its current contents. Conversely, if the file does not exist, a new file will be generated.

```
with open("output.txt", "w") as file:
  # File operations go here
```

– Writing content to the file:
The write() function is employed for the purpose of writing information to the file. It has the capability to write various types of data, such as strings, numbers, or any other data format that can be transformed into a string.

```
with open("output.txt", "w") as file:
  file.write("This is a sample sentence.")
```

– Appending to a file:
To append new content to an existing file without replacing its current content, it is possible to open the file in append mode ('a'). Subsequently, the write() method will append the new content to the conclusion of the file.

```
with open("output.txt", "a") as file:
  file.write("\nAppending new content.")
```

– **Writing multiple lines:**

Multiple lines can be written to a file either through the repeated utilization of the write() method or by supplying a sequence of strings to the writelines() method.

```
lines = ["Line 1\n", "Line 2\n", "Line 3\n"]
with open("output.txt", "w") as file:
  file.writelines(lines)
```

2.7 Working with Libraries

In Python, libraries (also known as modules or packages) are prewritten collections of code that provide functionality beyond the basic capabilities of the Python language. Working with libraries is a fundamental aspect of Python development, allowing us to leverage existing code to solve specific problems efficiently.

2.7.1 Importing Libraries

Importing libraries in Python is an indispensable component of programming, as it enables us to exploit pre-existing code and functionalities created by other individuals. The process of importing can be accomplished through various methods, and the following instances provide illustrations of distinct approaches. This allows us to avail ourselves of an extensive range of functionalities, thereby enhancing the efficiency and manageability of our code.

– **Importing the entire library:**

```
# Example: Using the math library for square root
import math

result = math.sqrt(25)
print(result) # Output: 5.0
```

The import keyword is used in this instance to import the entire math library. Subsequently, the square root of 25 is calculated using the math.sqrt() function.

– **Importing specific modules or functions:**

```
# Example: Importing only the sqrt function from the math library
from math import sqrt
```

```
result = sqrt(25)
print(result) # Output: 5.0
```

In this case, only the sqrt function from the math library is imported. This approach eliminates the need to prefix the function with the library name when used.

– **Importing with an alias:**

```
# Example: Using an alias for the pandas library
import pandas as pd

data = pd.read_csv("data.csv")
print(data.head())
```

Here, the pandas library is imported with the alias pd. This is a common convention to simplify code and make it more readable. The pd alias is then used to call functions from the pandas library.

– **Importing all modules from a library:**

```
# Example: Importing all modules from the datetime library
from datetime import *

current_date = date.today()
print(current_date) # Output: 2023-12-12
```

Importing all modules using the * wildcard allows us to use all functions and classes without explicitly mentioning them. However, this approach is generally discouraged to avoid name clashes.

2.7.2 Popular Python Libraries Overview

The Python libraries form the backbone of various Python applications, providing solutions across different domains, including data science, machine learning, web development, and more. Depending on our project requirements, we can choose the libraries that best suit our needs.

NumPy
– **Description:** NumPy, which is short for numerical Python, encompasses a comprehensive collection of numerical operation functions specifically designed for Python.

Main Features

- Efficient manipulation of large, homogeneous arrays can be achieved through the use of multidimensional arrays.
- Mathematical functions: Offer an extensive assortment of mathematical functions to facilitate array operations.

Use Cases

- Scientific computing and data analysis.
- Linear algebra operations.
- Signal processing and image analysis.

Pandas

- **Description:** Pandas is a library used for manipulating and analyzing data.

Main Features

- DataFrame: A two-dimensional table for data manipulation.
- Series: A one-dimensional labeled array.
- Data cleaning, merging, and reshaping tools.

Use Cases

- Data exploration and analysis.
- Data cleaning and preparation.
- Time series data analysis.

Matplotlib

- **Description:** Matplotlib is an esteemed library for generating visualizations, encompassing the realms of static, animated, and interactive visualizations.

Main Features

- Line plots, scatter plots, bar plots, etc.
- Support for LaTeX for mathematical expressions.
- Customizable plots and styles.

Use Cases

- Data visualization for analysis and presentation.
- Creating publication-quality plots.

Requests
– **Description:** Requests is a library designed to facilitate the execution of HTTP requests.

Main Features
– HTTP methods (GET, POST, PUT, DELETE, etc.).
– Session handling and cookie support.
– Asynchronous requests with **asyncio**.

Use Cases
– Web scraping and data extraction.
– Interacting with RESTful APIs.
– Sending HTTP requests and handling responses.

Scikit-learn
– **Description:** Scikit-learn, a library for classical machine learning algorithms, is a tool widely used in the field of machine learning.

Main Features
– Classification, regression, clustering, and dimensionality reduction algorithms can be categorized as different types of computational techniques for data analysis.
– Model selection and evaluation tools.
– Support for preprocessing and feature engineering.

Use Cases
– Building and evaluating machine learning models.
– Data analysis and exploration.

TensorFlow and PyTorch
– **Description:** TensorFlow and PyTorch are deep learning libraries.

Main Features
– Define, train, and deploy neural networks.
– Support for automatic differentiation.
– Broad ecosystem for machine learning and deep learning.

Use Cases
- Deep learning model development.
- Natural language processing and computer vision tasks.

Django and Flask
- **Description:** Django and Flask are web frameworks for building web applications.

Main Features
- Django: High-level framework with built-in features (admin, authentication, etc.).
- Flask: Micro-framework for lightweight and flexible applications.

Use Cases
- Developing web applications and APIs.
- Rapid development and scalability.

Beautiful Soup
- **Description:** Beautiful Soup is a web scraping library for pulling data out of HTML and XML files.

Main Features
- Parses HTML and XML documents.
- Navigates the parse tree and searches for specific elements.

Use Cases
- Scraping data from websites.
- Extracting information from HTML and XML.

SQLAlchemy
- **Description:** SQLAlchemy is a library that serves as a toolkit for SQL operations and also provides functionality for object-relational mapping (ORM).

Main Features
- SQL expression language and ORM.
- Connection pooling and transaction management.

- Database interaction in Python.
- Object-relational mapping for databases.

OpenCV
- **Description:** OpenCV is a computer vision library for image and video processing.

Main Features
- Image and video manipulation.
- Feature extraction and object detection.

Use Cases
- Computer vision applications.
- Image and video analysis.

2.8 Object-Oriented Programming in Python

Object-oriented programming (OOP) is a programming paradigm that employs the utilization of "objects" to systematize and structure code. Objects are exemplifications of classes, which are data types generated by users that encapsulate both data (attributes) and the procedures that manipulate the data (methods). Python is a programming language that adheres to the principles of object-oriented programming, and these principles are intricately incorporated into its syntax and design.

2.8.1 Classes and Objects

Classes
- A class serves as a blueprint or a template for the creation of objects, specifying their attributes and methods.
- The definition of classes in Python employs the use of the keyword "class."

The structure for declaring a class in Python is as shown:

```
class ClassName:
  def __init__(self, parameter1, parameter2, ...):
    # Constructor or initializer method
    # Set up instance attributes
```

```
def method1(self, parameter1, parameter2, ...):
  # Method 1 definition
  # Access instance attributes using self
def method2(self, parameter1, parameter2, ...):
  # Method 2 definition
  # Access instance attributes using self
```

- The class keyword is employed for the purpose of declaring a class. In the pro-vided instance, the name of the class is denoted by ClassName.
- Constructor (_init_) method:
  - The _init_ method, which is referred to as the "constructor," is a distinctive method that is automatically executed upon the creation of an object from the class.
  - The initialization of the object's attributes is performed. The self parameter is employed to refer to the instance of the class and to make references to in-stance attributes.
- Other methods:
  - Additional methods within the class are defined like regular functions, taking self as the first parameter.
  - These methods can perform various actions and access instance attributes.

Example

```
class Car:
  def __init__(self, make, model, year):
    self.make = make
    self.model = model
    self.year = year

  def display_info(self):
    return f"{self.year} {self.make} {self.model}"
```

The given example demonstrates the implementation of a class called Car. This class possesses the attributes of make, model, and year, as well as a method named dis-play_info. The initialization method, _init_, is responsible for assigning values to the attributes of the Car object.

Objects

In Python, an object represents an exemplification of a class. A class serves as a design that specifies characteristics and functionalities, while an object embodies a tangible manifestation of that design. Objects play a vital role in Python since they enable us to simulate and engage with real-world entities within our code. The establishment of objects contributes to upholding a modular and structured framework, thereby enhancing the readability and manageability of our code.

– **Creating an object:**
To instantiate an instance of the class, one invokes the class as though it were a function. By doing so, the constructor (_init_) method is invoked, passing the specified initial values.

```
# Creating an object of the class
object_name = ClassName(initial_value1, initial_value2, ...)

# Creating objects of the Car class
car1 = Car("Toyota", "Camry", 2022)
car2 = Car("Honda", "Civic", 2021)
```

Here, car1 and car2 are instances of the Car class. The _init_ method is automatically called when creating these objects, initializing their attributes.

– **Accessing attributes and calling methods:**
We can access attributes using the dot (.) notation. In this case, car1.make returns the value of the make attribute. Similarly, car2.display_info() calls the display_info method.

```
# Accessing attributes and calling methods
print(car1.make) # Output: Toyota
print(car2.display_info()) # Output: 2021 Honda Civic
```

Example 1

```
class Car:
  def __init__(self, make, model, year):
    self.make = make
    self.model = model
    self.year = year

  def display_info(self):
    return f"{self.year} {self.make} {self.model}"

# Creating objects of the Car class
car1 = Car("Toyota", "Camry", 2022)
car2 = Car("Honda", "Civic", 2021)
```

```
# Accessing attributes and calling methods
print(car1.make) # Output: Toyota
print(car2.display_info()) # Output: 2021 Honda Civic
```

This example demonstrates the creation of a simple Car class, instantiation of objects (car1 and car2), and accessing their attributes and methods.

Example 2

```
class Dog:
    def __init__(self, name, age):
      self.name = name
      self.age = age

  def bark(self):
    return "Woof!"

# Creating an object of the Dog class
my_dog = Dog("Buddy", 3)

# Accessing attributes and calling methods
print(my_dog.name)       # Output: Buddy
print(my_dog.bark())     # Output: Woof!
```

In this particular instance, the class is denoted as "Dog," while an object named "my_dog" is created from the aforementioned class. The initialization method, "__init__," serves to establish the attributes (name and age), while the bark method acts as a function connected to the Dog class, capable of being invoked on instances of the class. Subsequently, the object my_dog possesses the ability to access its attributes and invoke methods that have been defined within the class.

2.8.2 Inheritance and Polymorphism

Inheritance in Python

In the realm of object-oriented programming, the notion of inheritance holds great significance as it permits a fresh class to acquire attributes and methods from a pre-existing class. This pre-existing class is commonly known as the "base class" or "parent class," while the newly formed class takes on the role of the derived class or child class. By taking advantage of inheritance, one can foster the reuse of code and the establishment of a hierarchical structure encompassing various classes.

```python
# Base class
class Animal:
    def __init__(self, name):
        self.name = name

    def speak(self):
        return "Some generic sound"

# Derived class (inherits from Animal)
class Dog(Animal):
    def speak(self):
        return "Woof!"

# Creating objects
animal = Animal("Generic Animal")
dog = Dog("Buddy")

# Calling the speak method
print(animal.speak()) # Output: Some generic sound
print(dog.speak()) # Output: Woof!
```

In this particular instance, the base class Animal possesses a method known as speak. The Dog class, derived from Animal, supersedes the speak method. Both classes, namely Animal and Dog, can be utilized, and the speak method exhibits distinct behavior contingent upon the class.

Types of Inheritance

1. **Single inheritance:** A class acquires the attributes and behaviors of a single base class. For example, the derived class is defined as class DerivedClass(BaseClass).
2. **Multiple inheritance:** A class obtains the attributes and behaviors of more than one base class. For example, the derived class is defined as class DerivedClass (BaseClass1, BaseClass2, . . .).
3. **Multilevel inheritance:** A class gains the attributes and behaviors of another class, which itself inherits from a base class. For example, the derived class is defined as class DerivedClass(IntermediateClass).

4. **Hierarchical inheritance:** Multiple classes inherit the attributes and behaviors of a single base class. For example, the derived classes are defined as class DerivedClass1(BaseClass) and class DerivedClass2(BaseClass).
5. **Hybrid inheritance:** A combination of two or more types of inheritance is employed. For example, a class may inherit from one class using multiple inheritance and from another class using single inheritance.

Example of Single Inheritance

```python
# Base class
class Animal:
    def __init__(self, name):
        self.name = name

    def speak(self):
        return "Some generic sound"

# Derived class (inherits from Animal)
class Dog(Animal):
    def bark(self):
        return "Woof!"

# Creating objects
animal = Animal("Generic Animal")
dog = Dog("Buddy")

# Accessing methods from the base and derived classes
print(animal.speak()) # Output: Some generic sound
print(dog.speak()) # Output: Some generic sound
print(dog.bark()) # Output: Woof!
```

In this particular instance, the Animal class serves as the fundamental class, while the Dog class functions as the subclass. The Dog class acquires the speak method from its parent class Animal.

Example of Multiple Inheritance

```python
# Base classes
class Engine:
    def start(self):
        return "Engine started"
```

```
class Electric:
  def charge(self):
   return "Charging electric power"

# Derived class (inherits from both Engine and Electric)
class HybridCar(Engine, Electric):
  def drive(self):
   return "Driving in hybrid mode"

# Creating an object
hybrid_car = HybridCar()

# Accessing methods from the base classes
print(hybrid_car.start()) # Output: Engine started
print(hybrid_car.charge()) # Output: Charging electric power
print(hybrid_car.drive()) # Output: Driving in hybrid mode
```

The example demonstrates the utilization of a derived class called "HybridCar," which inherits from both the Engine and Electric base classes. This enables the HybridCar class to have access to the methods provided by both of its base classes.

Example of Multilevel Inheritance

```
# Base class
class Animal:
  def speak(self):
   return "Some generic sound"

# Intermediate class (inherits from Animal)
class Dog(Animal):
  def bark(self):
   return "Woof!"

# Derived class (inherits from Dog)
class Poodle(Dog):
  def dance(self):
   return "Poodle is dancing"

# Creating an object
poodle = Poodle()
```

```
# Accessing methods from all levels of inheritance
print(poodle.speak()) # Output: Some generic sound
print(poodle.bark()) # Output: Woof!
print(poodle.dance()) # Output: Poodle is dancing
```

In this particular instance, Poodle represents a subclass that acquires characteristics from Dog, which, in turn, acquires characteristics from the parent class Animal. It possesses the capability to access methods from all levels of inheritance.

Polymorphism in Python

Polymorphism enables the utilization of objects from diverse classes as objects of a shared base class. It permits the representation of various types of objects through a singular interface (method). Polymorphism is accomplished through method overriding, wherein the child class possesses a method with the identical name as the method in the parent class.

```
class Shape:
    def area(self):
        return "Some generic area calculation"

class Square(Shape):
    def __init__(self, side):
        self.side = side

    def area(self):
        return self.side ** 2

class Circle(Shape):
    def __init__(self, radius):
        self.radius = radius

    def area(self):
        return 3.14 * self.radius ** 2

# Using polymorphism
shapes = [Square(5), Circle(3)]
for shape in shapes:
    print(f"Area: {shape.area()}")
```

```
# Output
# Area: 25
# Area: 28.26
```

In this particular instance, the class Shape serves as the fundamental class housing a method for computing area. The classes Square and Circle are subclasses of Shape and possess an overridden version of the area method. The list shapes encompasses objects from both classes, employing the identical method (area) to determine the area, thereby exemplifying the concept of polymorphism.

Summary

- Python syntax places a strong emphasis on readability, employing indentation to denote block structure.
- The correct use of indentation is of utmost importance in Python, as it serves as a crucial indicator of the underlying block structure.
- Comments, which serve as a form of documentation, are denoted by a # symbol. Python offers support for a variety of data types, encompassing integers, floats, strings, and booleans.
- Variables are utilized to store data and manipulate it as needed. Lists are mutable, meaning they can be modified, while tuples are immutable, meaning they cannot be changed.
- Dictionaries employ key-value pairs, while sets consist solely of unique elements.
- Python is an object-oriented language, with classes and objects serving as its core concepts.
- A class functions as a blueprint for creating objects, while objects are instances of classes.
- Inheritance allows a class to inherit attributes and methods from another class.
- Polymorphism enables objects of different types to be treated as if they were objects of a common type.

Exercise (MCQs)

1. **What is the primary purpose of indentation in Python syntax?**
   A. Enhancing aesthetics
   B. Enforcing code style
   C. Indicating block structure
   D. Improving execution speed

2. **Which character is used to indicate a comment in Python?**
   A. //   B. #   C. –   D. /* */

3. **What is the purpose of variables in Python?**
   A. To store data
   B. To perform mathematical operations
   C. To create loops
   D. To define functions

4. **Which of the following is a primitive data type in Python?**
   A. List   B. Tuple   C. String   D. Dictionary

5. **Which data type is mutable in Python?**
   A. List   B. Tuple   C. String   D. Dictionary

6. **What does a set in Python contain?**
   A. Duplicate elements
   B. Ordered elements
   C. Unique elements
   D. Key-value pairs

7. **How is an element accessed in a list or tuple in Python?**
   A. Using dot notation
   B. Using square brackets and index
   C. Using parentheses and index
   D. Using the get method

8. **What is a class in Python?**
   A. A function
   B. A module
   C. A blueprint for creating objects
   D. A loop structure

9. **In OOP, what are instances of classes called?**
   A. Objects   B. Functions   C. Variables   D. Methods

10. **What does inheritance allow in Python?**
   A. Code duplication
   B. Code reuse
   C. Method overloading
   D. Variable overloading

11. **Which type of inheritance involves a class inheriting from more than one base class?**
    A. Single inheritance
    B. Multiple inheritance
    C. Multilevel inheritance
    D. Hierarchical inheritance

Answers

1. C
2. B
3. A
4. C
5. A
6. C
7. B
8. C
9. A
10. B
11. B

Fill in the Blanks

1. Proper _____ is crucial in Python to indicate block structure.
2. Comments in Python start with the _____ character.
3. Python supports various data types, including integers, floats, strings, and _____.
4. A _____ data type represents a single value.
5. Lists in Python are _____, while tuples are _____.
6. Dictionaries in Python use _____ pairs, while sets contain _____ elements.
7. In Python, elements in a list or tuple are accessed using square brackets and
8. In Python, a class is a _____ for creating objects.
9. Instances of classes in OOP are called _____.
10. Inheritance in Python allows a class to inherit attributes and methods from _____ class(es).
11. _____ inheritance involves a class inheriting from more than one base class.

Answers

1. indentation
2. #
3. booleans
4. primitive
5. mutable, immutable
6. key-value, unique
7. index
8. blueprint
9. objects
10. another
11. multiple

Descriptive Questions

1. Explain the significance of proper indentation in Python syntax and how it influences the structure of the code.
2. Provide an overview of primitive data types in Python and explain the purpose of variables in the context of Python programming.
3. Discuss the differences between lists and tuples in Python, emphasizing their mutability or immutability.
4. Explain the key characteristics of dictionaries and sets in Python, highlighting their use cases and unique properties.
5. Define the concepts of classes and objects in Python's object-oriented programming paradigm, providing examples for better understanding.
6. Elaborate on the concept of inheritance in Python, discussing how it enables code reuse. Provide an example to illustrate polymorphism.
7. Describe the various types of inheritance in Python, including single, multiple, multilevel, hierarchical, and hybrid inheritance.
8. Walk through the polymorphism example involving Shape, Square, and Circle classes. Explain how the common interface (area method) is utilized.
9. Explore the control statements in Python, including if, for, and while statements. Provide examples to demonstrate their usage.
10. Discuss the role of functions in Python and explain the process of defining functions. Additionally, explain the concept of modules and how they enhance code organization.
11. Provide an overview of working with files in Python, explaining the open() function and file input/output operations.
12. Explain the importance of libraries in Python programming and discuss the process of importing libraries. Provide examples of popular Python libraries.

13. Delve deeper into object-oriented programming concepts, specifically focusing on defining classes, creating objects, and encapsulating attributes and methods.
14. Elaborate on file input/output operations in Python, including reading from and writing to files. Explain the with statement for handling files.
15. Provide a detailed explanation of conditional statements in Python, including the syntax and usage of if, elif, and else statements.
16. Write a Python program that takes a list of numbers, squares each element, and prints the resulting list.
17. Create a tuple containing the names of your favorite fruits. Write a program that asks the user for input and checks if the fruit is in the tuple.
18. Design a program that prompts the user to enter information about a book (title, author, and publication year) and stores it in a dictionary. Print the dictionary at the end.
19. Implement a Python program with classes representing geometric shapes (e.g., Circle, Square) inheriting from a common base class. Use polymorphism to calculate and print the area of each shape.
20. Create a text file with some content. Write a Python program that reads the content of the file, counts the number of words, and prints the result.
21. Write a function that takes a list of numbers as input and returns the sum of all the even numbers in the list.
22. Create a Python module that defines a function to calculate the area of a rectangle. In another program, import the module and use the function to calculate the area of a rectangle.
23. Write a program that takes two sets as input from the user and prints the union, intersection, and difference of the sets.
24. Design a simple movie database using classes. Create classes for movies, directors, and actors, allowing users to add and retrieve information about movies, directors, and actors.
25. Write a program that asks the user for their age. Based on the age, print different messages such as "You're a child," "You're a teenager," or "You're an adult."

Chapter 3
Data Preprocessing in Python

3.1 Numerical and Scientific Computing Using NumPy and SciPy

In this segment, we delve into the fundamental elements of numerical and scientific computation employing two potent Python libraries – NumPy and SciPy. These libraries assume a pivotal function in scientific computation, furnishing a basis for manipulating extensive, multidimensional arrays and executing diverse mathematical computations.

3.1.1 Numerical Computations with NumPy

– Introduction to NumPy

NumPy, which is an abbreviation for Numerical Python, constitutes a robust open-source Python library that furnishes assistance for extensive, multidimensional arrays and matrices. Furthermore, it encompasses a compilation of sophisticated mathematical functions to carry out operations on these arrays. Notably, it emerges as an indispensable library for scientific computation in Python and serves as the underpinning for diverse other libraries and tools in the realm of data science and machine learning.

Here are key aspects of NumPy that contribute to its significance:

1. **Arrays:**
    Multidimensional data structures: NumPy presents the ndarray, an object that is capable of representing arrays with multiple dimensions such as vectors, matrices, and arrays with higher dimensions. This feature enables the storage and manipulation of extensive datasets in a manner that is efficient.
    Element-wise operations: NumPy facilitates element-wise computations, thereby enabling mathematical operations to be executed on complete arrays without necessitating explicit iterations. This results in the production of succinct and effective code.

2. **Mathematical operations:**
    Universal functions (ufuncs): NumPy offers an extensive assortment of universal functions (ufuncs) that perform element-wise computations on arrays. These ufuncs encompass a broad spectrum of mathematical operations, encompassing fundamental arithmetic, trigonometry, logarithms, and various others.

https://doi.org/10.1515/9783110697186-003

Linear algebra: NumPy incorporates an extensive collection of functions dedicated to operations in the field of linear algebra, encompassing tasks such as the multiplication of matrices, decomposition of eigenvalues, as well as the resolution of linear systems of equations.

3. **Performance:**
Efficient data storage: NumPy arrays are executed in the programming languages C and Fortran, thereby facilitating proficient storage and manipulation of numerical data. This capability is of utmost significance when managing extensive datasets and executing intricate computations.
Broadcasting: The broadcasting mechanism of NumPy facilitates the execution of operations on arrays with different shapes and sizes. This feature simplifies the process of performing operations on arrays with varying dimensions.

4. **Integration with other libraries:**
Interoperability: NumPy effortlessly integrates with various libraries and resources within the Python ecosystem, including SciPy, Matplotlib, and scikit-learn, each serving distinct purposes such as scientific computing, plotting and visualization, and machine learning, respectively.

5. **Applications:**
Scientific computing: NumPy finds extensive applications in the field of scientific computation for endeavors encompassing data analysis, simulations, and the resolution of mathematical quandaries.
Data science and machine learning: Many libraries used in the fields of data science and machine learning, such as Pandas and scikit-learn, heavily depend on NumPy arrays to represent and manipulate data.

6. **Community and documentation:**
Active community: The presence of an extensive and engaged group of developers and contributors in the NumPy community guarantees consistent updates, resolution of programming errors, and access to a diverse array of available resources.
Documentation: The documentation of NumPy is comprehensive and meticulously maintained, offering thorough elucidations of functions, illustrative instances, and optimal methodologies.

NumPy constitutes an indispensable instrument for any Python developer involved in numerical and scientific computation. The efficacy, user-friendliness, and integration potential it possesses render it a fundamental element of the Python ecosystem for the fields of data science and computational undertakings.

- **Array creation and manipulation**
  - NumPy offers a multitude of methods for generating arrays, including np. array(), np.zeros(), np.ones(), and np.arange(). These methods enable the user to initialize arrays with designated values, zeros, ones, or to generate arrays with a specified range of values. The np.array() function facilitates the conversion of pre-existing Python lists or tuples into NumPy arrays.
  - Multidimensional arrays can be created using nested lists or by reshaping existing arrays using methods like reshape().
  - NumPy arrays possess the capacity to enable robust indexing and slicing operations. The retrieval of array elements is facilitated through the implementation of square bracket notation, while the extraction of array slices is accomplished through the utilization of the colon (:) operator. This feature in turn allows for the efficient and succinct extraction of subarrays.
  - NumPy offers a range of functions for the manipulation of arrays, including np reshape(), np flatten(), and np.concatenate(). These functions enable the modification of an array's shape, the flattening of its structure, and the concatenation of multiple arrays.
  - Transposition, achieved with np.transpose() or the.T attribute, is a common operation for rearranging array dimensions.

Array Creation

Using np.array()

The np.array() function serves as a fundamental means to generate arrays within the NumPy library. This function accepts a sequence-like object (such as a list or a tuple) as its input and subsequently yields a NumPy array.

Example 1: Creating a 1D array:

```
import numpy as np

# Creating a 1D array from a Python list
arr1d = np.array([1, 2, 3, 4, 5])
print("1D Array:")
print(arr1d)
```

In this particular instance, we generate a one-dimensional array (arr1d) by employing the np.array() function on a Python list [1, 2, 3, 4, 5]. The resultant array may be utilized for a variety of numerical computations.

Example 2: Creating a 2D array:

```
# Creating a 2D array from a nested Python list
arr2d = np.array([[1, 2, 3], [4, 5, 6]])
print("\n2D Array:")
print(arr2d)
```

A 2D array (arr2d) is generated from a nested Python list in this instance. The outer list symbolizes rows, while the inner lists symbolize the elements of each row. Consequently, the resulting structure is a 2D array.

Example 3: Creating an array with mixed data types:

```
# Creating an array with mixed data types
mixed_array = np.array([1, 2.5, "hello"])
print("\nMixed Data Type Array:")
print(mixed_array)
```

NumPy arrays possess homogeneity, denoting the preference for elements of an identical data type. Nevertheless, NumPy undertakes the endeavor to convert elements into a shared data type. In the given illustration, the array includes integers along with a string, hence NumPy alters all the elements to a common data type, specifically Unicode.

Example 4: Specifying data type:

```
# Specifying the data type of the array
arr_float = np.array([1, 2, 3], dtype=float)
print("\nArray with Specified Data Type (float):")
print(arr_float)
```

We have the option to explicitly indicate the data type of the array by utilizing the dtype parameter. In the given instance, we generate a one-dimensional array consisting of integers and specifically designate it as a float.

Using np.zeros()

The np.zeros() function is employed to generate an array that contains solely zeros. As an argument, it accepts the shape of the array.

Example 1: Creating a 1D array of zeros:

```
import numpy as np

# Creating a 1D array filled with zeros
zeros_1d = np.zeros(5)
print("1D Array of Zeros:")
print(zeros_1d)
```

In this particular instance, a one-dimensional array (zeros_1d) consisting of five elements, all of which are initially set to zero, is generated through the utilization of the np.zeros() function.

Example 2: Creating a 2D array of zeros:

```
# Creating a 2D array filled with zeros
zeros_2d = np.zeros((3, 4)) # 3 rows, 4 columns
print("\n2D Array of Zeros:")
print(zeros_2d)
```

Here, a 2D array (zeros_2d) with three rows and four columns, all initialized to zero, is created using np.zeros().

Using np.ones()

The np.ones() function is similar to np.zeros(), but it creates an array filled with ones.

Example 1: Creating a 1D array of ones:

```
# Creating a 1D array filled with ones
ones_1d = np.ones(6)
print("\n1D Array of Ones:")
print(ones_1d)
```

This example demonstrates the creation of a 1D array (ones_1d) with six elements, all initialized to one, using np.ones().

Example 2: Creating a 2D array of ones:

```
# Creating a 2D array filled with ones
ones_2d = np.ones((2, 3)) # 2 rows, 3 columns
print("\n2D Array of Ones:")
print(ones_2d)
```

In this particular instance, a two-dimensional array (referred to as ones_2d) is generated through the utilization of the np.ones() function. This array consists of two rows
and three columns, all of which are initially set to a value of one.

Both np.zeros() and np.ones() allow you to specify additional parameters like the
data type using the dtype parameter.

Example 3: Specifying data type with np.zeros():

```
# Creating a 1D array filled with zeros with a specified data type
(float)
zeros_float = np.zeros(4, dtype=float)
print("\n1D Array of Zeros with Specified Data Type (float):")
print(zeros_float)
```

In this example, a 1D array (zeros_float) with a specified data type (float) is created
using np.zeros().

Example 4: Specifying data type with np.ones():

```
# Creating a 2D array filled with ones with a specified data type (int)
ones_int = np.ones((3, 2), dtype=int)
print("\n2D Array of Ones with Specified Data Type (int):")
print(ones_int)
```

Here, a 2D array (ones_int) with a specified data type (int) is created using np.ones().

Using np.arange()

The np.arange() function is utilized to generate an array that contains values that are
evenly spaced within a specified range. It bears resemblance to the pre-existing range()
function in Python; however, it yields a NumPy array.

Example: Creating a 1D array with np.arange()

```
import numpy as np
# Creating a 1D array with values from 0 to 9
arr1d = np.arange(10)
print("1D Array:")
print(arr1d)
```

In this example, a 1D array (arr1d) is created using np.arange(10). The array contains values from 0 to 9 (exclusive). The np.arange() function is versatile and can take parameters like start, stop, and step to customize the array.

Customizing np.arange() Parameters

```
# Creating a 1D array with values from 2 to 10 (exclusive) with a step
of 2
arr_custom = np.arange(2, 10, 2)
print("\nCustomized 1D Array:")
print(arr_custom)
```

In this particular illustration, the np.arange() method is employed with the specified arguments start = 2, stop = 10 (exclusive), and step = 2. Consequently, a one-dimensional array (arr_custom) is obtained, which comprises the elements [2, 4, 6, 8].

Floating-Point Values with np.arange()

```
# Creating a 1D array with floating-point values
arr_float = np.arange(0, 1, 0.1)
print("\n1D Array with Floating-Point Values:")
print(arr_float)
```

The np.arange() function is utilized in this context to generate a one-dimensional array (arr_float) comprising floating-point values ranging from 0 to 1, exclusive, with an increment of 0.1.

Specifying Data Type with np.arange()

```
# Creating a 1D array with specified data type (float)
arr_float_dtype = np.arange(5, dtype=float)
```

```
print("\n1D Array with Specified Data Type (float):")
print(arr_float_dtype)
```

The dtype parameter enables us to specify the data type of the resulting array. In the present case, an array of dimension 1 (arr_float_dtype) is generated with values ranging from 0 to 4, while a particular data type (float) is assigned to it.

Reshaping Arrays Using reshape()

Reshaping arrays constitutes a critical operation within the context of NumPy, entailing the modification of the shape or dimensions of an extant array. The manipulation of the reshape() method within NumPy represents a widely employed approach to attain this objective.

Example 1: Reshaping a 1D array to a 2D array:

```
import numpy as np

# Creating a 1D array
arr1d = np.arange(6)
print("Original 1D Array:")
print(arr1d)

# Reshaping to a 2D array with 2 rows and 3 columns
arr2d = arr1d.reshape(2, 3)
print("\nReshaped 2D Array:")
print(arr2d)
```

In this particular illustration, we commence with a one-dimensional array, denoted as arr1d, which has been generated through the utilization of np.arange(). Subsequently, we employ the reshape() function to convert it into a two-dimensional array, referred to as arr2d, encompassing two rows and three columns.

Example 2: Reshaping a 1D array to a 3D array:

```
# Reshaping to a 3D array with 2 planes, 2 rows, and 3 columns
arr3d = arr1d.reshape(2, 2, 3)
print("\nReshaped 3D Array:")
print(arr3d)
```

In this particular scenario, we proceed to transform the identical one-dimensional array (arr1d) into a three-dimensional array (arr3d) comprising two planes, two rows, and three columns.

Example 3: Reshaping a 2D array to a Flattened 1D array:

```
# Creating a 2D array
arr2d_original = np.array([[1, 2, 3], [4, 5, 6]])
print("\nOriginal 2D Array:")
print(arr2d_original)

# Reshaping to a flattened 1D array
arr_flattened = arr2d_original.reshape(-1)
print("\nFlattened 1D Array:")
print(arr_flattened)
```

Here, we commence by utilizing a 2D array, denoted as arr2d_original, and proceed to employ the reshape() method with the objective of generating a 1D array that has been flattened, referred to as arr_flattened. The incorporation of the -1 argument within the reshape() method automatically undertakes the task of ascertaining the dimensions of the remaining dimension.

Array Manipulation

Array manipulation in NumPy involves various operations to modify the shape, content, and structure of arrays.

Indexing and Slicing

NumPy arrays facilitate the execution of robust indexing and slicing operations.

```
import numpy as np
# Creating a 2D array
arr2d = np.array([[1, 2, 3], [4, 5, 6], [7, 8, 9]])
print("Original 2D Array:")
print(arr2d)

# Accessing elements using indexing
print("\nElement at row 1, column 2:", arr2d[1, 2])
```

```
# Slicing 1D array
print("Sliced row 2:", arr2d[1, :])

# Slicing 2D array
print("Sliced subarray:")
print(arr2d[:2, 1:])
```

Array Concatenation

Combining multiple arrays along an existing axis.

```
# Creating two arrays
arr1 = np.array([1, 2, 3])
arr2 = np.array([4, 5, 6])

# Concatenating 1D arrays
concatenated_arr = np.concatenate([arr1, arr2])
print("Concatenated 1D Array:")
print(concatenated_arr)

# Creating two 2D arrays
arr2d_1 = np.array([[1, 2], [3, 4]])
arr2d_2 = np.array([[5, 6]])

# Concatenating 2D arrays along rows (axis=0)
concatenated_2d_arr = np.concatenate([arr2d_1, arr2d_2], axis=0)
print("\nConcatenated 2D Array along Rows:")
print(concatenated_2d_arr)
```

Transposition

Changing the order of axes, swapping rows with columns.

```
# Creating a 2D array
arr2d_original = np.array([[1, 2, 3], [4, 5, 6]])
print("Original 2D Array:")
print(arr2d_original)

# Transposing the 2D array
```

```
arr2d_transposed = arr2d_original.T
print("\nTransposed 2D Array:")
print(arr2d_transposed)
```

Reshaping

Changing the shape or dimensions of an array.

```
# Creating a 1D array
arr1d = np.arange(6)
print("Original 1D Array:")
print(arr1d)

# Reshaping to a 2D array with 2 rows and 3 columns
arr2d_reshaped = arr1d.reshape(2, 3)
print("\nReshaped 2D Array:")
print(arr2d_reshaped)
```

Splitting Arrays

Dividing an array into multiple subarrays along a specified axis can be achieved through the process of array partitioning.

```
# Creating a 1D array
arr1d_to_split = np.array([1, 2, 3, 4, 5, 6])

# Splitting the 1D array into three parts
split_arr = np.split(arr1d_to_split, [2, 4])
print("Split Arrays:")
print(split_arr)
```

Adding/Removing Elements

Modifying an array involves altering its size and content.

```
# Creating a 1D array
arr1d_original = np.array([1, 2, 3, 4, 5])
```

```
# Appending an element
arr1d_appended = np.append(arr1d_original, 6)
print("Appended 1D Array:")
print(arr1d_appended)

# Removing an element by index
arr1d_removed = np.delete(arr1d_original, 2)
print("\nArray after removing element at index 2:")
print(arr1d_removed)
```

– Basic numerical operations

Basic numerical operations in NumPy encompass the execution of mathematical operations on arrays or the interaction between arrays. NumPy facilitates element-wise operations, wherein the operation is individually applied to each element of the array.

Element-wise operations

Element-wise computations involve the execution of fundamental arithmetic operations including but not limited to addition, subtraction, multiplication, and division.

```
import numpy as np

# Creating two arrays
arr1 = np.array([1, 2, 3])
arr2 = np.array([4, 5, 6])

# Addition
result_addition = arr1 + arr2
print("Addition:", result_addition)

# Subtraction
result_subtraction = arr1 - arr2
print("Subtraction:", result_subtraction)

# Multiplication
result_multiplication = arr1 * arr2
print("Multiplication:", result_multiplication)

# Division
result_division = arr1 / arr2
print("Division:", result_division)
```

Mathematical Functions

NumPy offers an array of mathematical operations that act on each element, thereby granting a diverse array of mathematical functions.

```python
# Creating an array
arr = np.array([1, 2, 3, 4, 5])

# Square root
result_sqrt = np.sqrt(arr)
print("Square Root:", result_sqrt)

# Exponential
result_exp = np.exp(arr)
print("Exponential:", result_exp)

# Logarithm (natural logarithm)
result_log = np.log(arr)
print("Natural Logarithm:", result_log)

# Trigonometric functions
result_sin = np.sin(arr)
print("Sine:", result_sin)

result_cos = np.cos(arr)
print("Cosine:", result_cos)
```

Aggregation and Reduction

Aggregation functions perform a calculation on the entire array, reducing it to a single value.

```python
# Summation
sum_result = np.sum(arr)
print("Sum:", sum_result)

# Mean
mean_result = np.mean(arr)
print("Mean:", mean_result)
```

```
# Minimum and Maximum
min_value = np.min(arr)
max_value = np.max(arr)
print("Minimum:", min_value)
print("Maximum:", max_value)
```

– **Advanced array operations**

Advanced array operations in NumPy involve more complex and specialized operations that go beyond basic arithmetic and mathematical functions.

Broadcasting

The utilization of broadcasting in NumPy facilitates the execution of operations on arrays that possess distinct shapes and sizes. This functionality automatically extends smaller arrays to align with the dimensions of larger arrays.

```
import numpy as np

# Creating a 2D array
arr2d = np.array([[1, 2, 3], [4, 5, 6]])

# Broadcasting a scalar to the entire array
result_broadcasting = arr2d + 10
print("Broadcasting Result:")
print(result_broadcasting)
```

The scalar 10 is uniformly distributed to all elements of the 2D array arr2d in this particular instance.

Vectorization

Vectorization is a key concept in NumPy, where operations are applied to entire arrays instead of individual elements using explicit loops. It leads to more readable and computationally efficient code.

```
# Using vectorized operations for element-wise square
arr = np.array([1, 2, 3, 4, 5])
result_squared = arr**2
print("Vectorized Square Operation:")
print(result_squared)
```

In this instance, the operation of squaring is executed on each individual element within the array, eliminating the necessity for explicit loops.

Universal Functions (ufuncs)

Universal functions refer to functions that perform operations on arrays in an element-wise manner. These functions are an essential component of the functionality offered by the NumPy library, as they enable optimized and efficient computations for a variety of mathematical operations.

```
# Using a ufunc for element-wise square root
arr = np.array([1, 4, 9, 16, 25])
result_sqrt = np.sqrt(arr)
print("Element-wise Square Root using ufunc:")
print(result_sqrt)
```

Here, the np.sqrt() function is a universal function that applies the square root operation element-wise to the array.

Array Broadcasting

Broadcasting is an influential characteristic that empowers NumPy to execute operations on arrays of diverse forms and dimensions. It automatically adapts the shape of smaller arrays to correspond with the larger one, thereby enabling effective element-wise operations without the requirement for explicit looping.

```
# Broadcasting a 1D array to a 2D array
arr1d = np.array([1, 2, 3])
arr2d = np.array([[10, 20, 30], [40, 50, 60]])

result_broadcasting_2d = arr1d + arr2d
print("Broadcasting 1D array to 2D array:")
print(result_broadcasting_2d)
```

In this particular instance, the 1D array arr1d is subjected to broadcasting, where it is expanded to fit the dimensions of each row within the 2D array arr2d.

3.1.2 Scientific Computations with SciPy

SciPy, a Python library employed for scientific and technical computation, is an open-source platform. It enhances the functionalities of NumPy by offering supplementary modules for diverse purposes including optimization, signal processing, statistical operations, linear algebra, and beyond. Researchers, scientists, and engineers working in diverse disciplines find SciPy to be an indispensable resource.

Key Features

Extensive functionality: SciPy encompasses an extensive assortment of mathematical and scientific computational operations, rendering it an all-inclusive library catering to a multitude of academic domains.

Integration with NumPy: SciPy seamlessly integrates with NumPy, thereby enhancing the capabilities of both libraries and creating a robust environment for numerical computation.

Interdisciplinary tools: The SciPy library comprises a range of modules that encompass optimization, interpolation, signal and image processing, statistical analysis, and other functionalities. This wide range of capabilities renders it well-suited for an extensive variety of applications.

Open source and community-driven: Being an open-source project, SciPy benefits from a large community of contributors, ensuring regular updates, bug fixes, and the inclusion of new features.

Installation and Setup

To leverage the capabilities of SciPy, it is highly advisable to ensure its simultaneous installation with NumPy and other indispensable libraries. The installation process entails utilizing a package manager such as pip. To accomplish this, one must open a terminal or command prompt and execute the necessary commands:

```
pip install scipy
```

This command will install the latest version of SciPy and its dependencies.

Verifying the Installation

After installation, you can verify it by importing SciPy in a Python script or the Python interactive environment:

```
import scipy

# Check the version
print("SciPy Version:", scipy.__version__)
```

If there are no errors, and the version is printed, SciPy is successfully installed.

Dependencies

SciPy relies on NumPy, so it is crucial to have NumPy installed. NumPy can be installed separately or, as mentioned earlier, along with SciPy. Other optional dependencies exist for specific modules within SciPy, such as Matplotlib for plotting functionalities.

Setting Up a Virtual Environment

For a clean and isolated environment, consider setting up a virtual environment before installing SciPy. This step ensures that the dependencies do not interfere with the global Python environment.

```
# Creating a virtual environment
python -m venv myenv

# Activating the virtual environment
# On Windows
.\myenv\Scripts\activate
# On macOS/Linux
source myenv/bin/activate
```

After activation, install SciPy as mentioned earlier.

– Basics of scientific computing with SciPy

Arrays and matrices

Arrays and matrices are fundamental data structures in scientific computing. SciPy builds upon NumPy's array capabilities. It extends these functionalities to include specialized functions and data structures for scientific applications.

```
import numpy as np
from scipy import linalg # Importing SciPy's linear algebra module

# Creating a 1D array
arr_1d = np.array([1, 2, 3])
```

```
# Creating a 2D matrix
matrix_2d = np.array([[1, 2, 3], [4, 5, 6], [7, 8, 9]])

print("1D Array:")
print(arr_1d)
print("\n2D Matrix:")
print(matrix_2d)
```

Linear algebra operations

Linear system solution
SciPy offers a variety of functions that can be utilized to solve systems of linear equations, such as the function scipy.linalg.solve().

Consider the linear system

2x + y = 8

3x − y = 1

```
# Coefficient matrix
coeff_matrix = np.array([[2, 1], [3, -1]])

# Right-hand side
rhs_vector = np.array([8, 1])

# Solving the linear system
solution = linalg.solve(coeff_matrix, rhs_vector)

print("Solution to the Linear System:")
print(solution)
```

Eigenvalues and Eigenvectors
Eigenvalues and eigenvectors are crucial in various scientific applications. SciPy's scipy.linalg.eig() computes eigenvalues and eigenvectors.

Consider a matrix

$$A = \begin{bmatrix} 4 & -2 \\ 1 & 1 \end{bmatrix}$$

```
# Matrix A
matrix_A = np.array([[4, -2], [1, 1]])
```

```
# Computing eigenvalues and eigenvectors
eigenvalues, eigenvectors = linalg.eig(matrix_A)

print("Eigenvalues:")
print(eigenvalues)
print("\nEigenvectors:")
print(eigenvectors)
```

Singular Value Decomposition (SVD)

SVD is a factorization method widely used in numerical linear algebra. SciPy's scipy.linalg.svd() computes the SVD of a matrix.

Consider a matrix

$$B = \begin{bmatrix} 1 & 2 \\ 2 & 3 \end{bmatrix}$$

```
# Matrix B
matrix_B = np.array([[1, 2], [2, 3]])

# Computing Singular Value Decomposition
U, S, Vt = linalg.svd(matrix_B)

print("U matrix:")
print(U)
print("\nS matrix (singular values):")
print(S)
print("\nVt matrix (transpose of V):")
print(Vt)
```

Numerical Integration

SciPy provides powerful numerical integration methods through scipy.integrate. The quad() function is commonly used.

Consider integrating $f(x) = x^2$ over the interval $[0, 1]$

```
from scipy import integrate

# Function to integrate
def func(x):
 return x**2
```

```
# Numerical integration
result, error = integrate.quad(func, 0, 1)

print("Result of Numerical Integration:")
print(result)
```

Numerical Differentiation

scipy.misc.derivative() computes the derivative of a function at a given point using numerical methods.

Consider differentiating $g(x) = e^x$ at $x = 2$

```
from scipy.misc import derivative
# Function to differentiate
def func_g(x):
 return np.exp(x)

# Numerical differentiation
derivative_at_2 = derivative(func_g, 2.0, dx=1e-6)

print("Result of Numerical Differentiation at x=2:")
print(derivative_at_2)
```

3.2 Loading Data with Pandas

3.2.1 DataFrame and Series

DataFrame

A DataFrame is a data structure in pandas that is two-dimensional and tabular in nature, closely resembling a table found in a relational database. It is composed of rows and columns, wherein each column can possess a distinct data type.

Features

- Tabular structure: Data organized in rows and columns.
- Column names: Each column has a name or label.
- Index: Each row has an index, which can be explicitly set or autogenerated.
- Flexibility: Columns can have different data types.
- Extensibility: Supports the addition of new columns.

Example of creating a DataFrame:

```
import pandas as pd

# Creating a DataFrame from a dictionary
data = {'Name': ['Alice', 'Bob', 'Charlie'],
  'Age': [25, 30, 35],
  'City': ['New York', 'San Francisco', 'Los Angeles']}
df = pd.DataFrame(data)
print(df)
```

Output

```
     Name  Age            City
0   Alice   25        New York
1     Bob   30   San Francisco
2 Charlie   35     Los Angeles
```
Fig. 3.1: Creating a DataFrame.

Fig. 3.1 shows the results generated by a code snippet designed to create a pandas Data-Frame implementation. The visual diagram shows the structure and contents of the Data-Frame, including its rows, columns, and corresponding data objects stored in each cell.

Series
A Series refers to a singularly structured and labeled array in the pandas library. It is essentially a solitary column extracted from a DataFrame, but it is also capable of existing independently. The Series data structure has the capability to store various data types, encompassing integers, floating-point numbers, strings, and other forms of data.

Features
– One-dimensional: Consists of a single column or array of data.
– Labeled index: Each element in the Series has an index.
– Homogeneous data: All elements in a Series have the same data type.
– Similar to NumPy Arrays: Many operations available in NumPy arrays can be applied to Series.

Example of creating a Series
```
# Creating a Series from a list
ages = pd.Series([25, 30, 35], name='Age')

print(ages)
```

Output

```
0     25
1     30
2     35
Name: Age, dtype: int64
```
Fig. 3.2: Creating a Series.

Fig. 3.2 shows the results from the implementation rules responsible for creating the pandas Series object. The visual diagram shows the layout and elements of the sequence, which is a one-dimensional labeled layout in the Panda library. The output shows the index labels associated with each value in the series, and provides a clear understanding of how data is organized and stored in this data structure.

Distinction	Series	DataFrame
1. Dimensionality:	One-dimensional structure.	Two-dimensional structure.
2. Elements:	A single column of data with an index.	Multiple columns of data organized in a tabular structure with both row and column indices.
3. Use Cases:	Suitable for representing a single variable or feature.	Suitable for representing a dataset with multiple variables, each as a column.
4. Flexibility:	Homogeneous data type for all elements.	Columns can have different data types.
5. Visualization:	Typically visualized as a single column of data.	Visualized as a table with multiple columns.
6. Operations:	Operations are typically applied to a single column of data.	Operations can be applied to entire columns or rows, providing more flexibility.

Methods to Create a DataFrame

From a Dictionary

The column names in a dictionary are derived from its keys, and the data is represented by the corresponding values.

```
import pandas as pd

# Creating a DataFrame from a dictionary
data_dict = {'Name': ['Alice', 'Bob', 'Charlie'],
  'Age': [25, 30, 35],
  'City': ['New York', 'San Francisco', 'Los Angeles']}
```

```
df_from_dict = pd.DataFrame(data_dict)

print("DataFrame from Dictionary:")
print(df_from_dict)
```

Output:

```
DataFrame from Dictionary:
      Name   Age           City
0    Alice    25       New York
1      Bob    30  San Francisco
2  Charlie    35    Los Angeles
```
Fig. 3.3: Create a DataFrame from dictionary.

From a List of Lists

Each individual list that is nested within the main list represents a single row, while the main list itself encompasses all of the rows.

```
# Creating a DataFrame from a list of lists
data_list = [['Alice', 25, 'New York'],
        ['Bob', 30, 'San Francisco'],
        ['Charlie', 35, 'Los Angeles']]
df_from_list = pd.DataFrame(data_list, columns=['Name', 'Age', 'City'])

print("\nDataFrame from List of Lists:")
print(df_from_list)
```

Output:

```
DataFrame from List of Lists:
      Name   Age           City
0    Alice    25       New York
1      Bob    30  San Francisco
2  Charlie    35    Los Angeles
```
Fig. 3.4: Create a DataFrame from list of lists.

From a NumPy Array

Utilizing a NumPy array to create a DataFrame.

```
import numpy as np

# Creating a DataFrame from a NumPy array
data_array = np.array([['Alice', 25, 'New York'],
  ['Bob', 30, 'San Francisco'],
  ['Charlie', 35, 'Los Angeles']])
```

```
df_from_array = pd.DataFrame(data_array, columns=['Name', 'Age',
'City'])
print("\nDataFrame from NumPy Array:")
print(df_from_array)
```

Output:

```
DataFrame from NumPy Array:
      Name Age           City
0    Alice  25       New York
1      Bob  30  San Francisco
2  Charlie  35    Los Angeles
```
Fig. 3.5: Create a DataFrame from NumPy array.

Methods to create a Series

Creating a Series from a List
A Series refers to a singular column extracted from a DataFrame.

```
# Creating a Series from a list
ages_list = [25, 30, 35]
ages_series = pd.Series(ages_list, name='Age')

print("Series from List:")
print(ages_series)
```

Output:

```
Series from List:
0    25
1    30
2    35
Name: Age, dtype: int64
```
Fig. 3.6: Create a Series from list.

Creating a Series from a NumPy Array
Similar to creating a Series from a list.

```
# Creating a Series from a NumPy array
ages_array = np.array([25, 30, 35])
ages_series_np = pd.Series(ages_array, name='Age')

print("\nSeries from NumPy Array:")
print(ages_series_np)
```

Output:

```
Series from NumPy Array:
0    25
1    30
2    35
Name: Age, dtype: int32
```
Fig. 3.7: Create a Series from NumPy array.

3.2.2 Data Manipulation with Pandas

Data manipulation with pandas is a fundamental element of Python data analysis. It provides a robust and flexible toolkit for cleaning, transforming, and reshaping datasets. Within this process, missing data can be effectively handled, and duplicate records can be identified and eliminated. Pandas facilitates seamless data transformation, including reshaping through pivot operations and melting wide-format data. The merging and concatenating of DataFrames allow for the integration of information from diverse sources. The GroupBy operation enables the grouping of data, thereby facilitating analysis of specific subsets, while aggregation functions offer insights into summarized information.

Pandas simplifies the handling of time series data by offering tools for resampling and shifting. Advanced data manipulation techniques involve the application of custom functions using apply and the utilization of vectorized operations for improved efficiency. The best practices in pandas data manipulation involve optimizing memory usage and employing clear and readable chaining operations. All in all, pandas equips data scientists and analysts with a comprehensive range of tools to efficiently manipulate and analyze data. This makes it an indispensable library in the Python ecosystem for data manipulation tasks.

Data Cleaning with Pandas

Data cleansing with pandas involves the preparation and refinement of datasets to ensure their suitability for analysis. Essential elements of data cleansing encompass the management of missing data as well as the identification and elimination of duplicate records. Pandas offers methods such as dropna() and fillna() to address missing values, while the drop_duplicates() function is employed to handle duplicated rows. These operations play a pivotal role in preserving data integrity and guaranteeing accurate analyses.

Furthermore, pandas grants the ability to explore and comprehend data through functions such as info() and describe(), which assist in the identification of outliers or anomalies. The versatility of pandas facilitates the manipulation of data, including the alteration of data types or the conversion of categorical variables. By utilizing these tools, data cleansing with pandas ensures that datasets remain consistent, comprehensive, and primed for meaningful analysis and insights.

Handling Missing Data

Dealing with missing data is an essential stage in the process of analyzing data, and pandas offers powerful tools to accomplish this objective. Two popular approaches entail the identification and management of missing values:

Identifying missing values:

Pandas facilitates the identification of missing values through the utilization of functions such as isnull() or info(). A notable illustration of this is the function df.isnull().sum(), which provides the tally of missing values in every column.

```
import pandas as pd
import numpy as np

# Creating a DataFrame with missing values
data = {'Name': ['Alice', 'Bob', np.nan, 'Charlie'],
 'Age': [25, np.nan, 35, 40],
 'City': ['New York', 'San Francisco', 'Los Angeles', np.nan]}
df = pd.DataFrame(data)

# Identifying missing values using isnull() and sum()
missing_values_count = df.isnull().sum()

print("DataFrame with Missing Values:")
print(df)
print("\nMissing Values Count:")
print(missing_values_count)
```

Output:

```
DataFrame with Missing Values:
      Name   Age          City
0    Alice  25.0      New York
1      Bob   NaN  San Francisco
2      NaN  35.0   Los Angeles
3  Charlie  40.0          NaN

Missing Values Count:
Name    1
Age     1
City    1
dtype: int64
```

Fig. 3.8: Missing values count in DataFrame.

Handling missing values:

Once recognized, absent values can be resolved using techniques such as dropna() to eliminate rows or columns containing incomplete information, or fillna() to substitute missing values with designated values. To illustrate, df.fillna(0) effectively substitutes all NaN values in a DataFrame with zeros.

```
# Handling missing values using dropna()
df_cleaned_dropna = df.dropna()

# Handling missing values using fillna()
df_cleaned_fillna = df.fillna({'Name': 'Unknown', 'Age': 0, 'City':
'Unknown'})

print("\nDataFrame after Dropna:")
print(df_cleaned_dropna)
print("\nDataFrame after Fillna:")
print(df_cleaned_fillna)
```

Output:

```
DataFrame after Dropna:
      Name   Age      City
0    Alice  25.0  New York

DataFrame after Fillna:
        Name   Age            City
0      Alice  25.0        New York
1        Bob   0.0   San Francisco
2    Unknown  35.0     Los Angeles
3    Charlie  40.0         Unknown
```
Fig. 3.9: Handling missing values in DataFrame.

In the given illustrations, we initially formed a DataFrame containing absent values. Subsequently, the isnull() sum() function is employed to determine the count of absent values in each column. To manage the absent values, we exhibited two approaches: dropna() for eliminating rows with absent values and fillna() for substituting absent values with predetermined values. These techniques provide adaptability in addressing absent data according to the particular requirements of the analysis.

Dealing with Duplicates

Dealing with duplicates constitutes a pivotal component of data cleansing in the pandas library, as it guarantees the integrity of the data and safeguards against skewed analyses. The identification of duplicate rows can be accomplished by utilizing the duplicated() method, allowing for the exploration of redundant records based on either

column values or the entire row. The drop_duplicates() function facilitates the elimination of duplicate rows, resulting in a DataFrame that exclusively contains unique
records. The strategic management of duplicates is imperative in order to preserve
the accuracy of analyses and to prevent biases that may arise from repeated data
points. These operations possess particular value when working with extensive datasets or when integrating data from multiple sources, as they ensure that the resulting
DataFrame accurately represents the underlying information.

Identifying uplicates:

Identifying and handling duplicate rows is crucial to maintaining data integrity.
Pandas provides methods to identify duplicate rows based on column values or the
entire row.

```
import pandas as pd

# Creating a DataFrame with duplicate rows
data = {'Name': ['Alice', 'Bob', 'Alice', 'Charlie', 'Bob'],
 'Age': [25, 30, 25, 35, 30],
 'City': ['New York', 'San Francisco', 'New York', 'Los Angeles', 'San
Francisco']}
df = pd.DataFrame(data)

# Identifying duplicates using duplicated()
duplicates = df[df.duplicated()]

print("DataFrame with Duplicates:")
print(df)
print("\nIdentified Duplicates:")
print(duplicates)
```

Output:

```
DataFrame with Duplicates:
      Name  Age                City
0    Alice   25            New York
1      Bob   30       San Francisco
2    Alice   25            New York
3  Charlie   35         Los Angeles
4      Bob   30       San Francisco

Identified Duplicates:
    Name  Age                City
2  Alice   25            New York
4    Bob   30       San Francisco
```

Fig. 3.10: Identifying duplicate values in DataFrame.

Removing duplicates

Removing duplicate rows is accomplished using the drop_duplicates() function. This ensures that the DataFrame contains only unique records.

```
# Removing duplicates using drop_duplicates()
df_no_duplicates = df.drop_duplicates()

print("\nDataFrame after Removing Duplicates:")
print(df_no_duplicates)
```

Output:

```
DataFrame after Removing Duplicates:
       Name   Age              City
0     Alice    25          New York
1       Bob    30     San Francisco
3   Charlie    35       Los Angeles
```

Fig. 3.11: Removing duplicate values in DataFrame.

The identification of duplicate rows in the DataFrame was conducted through the utilization of the duplicated() method in this particular instance. The resulting DataFrame, denoted as duplicates, showcases the duplicate rows that were identified. Subsequently, the removal of duplicate rows was carried out by means of the drop_duplicates() function, thereby generating a DataFrame devoid of any duplicates. These operations are of utmost importance in guaranteeing the accuracy of the data and ensuring that the analyses conducted are not distorted by the presence of redundant information.

Data Transformation and Reshaping

Data transformation and reshaping in pandas involve restructuring datasets to better suit analytical needs. This process is crucial for converting data between different formats, aggregating information, and preparing it for further analysis. Key techniques include:

Reshaping with pivot

The employment of the pivot function in the pandas library acts as a powerful tool to enable the conversion of data from a lengthy configuration to a broad arrangement. This specific feature offers significant benefits when dealing with datasets that are structured in a stacked or vertical manner, thus requiring a transformation into a horizontal or tabular format. Essential elements in this procedure include the index, columns, and values, which collectively determine the framework of the resulting DataFrame.

```
import pandas as pd

# Creating a DataFrame
data = {'Date': ['2022-01-01', '2022-01-01', '2022-01-02', '2022-01-
02'],
 'Category': ['A', 'B', 'A', 'B'],
 'Value': [10, 20, 15, 25]}
df = pd.DataFrame(data)

# Reshaping with pivot
df_pivot = df.pivot(index='Date', columns='Category', values='Value')

print("Original DataFrame:")
print(df)
print("\nDataFrame after Pivot:")
print(df_pivot)
```

Output:

```
Original DataFrame:
        Date Category  Value
0  2022-01-01        A     10
1  2022-01-01        B     20
2  2022-01-02        A     15
3  2022-01-02        B     25

DataFrame after Pivot:
Category     A   B
Date
2022-01-01  10  20
2022-01-02  15  25
```

Fig. 3.12: Reshaping with pivot.

In this example, the original DataFrame has a long format, with each date having separate rows for categories A and B. After applying pivot, the data is reshaped into a
wide format, with dates as the index and categories as columns, providing a clearer
tabular structure.

Melting data:

The utilization of the melt function in the pandas library is paramount in the conversion of wide-format data to long-format. This becomes particularly valuable in situations
where the data is arranged in a tabular or horizontal structure and necessitates transformation into a stacked or vertical format.

The inclusion of the id_vars, var_name, and value_name parameters in the method
affords the opportunity for customization of the melted DataFrame.

```
import pandas as pd

# Creating a DataFrame
data = {'Date': ['2022-01-01', '2022-01-02'],
  'Category_A': [10, 15],
  'Category_B': [20, 25]}
df = pd.DataFrame(data)

print("Original DataFrame:")
print(df)

# Melting data with the melt function
df_melted = pd.melt(df, id_vars=['Date'], var_name='Category',
value_name='Value')

print("\nDataFrame after Melting:")
print(df_melted)
```

Output:

```
Original DataFrame:
        Date  Category_A  Category_B
0  2022-01-01          10          20
1  2022-01-02          15          25

DataFrame after Melting:
        Date    Category  Value
0  2022-01-01  Category_A     10
1  2022-01-02  Category_A     15
2  2022-01-01  Category_B     20
3  2022-01-02  Category_B     25
```

Fig. 3.13: Melting the data.

3.3 Data Cleaning and Transformation

Data cleansing and data transformation are fundamental stages in the data preprocessing pipeline, with the objective of enhancing the quality and utility of the dataset
for analysis or modeling purposes. The process of data cleansing entails the identification and rectification of errors, discrepancies, and missing values within the dataset.
This may involve the elimination of duplicate records, the handling of missing
data through imputation or deletion, and the correction of erroneous values. On the
other hand, data transformation encompasses the reorganization or restructuring of
the data to render it suitable for analysis or modeling. This may encompass the encod-

ing of categorical variables, the scaling of numerical characteristics, or the creation of new characteristics through the application of feature engineering techniques.

Furthermore, data transformation may entail the aggregation or summarization of data, the creation of derived variables, or the implementation of dimensionality reduction. By ensuring that the dataset is free from impurities, exhibits consistency, and adheres to appropriate formatting, the processes of data cleansing and transformation facilitate more precise and dependable analyses, thereby leading to enhanced insights and decision-making capabilities.

3.3.1 Handling Missing Data

Handling missing data is a crucial aspect of data preprocessing, ensuring the robustness and accuracy of analyses and models. There exist various strategies to address missing data, including imputation, deletion, and modeling. Imputation entails estimating missing values by utilizing other available data, such as utilizing the mean, median, or mode for numerical variables or employing the most frequent category for categorical variables.

Deletion involves eliminating records or features with missing values, either entirely or partially, which can be appropriate if the missing data is minimal and random. Modeling entails treating missing values as a distinct category or employing machine learning algorithms to predict missing values based on other variables.

```python
import pandas as pd
from sklearn.impute import SimpleImputer

# Sample dataset with missing values
data = {'Age': [30, None, 50, 60],
 'Income': [50000, 60000, None, 80000],
 'Education_Level': [12, 16, 18, None]}
df = pd.DataFrame(data)

# Imputation using mean
imputer = SimpleImputer(strategy='mean')
df_imputed = pd.DataFrame(imputer.fit_transform(df), columns=df.columns)

print("Original DataFrame:")
print(df)
print("\nDataFrame after Imputation:")
print(df_imputed)
```

Output:

```
Original DataFrame:
    Age   Income  Education_Level
0  30.0  50000.0             12.0
1   NaN  60000.0             16.0
2  50.0      NaN             18.0
3  60.0  80000.0              NaN

DataFrame after Imputation:
         Age         Income  Education_Level
0  30.000000  50000.000000        12.000000
1  46.666667  60000.000000        16.000000
2  50.000000  63333.333333        18.000000
3  60.000000  80000.000000        15.333333
```

Fig. 3.14: Imputing missing values in DataFrame.

In this particular instance, there are absent values in the columns denoted as 'Age', 'Income,' and 'Education_Level'. To address this issue, we employ the utilization of the SimpleImputer module from the renowned scikit-learn library to impute the missing values with the mean value of each corresponding column. The resultant DataFrame encompasses the imputed values, thereby guaranteeing the wholeness of the dataset and facilitating further analysis and modeling endeavors.

3.3.2 Data Type Conversions

Data type conversions play a vital role in the preprocessing of data, as they allow for the representation of data in a manner that is suitable for analysis, modeling, or storage. This process entails the alteration of data from one type to another, for instance, the conversion of strings into numerical values or the transformation of categorical variables into numerical representations.

The conversions of data types serve to guarantee the consistency of data and its compatibility with various algorithms and tools. To illustrate, the conversion of categorical variables into numerical format, accomplished through the utilization of encoding techniques like one-hot encoding or label encoding, facilitates the effective processing of such variables by machine learning algorithms. Likewise, the conversion of numerical values from one data type to another, such as the transition from integers to floats, may become necessary in order to address precision or scaling requirements.

```
import pandas as pd

# Sample DataFrame with mixed data types
data = {'ID': ['001', '002', '003', '004'],
```

```
 'Age': [30, 40, 50, 60],
 'Income': ['50000', '60000', '70000', '80000'],
 'Education_Level': [12.5, 16.2, 18.9, 20.7]}
df = pd.DataFrame(data)

# Convert 'ID' column from string to integer
df['ID'] = df['ID'].astype(int)

# Convert 'Income' column from string to integer
df['Income'] = df['Income'].astype(int)

print("DataFrame after Data Type Conversions:")
print(df)
```

Output:

```
DataFrame after Data Type Conversions:
   ID  Age  Income  Education_Level
0   1   30   50000             12.5
1   2   40   60000             16.2
2   3   50   70000             18.9
3   4   60   80000             20.7
```

Fig. 3.15: Data type conversion.

In this example, we have a DataFrame with mixed data types. We convert the 'ID' and 'Income' columns from strings to integers using the astype method in pandas, ensuring consistency and enabling numerical operations or analysis of these columns. Similarly, other data type conversions can be performed as needed to prepare the data for further processing or modeling.

3.4 Feature Engineering

Feature engineering involves the process of transforming raw data into a format that is more suitable for machine learning algorithms, with the goal of improving the performance of the model. It encompasses the selection, creation, and modification of features to extract meaningful patterns and insights from the data. This may include converting categorical variables into numerical representations using techniques like one-hot encoding or label encoding. Additionally, feature engineering includes feature scaling, which standardizes or normalizes numerical features to ensure consistency and comparability across different scales. Moreover, it involves techniques for reducing data dimensionality, such as principal component analysis (PCA) and feature selection methods that aim to decrease the number of features and eliminate irrelevant or redundant ones. The effective implementation of feature engineering can significantly enhance the accuracy, interpretability, and generalization of the model to new data, making it a critical step in the machine learning pipeline.

3.4.1 Encoding Categorical Variables

Encoding categorical variables is an essential step in feature engineering, especially for tasks related to machine learning. It involves transforming categorical data into a numerical format that algorithms can understand. One common technique is called "one-hot encoding," where each category is represented by a binary value (0 or 1) in a separate column. This approach preserves the categorical information without imposing any ordinality. Another approach is label encoding, where each category is assigned a unique integer. However, label encoding can introduce ordinality that is not present in the original data, potentially misleading the algorithm. Therefore, selecting the appropriate encoding method is crucial to ensure an accurate representation of categorical variables during the model training process.

One-Hot Encoding

One-hot encoding is a technique that is used to convert categorical variables into a numerical format that is suitable for machine learning algorithms. In this methodology, each category is represented as a binary vector, where only one bit is assigned a value of 1 to indicate the presence of the respective category. This approach ensures that the categorical information is preserved without introducing any form of ordinality. For example, if we have three categories, namely 'Red', 'Green', and 'Blue', they would be encoded as [1, 0, 0], [0, 1, 0], and [0, 0, 1], respectively.

```python
import pandas as pd

# Sample categorical data
data = {'Color': ['Red', 'Green', 'Blue', 'Red', 'Blue']}
df = pd.DataFrame(data)

# One-hot encoding
one_hot_encoded = pd.get_dummies(df['Color'])

print("Original DataFrame:")
print(df)
print("\nOne-hot Encoded DataFrame:")
print(one_hot_encoded)
```

Output:

```
Original DataFrame:
    Color
0     Red
1   Green
2    Blue
3     Red
4    Blue

One-hot Encoded DataFrame:
    Blue   Green    Red
0  False   False   True
1  False   True   False
2   True   False  False
3  False   False   True
4   True   False  False
```
Fig. 3.16: One-hot encoding.

In this specific instance, the categorical variable 'Color' is transformed into binary vectors through the process of one-hot encoding, which conveys the existence or non-existence of each category. This particular conversion allows machine learning algorithms to effectively understand and make use of categorical data.

Label Encoding

Label encoding is a method utilized to convert categorical variables into a numerical format by assigning a unique integer to each category. This specific technique entails replacing each category with a numerical value, starting from 0 and progressing up to n-1, where n represents the number of distinct categories. While its simplicity is evident, it is crucial to acknowledge that label encoding may unintentionally introduce a semblance of order to the data, thereby implying a meaningful ranking among categories that may not actually exist. For instance, if we were to examine three categories: 'Red', 'Green', and 'Blue', they would be encoded as 0, 1, and 2, respectively.

```
from sklearn.preprocessing import LabelEncoder
import pandas as pd

# Sample categorical data
data = {'Color': ['Red', 'Green', 'Blue', 'Red', 'Blue']}
df = pd.DataFrame(data)

# Label encoding
label_encoder = LabelEncoder()
df['Color_LabelEncoded'] = label_encoder.fit_transform(df['Color'])
```

```
print("Original DataFrame:")
print(df[['Color']])
print("\nLabel Encoded DataFrame:")
print(df[['Color_LabelEncoded']])
```

Output:

```
Original DataFrame:
    Color
0     Red
1   Green
2    Blue
3     Red
4    Blue

Label Encoded DataFrame:
   Color_LabelEncoded
0                   2
1                   1
2                   0
3                   2
4                   0
```

Fig. 3.17: Label encoding.

In this example, the categorical variable 'Color' has been encoded with labels that represent numerical values. Every distinct category is given a numerical label according to its sequential appearance in the data. Nevertheless, prudence is advised when utilizing label encoding, particularly in scenarios where the categorical variable lacks inherent ordinality. This is due to the potential for machine learning algorithms to misinterpret the encoded labels, resulting in misinterpretation of the data.

3.4.2 Feature Scaling

Feature scaling is a preprocessing technique used to standardize or normalize the range of numerical features in a given dataset. The main aim is to ensure that all features have comparable scales, thereby reducing the possibility of certain features dominating others during model training. Standardization involves transforming the data to have a mean of 0 and a standard deviation of 1, while normalization scales the data to a range of 0 to 1.

The practice of feature scaling carries particular significance for algorithms that heavily rely on distance-based metrics, such as k-nearest neighbors and support vector machines. Moreover, it is also crucial for optimization algorithms driven by gradient descent, such as linear regression and neural networks. By bringing all features to a comparable scale, feature scaling has the potential to bolster convergence speed, prevent numerical instability, and enhance the performance and interpretability of machine learning models. Various methods are commonly employed for feature scaling, including Min-Max Scaling, Z-score Scaling, and Robust Scaling.

Standardization

Standardization is a method used to normalize numerical features by transforming them to have a mean of 0 and a standard deviation of 1. This procedure involves subtracting the mean of each feature from its respective values and dividing the result by the standard deviation.

The utilization of standardization is beneficial for algorithms that assume the input data adheres to a normal distribution and assigns equal significance to all features. It ensures that features with larger scales do not dominate the learning process. For example, in a dataset that encompasses features like age, income, and education level, which exhibit varying scales, standardization would enable comparison among these features.

```
from sklearn.preprocessing import StandardScaler
import pandas as pd

# Sample numerical data
data = {'Age': [30, 40, 50, 60],
 'Income': [50000, 60000, 70000, 80000],
 'Education_Level': [12, 16, 18, 20]}
df = pd.DataFrame(data)

# Standardization
scaler = StandardScaler()
df_scaled = pd.DataFrame(scaler.fit_transform(df), columns=df.columns)

print("Original DataFrame:")
print(df)
print("\nStandardized DataFrame:")
print(df_scaled)
```

Output:

```
Original DataFrame:
   Age  Income  Education_Level
0   30   50000               12
1   40   60000               16
2   50   70000               18
3   60   80000               20

Standardized DataFrame:
        Age    Income  Education_Level
0 -1.341641 -1.341641        -1.521278
1 -0.447214 -0.447214        -0.169031
2  0.447214  0.447214         0.507093
3  1.341641  1.341641         1.183216
```

Fig. 3.18: Standardization of DataFrame.

In this instance, the initial numerical data depicting age, income, and education level is standardized through the utilization of the StandardScaler implemented in scikit-learn. Each individual characteristic is adjusted in such a way that it possesses an average value of 0 and a standard deviation of 1, thereby rendering them amenable to comparison across varying scales. This safeguard guarantees that no individual characteristic holds undue influence over the process of learning in machine learning algorithms that heavily rely on numerical data.

Normalization

Normalization is a technique for scaling features, which transforms numerical data into a standardized scale that typically ranges from 0 to 1. This process entails adjusting the values of each feature so that they fall within this range, while simultaneously preserving their relative relationships.

Normalization is particularly advantageous when the magnitudes of the features exhibit substantial variation, as it ensures that all features contribute equitably to the learning procedure. It is extensively employed in algorithms that mandate input data to be confined within a specific range, such as neural networks and distance-based algorithms like k-nearest neighbors. To elaborate, for instance, if we possess features such as age, income, and education level that possess dissimilar scales, normalization would unify them onto a standardized scale, thereby facilitating direct comparability.

```
from sklearn.preprocessing import MinMaxScaler
import pandas as pd

# Sample numerical data
data = {'Age': [30, 40, 50, 60],
  'Income': [50000, 60000, 70000, 80000],
  'Education_Level': [12, 16, 18, 20]}
```

```
df = pd.DataFrame(data)

# Normalization
scaler = MinMaxScaler()
df_normalized = pd.DataFrame(scaler.fit_transform(df), columns=df.
columns)

print("Original DataFrame:")
print(df)
print("\nNormalized DataFrame:")
print(df_normalized)
```

Output:

```
Original DataFrame:
    Age  Income  Education_Level
0   30   50000               12
1   40   60000               16
2   50   70000               18
3   60   80000               20

Normalized DataFrame:
        Age    Income  Education_Level
0  0.000000  0.000000             0.00
1  0.333333  0.333333             0.50
2  0.666667  0.666667             0.75
3  1.000000  1.000000             1.00
```

Fig. 3.19: Normalization of DataFrame.

In this instance, the initial numeric information signifying age, income, and level of education undergoes normalization by utilizing the MinMaxScaler from scikit-learn. The values of each characteristic are adjusted to a span ranging from 0 to 1, thereby maintaining their relative associations while guaranteeing consistency across various scales. This facilitates equitable comparisons between characteristics and averts the prevalence of any individual attribute in machine learning algorithms, thereby upholding the integrity of the learning process.

3.5 Data Visualization with Matplotlib and Seaborn

The utilization of Matplotlib and Seaborn for data visualization is indispensable when it comes to thoroughly exploring, meticulously analyzing, and effectively communicating insights obtained from data. Matplotlib, a widely utilized plotting library in Python, provides a significant level of customization in generating a wide range of static plots, including line plots, scatter plots, histograms, bar plots, and more. It empowers users with precise control over various plot elements, such as colors, markers, labels, and annotations.

Seaborn, constructed atop Matplotlib, furnishes a more advanced interface for crafting informative and visually appealing statistical graphics. By providing convenient functions for plotting data with minimal code, it simplifies the otherwise intricate process of generating complex visualizations. Seaborn excels in the production of visually captivating plots for statistical analysis, including specialized ones like violin plots, box plots, pair plots, and heatmaps.

Collectively, Matplotlib and Seaborn constitute a potent toolkit for data visualization, enabling analysts and data scientists to swiftly and effectively explore patterns, trends, and relationships within datasets. These libraries facilitate the creation of plots of publication-quality, thereby enhancing data storytelling and presentation, thereby rendering them indispensable tools in the workflow of data analysis.

3.5.1 Basic Plotting with Matplotlib

Plotting with Matplotlib is an essential aspect of data visualization, enabling the creation of various plots to examine data distributions, trends, and relationships. Matplotlib, a versatile Python plotting library, provides a flexible and intuitive interface for producing high-quality static visualizations suitable for publication. By utilizing Matplotlib, analysts and researchers can generate different types of plots, including line plots, scatter plots, bar plots, histograms, pie charts, box plots, violin plots, heatmaps, area plots, and contour plots.

These plots serve distinct objectives, permitting users to examine numerical distributions, compare categorical variables, visualize relationships between variables, identify outliers, and explore patterns within data. Whether visualizing time series data, investigating correlations, or presenting categorical distributions, Matplotlib provides the necessary tools for creating informative and insightful visualizations.

The establishment of the foundation of data exploration and analysis workflows is accomplished through the utilization of basic plotting techniques in Matplotlib. These techniques provide critical understandings of datasets that can assist in decision-making, enable discoveries, and effectively convey findings. Attaining expertise in basic plotting with Matplotlib is essential for practitioners in the field of data science and analysis, as it is a fundamental skill that allows for the extraction of actionable insights from data.

Line Plot

Line plots are employed to represent the trajectory of data points across an unbroken duration. They are constructed by joining the data points with linear segments. For instance, one could construct a line plot to depict the variation in stock prices over a given period of time.

```python
import matplotlib.pyplot as plt

x = [1, 2, 3, 4, 5]
y = [2, 3, 5, 7, 11]

plt.plot(x, y)
plt.xlabel('X-axis')
plt.ylabel('Y-axis')
plt.title('Line Plot Example')
plt.show()
```

Output:

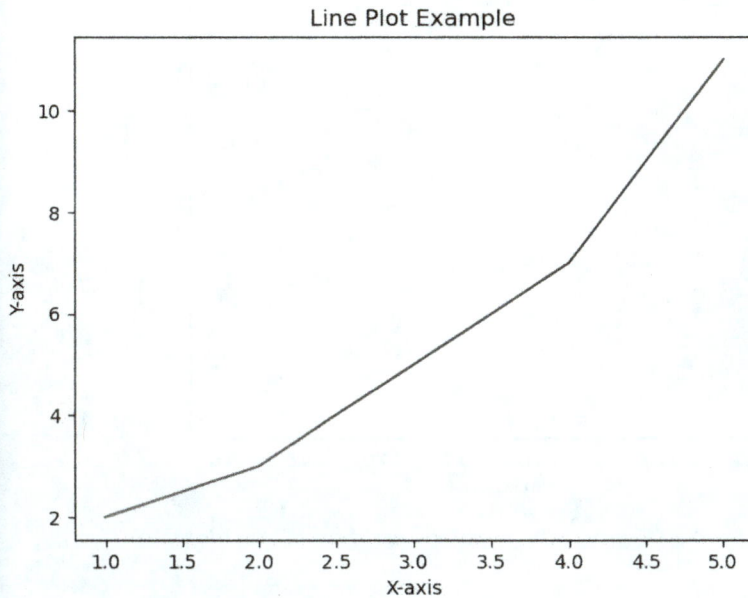

Fig. 3.20: Line plot.

Scatter Plot
Scatter plots exhibit individual data points as markers on a Cartesian plane, rendering them well-suited for illustrating the correlation between two numerical variables. For instance, one can create a plot to depict the connection between the mileage of a car and its corresponding price.

```
import matplotlib.pyplot as plt

x = [1, 2, 3, 4, 5]
y = [2, 3, 5, 7, 11]

plt.scatter(x, y)
plt.xlabel('X-axis')
plt.ylabel('Y-axis')
plt.title('Scatter Plot Example')
plt.show()
```

Output:

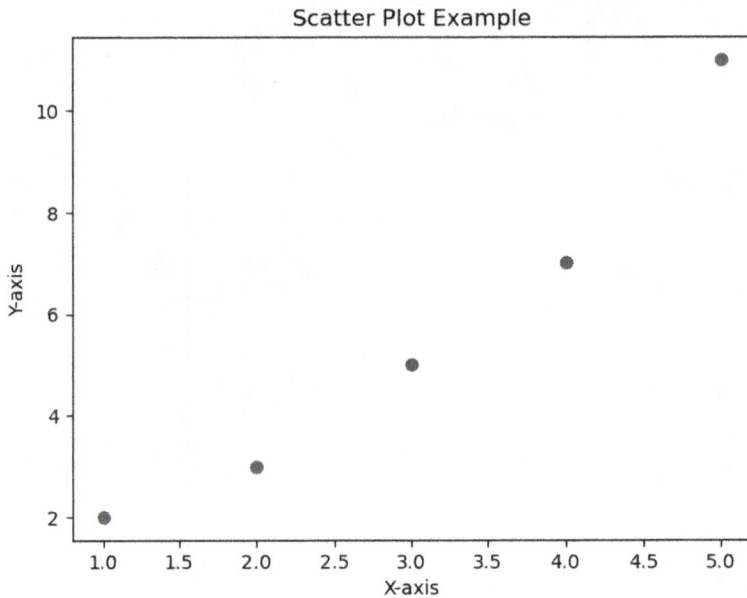

Fig. 3.21: Scatter plot.

Bar Plot

Bar plots depict categorical data using rectangular bars, where the length of each bar signifies the value of the corresponding category. Such visualizations prove valuable in the task of comparing the quantities associated with various categories. For instance, they are employed to assess the sales performance of different products.

```
import matplotlib.pyplot as plt

categories = ['A', 'B', 'C', 'D']
values = [10, 20, 15, 25]

plt.bar(categories, values)
plt.xlabel('Categories')
plt.ylabel('Values')
plt.title('Bar Plot Example')
plt.show()
```

Output:

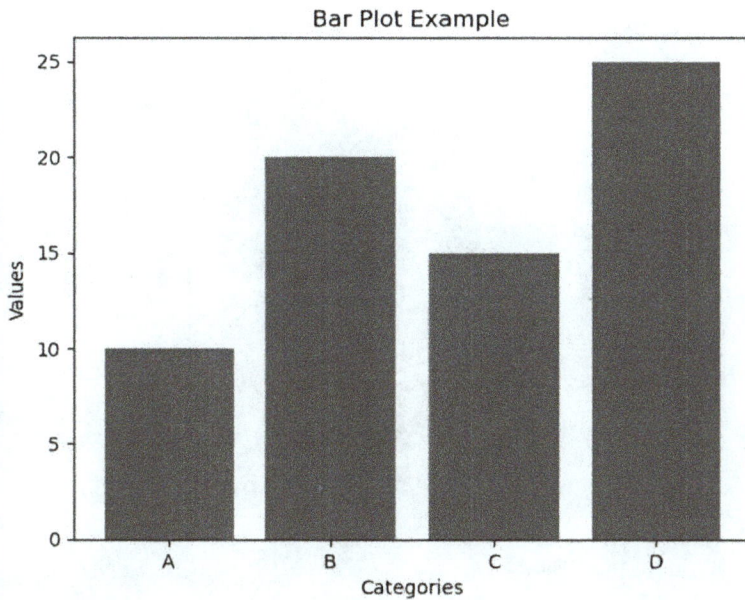

Fig. 3.22: Bar plot.

Histogram

Histograms depict the distribution of quantitative data by partitioning the data into intervals and enumerating the quantity of data points within each interval. They serve as a valuable tool for comprehending the frequency distribution of a specific variable. An instance where histograms are applicable is when visualizing the age distribution within a population.

```
import matplotlib.pyplot as plt

data = [1, 2, 2, 3, 3, 3, 4, 4, 4, 4, 5, 5, 5, 5, 5]

plt.hist(data, bins=5)
plt.xlabel('Values')
plt.ylabel('Frequency')
plt.title('Histogram Example')
plt.show()
```

Output:

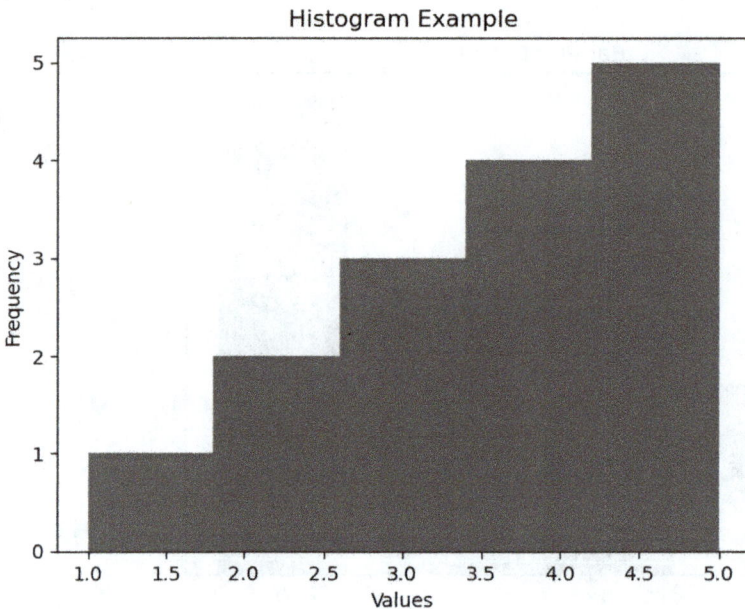

Fig. 3.23: Histogram plot.

Pie Chart

Pie charts depict categorical information by dividing a circle into slices, with each slice denoting a specific category and its magnitude indicating the proportion of that category in the entirety. These charts serve a practical purpose in demonstrating the makeup of an entire entity, such as the allocation of expenses in a budget.

```
import matplotlib.pyplot as plt

sizes = [15, 30, 45, 10]
```

```
labels = ['A', 'B', 'C', 'D']

plt.pie(sizes, labels=labels, autopct='%1.1f%%')
plt.title('Pie Chart Example')
plt.show()
```

Output:

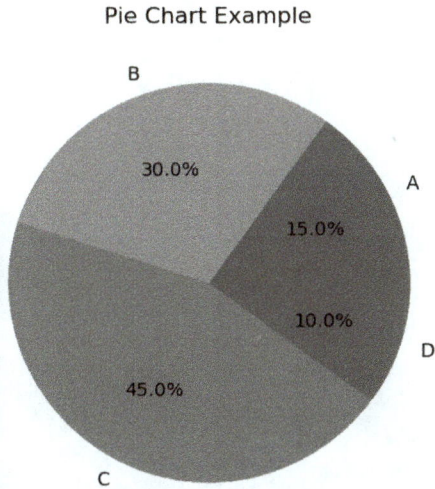

Fig. 3.24: Pie chart.

Box Plot

Box plots, alternatively referred to as box-and-whisker plots, serve the purpose of graphically representing the distribution of numerical data, thereby exhibiting the median, quartiles, and outliers. Their value lies in the identification of outliers and the comprehension of the data's dispersion and central tendency. For instance, they can be employed to contrast the distribution of test scores among various student groups.

```
import matplotlib.pyplot as plt
import numpy as np

np.random.seed(10)
data = np.random.normal(0, 1, 100)

plt.boxplot(data)
plt.title('Box Plot Example')
plt.show()
```

Output:

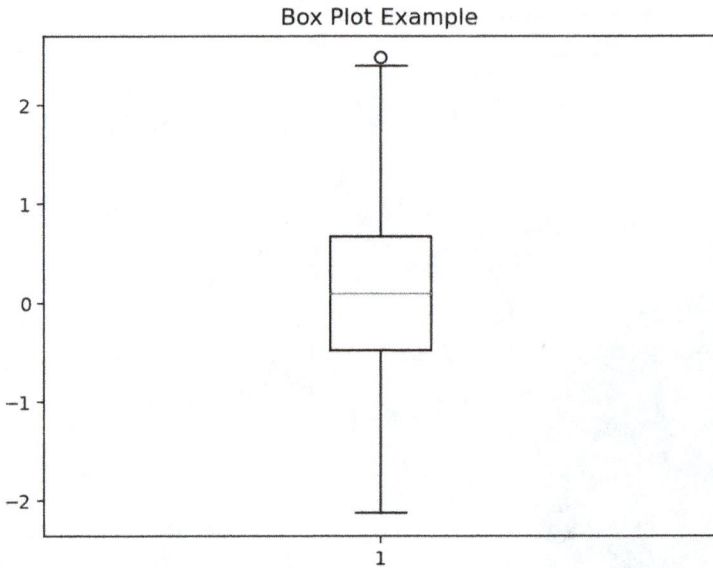

Fig. 3.25: Box plot.

Violin Plot

Violin plots amalgamate a box plot and a kernel density plot to exhibit the distribution of numerical data. They offer a more intricate perspective of the distribution of data in comparison to box plots. For instance, they can be utilized to visualize the distribution of heights among diverse age groups.

```
import matplotlib.pyplot as plt
import seaborn as sns
import numpy as np

np.random.seed(10)
data = np.random.normal(0, 1, 100)

sns.violinplot(data)
plt.title('Violin Plot Example')
plt.show()
```

Output:

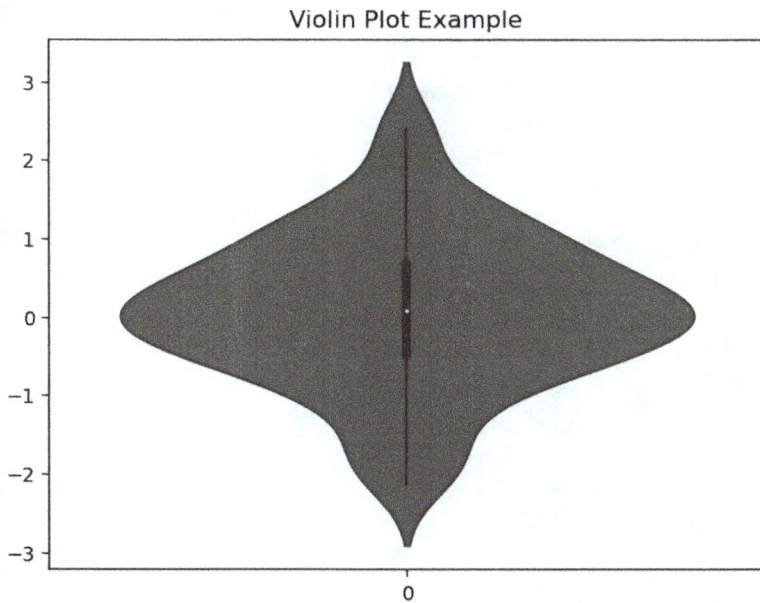

Fig. 3.26: Violin plot.

Heatmap

Heatmaps visualize data in a tabular format by assigning colors to cells based on their values. They are commonly used to visualize correlations or relationships in large datasets. Example: visualizing the correlation matrix of numerical variables in a dataset.

```python
import matplotlib.pyplot as plt
import seaborn as sns
import numpy as np

np.random.seed(10)
data = np.random.rand(10, 10)

sns.heatmap(data, annot=True, cmap='YlGnBu')
plt.title('Heatmap Example')
plt.show()
```

Output:

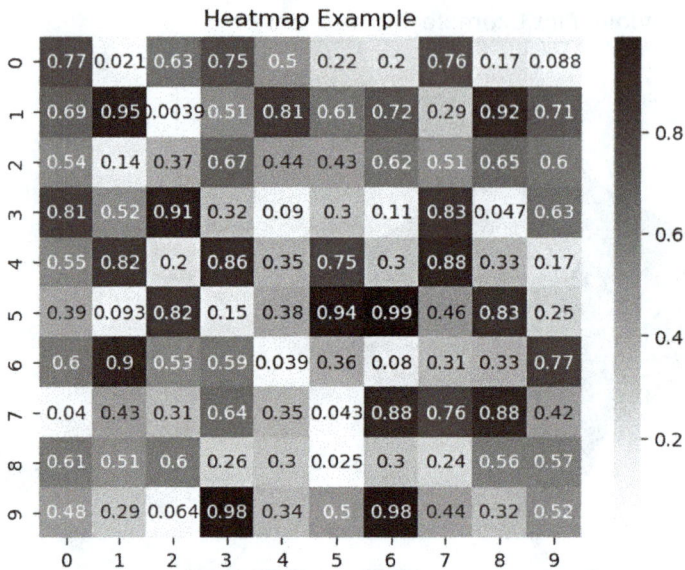

	0	1	2	3	4	5	6	7	8	9
0	0.77	0.021	0.63	0.75	0.5	0.22	0.2	0.76	0.17	0.088
1	0.69	0.95	0.0039	0.51	0.81	0.61	0.72	0.29	0.92	0.71
2	0.54	0.14	0.37	0.67	0.44	0.43	0.62	0.51	0.65	0.6
3	0.81	0.52	0.91	0.32	0.09	0.3	0.11	0.83	0.047	0.63
4	0.55	0.82	0.2	0.86	0.35	0.75	0.3	0.88	0.33	0.17
5	0.39	0.093	0.82	0.15	0.38	0.94	0.99	0.46	0.83	0.25
6	0.6	0.9	0.53	0.59	0.039	0.36	0.08	0.31	0.33	0.77
7	0.04	0.43	0.31	0.64	0.35	0.043	0.88	0.76	0.88	0.42
8	0.61	0.51	0.6	0.26	0.3	0.025	0.3	0.24	0.56	0.57
9	0.48	0.29	0.064	0.98	0.34	0.5	0.98	0.44	0.32	0.52

Fig. 3.27: Heatmap.

Area Plot

Area plots are similar to line plots but fill the area below the line, making them useful for visualizing cumulative data or stacked data. For example, visualizing the cumulative sales over time for different product categories.

    import matplotlib.pyplot as plt

```
import matplotlib.pyplot as plt

x = [1, 2, 3, 4, 5]
y1 = [1, 2, 3, 4, 5]
y2 = [1, 4, 9, 16, 25]

plt.fill_between(x, y1, color='skyblue', alpha=0.4)
plt.fill_between(x, y2, color='orange', alpha=0.4)
plt.title('Area Plot Example')
plt.show()
```

Output:

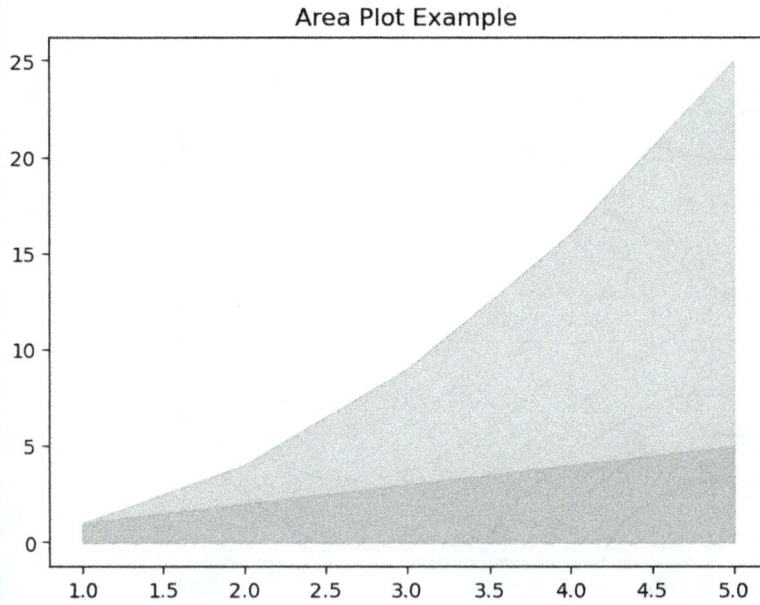

Fig. 3.28: Area plot.

Contour Plot

Contour plots represent three-dimensional data in two dimensions by showing contours or lines of constant values. They are commonly used for visualizing geographical or scientific data. For example, visualizing elevation data on a map.

```python
import matplotlib.pyplot as plt
import numpy as np

x = np.linspace(-3, 3, 100)
y = np.linspace(-3, 3, 100)
X, Y = np.meshgrid(x, y)
Z = np.sin(X) + np.cos(Y)

plt.contour(X, Y, Z)
plt.title('Contour Plot Example')
plt.show()
```

Output:

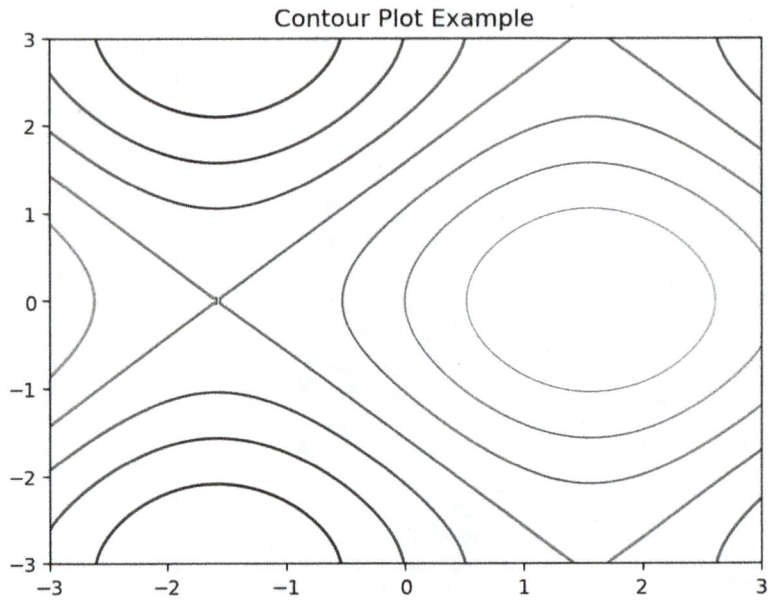

Fig. 3.29: Contour plot.

3.5.2 Advanced Visualizations with Seaborn

Seaborn, an advanced visualization tool, provides robust features for the demonstration of data, exhibiting superior capabilities when contrasted with fundamental plotting libraries such as Matplotlib. Seaborn is constructed upon Matplotlib, delivering an interface at a higher level, which enables the creation of statistically informative and visually captivating graphics.

Here's a sample structure for the "dataset.csv" file:

```
x_variable,y_variable,category
1,2,A
2,3,B
3,4,A
4,5,B
5,6,A
6,7,B
```

Pair Plot

Pair plots depict the pairwise associations among variables in a dataset by presenting scatter plots for numerical variables and histograms for the diagonal axes.

```python
import seaborn as sns
import pandas as pd

data = pd.read_csv('dataset.csv')
sns.jointplot(x='x_variable', y='y_variable', data=data, kind='scatter')
```

Output:

```
<seaborn.axisgrid.PairGrid at 0x218f9693950>
```

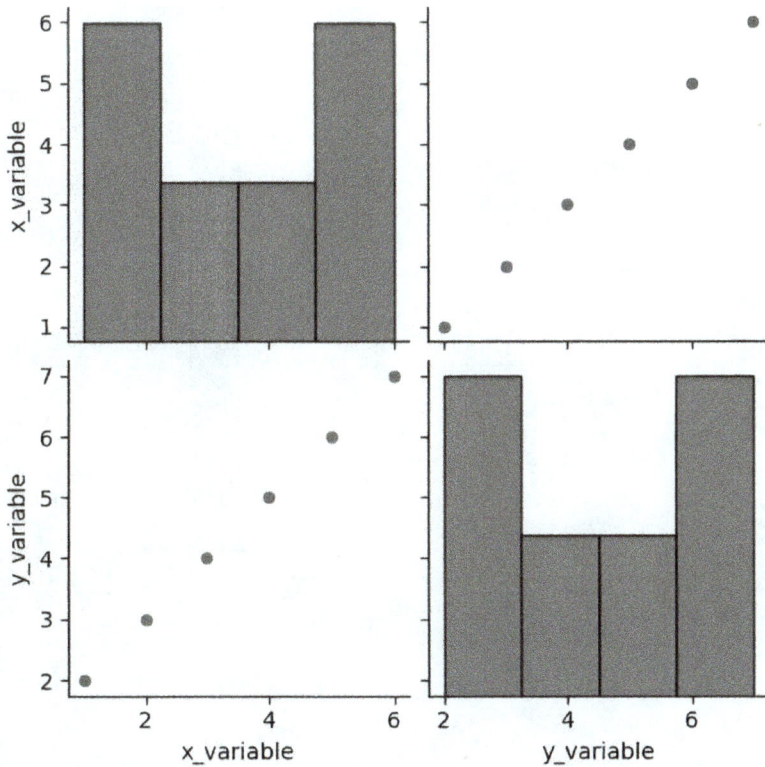

Fig. 3.30: Pair plot.

Joint Plot

Joint plots integrate scatter plots and histograms to visually represent the correlation between two quantitative variables in addition to their respective distributions.

```
import seaborn as sns
import pandas as pd

data = pd.read_csv('dataset.csv')
sns.jointplot(x='x_variable', y='y_variable', data=data, kind='scatter')
```

Output:

```
<seaborn.axisgrid.JointGrid at 0x218fa33d6d0>
```

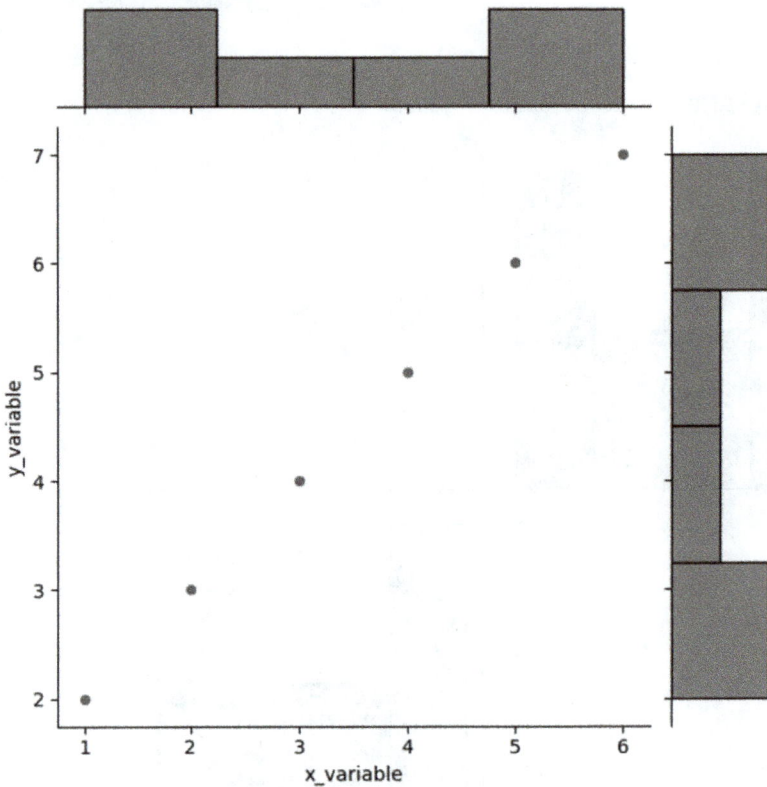

Fig. 3.31: Joint plot.

PairGrid

PairGrid allows customization of pair plots by providing access to individual subplots, facilitating detailed exploration of pairwise relationships.

```
import seaborn as sns
import pandas as pd
```

```
data = pd.read_csv('dataset.csv')
g = sns.PairGrid(data)
g.map(sns.scatterplot)
```

Output:

```
<seaborn.axisgrid.PairGrid at 0x218fce7a950>
```

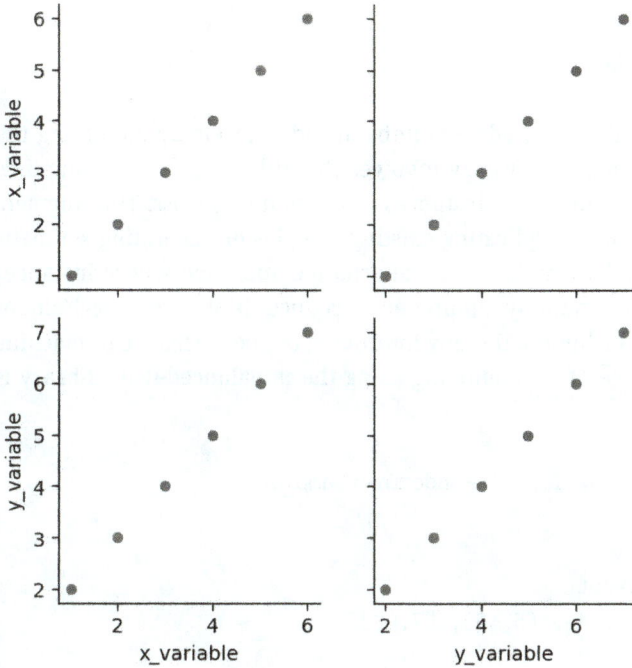

Fig. 3.32: Pair grid.

3.6 Handling Imbalanced Data

Handling imbalanced data is an imperative undertaking within the realm of machine learning, where the quantity of samples in one category significantly surpasses the quantity of samples in another category.

Imbalanced datasets pose challenges in the training of models because algorithms tend to favor the category with a larger number of samples, leading to biased predictions and inferior performance for categories with fewer samples. To address this issue, various methodologies are employed, including resampling techniques such as oversampling (increasing the number of samples in the minority category) and under-sampling (reducing the number of samples in the majority category).

Furthermore, synthetic data generation techniques such as SMOTE (Synthetic Minority Over-sampling Technique) and ADASYN (Adaptive Synthetic Sampling) are utilized to generate artificial data points for the minority category, thus achieving a balanced dataset. Handling imbalanced data ensures that machine learning models are trained on datasets that are more representative, resulting in improved performance and generalization across all categories.

3.6.1 Resampling Techniques

Resampling methods are utilized to address imbalanced datasets by modifying the classes' distribution. One common strategy involves the utilization of oversampling, which entails increasing the number of instances in the minority class. This augmentation can be achieved by either replicating existing samples or generating synthetic data points. In contrast, undersampling is an alternative approach where instances from the majority class are randomly eliminated to reduce its size. Both techniques aim to equalize the class distribution, thereby improving the performance of machine learning models. An example of oversampling using the imbalanced-learn library is provided:

```python
from imblearn.over_sampling import RandomOverSampler
import numpy as np

# Sample imbalanced dataset
X = np.array([[1, 2], [3, 4], [5, 6], [7, 8]])
y = np.array([0, 0, 1, 1])

# Instantiate RandomOverSampler
ros = RandomOverSampler()

# Resample dataset
X_resampled, y_resampled = ros.fit_resample(X, y)

print("Original class distribution:", np.bincount(y))
print("Resampled class distribution:", np.bincount(y_resampled))
```

In this particular instance, the initial step involves establishing an imbalanced dataset consisting of two distinct classes. Subsequently, we employ the RandomOverSampler function, sourced from the imbalanced-learn library, in order to oversample the minority class. Lastly, we display the class distributions both prior to and subsequent to the resampling process, enabling us to observe the resultant balancing effect.

Here's a programming example of undersampling using the imbalanced-learn library:

```
from imblearn.under_sampling import RandomUnderSampler
import numpy as np

# Sample imbalanced dataset
X = np.array([[1, 2], [3, 4], [5, 6], [7, 8], [9, 10]])
y = np.array([0, 0, 1, 1, 1])

# Instantiate RandomUnderSampler
rus = RandomUnderSampler()

# Resample dataset
X_resampled, y_resampled = rus.fit_resample(X, y)

print("Original class distribution:", np.bincount(y))
print("Resampled class distribution:", np.bincount(y_resampled))
```

In this particular instance, we establish a representative imbalanced dataset consisting of two distinct classes. To achieve undersampling, we employ the RandomUnderSampler function from the imbalanced-learn library. By invoking the fit_resample method, we execute the undersampling operation. Ultimately, we demonstrate the effects of balancing by displaying the class distributions prior to and subsequent to undersampling.

3.6.2 Synthetic Data Generation

Synthetic data generation approaches are employed to address the problem of class imbalance in datasets, with a particular emphasis on the minority class. Methods such as SMOTE and ADASYN produce synthetic instances for the minority class by utilizing existing data points.

SMOTE accomplishes this by creating synthetic samples through interpolation between instances of the minority class, while ADASYN adjusts the generation process by considering the density of samples in the feature space. These approaches aid in mitigating the impact of class imbalance by augmenting the dataset with artificially generated data points, thereby enhancing the performance of machine learning models.

An illustrative example showcasing the application of SMOTE is presented below:

```python
from imblearn.over_sampling import SMOTE
import numpy as np

# Sample imbalanced dataset
X = np.array([[1, 2], [3, 4], [5, 6], [7, 8]])
y = np.array([0, 0, 1, 1])

# Instantiate SMOTE
smote = SMOTE()

# Generate synthetic samples
X_synthetic, y_synthetic = smote.fit_resample(X, y)

print("Original class distribution:", np.bincount(y))
print("Synthetic class distribution:", np.bincount(y_synthetic))
```

In this instance, SMOTE is utilized to produce artificial data points for the underrepresented class within the dataset that exhibits imbalance. The fit_resample technique is utilized to execute the generation of synthetic data, and the resultant distributions of classes both before and after the application of SMOTE are compared to observe the effect of achieving balance.

Here is an illustrative programming example showcasing the utilization of ADASYN (Adaptive Synthetic Sampling) for the purpose of creating synthetic data points for the underrepresented class within an imbalanced dataset:

```python
from imblearn.over_sampling import ADASYN
import numpy as np

# Sample imbalanced dataset
X = np.array([[1, 2], [3, 4], [5, 6], [7, 8]])
y = np.array([0, 0, 1, 1])

# Instantiate ADASYN
adasyn = ADASYN()

# Generate synthetic samples
X_synthetic, y_synthetic = adasyn.fit_resample(X, y)

print("Original class distribution:", np.bincount(y))
print("Synthetic class distribution:", np.bincount(y_synthetic))
```

In this particular instance, we are presented with a dataset that exhibits an imbalance in terms of the number of instances belonging to each class, whereby the minority class possesses a smaller number of instances. To address this issue, we apply the ADASYN algorithm, which serves to generate synthetic data points specifically for the minority class. Subsequently, the fit_resample method is invoked to carry out the generation of synthetic data. Finally, to observe the effect of the balancing process, we proceed to display the class distributions both before and after the application of ADASYN.

Summary

- Numerical and scientific computing using NumPy and SciPy: Covered array creation, manipulation, and various numerical operations using NumPy and SciPy libraries.
- Loading data with pandas: Introduction to pandas library for data manipulation and analysis, including DataFrame and Series, along with data manipulation techniques.
- Data cleaning and transformation: Discussed strategies for handling missing data and data type conversions in datasets.
- Feature engineering: Covered techniques such as encoding categorical variables and feature scaling for preparing data for machine learning.
- Data visualization with Matplotlib and Seaborn: Introduced Matplotlib and Seaborn libraries for data visualization, including basic and advanced plotting techniques.
- Handling imbalanced data: Discussed challenges posed by imbalanced datasets in machine learning and techniques like resampling and synthetic data generation to address class imbalance.

Exercise (MCQs)

1. **What is the purpose of indentation in Python syntax?**
   a) To indicate comments
   b) To separate code blocks
   c) To denote data types
   d) To define class attributes

2. **Which library is commonly used for numerical and scientific computing in Python?**
   a) Pandas   b) Matplotlib   c) NumPy   d) Seaborn

3. **What is the primary data structure in pandas for storing and manipulating data?**
   a) Arrays   b) Lists   c) DataFrame   d) Tuples

4. **Which technique is used for handling missing data in pandas?**
   a) Resampling
   b) Feature scaling
   c) Data type conversion
   d) Imputation

5. **What is the purpose of feature scaling in machine learning?**
   a) To convert categorical variables into numerical representations
   b) To balance imbalanced datasets
   c) To standardize or normalize features
   d) To visualize data distributions

6. **Which library is commonly used for data visualization in Python?**
   a) NumPy   b) SciPy   c) Pandas   d) Matplotlib

7. **Which plot type is used for visualizing pairwise relationships between variables in Seaborn?**
   a) Scatter plot   b) Pair plot   c) Histogram   d) Heatmap

8. **What technique is commonly used to address class imbalance in machine learning datasets?**
   a) Oversampling
   b) Feature engineering
   c) Data cleaning
   d) Dimensionality reduction

9. **What is the purpose of synthetic data generation techniques like SMOTE and ADASYN?**
   a) To create artificial data points for majority classes
   b) To remove outliers from datasets
   c) To convert categorical variables into numerical representations
   d) To standardize features in datasets

10. **Which of the following is not a feature engineering technique?**
    a) Encoding categorical variables
    b) Feature scaling
    c) Data imputation
    d) Dimensionality reduction

Answers

1. b
2. c
3. c
4. d
5. c
6. d
7. b
8. a
9. a
10. a

Fill in the Blanks

1. _____ and _____ are libraries commonly used for numerical and scientific computing tasks in Python.
2. In pandas, the primary data structure for storing and manipulating data is called _____.
3. Resampling techniques such as _____ and _____ are used to address class imbalance in machine learning datasets.
4. Feature scaling techniques aim to standardize or normalize the _____ of features in datasets.
5. Matplotlib and Seaborn are popular libraries used for _____ in Python.
6. Pair plots are used in Seaborn to visualize _____ relationships between variables.
7. SMOTE and ADASYN are techniques used for generating _____ data points in imbalanced datasets.
8. _____ and _____ are methods used for encoding categorical variables in feature engineering.
9. Data cleaning involves handling _____ values and converting data types for analysis.
10. Classes serve as blueprints for creating _____ in object-oriented programming.

Answers

1. NumPy, SciPy
2. DataFrame
3. oversampling, undersampling

4. scale
5. data visualization
6. pairwise
7. synthetic
8. Label encoding, one-hot encoding
9. missing
10. objects

Descriptive Questions

1. Explain the importance of proper indentation in Python syntax and how it impacts the readability of code.
2. Describe the role of pandas in data manipulation and analysis, and provide examples of DataFrame operations.
3. Discuss the significance of feature engineering in machine learning and explain the difference between encoding categorical variables and feature scaling.
4. Explain the process of data visualization using Matplotlib and Seaborn, and provide examples of basic and advanced plotting techniques.
5. Describe the challenges posed by imbalanced datasets in machine learning and discuss techniques such as resampling and synthetic data generation to address class imbalance.
6. Explain the concept of feature scaling and discuss its importance in preparing data for machine learning models.
7. Discuss the role of comments in Python code and how they contribute to code documentation and readability.
8. Explain the concept of object-oriented programming in Python, including classes, objects, inheritance, and polymorphism.
9. Discuss the strategies for handling missing data in datasets and the importance of data imputation in data preprocessing.
10. Describe the process of encoding categorical variables in feature engineering and discuss the differences between label encoding and one-hot encoding.
11. Write a Python program that creates a 2D NumPy array and performs the following operations:
    a. Compute the mean, median, and standard deviation of the array.
    b. Reshape the array into a different shape.
    c. Perform element-wise addition and multiplication with another array.
12. Write a Python program that loads a CSV file using pandas and performs the following operations:
    a. Display the first few rows of the DataFrame.
    b. Calculate summary statistics for numerical columns.
    c. Convert a categorical column to numerical one using label encoding.

13. Write a Python program that generates a line plot using Matplotlib to visualize a time series dataset.
    a. Include labels for the x and y axes.
    b. Add a title to the plot.
    c. Customize the line style and color.
14. Write a Python program that loads an imbalanced dataset and implements over-sampling using the SMOTE technique from the imbalanced-learn library.
    a. Display the class distribution before and after oversampling.
    b. Train a simple machine learning model (e.g., logistic regression) on the balanced dataset and evaluate its performance.
15. Write a Python program that preprocesses a dataset for machine learning using feature engineering techniques.
    a. Encode categorical variables using one-hot encoding.
    b. Scale numerical features using Min-Max scaling or standardization.
    c. Split the dataset into training and testing sets for model evaluation.

Chapter 4
Foundations of Machine Learning

The underpinning on which the entire realm of machine learning operates is constituted by the bedrock of this discipline. These bedrock elements encompass indispensable principles and concepts that serve as the foundation for the formulation, construction, and assessment of machine learning algorithms. At its core, the objective of machine learning is to facilitate computers in obtaining knowledge from data without the necessity of explicit programming. This chapter thoroughly explores the fundamental facets that hold paramount importance for every practitioner to apprehend to adeptly navigate the intricate terrain of machine learning.

A fundamental initial step in comprehending machine learning resides in differentiating between supervised and unsupervised learning. The incorporation of labeled data characterizes supervised learning, while unsupervised learning operates without such labeling. Subsequent examination is conducted within the subsections to clarify the notions of classification versus regression and clustering versus association. These notions offer insight into the varied forms of learning tasks and their corresponding applications.

The significance of achieving a delicate equilibrium between the ability to capture intricate patterns in data and the capability to generalize to unobserved instances is emphasized by the concepts of overfitting and regularization. Overfitting pertains to the scenario in which a model becomes excessively tailored to the training data, resulting in inadequate performance on unseen data. Techniques for regularization, such as the Bias-Variance Trade-off and L1/L2 Regularization, offer methods to alleviate overfitting and enhance the resilience of models.

Evaluation metrics play a crucial role in assessing the performance of machine learning models. This chapter provides an overview of metrics tailored for both classification and regression tasks. These metrics offer valuable insights into the accuracy, precision, recall, and other key measures of model performance.

Cross-validation arises as an essential instrument for the evaluation and choice of models. It diminishes the possibility of overfitting by methodically dividing data into training and validation sets. A comprehensive explanation of diverse techniques, such as k-fold cross-validation, leave-one-out, and stratified K-old, empowers professionals to proficiently validate their models.

The basic essence of machine learning is to provide learners with the necessary fundamental principles and methodologies that are required to begin the process of constructing intelligent systems. These foundations establish a strong and stable basis for the subsequent exploration of more sophisticated concepts and techniques in later chapters.

https://doi.org/10.1515/9783110697186-004

4.1 Supervised vs Unsupervised Learning

Supervised and unsupervised learning are two fundamental frameworks in the field of machine learning, each addressing distinct categories of learning tasks and methodologies.

Supervised learning, which focuses on the training of a model using labeled information, involves associating each input data point with an output label or target. The primary objective is to establish a mapping from inputs to outputs, allowing the model to generate predictions on new data. Supervised learning is commonly used in classification tasks, where the aim is to assign input instances to specific categories or labels, as well as regression tasks, where the goal is to forecast a continuous value. Prominent algorithms in supervised learning include decision trees, support vector machines, and neural networks.

In contrast, unsupervised learning deals with unlabeled data, requiring the model to identify underlying patterns or structures without explicit guidance. Instead of making predictions for specific outputs, unsupervised learning algorithms aim to uncover inherent relationships or groupings within the data. Clustering algorithms, such as K-means and hierarchical clustering, segment the data into distinct clusters based on similarities, while association algorithms, like Apriori, discover rules or associations between different attributes. Unsupervised learning is particularly advantageous for anomaly detection, data compression, and feature extraction tasks.

Supervised learning relies on labeled data to learn the correlations between inputs and outputs, enabling prediction tasks. In contrast, unsupervised learning operates on unlabeled data to reveal hidden structures or patterns, providing insights and understanding of raw data without explicit guidance. Both paradigms play significant roles in various machine learning applications, each offering distinct advantages and challenges depending on the problem and available data.

Types of Supervised Learning

Classification: The aim of classification is to generate forecasts pertaining to the categorical class designations of novel instances by leveraging prior observations. This approach is utilized when the output variable assumes categorical values. Examples that demonstrate this concept include the identification of email spam, analysis of sentiment, and medical diagnosis.

Regression: Regression entails the estimation of a continuous output value by relying on input features. This approach is utilized when the output variable assumes numerical values. Instances of this include predicting house prices, stock prices, and temperature forecasting.

Types of Unsupervised Learning

Clustering: Clustering algorithms partition data points into clusters or groups according to their similarity. The objective is to discover natural groupings in the data without any predetermined labels. Customer segmentation, document clustering, and image segmentation are common examples of this.

Association: Association rule learning is a method that identifies interesting relationships or associations between variables in large datasets. The main focus is on finding patterns of co-occurrence or correlation among items. Market basket analysis is a specific application of association rule learning that aims to discover items that are frequently purchased together. Recommendation systems, on the other hand, suggest related products or content based on user behavior. Both of these examples illustrate the use of association rule learning in practice.

Supervised and unsupervised learning methods, which span a broad array of techniques and algorithms, serve as indispensable tools for tackling diverse real-world challenges in domains including finance, healthcare, e-commerce, and beyond.

4.1.1 Classification vs Regression

Classification and regression, two cardinal categories of supervised learning tasks within the realm of machine learning, each fulfill unique objectives and require specific approaches.

In the domain of categorization, the aim is to allocate input data points to preexisting classes or labels. This methodology is typically utilized when the output variable demonstrates a categorical character. For instance, in the sphere of detecting email spam, the objective is to classify emails as either "spam" or "not spam" based on various attributes such as the sender, subject, and content. Similarly, in the analysis of sentiment, textual data is classified as "positive," "negative," or "neutral" depending on the sentiment expressed. Prominent algorithms employed for categorization encompass logistic regression, decision trees, and support vector machines.

In contrast, regression involves the prediction of a continuous output value using input features. This approach is used when the output variable has numerical characteristics. For example, in the field of real estate, regression can be used to forecast house prices based on factors such as location, size, and amenities. In the domain of stock market analysis, regression models can be employed to predict future stock prices by analyzing historical data and market indicators. Common regression techniques include linear regression, polynomial regression, and decision tree regression.

To exemplify, let us examine a straightforward classification problem: forecasting if a loan applicant of a bank will fail to pay their loan or not. The input characteristics in this situation could consist of the applicant's credit score, earnings, and debt-to-income ratio, while the output would be a binary tag indicating either "default" or "no default." A logistic regression model can be educated on past data to categorize potential loan applicants based on these characteristics.

In contrast, suppose we have an interest in predicting the price of a dwelling based on its dimensions, number of bedrooms, and geographical location. This scenario introduces a regression issue as the output variable, specifically the dwelling price, exhibits a continuous characteristic. In this instance, a linear regression model can be utilized to establish the connection between the input attributes and the dwelling prices by employing a dataset consisting of past real estate transactions. Consequently, this grants us the capability to generate predictions regarding the price of newly constructed dwellings.

Classification involves the classification of data into classes or labels, whereas regression concentrates on the prediction of numerical values. A comprehensive understanding of the differences between these two types of supervised learning tasks is crucial when choosing appropriate algorithms and methodologies to effectively tackle various real-world problems.

Types of Classification

Binary classification: In the realm of binary classification, the aim is to categorize instances into either of two separate categories. Instances may encompass the identification of spam (differentiating emails into spam or non-spam), the detection of fraud (distinguishing between fraudulent and non-fraudulent transactions), and medical diagnosis (ascertaining the existence or absence of a disease).

Multiclass classification: Multiclass classification pertains to the process of classifying instances into multiple distinct classes or categories. Instances may include recognizing handwritten digits (ranging from 0 to 9), conducting sentiment analysis (identifying instances as positive, negative, or neutral), and classifying documents into various topics.

Types of Regression

Linear regression: Linear regression constructs a model that represents the correlation between a reliant variable and one or multiple autonomous variables using a linear equation. Its application lies in the forecast of continuous numerical values. Instances include the anticipation of housing costs based on the area and quantity of bedrooms, the prediction of stock prices utilizing historical data, and the estimation of sales revenue by taking marketing expenses into account.

Polynomial regression: Polynomial regression extends the scope of linear regression by employing a polynomial function to fit the data, rather than a mere straight line. This methodology effectively captures intricate nonlinear associations between the variables. Illustrative instances encompass the prediction of a projectile's trajectory, the modeling of temporal temperature fluctuations, and the fitting of growth curves in the realm of biology.

Logistic regression: Despite being named as such, logistic regression is utilized as a classification algorithm for tasks involving binary classification. It constructs a model to determine the probability that a given instance is part of a particular class by employing a logistic function. Instances of its application include predicting the probability of a customer making a purchase, estimating the likelihood of a patient having a specific disease based on medical tests, and forecasting the probability of defaulting on a loan.

Ridge and Lasso regression: Ridge and Lasso regression are methods utilized to regularize linear regression models by integrating a penalty term into the cost function. These methods assist in mitigating overfitting and improving the generalization capability of the model. Ridge regression incorporates a penalty term that is directly proportional to the square of the coefficients' magnitude, whereas Lasso regression incorporates a penalty term that is directly proportional to the absolute value of the coefficients. These methods are particularly advantageous when dealing with multicollinearity and datasets with high dimensionality.

Classification and regression techniques, which are essential tools in the field of machine learning, are widely used in diverse domains including finance, healthcare, marketing, and engineering.

4.1.2 Clustering vs Association

Clustering and association are two separate categories of unsupervised learning tasks in the realm of machine learning, each serving different purposes and employing varied methodologies.

Clustering entails the process of grouping similar data points together based on their inherent characteristics, without any predefined labels. The primary aim is to discover inherent groupings or clusters within the data. For example, in the context of customer segmentation, clustering algorithms can effectively divide customers into distinct groups based on their purchasing behavior, demographics, or other relevant features. A well-known algorithm for clustering is the K-means algorithm, which assigns data points to clusters by minimizing the distance between each point and the centroid of its assigned cluster. Another technique, called "hierarchical clustering," constructs a hierarchical structure of clusters by recursively merging or splitting clusters based on their similarity.

On the contrary, association rule learning seeks to uncover intriguing connections or associations amidst various variables within extensive datasets. The primary emphasis resides in the identification of patterns of co-occurrence or correlation among items. An exemplary illustration of this phenomenon is market basket analysis, where association rules are employed to unveil the relationships between products that are frequently purchased together during transactions. The Apriori algorithm is commonly employed for this endeavor, as it systematically generates potential itemsets and eliminates those that fail to satisfy the minimum support criteria, thus effectively identifying frequent itemsets and association rules.

To exemplify, let us contemplate a retail establishment that desires to scrutinize customer acquisition data. By employing clustering, the establishment can effectively classify customers into discrete categories based on their preferences when it comes to procuring merchandise. This invaluable data can subsequently be employed to fabricate targeted marketing strategies or personalized recommendations. Meanwhile, association analysis can reveal patterns such as "customers who acquire diapers are inclined to also obtain baby formula," thus enabling the establishment to optimize the positioning of products or promotional undertakings.

In summary, the focus of clustering is on the identification of natural groupings or clusters within data. On the other hand, association rule learning is primarily concerned with the discovery of relationships or patterns of co-occurrence among variables. The utilization of both approaches is extremely valuable in the process of uncovering insights and patterns within unlabeled data. Ultimately, this enables businesses to make well-informed decisions and enhance their operational efficiency.

Types of Clustering

K-means clustering: The technique of K-means clustering divides the data into a preestablished quantity (k) of clusters, aiming to minimize the distance between data points and the centroid of their designated cluster. This iterative process updates centroids until convergence is reached. K-means clustering is extensively utilized owing to its straightforwardness and effectiveness, although it necessitates the prior specification of the cluster count.

Hierarchical clustering: Hierarchical clustering, conversely, builds a dendrogram, a tree-like arrangement, through iterative merging or splitting of clusters based on the similarity of data points. It does not require the prior specification of cluster numbers and can yield a valuable understanding of the hierarchical composition of the data. Two frequently employed techniques in hierarchical clustering are agglomerative (bottom-up) and divisive (top-down) clustering.

DBSCAN: Density-based clustering (DBSCAN) is a clustering algorithm that detects clusters by taking into account areas of high density that are separated by areas of low density. This method can identify clusters of various shapes and is robust against noise and outliers. DBSCAN, abbreviated from density-based spatial clustering of applications with noise, is a widely used density-based clustering algorithm that necessitates the specification of two parameters: epsilon, which denotes the maximum distance between points for them to be considered part of the same cluster, and minPts, which represents the minimum number of points required to form a dense region.

Mean shift clustering: Mean shift clustering, on the other hand, is a clustering technique devoid of parameters that detects clusters through the displacement of centroids towards areas of heightened data density. Comparable to hierarchical clustering, it does not necessitate the a priori specification of cluster quantity and can autonomously ascertain the optimal number of clusters based on the distribution of data.

Types of Association

Apriori algorithm: The Apriori algorithm, which is widely recognized, is a notable algorithm for learning association rules. This algorithm is employed to identify frequent itemsets in transactional datasets. By generating candidate itemsets and subsequently eliminating ones that do not meet the minimum support criteria, the algorithm effectively identifies frequent itemsets. From these frequent itemsets, association rules are derived, thereby providing valuable insights into the probability of one item being purchased given the purchase of another item.

FP-growth algorithm: The FP-growth algorithm presents an alternative technique for mining frequent itemsets in transactional datasets. It employs the construction of a concise data structure called the FP-tree (frequent pattern tree) to efficiently identify frequent itemsets, eliminating the need for explicit generation of candidate itemsets. This property renders it especially advantageous for processing large datasets containing a substantial number of transactions.

Eclat algorithm: The Eclat algorithm is an additional and widely recognized algorithm for association rule learning. It explores frequent itemsets by intersecting transaction tidsets. Through the utilization of the downward closure property of support, it effectively detects frequent itemsets.

PrefixSpan algorithm: The PrefixSpan algorithm, conversely, is utilized specifically to extract sequential patterns in sequence databases. It employs a recursive approach to generate frequent sequences through the extension of prefix patterns, subsequently optimizing the search space to effectively discern frequent sequential patterns.

Various types of clustering and association techniques play a crucial role in the domain of data mining and pattern recognition. They facilitate the identification of significant patterns and valuable insights from extensive datasets across a wide range of fields, including market basket analysis, customer segmentation, and recommendation systems.

4.2 Overfitting and Regularization

Overfitting and regularization are two fundamental concepts in machine learning, particularly within the context of training predictive models. The occurrence of over-fitting transpires when a model acquires an excessive comprehension of the training data, encompassing noise or random fluctuations in the data rather than the underlying patterns. Consequently, the model exhibits satisfactory performance on the training data but demonstrates inadequate generalization to unseen data. This can result in below-average performance and incorrect predictions in real-world circumstances. Regularization, on the other hand, is a technique utilized to address overfitting by incorporating a penalty term into the loss function of the model. This penalty discourages the presence of intricate models with high variance by imposing limitations on the model parameters.

L2 regularization, known as "Ridge regularization," is a prevalent form of regularization that involves adding a penalty term to the loss function. This penalty term is proportional to the squared magnitude of the model's weights. L1 regularization, also known as "Lasso regularization," is another form of regularization that includes a penalty term proportional to the absolute magnitude of the model's weights. These regularization techniques are effective in preventing overfitting by encouraging simpler models with smaller coefficients. As a result, they reduce model complexity and improve generalization performance.

Regularization methods can be optimized by modifying hyperparameters, such as the regularization factor, which controls the balance between accurately fitting the training data and reducing model complexity. The selection of appropriate hyperparameters is often accomplished through the utilization of cross-validation, which assesses the model's effectiveness on a distinct validation dataset.

Overfitting occurs when a model acquires noise or irrelevant patterns from the training data, leading to insufficient generalization performance. The use of regularization techniques, such as L2 and L1 regularization, can mitigate overfitting by penalizing complex models and advocating for simplicity. To construct models that effectively generalize to unseen data and provide accurate predictions in real-world scenarios, it is imperative to employ appropriate regularization and conduct hyperparameter tuning.

4.2.1 Bias-Variance Trade-Off

The concept of balancing bias and variance is a fundamental aspect of the domain of machine learning. This balance is essential to attain an equilibrium between the bias and variance of a specific model. Bias represents the difference between the model's expected prediction and the true value, while variance measures the variability in the model's predictions across various training datasets.

Let us consider a simple example that involves the application of a polynomial regression model to a collection of data points. Suppose we have a dataset that consists of only one characteristic, labeled as "x," and its associated target variable, labeled as "y." Our aim is to construct a polynomial regression model that can effectively forecast the value of "y" based on "x". To accomplish this task, we can express our model in the following manner:

$$y = \beta_0 + \beta_1 x + \beta_2 x2 + \ldots + \beta_{nxn} + \epsilon$$

where ϵ represents the error term, and $\beta_0, \beta_1, \ldots, \beta_n$ are the coefficients of the polynomial terms.

The model's bias can be measured by determining the disparity between the anticipated forecast of the model and the actual value, which can be computed as:

$$\text{Bias}(\hat{f}(x)) = E[\hat{f}(x)] - f(x)$$

where $\hat{f}(x)$ represents the predicted value by the model, $f(x)$ is the true value, and $E[\hat{f}(x)]$ is the expected value of the predictions over different training datasets.

On the contrary, the model's variance quantifies the amount of variation in predictions at a specific point when considering different instances of the model. It can be determined by performing calculations:

$$\text{Var}(\hat{f}(x)]) = E[\hat{f}(x) - E[\hat{f}(x)])^2]$$

The aim is to identify a model that attains an optimal balance between bias and variance. A model that displays a high level of bias but a low level of variance, like a linear regression model, may oversimplify the underlying relationship within the data, thus resulting in systematic errors (underfitting). On the other hand, a model that exhibits low bias but high variance, such as a high-degree polynomial regression model, may capture the noise present in the training data, leading to an increased susceptibility to fluctuations in the training set (overfitting).

To exemplify the trade-off between bias and variance, we shall examine the process of fitting polynomial regression models to a specific dataset, where the degrees of the polynomials differ. In this scenario, as the degree of the polynomial rises, the bias decreases (resulting in a more flexible model capable of capturing more complex relationships within the data), while the variance increases (causing the model to be more sensitive to fluctuations in the training data).

By choosing the suitable degree of a polynomial, our aim is to find a harmonious equilibrium between bias and variance that reduces the total error (the sum of the squared bias and variance). This objective is frequently achieved through methods like cross-validation or regularization, which work to address overfitting by penalizing overly complex models.

In summary, the bias-variance trade-off highlights the fundamental trade-off that exists between the bias and variance of machine learning models. Understanding this

trade-off is essential when choosing the appropriate complexity of a model and preventing cases of underfitting or overfitting in real-world applications.

The concept of balancing bias and variance is a pivotal principle in the domain of
machine learning. It entails achieving an equilibrium between a model's capacity to
precisely grasp the intrinsic patterns within a dataset (reduced bias) and its adaptability
to various datasets (reduced variance). Numerous Python libraries are accessible, providing resources and methodologies for comprehending and handling this trade-off.

scikit-learn, a Python library, is extensively employed for a range of machine
learning undertakings, encompassing both supervised and unsupervised learning. Although scikit-learn does not furnish distinct functions for measuring bias and variance, it does present an array of instruments for assessing models. These instruments
consist of cross-validation, learning curves, and validation curves, which serve the
purpose of evaluating the bias and variance of a model.

An example of utilizing learning curves in scikit-learn to visually represent the
bias-variance trade-off is as follows:

```python
import numpy as np
import matplotlib.pyplot as plt
from sklearn.datasets import load_iris
from sklearn.model_selection import learning_curve
from sklearn.linear_model import LogisticRegression

# Load Iris dataset
iris = load_iris()
X, y = iris.data, iris.target

# Define model
model = LogisticRegression()

# Plot learning curves
train_sizes, train_scores, test_scores = learning_curve(model, X, y,
cv=5)
train_mean = np.mean(train_scores, axis=1)
train_std = np.std(train_scores, axis=1)
test_mean = np.mean(test_scores, axis=1)
test_std = np.std(test_scores, axis=1)

plt.plot(train_sizes, train_mean, color='blue', marker='o',
label='Training accuracy')
plt.fill_between(train_sizes, train_mean - train_std, train_mean +
train_std, alpha=0.15, color='blue')
plt.plot(train_sizes, test_mean, color='green', linestyle='--',
```

```
marker='s', label='Validation accuracy')
plt.fill_between(train_sizes, test_mean - test_std, test_mean +
test_std, alpha=0.15, color='green')

plt.xlabel('Number of training samples')
plt.ylabel('Accuracy')
plt.legend()
plt.show()
```

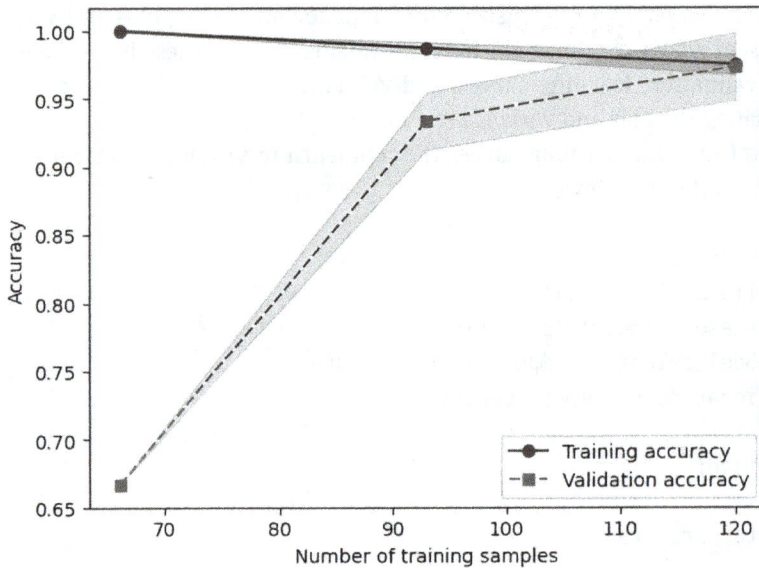

Fig. 4.1: Number of samples vs accuracy.

Fig. 4.1 presents a visual representation of the bias-variance tradeoff, illustrating the relationship between the number of samples and the model's accuracy. The graph depicts how the model's performance, measured by its accuracy, varies as the size of the training dataset changes.

TensorFlow and Keras: TensorFlow and its associated high-level API, Keras, provide a diverse range of tools and methodologies for the construction and training of deep learning models. These libraries furnish functionalities that enable the implementation of regularization techniques, dropout, and early stopping, all of which serve to effectively address the bias-variance trade-off.

```
import tensorflow as tf
from tensorflow.keras.models import Sequential
from tensorflow.keras.layers import Dense, Dropout
```

```
from sklearn.datasets import load_iris
from sklearn.model_selection import train_test_split

# Load Iris dataset
iris = load_iris()
X, y = iris.data, iris.target

# Split data into train and test sets
X_train, X_test, y_train, y_test = train_test_split(X, y, test_size=0.2,
random_state=42)

# Define model with dropout regularization
model = Sequential([
    Dense(64, activation='relu', input_shape=(4,)),
    Dropout(0.2),
    Dense(3, activation='softmax')
])

# Compile the model
model.compile(optimizer='adam', loss='sparse_categorical_crossentropy',
metrics=['accuracy'])

# Train the model
history = model.fit(X_train, y_train, epochs=50, batch_size=32,
validation_data=(X_test, y_test))
```

4.2.2 L1 and L2 Regularization

L1 and L2 regularization are techniques utilized to address the problem of overfitting in machine learning models by introducing supplementary penalizing terms into the cost function. These regularization approaches aim to encourage the creation of simpler models by penalizing significant coefficient values, although each technique uniquely accomplishes this.

Let us examine a linear regression model enhanced by the addition of L1 and L2 regularization. The traditional linear regression model aims to minimize the sum of squared residuals, also referred to as ordinary least squares, which is mathematically represented as:

$$J(\theta) = \frac{1}{2m} \sum_{i=1}^{m} \left(h_\theta\left(x^{(i)}\right) - y^{(i)} \right)^2$$

where $J(\theta)$ is the cost function, $h_\theta(x^{(i)})$ is the predicted value for the ith example, $y^{(i)}$ is the true value, and m is the number of training examples.

In the context of regularization in the L2 norm, which is alternatively referred to as "Ridge regularization," an additional term is incorporated into the cost function that is directly proportional to the square of the magnitude of the coefficients of the model:

$$J_{L2}(\theta) = J(\theta) + \lambda \sum_{j=1}^{n} \theta_j^2$$

the regularization parameter, denoted by λ, and the number of features, denoted by n, are the key components in this context. The regularization parameter is responsible for governing the intensity of regularization, with higher values resulting in a more robust regularization.

In the context of L1 regularization, which is also referred to as "Lasso regularization," an additional term is incorporated into the cost function that is directly proportional to the absolute value of the coefficients of the model:

$$J_{L1}(\theta) = J(\theta) + \lambda \sum_{j=1}^{n} \left| \theta^j \right|$$

The strength of regularization is controlled by the regularization parameter λ, just like L2 regularization.

To elucidate the disparity between L1 and L2 regularization, we shall contemplate a rudimentary instance of linear regression comprising of two features ($n = 2$). Let us assume that we possess a dataset consisting of five training examples:

$$x^{(1)} = [1, 2], y^{(1)} = 3$$
$$x^{(2)} = [1, 3], y^{(2)} = 4$$
$$x^{(3)} = [1, 4], y^{(3)} = 5$$
$$x^{(4)} = [1, 5], y^{(4)} = 6$$
$$x^{(5)} = [1, 6], y^{(5)} = 7$$

We fit a linear regression model to this dataset using both L1 and L2 regularization with $\lambda = 0.1$. After training the models, we examine the values of the coefficients θ_0 and θ_1.

With L2 regularization, the resulting coefficients might be:

$$\theta_0 = 0.5$$
$$\theta_1 = 0.9$$

With L1 regularization, the resulting coefficients might be:

$$\theta_0 = 0.7$$
$$\theta_1 = 0.8$$

In this specific case, it is evident that L2 regularization demonstrates a tendency to gradually decrease the coefficients toward zero to a greater extent when compared to L1 regularization. Conversely, L1 regularization illustrates a propensity to reduce the coefficients completely to zero, thereby effectively performing feature selection by eliminating irrelevant features. This occurrence can be attributed to the fact that the L1 penalty possesses the property of generating sparse solutions, which can be beneficial in situations where feature sparsity is desirable.

In summary, L1 and L2 regularization are methods used to prevent overfitting in machine learning models by penalizing the coefficients with high values. L2 regularization penalizes the squared magnitude of the coefficients, while L1 regularization penalizes the absolute magnitude. It is crucial to understand the differences between these regularization methods to choose the most suitable technique and effectively control model complexity.

Several libraries in Python offer implementations of L1 and L2 regularization methods, which are frequently employed in machine learning to mitigate overfitting and enhance the generalization capability of models. scikit-learn and TensorFlow/ Keras are two commonly utilized libraries for this purpose. In the subsequent section, I will elucidate the usage of these libraries in performing L1 and L2 regularization, illustrated through an example employing the Iris dataset.

scikit-learn: Scikit-learn provides linear models that support L1 and L2 regularization. These models include LogisticRegression, LinearRegression, and Ridge, among others.

```
from sklearn.datasets import load_iris
from sklearn.model_selection import train_test_split
from sklearn.preprocessing import StandardScaler
from sklearn.linear_model import LogisticRegression

# Load Iris dataset
iris = load_iris()
X, y = iris.data, iris.target

# Split data into train and test sets
X_train, X_test, y_train, y_test = train_test_split(X, y, test_size=0.2,
random_state=42)

# Standardize features
scaler = StandardScaler()
X_train_scaled = scaler.fit_transform(X_train)
X_test_scaled = scaler.transform(X_test)
# Train Logistic Regression model with L1 regularization
model = LogisticRegression(penalty='l1', solver='liblinear', C=1.0) # C
```

```
is the inverse of regularization strength
model.fit(X_train_scaled, y_train)

# Evaluate model
accuracy = model.score(X_test_scaled, y_test)
print("Accuracy:", accuracy)
```

Accuracy: 0.9666666666666667

TensorFlow/Keras: TensorFlow and its high-level API Keras provide an assortment of regularizers that can be implemented in the layers of a neural network. These regularizers encompass l1, l2, and l1_l2.

```
import tensorflow as tf
from sklearn.datasets import load_iris
from sklearn.model_selection import train_test_split
from sklearn.preprocessing import StandardScaler

# Load Iris dataset
iris = load_iris()
X, y = iris.data, iris.target

# Split data into train and test sets
X_train, X_test, y_train, y_test = train_test_split(X, y, test_size=0.2,
random_state=42)

# Standardize features
scaler = StandardScaler()
X_train_scaled = scaler.fit_transform(X_train)
X_test_scaled = scaler.transform(X_test)

# Define a simple neural network model with L2 regularization
model = tf.keras.Sequential([
    tf.keras.layers.Dense(64, activation='relu', kernel_regularizer=tf.
keras.regularizers.l2(0.01)),
    tf.keras.layers.Dense(3, activation='softmax')
])

# Compile the model
model.compile(optimizer='adam', loss='sparse_categorical_crossentropy',
metrics=['accuracy'])
```

```
# Train the model
model.fit(X_train_scaled, y_train, epochs=50, batch_size=32,
validation_data=(X_test_scaled, y_test))

# Evaluate the model
test_loss, test_accuracy = model.evaluate(X_test_scaled, y_test)
print("Test Accuracy:", test_accuracy)
```

In both instances, the application of L1 and L2 regularization serves to mitigate the issue of overfitting. L1 regularization entails the inclusion of a penalty that corresponds to the absolute value of the coefficient's magnitude, whereas L2 regularization incorporates a penalty that corresponds to the square of the coefficient's magnitude. By adjusting the regularization strength parameter, such as C for scikit-learn's LogisticRegression or kernel_regularizer for TensorFlow/Keras layers, one can effectively regulate the degree of regularization that is implemented.

4.3 Evaluation Metrics

Evaluation metrics are essential instruments for assessing the effectiveness of machine learning models, providing valuable information on the model's ability to generalize and make accurate predictions on new data. These metrics measure various aspects of model performance, such as accuracy, precision, recall, and F1 score, among others. The understanding and choice of appropriate evaluation metrics are crucial for evaluating the effectiveness of a model and guiding strategies to improve its performance.

Accuracy is a commonly used evaluation metric for classification tasks, which assesses the proportion of correctly classified instances out of the total number of instances. However, solely relying on accuracy may not provide a comprehensive representation of model performance, especially when dealing with imbalanced datasets where one class is dominant. In such cases, precision and recall become essential metrics. Precision measures the proportion of true positive predictions among all positive predictions, while recall measures the proportion of true positive predictions among all actual positive instances. The F1 score, which is the harmonic mean of precision and recall, achieves a balance between these two metrics, making it a suitable choice for imbalanced datasets.

In the context of regression tasks, the evaluation metrics encompass three measures: mean squared error (MSE), mean absolute error (MAE), and R-squared (R^2) score. MSE serves as a quantification of the average squared difference between the predicted and true values, while MAE provides a measure of the average absolute difference. On the other hand, the R^2 score quantifies the degree to which the model explains the variance, with higher values indicating a stronger fit.

The area under the receiver operating characteristic curve (AUC-ROC) and the area under the precision-recall curve (AUC-PR) are additional evaluation metrics that are commonly utilized in binary classification tasks. AUC-ROC assesses the balance between the sensitivity (true positive rate) and the false positive rate, providing valuable insights into the model's capacity to distinguish between positive and negative instances across different thresholds. In the context of imbalanced datasets where precision and recall are of utmost importance, AUC-PR concisely summarizes the performance of the precision-recall curve.

Cross-validation is a commonly used method for assessing model performance, particularly in situations where there is a lack of data. It involves partitioning the dataset into several subsets, training the model on one subset, and then assessing its performance on the remaining subset. This procedure is repeated multiple times, and the average performance across the subsets is calculated to obtain a reliable estimate of the model's performance.

In summary, the assessment criteria play a pivotal role in the assessment of the effectiveness of machine learning models in various tasks and datasets. Through careful selection of suitable assessment criteria and utilization of methods like cross-validation, experts can gain a valuable understanding of model performance and make informed choices to improve model accuracy and generalizability.

4.3.1 Metrics for Classification

The assessment of the efficacy of machine learning models in tasks involving categorical output variables is heavily reliant on metrics for classification. These metrics provide valuable insights into the model's capacity to accurately categorize instances into various classes, allowing for the evaluation of its accuracy, precision, recall, and other performance-related factors.

Accuracy is a noteworthy indicator among the fundamental metrics employed in classification. It measures the ratio of accurately classified instances to the total number of instances. The calculation for accuracy entails the application of the subsequent formula:

$$\text{Accuracy} = \frac{\text{TP} + \text{TN}}{\text{TP} + \text{TN} + \text{FP} + \text{FN}}$$

TP represents the count of accurate positive predictions, TN represents the count of accurate negative predictions, FP represents the count of inaccurate positive predictions, and FN represents the count of inaccurate negative predictions.

However, accuracy in isolation may not provide a comprehensive representation of the model's performance, especially in datasets that demonstrate an unequal distribution, where one class dominates the others. In such circumstances, precision and recall assume crucial roles as metrics. Precision measures the proportion of correct positive predictions relative to all positive predictions, and it can be calculated as follows:

$$Precision = \frac{TP}{TP + FP}$$

Recall, also referred to as sensitivity or true positive rate, quantifies the ratio of accurate positive forecasts in relation to the entirety of genuine positive occurrences, and its computation can be accomplished by:

$$Recall = \frac{TP}{TP + FN}$$

The F1 score, known as the harmonic mean of precision and recall, offers an equilibrium between these two metrics and proves particularly advantageous when dealing with imbalanced datasets. One can compute it using the subsequent formula:

$$F1 = 2* \frac{Precision* Recall}{Precision + Recall}$$

Let us examine a numerical illustration to elucidate the aforementioned metrics. Let us assume that we are faced with a binary classification quandary, wherein we aim to forecast whether an email is spam (positive class) or not spam (negative class). Consequently, we possess a dataset containing precisely 100 emails, of which 80 are classified as not spam and 20 are classified as spam. Subsequently, we proceed to train a classification model and acquire the ensuing confusion matrix.

True/predicted	Not spam	Spam
Not spam	70	5
Spam	10	15

Using this matrix of confusion, we can derive the accuracy, precision, recall, and F1 score of the model.

Accuracy = (70 + 15) / (70 + 5 + 10 + 15) = 85%

Precision = 70 / (70 + 10) = 87.5%

Recall = 70 / (70 + 5) = 93.3%

F1 score = 2 * (0.875 * 0.933) / (0.875 + 0.933) = 90.3%

In this particular instance, the model achieved a level of correctness of 85%, signifying that 85% of the forecasts were accurate. The precision of 87.5% signifies that among all emails predicted as spam, 87.5% were in fact spam. The recall of 93.3% indicates that the model accurately identified 93.3% of all genuine spam emails. The F1 score of 90.3% offers a balanced evaluation of precision and recall, taking into account both false positives and false negatives.

Metrics for classification offer valuable insights into the performance of a model by quantifying its accuracy, precision, recall, and F1 score. Comprehending these metrics is vital for assessing the efficacy of classification models and making well-informed decisions in applications of machine learning.

Several Python libraries offer functionality for computing metrics commonly used for evaluating classification models.

scikit-learn: Scikit-learn, a machine learning library extensively employed in Python, furnishes a broad range of tools for the purpose of classification analysis. Within this library, one can find functions that enable the computation of diverse classification metrics, encompassing accuracy, precision, recall, F1 score, and area under the ROC curve (ROC AUC).

```
from sklearn.metrics import accuracy_score, precision_score,
recall_score, f1_score, roc_auc_score

# Compute accuracy
accuracy = accuracy_score(y_true, y_pred)

# Compute precision
precision = precision_score(y_true, y_pred)

# Compute recall
recall = recall_score(y_true, y_pred)

# Compute F1 score
f1 = f1_score(y_true, y_pred)

# Compute ROC AUC score
roc_auc = roc_auc_score(y_true, y_pred_proba)
```

TensorFlow and PyTorch: While TensorFlow and PyTorch are primarily deep learning libraries, they also offer functionality for computing classification metrics. These libraries are particularly useful when working with neural network models.

```
import tensorflow as tf

# Compute accuracy
accuracy = tf.keras.metrics.Accuracy()
accuracy.update_state(y_true, y_pred)
accuracy_result = accuracy.result().numpy()
```

```
# Compute precision, recall, and F1 score
precision, recall, f1 = tf.keras.metrics.Precision(), tf.keras.metrics.
Recall(), tf.keras.metrics.F1Score()
precision.update_state(y_true, y_pred)
recall.update_state(y_true, y_pred)
f1.update_state(y_true, y_pred)
precision_result = precision.result().numpy()
recall_result = recall.result().numpy()
f1_result = f1.result().numpy()
```

Pandas and NumPy: Pandas and NumPy constitute essential libraries utilized for the manipulation of data and numerical computations within the Python programming language. Despite their lack of dedicated functions for the computation of classification metrics, they are frequently employed in tandem with other libraries to preprocess data and manually derive metrics.

```
import numpy as np
import pandas as pd


# Compute accuracy
accuracy = np.mean(y_true == y_pred)


# Compute precision
true_positives = np.sum((y_true == 1) & (y_pred == 1))
false_positives = np.sum((y_true == 0) & (y_pred == 1))
precision = true_positives / (true_positives + false_positives)


# Compute recall
false_negatives = np.sum((y_true == 1) & (y_pred == 0))
recall = true_positives / (true_positives + false_negatives)


# Compute F1 score
f1 = 2 * (precision * recall) / (precision + recall)
```

4.3.2 Metrics for Regression

Metrics for regression are essential in evaluating the effectiveness of machine learning models when the output variable is continuous. These metrics provide valuable insights into the model's ability to accurately predict numerical values and assist in evaluating its precision, accuracy, and other performance-related aspects.

One of the main metrics used for regression analysis is the MSE, which measures the average squared difference between predicted and actual values. Its calculation involves the use of the following formula:

$$\text{MSE} = \frac{1}{n} \sum_{i=1}^{n} (y_i - \hat{y}_i)^2$$

where n is the number of instances, y_i is the true value, and $\hat{y}_i$ is the predicted value for the ith instance.

MAE is another metric that is frequently employed. It quantifies the average absolute disparity between the predicted and actual values. The calculation involves determining the absolute difference:

$$\text{MAE} = \frac{1}{n} \sum_{i=1}^{n} |y_i - \hat{y}_i|$$

where $|\cdot|$ denotes the absolute value.

The root mean squared error (RMSE) is an alternative form of MSE which offers an assessment of the standard deviation of the residuals. By taking the square root of MSE, RMSE can be computed:

$$\text{RMSE} = \sqrt{\text{MSE}}$$

These metrics provide different perspectives on model performance. MSE and RMSE penalize large errors more heavily, making them sensitive to outliers. MAE, on the other hand, treats all errors equally and is more robust to outliers.

Let's consider a numerical example to illustrate these metrics. Suppose we have a dataset with five instances:

$$(x_1, y_1) = (1, 3)$$
$$(x_2, y_2) = (2, 5)$$
$$(x_3, y_3) = (3, 7)$$
$$(x_4, y_4) = (4, 9)$$
$$(x_5, y_5) = (5, 11)$$

A regression model is utilized to make predictions on y by taking x as input. The following predictions are made by the model:

$$\hat{y}_1 = 2$$
$$\hat{y}_2 = 4$$
$$\hat{y}_3 = 6$$
$$\hat{y}_4 = 8$$
$$\hat{y}_5 = 10$$

Using these estimations, it is feasible to compute the MSE, MAE, and RMSE of the model:

$$\text{MSE} = \frac{1}{5}\sum_{i=1}^{5}(y_i - \hat{y}_i)^2 = \frac{1}{5}\times(0^2 + 1^2 + 1^2 + 1^2 + 1^2) = 0.8$$

$$\text{MAE} = \frac{1}{5}\sum_{i=1}^{5}|y_i - \hat{y}_i| = \frac{1}{5}\times(0 + 1 + 1 + 1 + 1) = 0.8$$

$$\text{RMSE} = \sqrt{\text{MSE}} = \sqrt{0.8} \approx 0.894$$

The aforementioned illustration showcases the accomplishment of the model in achieving a MSE of 0.8. This numerical value essentially represents the average of the squared differences between the predicted and actual values, amounting to 0.8. The MAE, also standing at 0.8, signifies the average absolute difference between the predicted and actual values. Moreover, the RMSE, which is approximately 0.894, acts as a gauge for the standard deviation of the residuals, thereby offering valuable insight into the typical error associated with the model's predictions.

In summary, regression metrics, such as MSE, MAE, and RMSE, provide significant insights into the performance of a model by assessing its accuracy and precision. A comprehensive understanding of these metrics is imperative when evaluating the effectiveness of regression models and making well-informed decisions in the field of machine learning applications.

Several Python libraries provide functionality for computing metrics commonly used for evaluating regression models. Here are some popular ones:

scikit-learn: Scikit-learn, a Python machine learning library that is extensively utilized, provides an extensive array of tools for the analysis of regression. It encompasses functionalities for the computation of diverse regression metrics, including but not limited to MSE, MAE, and R^2 score.

```
from sklearn.metrics import mean_squared_error, mean_absolute_error,
r2_score

# Compute Mean Squared Error
mse = mean_squared_error(y_true, y_pred)

# Compute Mean Absolute Error
mae = mean_absolute_error(y_true, y_pred)

# Compute R-squared score
r2 = r2_score(y_true, y_pred)
```

TensorFlow and PyTorch: While TensorFlow and PyTorch are primarily deep learning libraries, they also offer functionality for computing regression metrics. These libraries are particularly useful when working with neural network models.

```python
import torch
import torch.nn as nn

# Define a custom loss function (e.g., Mean Squared Error)
criterion = nn.MSELoss()

# Compute Mean Squared Error
mse = criterion(y_pred, y_true)

# Optionally, compute Mean Absolute Error and R-squared score manually
mae = torch.mean(torch.abs(y_pred - y_true))
r2 = 1 - (torch.sum((y_true - y_pred)**2) / torch.sum((y_true - torch.
mean(y_true))**2))
```

Pandas and NumPy: Pandas and NumPy are essential libraries utilized to manipulate data and execute numerical computations within the Python programming language. Although these libraries do not offer dedicated functionalities for the calculation of regression metrics, they are frequently employed alongside other libraries to preprocess data and manually compute metrics.

```python
import numpy as np
import pandas as pd

# Compute Mean Squared Error using NumPy
mse = np.mean((y_true - y_pred)**2)

# Compute Mean Absolute Error using NumPy
mae = np.mean(np.abs(y_true - y_pred))

# Compute R-squared score using NumPy
r2 = 1 - (np.sum((y_true - y_pred)**2) / np.sum((y_true - np.mean
(y_true))**2))
```

4.4 Cross-Validation

Cross-validation is an essential procedure utilized in the domain of machine learning to evaluate the effectiveness of a model and deduce its capacity to generalize to unseen data. This technique involves dividing the dataset into several subsets, known as folds, where the model is trained on a portion of the data and assessed on the remaining portion. This iterative process is repeated multiple times, with each fold serving as the validation set precisely once. The application of cross-validation effectively tackles the issue of an excessively optimistic or pessimistic model performance resulting from stochastic fluctuations in the training and testing data partitions.

Among the various methodologies for cross-validation, one of the most prevalent approaches is commonly referred to as "k-fold cross-validation." This particular method entails dividing the dataset into k folds, with each fold being of equal size. The model is then trained on k-1 folds and evaluated on the remaining fold. This process is repeated k times, with each fold being used as the validation set once. Typically, the final performance metric is obtained by calculating the average of the performance metrics across all the folds. This k-fold cross-validation methodology is highly reliable in estimating the performance of the model and effectively addresses the variability introduced by random data partitions.

Another form of cross-validation is known as "leave-one-out cross-validation" (LOOCV), in which each instance in the dataset is used as a separate validation set, and the model is trained on the remaining instances. LOOCV offers significant benefits for datasets with limited size, as it provides a more accurate assessment of model performance. Nonetheless, this approach can be computationally intensive for datasets with a large number of instances.

Stratified k-fold cross-validation is an adaptation of the k-fold cross-validation approach that ensures that the class distribution of the original dataset is preserved in each fold. This is especially important when working with imbalanced datasets, where one class may have a lower representation. The utilization of stratified k-fold cross-validation guarantees that each class is proportionally represented in both the training and validation sets, leading to more reliable performance estimations.

Cross-validation is of utmost importance in the process of selecting models and tuning hyperparameters, as it enables the discovery of the most effective model structure and optimal values for hyperparameters. Through the comparison of model performance across various folds, practitioners are able to make well-informed choices and prevent overfitting to the training data.

Cross-validation may present a potential limitation in terms of computational cost, especially when confronted with vast datasets or intricate models. However, the advantages gained from acquiring a dependable evaluation of model performance frequently surpass the computational burden. Furthermore, the utilization of methods like parallelization and optimization can aid in mitigating the computational overhead linked with cross-validation.

Cross-validation is a crucial technique in the field of machine learning, used to estimate the performance of models and choose the most efficient one. By reducing the impact of random data partitions and offering reliable estimates of model generalization, cross-validation empowers practitioners to make informed decisions and build models that effectively generalize to new data.

4.4.1 k-Fold Cross-Validation

The utilization of k-fold cross-validation is a prevalent practice within the realm of machine learning, employed to evaluate the efficacy of a model. This technique entails the partitioning of the dataset into k folds, each of equivalent size. The model is subsequently trained on k-1 folds and assessed on the remaining fold. This procedure is iterated k times to ensure that every fold serves as the validation set exactly once. By computing the average performance metric across all folds, a comprehensive estimation of the model's effectiveness can be attained.

Let us consider a dataset that comprises 100 instances, and we choose to employ k-fold cross-validation with k = 5. In this particular scenario, the dataset is partitioned into 5 folds, each consisting of 20 instances.

During the initial iteration, Fold 1 is utilized as the validation set while Folds 2 to 5 are employed as the training set. The model is trained on Folds 2 to 5, and its performance is evaluated on Fold 1. The performance metric, such as accuracy, is computed for this specific iteration.

In the subsequent iteration, Fold 2 serves as the validation set, and Folds 1, 3, 4, and 5 are utilized as the training set. The model is trained on Folds 1, 3, 4, and 5, and its performance is assessed on Fold 2. The performance metric is calculated accordingly.

The remaining iterations involve repeating this process, where a distinct fold is used as the validation set for each iteration. Once all iterations are finished, the final estimation of the model's performance is obtained by averaging the performance metric across all folds.

k-Fold cross-validation provides several benefits. It allows for the efficient utilization of available data by including each instance in the dataset for training and validation purposes. This approach effectively reduces the variability introduced by random data splits, resulting in a more reliable estimation of the model's performance. Additionally, k-fold cross-validation ensures that the model's performance remains consistent across different subsets of the data, which is especially important when dealing with small datasets or evaluating models with limited data.

The computational complexity of k-fold cross-validation can pose a potential drawback, especially when working with large datasets or intricate models. However, the advantages of obtaining a reliable estimation of model performance generally outweigh the additional computational burden.

k-Fold cross-validation is a prominent approach employed to evaluate the performance of machine learning models. By systematically assessing the models across multiple folds, practitioners can acquire dependable estimates of model performance. This enables them to make informed decisions regarding model selection and hyperparameter tuning.

In the Python programming language, numerous libraries are available that facilitate the implementation of k-fold cross-validation. These libraries are widely used for evaluating the performance of machine learning models. Here are some popular Python libraries typically employed for k-fold cross-validation:

scikit-learn: Scikit-learn is an influential Python library for machine learning that offers extensive resources for data analysis and modeling. Within the sklearn model_selection module, it incorporates a flexible KFold class that enables the partitioning of the dataset into k folds, thereby facilitating cross-validation.

```
from sklearn.model_selection import KFold

# Initialize KFold with number of splits (k)
kf = KFold(n_splits=5, shuffle=True, random_state=42)

# Iterate over the splits
for train_index, test_index in kf.split(X):
    X_train, X_test = X[train_index], X[test_index]
    y_train, y_test = y[train_index], y[test_index]
    # Train and evaluate model
```

TensorFlow and PyTorch: TensorFlow and PyTorch, notwithstanding their main purpose as deep learning libraries, possess the capability to undertake k-fold cross-validation. Nonetheless, given the absence of dedicated built-in features for cross-validation, the process of implementing k-fold cross-validation may necessitate the inclusion of supplementary procedures.

```
import numpy as np
from sklearn.model_selection import KFold
import torch

# Assuming data X, y are already loaded
X = torch.tensor(X, dtype=torch.float32)
y = torch.tensor(y, dtype=torch.long)

# Initialize KFold with number of splits (k)
kf = KFold(n_splits=5, shuffle=True, random_state=42)
```

```
# Iterate over the splits
for train_index, test_index in kf.split(X.numpy(), y.numpy()):
    X_train, X_test = X[train_index], X[test_index]
    y_train, y_test = y[train_index], y[test_index]
    # Train and evaluate model
```

Pandas and NumPy: Pandas and NumPy are essential libraries in Python for the manipulation of data and the computation of numerical values. Despite their lack of inherent cross-validation capabilities, these libraries are frequently employed in tandem with other libraries to preprocess data and facilitate cross-validation.

```
import numpy as np
import pandas as pd
from sklearn.model_selection import KFold

# Assuming data X, y are already loaded into pandas DataFrames
kf = KFold(n_splits=5, shuffle=True, random_state=42)

# Iterate over the splits
for train_index, test_index in kf.split(X):
    X_train, X_test = X.iloc[train_index], X.iloc[test_index]
    y_train, y_test = y.iloc[train_index], y.iloc[test_index]
    # Train and evaluate model
```

4.4.2 Leave-One-Out and Stratified K-Fold

LOOCV and stratified k-fold cross-validation are two extensively utilized techniques for assessing the effectiveness of machine learning models.

LOOCV entails dividing the dataset into n folds, with n denoting the number of instances in the dataset. In each iteration, one instance is excluded and used as the validation set, while the model is trained on the remaining n-1 instances. This process is repeated n times, with each instance serving as the validation set once. LOOCV provides a precise evaluation of model performance, although it can be computationally demanding, especially for large datasets.

Let us illustrate the LOOCV methodology using a numerical example. We can assume that we have a dataset comprising 100 instances. In the first iteration, the model is trained on instances 2 to 100, and its performance is evaluated on instance 1. Moving on to the second iteration, the model is trained on instances 1 and 3 to 100, with the performance assessed on instance 2. This process is repeated for all instances, leading to the computation of a performance metric (such as accuracy) for each iteration. The final estimation of the model's performance is obtained by averaging the performance metrics across all instances.

Stratified k-fold cross-validation, a variant of K-fold cross-validation, ensures that each fold in the cross-validation process maintains the same class distribution as the original dataset. This is of particular importance when dealing with imbalanced datasets, where one class may be disproportionately represented. The stratified approach guarantees that each class is proportionately represented in both the training and validation sets, thus yielding more reliable performance estimates.

Let us expound upon the concept of stratified k-fold cross-validation through the use of a numerical illustration. Assume we are faced with a binary classification problem, which consists of a total of 100 instances. Out of these instances, 80 belong to class 0 while the remaining 20 belong to class 1. Our objective is to apply stratified k-fold cross-validation with a value of k equal to 5. By dividing the dataset into 5 folds, we ensure that each fold maintains the original dataset's class distribution. This guarantees that each fold contains a proportionate representation of both classes, resulting in more dependable performance evaluations.

LOOCV and stratified k-fold cross-validation are two powerful methodologies utilized for assessing the effectiveness of machine learning models. LOOCV provides an accurate evaluation of model performance, although it comes at the expense of computational overhead. On the other hand, stratified K-fold cross-validation ensures that each fold preserves the class distribution of the original dataset, leading to more reliable performance estimates, particularly when dealing with imbalanced datasets.

LOOCV and stratified k-fold cross-validation are commonly used methodologies for evaluating the effectiveness of machine learning models. Several Python libraries are available to facilitate the implementation of these methodologies.

scikit-learn: Scikit-learn is a widely recognized Python machine learning library renowned for providing effective tools for the analysis and modeling of data. It encompasses a wide range of functions and classes that facilitate the execution of various cross-validation techniques, including but not limited to LOOCV and stratified k-fold cross-validation.

LeaveOneOut: The LeaveOneOut class, which falls under the sklearn model_selection module, creates an instance of LOOCV. This technique generates train/test indices that divide the data into separate train/test sets, ensuring that each sample is used as a test set exactly once.

StratifiedKFold: The StratifiedKFold class, found in the sklearn model_selection module, is responsible for the implementation of Stratified k-fold cross-validation. This technique involves dividing the dataset into k folds, while also maintaining the proportion of samples for each class. By doing so, it ensures that each fold accurately represents the overall distribution of classes within the dataset.

```
from sklearn.model_selection import LeaveOneOut, StratifiedKFold
from sklearn.datasets import load_iris
from sklearn.linear_model import LogisticRegression
from sklearn.metrics import accuracy_score

# Load dataset
iris = load_iris()
X, y = iris.data, iris.target

# Example of Leave-One-Out Cross-Validation
loo = LeaveOneOut()
model = LogisticRegression()
accuracies_loo = []
for train_index, test_index in loo.split(X):
    X_train, X_test = X[train_index], X[test_index]
    y_train, y_test = y[train_index], y[test_index]
    model.fit(X_train, y_train)
    y_pred = model.predict(X_test)
    accuracies_loo.append(accuracy_score(y_test, y_pred))

mean_accuracy_loo = sum(accuracies_loo) / len(accuracies_loo)
print("Mean accuracy with LOOCV:", mean_accuracy_loo)

# Example of Stratified K-Fold Cross-Validation
skf = StratifiedKFold(n_splits=5, shuffle=True, random_state=42)
accuracies_skf = []
for train_index, test_index in skf.split(X, y):
    X_train, X_test = X[train_index], X[test_index]
    y_train, y_test = y[train_index], y[test_index]
    model.fit(X_train, y_train)
    y_pred = model.predict(X_test)
    accuracies_skf.append(accuracy_score(y_test, y_pred))

mean_accuracy_skf = sum(accuracies_skf) / len(accuracies_skf)
print("Mean accuracy with Stratified K-Fold:", mean_accuracy_skf)
```

TensorFlow and PyTorch: Although TensorFlow and PyTorch are primarily recognized as deep learning libraries, they can also be employed for implementing cross-validation techniques. However, compared to scikit-learn, additional steps may be required.

For TensorFlow: TensorFlow lacks built-in functions for cross-validation, thus necessitating manual dataset splitting and model training within a loop to implement LOOCV or stratified k-fold cross-validation. TensorFlow's flexibility allows for customization based on specified requirements.

For PyTorch: Similar to TensorFlow, PyTorch does not provide built-in functions for cross-validation. Cross-validation can be implemented manually using techniques like k-fold splitting within a loop, and subsequently, the model can be trained and assessed accordingly.

```python
import numpy as np
from sklearn.model_selection import StratifiedKFold
import torch
import torch.nn as nn
import torch.optim as optim


# Example using PyTorch
# Assuming data X, y are already loaded
X = torch.tensor(X, dtype=torch.float32)
y = torch.tensor(y, dtype=torch.long)


# Example of Stratified K-Fold Cross-Validation
skf = StratifiedKFold(n_splits=5, shuffle=True, random_state=42)
accuracies_skf = []
for train_index, test_index in skf.split(X.numpy(), y.numpy()):
    X_train, X_test = X[train_index], X[test_index]
    y_train, y_test = y[train_index], y[test_index]

    # Define model architecture
    model = nn.Sequential(
        nn.Linear(4, 64),
        nn.ReLU(),
        nn.Linear(64, 3)
    )

    # Define loss function and optimizer
    criterion = nn.CrossEntropyLoss()
    optimizer = optim.Adam(model.parameters(), lr=0.001)

    # Train the model
    for epoch in range(100):
```

```
        optimizer.zero_grad()
        outputs = model(X_train)
        loss = criterion(outputs, y_train)
        loss.backward()
        optimizer.step()

    # Evaluate the model
    with torch.no_grad():
        outputs = model(X_test)
        _, predicted = torch.max(outputs, 1)
        accuracy = (predicted == y_test).sum().item() / len(y_test)
        accuracies_skf.append(accuracy)

mean_accuracy_skf = np.mean(accuracies_skf)
print("Mean accuracy with Stratified K-Fold (PyTorch):",
mean_accuracy_skf)
```

These libraries provide effective and reliable resources for implementing cross-validation methods, enabling professionals to accurately assess the performance of models and make well-informed choices regarding model selection and fine-tuning of hyperparameters.

Summary

- The introduction pertains to fundamental concepts such as the dichotomy between supervised and unsupervised learning, the issue of overfitting, the concept of regularization, the assessment of evaluation metrics, and the utilization of cross-validation.
- Supervised learning entails the utilization of labeled data to train, whereas unsupervised learning revolves around the handling of unlabeled data.
- Supervised learning is concerned with making predictions based on input–output pairs, whereas unsupervised learning is primarily focused on the identification of patterns or structures within the data.
- Classification is a form of learning that involves the prediction of discrete class labels, while regression entails the prediction of continuous numeric values.
- For instance, classification can be applied to the prediction of species of iris flowers, while regression can be utilized to forecast house prices.
- Clustering is a procedure that involves the categorization of similar data points based on their characteristics, while association is concerned with the identification of patterns or relationships among variables. For example, clustering can be utilized to group customers based on their purchasing behavior, while association can be employed to identify frequent itemsets in market basket analysis.

- Overfitting occurs when a model becomes excessively fine-tuned to the training data and as a result, performs inadequately when presented with unseen data. To prevent overfitting, regularization techniques such as L1 and L2 are implemented to penalize large parameter values.
- Diverse evaluation metrics, including accuracy, precision, recall, F1 score, MSE, MAE, and R^2 are used to assess the performance of models.
- Cross-validation techniques such as k-Fold, Leave-One-Out, and stratified k-fold are employed to estimate the performance of models on unseen data.
- Python libraries such as scikit-learn, TensorFlow, PyTorch, and Yellowbrick provide a range of tools for implementing machine learning algorithms and techniques.
- Code examples serve to demonstrate the loading of datasets, the preprocessing of data, the training of models, and the evaluation of performance using appropriate metrics and cross-validation techniques.

Exercise (MCQs)

1. Which technique aims to prevent overfitting in machine learning models?
   A) Regularization
   B) Cross-validation
   C) Clustering
   D) Dimensionality reduction

2. What is the main difference between supervised and unsupervised learning?
   A) Supervised learning involves labeled data, while unsupervised learning involves unlabeled data.
   B) Supervised learning requires a larger dataset than unsupervised learning.
   C) Unsupervised learning always outperforms supervised learning.
   D) Supervised learning is used for classification, while unsupervised learning is used for regression.

3. What type of problem is predicting house prices?
   A) Classification   B) Regression   C) Clustering   D) Association

4. Which technique involves grouping similar data points together based on their features?
   A) Clustering   B) Association   C) Classification   D) Regression

5. What does L1 regularization penalize?
   A) Large parameter values
   B) Small parameter values
   C) Mean squared error
   D) Mean absolute error

6. Which metric is used to evaluate the performance of a classification model when the classes are imbalanced?

   A) Accuracy   B) Precision   C) Recall   D) F1 score

7. Which cross-validation technique involves dividing the dataset into k folds and using each fold as a test set exactly once?

   A) k-Fold cross-validation

   B) Leave-one-out cross-validation

   C) Stratified k-fold cross-validation

   D) Random split cross-validation

8. What does the bias-variance trade-off aim to balance?

   A) Model complexity and computational resources

   B) Model flexibility and interpretability

   C) Underfitting and overfitting

   D) Training time and testing time

9. Which Python library provides comprehensive tools for implementing machine learning algorithms and techniques?

   A) NumPy   B) TensorFlow   C) Matplotlib   D) Pandas

10. Which type of regularization encourages sparsity in the model?

    A) L1 regularization

    B) L2 regularization

    C) Both L1 and L2 regularization

    D) Neither L1 nor L2 regularization

11. Which metric is not affected by class imbalance?

    A) Accuracy   B) Precision   C) Recall   D) F1 score

12. Which metric penalizes large prediction errors more severely?

    A) Mean squared error (MSE)

    B) Mean absolute error (MAE)

    C) R-squared (R^2)

    D) Root mean squared error (RMSE)

13. Which cross-validation technique is computationally expensive but provides the most reliable estimate of model performance?

    A) k-Fold cross-validation

    B) Leave-one-out cross-validation

    C) Stratified k-fold cross-validation

    D) Random split cross-validation

14. Which visualization technique helps analyze the relationship between training size and model performance?
    A) Learning curves
    B) Validation curves
    C) Residual plots
    D) Confusion matrices

15. Which library offers high-level APIs for building and training deep learning models?
    A) Matplotlib   B) TensorFlow   C) Scikit-learn   D) PyTorch

16. Which technique is commonly used for reducing the dimensionality of high-dimensional datasets?
    A) Clustering
    B) Association
    C) Principal component analysis (PCA)
    D) K-nearest neighbors (KNN)

Answers

1. A) Regularization
2. A) Supervised learning involves labeled data, while unsupervised learning involves unlabeled data.
3. B) Regression
4. A) Clustering
5. A) Large parameter values
6. D) F1 score
7. A) k-Fold cross-validation
8. C) Underfitting and overfitting
9. B) TensorFlow
10. A) L1 regularization
11. A) Accuracy
12. A) Mean squared error (MSE)
13. B) Leave-one-out cross-validation
14. A) Learning curves
15. D) PyTorch
16. C) Principal component analysis (PCA)

Fill in the Blanks

1. In machine learning, overfitting occurs when the model learns to _____ the training data and performs poorly on unseen data.
2. Supervised learning involves _____ data for training, while unsupervised learning deals with _____ data.
3. Classification predicts _____ class labels, while regression predicts _____ numeric values.
4. Clustering groups _____ data points together based on their features, while association identifies _____ among variables.
5. L1 and L2 regularization techniques are used to prevent _____ in machine learning models.
6. The F1 score is a metric that combines both _____ and _____.
7. In k-fold cross-validation, the dataset is divided into _____ equal-sized folds.
8. The bias-variance trade-off balances model _____ and _____.
9. TensorFlow and PyTorch are popular libraries for building and training _____ models.
10. L1 regularization adds a penalty equivalent to the _____ of the magnitude of coefficients, while L2 regularization adds a penalty equivalent to the _____ of the magnitude of coefficients.
11. Precision measures the ratio of _____ predictions to _____ predictions.
12. MSE stands for _____ and is calculated as the average of squared _____ between predicted and actual values.
13. Keras, a high-level API for building neural networks, is now integrated into _____ as its official high-level API.
14. Principal component analysis (PCA) is a technique commonly used for reducing the _____ of high-dimensional datasets.

Answers

1. memorize
2. labeled, unlabeled
3. discrete, continuous
4. similar, patterns or relationships
5. overfitting
6. precision, recall
7. k
8. complexity, variance
9. neural network
10. absolute value, square
11. true positive, all positive

12. Mean Squared Error, errors
13. TensorFlow
14. scikit-learn
15. dimensionality

Descriptive Questions

1. Explain the concept of overfitting in machine learning and provide strategies to mitigate it.
2. Compare and contrast supervised and unsupervised learning techniques, providing examples of each.
3. Describe the difference between classification and regression tasks in machine learning, providing real-world examples.
4. Discuss the role of regularization techniques such as L1 and L2 in preventing overfitting, and explain how they work.
5. What are evaluation metrics in machine learning, and why are they important? Provide examples of commonly used metrics.
6. Explain the concept of cross-validation and its importance in evaluating machine learning models. Provide examples of cross-validation techniques.
7. Discuss the bias-variance trade-off in machine learning and how it impacts model performance. Provide examples to illustrate.
8. Describe the role of Python libraries such as scikit-learn, TensorFlow, and PyTorch in implementing machine learning algorithms.
9. What are some common techniques used for feature selection and dimensionality reduction in machine learning? Explain each briefly.
10. Discuss the advantages and disadvantages of different types of clustering algorithms in unsupervised learning.
11. Given a dataset with 100 samples and 10 features, how many data points would be in each fold in 5-fold cross-validation?
12. Calculate the mean squared error (MSE) for a regression model with actual values [5, 10, 15] and predicted values [4, 11, 16].
13. Suppose a classification model correctly predicts 80 out of 100 positive cases and 90 out of 100 negative cases. Calculate the accuracy, precision, recall, and F1 score.
14. Implement k-fold cross-validation with k = 3 on a dataset using Python and scikit-learn, and evaluate a logistic regression model.
15. Use L1 regularization with a logistic regression model to classify samples in the Iris dataset, and tune the regularization strength parameter to optimize model performance.
16. Compute the mean and standard deviation of a feature in the Iris dataset using NumPy.

Chapter 5
Classic Machine Learning Algorithms

Classic machine learning algorithms constitute the foundational framework of contemporary data science and serve as indispensable tools for the analysis and prediction of data. These algorithms encompass a broad range of techniques that are fundamental to the comprehension of the principles and applications of machine learning.

Linear regression, in spite of its simplicity, serves as a powerful algorithm utilized for the purpose of modeling the correlation between independent and dependent variables. It is extensively employed in the realm of predictive analytics and forecasting tasks, with variations such as Simple Linear Regression, Multiple Linear Regression, and Polynomial Regression, tailored to cater to different scenarios.

Logistic regression, despite its nomenclature, is a classification algorithm commonly employed for binary classification problems, such as the detection of spam or medical diagnosis. It estimates the probability that a given input belongs to a specific class and is particularly valuable when the relationship between features and the target variable is non-linear.

Decision Trees and Random Forests are algorithms that are widely used in both classification and regression tasks. Decision trees use recursive processes to divide the input space into regions, which makes them easy to interpret. Random Forests, on the other hand, comprise multiple decision trees, and they improve prediction accuracy and prevent overfitting by combining predictions from these trees.

Support Vector Machines (SVMs) are powerful supervised learning models that are utilized in both classification and regression tasks. They work by identifying the hyperplane that can best separate the classes in the feature space, which makes them highly effective in high-dimensional spaces and particularly suitable for complex datasets.

k-Means clustering is an unsupervised learning algorithm that is used to divide data into clusters. Its main objective is to group similar data points together while ensuring that dissimilar points are kept apart. This makes k-Means clustering useful in tasks such as customer segmentation and anomaly detection.

Principal Component Analysis (PCA) is a technique for reducing the dimensionality of data by transforming it into a lower-dimensional representation while preserving important information. It has various applications in data visualization, noise reduction, and speeding up learning algorithms.

Naive Bayes is a classifier that uses Bayes' theorem and assumes strong independence between features. Despite its simplicity, it performs well in practice and is widely used for tasks like text classification and spam filtering.

Ensemble methods, such as Boosting and Bagging, combine multiple base learners to improve predictive performance. AdaBoost trains weak learners sequentially, with

https://doi.org/10.1515/9783110697186-005

a focus on difficult instances to classify. Gradient Boosting constructs models step by step, optimizing for errors made by previous models.

5.1 Linear Regression

Linear regression is a statistical technique employed for the purpose of depicting the connection between one or more autonomous variables and a continuous reliant variable. It postulates that this connection is roughly linear, indicating that alterations in the autonomous variables are correspondingly linked to modifications in the reliant variable in a linear manner.

In the most basic configuration, referred to as Simple Linear Regression, there exists solely a single independent variable. The equation of the model is expressed as y = mx + b, wherein y symbolizes the dependent variable, x symbolizes the independent variable, m denotes the slope of the line (indicating the rate of alteration of y in relation to x), and b represents the y-intercept (which signifies the value of y when x equals zero).

In Multiple Linear Regression, the inclusion of two or more independent variables leads to the expansion of the model equation. This expanded equation encompasses all the variables, denoted as y = b0 + b1x1 + b2x2 + . . . + bnxn. Here, b0 represents the intercept, while b1, b2, . . ., bn correspond to the coefficients associated with the predictors x1, x2, . . ., xn.

The primary aim of linear regression is to identify the optimal line (or hyperplane, when considering multiple variables) that minimizes the total sum of squared discrepancies between the observed values of the dependent variable and the values predicted by the linear equation. This procedure is frequently accomplished through the utilization of the least squares method.

Linear regression models can be assessed using different metrics, such as the coefficient of determination (R^2), which quantifies the extent to which the independent variables account for the variability in the dependent variable, and hypothesis tests to determine the statistical significance of the regression coefficients.

The following are the underlying presumptions of linear regression: linearity, independence of the observations, homoscedasticity (constant variance of errors), normality of residuals (normal distribution of errors), and lack of multicollinearity (no significant dependency between independent variables).

Linear regression is extensively employed in diverse domains, encompassing the realms of economics, finance, social sciences, engineering, and natural sciences, to undertake a multitude of tasks, including prognosticating forthcoming results, comprehending associations amid variables, and assessing the impacts of interventions or treatments. Notwithstanding its uncomplicated nature, linear regression persists as one of the most potent and comprehensible instruments within the statistical arsenal.

5.1.1 Simple Linear Regression

Linear regression is extensively employed in diverse domains, encompassing the realms of economics, finance, social sciences, engineering, and natural sciences, to undertake a multitude of tasks, including prognosticating forthcoming results, comprehending associations amid variables, and assessing the impacts of interventions or treatments. Notwithstanding its uncomplicated nature, linear regression persists as one of the most potent and comprehensible instruments within the statistical arsenal.

The relationship between the independent and dependent variables is assumed by the model to be roughly linear. This connection can be stated mathematically as y = mx + b, where b stands for the y-intercept and m for the slope of the line, which represents the rate of change of y with respect to x.

The simple linear regression model minimizes the sum of squared differences between the values predicted by the linear equation and the actual values of the dependent variable in order to choose the most efficient line. This procedure is often carried out by applying the least squares method.

After fitting the model to the data, it may be used to understand the relationship between the variables and make predictions as well as draw conclusions. The correlation coefficient, often known as Pearson's r, which runs from −1 to 1, allows us to use simple linear regression to measure the strength and direction of the relationship between the variables.

The basic assumptions of simple linear regression are that the variables have a linear connection, the observations are independent of one another, the errors are homoscedastic (have a constant variance), and the residuals are normally distributed.

Simple linear regression is widely used for tasks including projecting future results, understanding causal links, and calculating the effect of one variable on another in a variety of domains, including economics, social sciences, engineering, and natural sciences. Even with its simplicity, simple linear regression is nevertheless a powerful and adaptable tool for data analysis and interpretation.

Now let's look at a straightforward example of simple linear regression, where the exam score of a student is predicted based on how many hours they studied. The procedures for performing the simple linear regression are listed below.

Step 1: Data Collection
Let's say we have gathered the information below:

Hours Studied (x)	Exam Score (y)
2	65
3	70
4	75
5	80
6	85

Step 2: Data Visualization

To see how study hours and exam scores relate to one another, first plot the data points on a scatter plot.

```
import matplotlib.pyplot as plt

hours_studied = [2, 3, 4, 5, 6]
exam_scores = [65, 70, 75, 80, 85]

plt.scatter(hours_studied, exam_scores)
plt.xlabel('Hours Studied')
plt.ylabel('Exam Score')
plt.title('Relationship Between Hours Studied and Exam Score')
plt.show()
```

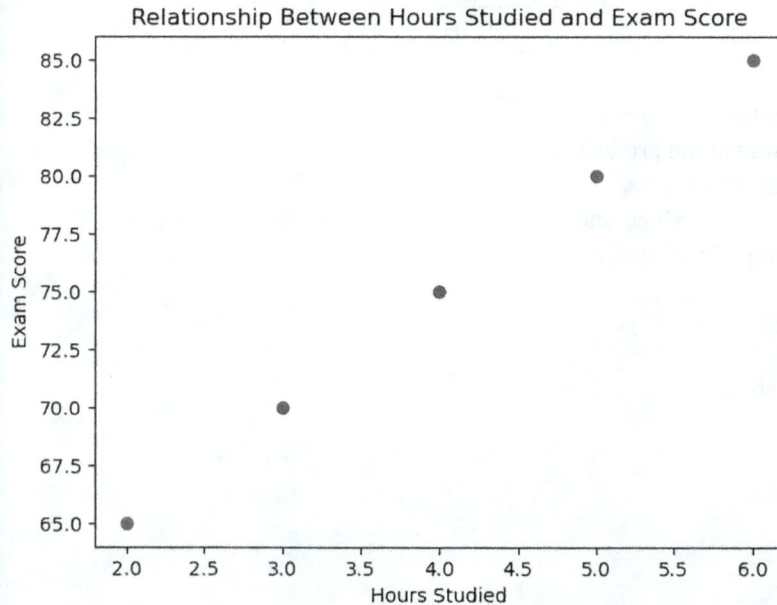

Fig. 5.1: Relationship between Hours Studies and Exam Score.

Fig. 5.1 presents a scatter plot of the relationship between the number of hours of study and the corresponding test scores before visually applying simple linear regression. The data points in the graph show the distribution of these two variables, allowing a preliminary examination of the potential relationship between study time and academic achievement.

Step 3: Model Fitting

Now, use the simple linear regression model to fit a line to the data.

The formula we'll use is $y = mx + b$. b

where:

– x is the number of study hours;
– m is the line's slope; and
– b is the y-intercept.
– y is the expected exam score.

Step 4: Calculating Slope (m) and Intercept (b)

Calculate m and b using the following formulas:

$$m = \frac{n(\sum xy) - (\sum x)(\sum y)}{n(\sum x^2) - (\sum x)^2}$$

$$b = \frac{\sum y - m(\sum x)}{n}$$

where:

– n is the number of data points,
– $\sum xy$ is the sum of the product of x and y,
– $\sum x$ is the sum of x values,
– $\sum y$ is the sum of y values, and
– $\sum x^2$ is the sum of the squares of x values.

For the above example:

– $n = 5$
– $\sum xy = 1550$
– $\sum x = 20$
– $\sum y = 375$
– $\sum x^2 = 90$

$$m = \frac{5 * 1550 - 20 * 375}{5 * 90 - 20^2}$$

$$m = \frac{7750 - 7500}{450 - 400}$$

$$m = \frac{250}{50}$$

$$m = 5$$

$$b = \frac{375 - 5 * 20}{5}$$

$$b = \frac{375 - 100}{5}$$

$$b = \frac{275}{5}$$

$$b = 55$$

After calculating, the slope m = 5 and y-intercept b = 55.
   The best fit line fitted on the data is:

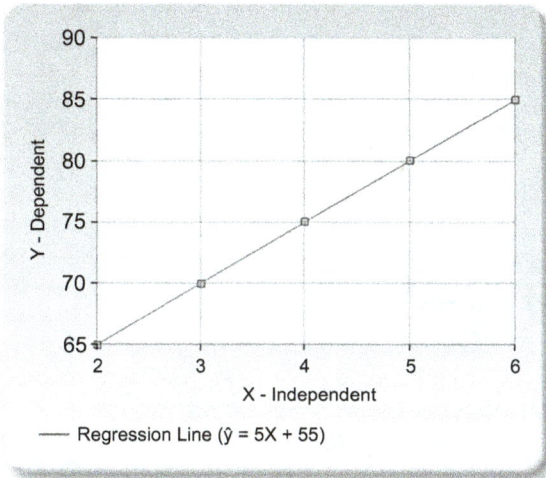

Fig. 5.2: Linear Regression Best fit line.

Fig. 5.2 shows a linear regression best fit line superimposed on a scatter plot of test scores versus hours of practice. A line of best fit is a linear model calculated to best represent the relationship between two variables, minimizing the deviation between the actual data points and the predicted values on the line.

Step 5: Making Predictions
Make predictions for new data points using the equation of line. For instance, we can forecast a student's exam score as follows if they study for seven hours:

$$y = (5 \times 7) + 55 = 90$$

So, the predicted exam score for a student who studies 7 h is 85.

Step 6: Evaluating the Model

In order to determine how well our model matches the data, we can finally analyze its performance using measures like Mean Squared Error (MSE) or R^2.

Python Code to evaluate the model:

```python
import numpy as np

# Given data
hours_studied = np.array([2, 3, 4, 5, 6])
exam_scores = np.array([65, 70, 75, 80, 85])

# Step 1: Calculate Predictions
predictions = 5 * hours_studied + 55

# Step 2: Calculate Residuals
residuals = exam_scores - predictions

# Step 3: Calculate Mean Squared Error
mse = np.mean(residuals**2)

# Step 4: Calculate Total Sum of Squares
tss = np.sum((exam_scores - np.mean(exam_scores))**2)

# Step 5: Calculate Residual Sum of Squares
rss = np.sum(residuals**2)

# Step 6: Calculate R^2
r_squared = 1 - (rss / tss)

print("Mean Squared Error :", mse)
print("R^2:", r_squared)
```

Mean Squared Error: 0.0

R^2: 1.0

Thus, the R^2 value is 1.00 and the MSE is 0.0. These measurements show how well the model matches the data, with the number of hours studied accounting for almost 100% of the variation in exam scores.

Let's look at another scenario in which we wish to estimate a house's cost depending on its square footage. We will use the scikit-learn toolkit and Python to do simple linear regression.

sklearn.linear_model
This module in scikit-learn contains various classes for linear models, including regression models.

LinearRegression class
- To fit a linear regression model to data, use the **LinearRegression** class offered by **sklearn.linear_model**.
- Modeling the relationship between a dependent variable and one or more independent variables using a linear technique is known as linear regression.
- In simple linear regression (as used in the example), there is only one independent variable. However, scikit-learn's **LinearRegression** class can handle multiple independent variables as well (Multiple Linear Regression).
- Ordinary least squares (OLS) regression is implemented by the **LinearRegression** class. It finds the best-fitting line (or hyperplane) through the data points by minimizing the sum of squared residuals.
- The **predict()** function can be used to create predictions once the model has been trained using training data via the **fit()** method.

Here's the code:

```
import numpy as np
from sklearn.linear_model import LinearRegression
import matplotlib.pyplot as plt

# Example data: House size (in square feet) and corresponding prices
house_sizes = np.array([800, 1000, 1200, 1500, 1800]).reshape(-1, 1) #
Reshape to make it a column vector
house_prices = np.array([100000, 150000, 180000, 210000, 250000])

# Step 1: Create and fit the model
model = LinearRegression()
model.fit(house_sizes, house_prices)

# Step 2: Make predictions
predicted_prices = model.predict(house_sizes)

# Step 3: Visualize the data and the regression line
plt.scatter(house_sizes, house_prices, color='blue', label='Actual
Prices')
plt.plot(house_sizes, predicted_prices, color='red', label='Predicted
Prices')
```

```
plt.xlabel('House Size (sqft)')
plt.ylabel('House Price ($)')
plt.title('Simple Linear Regression: House Price Prediction')
plt.legend()
plt.show()

# Step 4: Print the slope (coefficient) and intercept of the line
print("Slope (Coefficient):", model.coef_[0])
print("Intercept:", model.intercept_)

# Step 5: Evaluate the model (optional)
mse = np.mean((predicted_prices - house_prices) ** 2)
r_squared = model.score(house_sizes, house_prices)
print("Mean Squared Error (MSE):", mse)
print("R^2 Score:", r_squared)
```

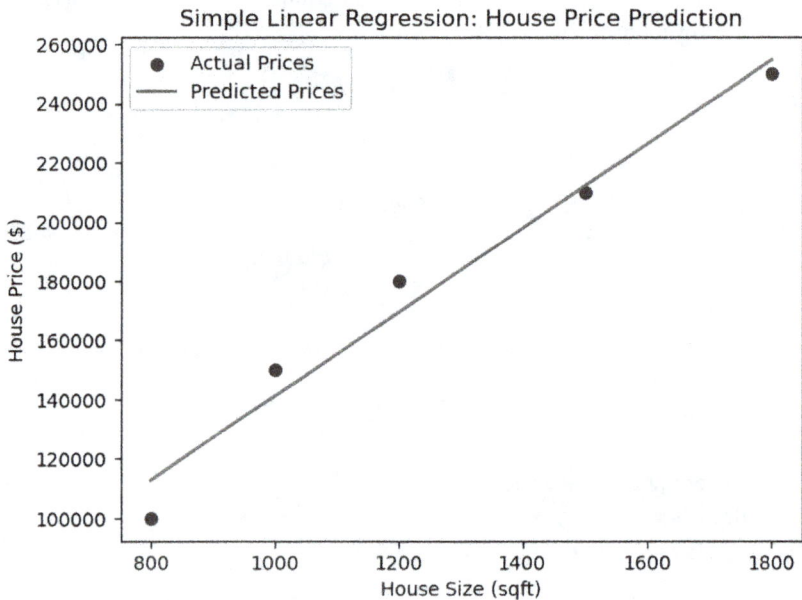

```
Slope (Coefficient): 141.77215189873414
Intercept: -632.911392405018
Mean Squared Error (MSE): 75443037.97468361
R^2 Score: 0.9711609182053962
```

Fig. 5.3: Sample linear regression: house price prediction.

Fig. 5.3 shows an example of using linear regression to predict house prices based on property size. The Scatter plot shows the relationship between the square footage or total living area of the homes and their corresponding sale prices. The line of best fit, estimated using linear regression techniques, is superimposed on the data points, representing a linear model that aims to capture the relationship between household size and the objective variable of house price.

5.1.2 Multiple Linear Regression

An extension of simple linear regression, multiple linear regression allows correlations to be modeled between a dependent variable and several independent variables. It suggests that the independent and dependent variables have a linear relationship. The model's equation has the following format:

$$y = b0 + b1x1 + b2x2 + \ldots + bnxn$$

The dependent variable in this equation is y, while the independent variables are x1, x2, . . ., xn. With respect to each independent variable, the coefficients (or weights) b0, b1, b2, . . ., bn correspond. Interestingly, the intercept term is b0.

Methods like ordinary least squares (OLS), which minimize the sum of squared discrepancies between actual and predicted values, are used to estimate the coefficients. Metrics like MSE and R2 are used to assess the model's performance and determine its goodness of fit.

Multiple linear regression enables the modeling of more intricate relationships and interactions among multiple predictors, making it a versatile tool in diverse fields such as finance, economics, engineering, and social sciences. However, it assumes linearity, independence of predictors, constant variance of errors, and normally distributed residuals, all of which should be examined before interpretation.

A multiple linear regression model's coefficients are interpreted by evaluating each independent variable's effect on the dependent variable while holding the other variables constant. Assuming that all other variables stay constant, the coefficients show how the dependent variable changes for every unit change in the corresponding independent variable.

Multiple linear regression can be performed using various methods, each with its advantages and disadvantages.

The Ordinary Least Squares (OLS) Method
A popular strategy for fitting a multiple linear regression model to a given dataset is ordinary least squares (OLS). Finding the regression model's coefficients, or weights, is its main goal in order to reduce the sum of squared differences between the dependent variable's observed and predicted values. The OLS method is computationally efficient and produces objective estimations of the coefficients.

- The most common method used to fit a multiple linear regression model is ordinary least squares.
- Its goal is to reduce the total sum of squared differences between the dependent variable's expected and observed values.
- OLS estimates the coefficients (weights) for the independent variables by determining the values that minimize the residual sum of squares (RSS).
- This approach yields unbiased coefficient estimates and is computationally efficient and simple to apply.

To execute OLS in Python, the statsmodels library can be employed, which offers a convenient interface for fitting statistical models, including linear regression. Below is an outline of the steps involved in performing OLS using statsmodels:

```python
import numpy as np
import pandas as pd
import statsmodels.api as sm

# Example dataset
data = {
    'X1': [1, 2, 3, 4, 5],
    'X2': [2, 3, 4, 5, 6],
    'Y': [2, 3, 4, 5, 6]
}
df = pd.DataFrame(data)

# Add intercept term to independent variables
X = sm.add_constant(df[['X1', 'X2']])
y = df['Y']

# Fit OLS model
model = sm.OLS(y, X).fit()

# Print summary of the model
print(model.summary())
```

- Import the required libraries first: statsmodels, pandas for dataset processing, and numpy for numerical operations.api as standard for OLS model fitting.
- Describe a sample dataset that has the dependent variable Y and the independent variables X1 and X2.
- Use Pandas to structure the data into a DataFrame df.

- Use sm to add an intercept term to the independent variables in order to fit the OLS model.add_constant() function, which augments the DataFrame with a one-column representation of the intercept term.
- Specify which variables are dependent (y) and which are independent (X).
- Fit OLS model using sm.OLS(y, X).fit(), pass the dependent variable y and the independent variables X.
- Finally, print the summary of the fitted model using **model.summary()**, which provides detailed information about the regression coefficients, standard errors, p-values, and goodness-of-fit statistics such as R-squared and adjusted R-squared.

```
                            OLS Regression Results
==============================================================================
Dep. Variable:                      Y   R-squared:                       1.000
Model:                            OLS   Adj. R-squared:                  1.000
Method:                 Least Squares   F-statistic:                 3.977e+30
Date:                Fri, 16 Feb 2024   Prob (F-statistic):           2.78e-46
Time:                        10:54:44   Log-Likelihood:                 164.57
No. Observations:                   5   AIC:                            -325.1
Df Residuals:                       3   BIC:                            -325.9
Df Model:                           1
Covariance Type:            nonrobust
==============================================================================
                 coef    std err          t      P>|t|      [0.025      0.975]
------------------------------------------------------------------------------
const          0.3333   1.26e-15   2.64e+14      0.000       0.333       0.333
X1             0.3333   8.69e-16   3.84e+14      0.000       0.333       0.333
X2             0.6667   4.09e-16   1.63e+15      0.000       0.667       0.667
==============================================================================
Omnibus:                          nan   Durbin-Watson:                   0.033
Prob(Omnibus):                    nan   Jarque-Bera (JB):                0.545
Skew:                          -0.111   Prob(JB):                        0.762
Kurtosis:                       1.398   Cond. No.                     1.77e+16
==============================================================================

Notes:
[1] Standard Errors assume that the covariance matrix of the errors is correctly specified.
[2] The smallest eigenvalue is 4.75e-31. This might indicate that there are
strong multicollinearity problems or that the design matrix is singular.
```

Fig. 5.4: The ordinary least squares (OLS) method.

Fig. 5.4 provides a visual representation of the ordinary least squares (OLS) method, which is a fundamental technique employed in linear regression analysis.

The OLS regression model is summarized in the program output, which is displayed above. It includes data like coefficients, standard errors, p-values, R-squared, and more. This synopsis sheds light on the connections between the independent and dependent variables as well as the model's general goodness-of-fit.

Gradient Descent Method

By modifying a model's coefficients or parameters, the iterative optimization process known as Gradient Descent is used to minimize a specified cost function. Gradient Descent is a technique used specifically in linear regression to choose the best coefficients for mini-mizing the cost function, which is commonly expressed as the Mean Squared Error. To do this, update the coefficients in the opposite direction as the cost function's gradient.

- One popular optimization approach that seeks to reduce the cost function – such as the Mean Squared Error – is gradient descent. The coefficients are adjusted iteratively to accomplish this.
- Gradient fall, when used in multiple linear regression, updates the coefficients by advancing in the direction of the cost function's steepest fall.
- Gradient Descent can be used by processing the data in batches or mini-batches when faced with massive datasets that are too big to store into memory.
- It is noteworthy, therefore, that Gradient Descent might not converge to the in-tended global minimum, but rather to a local minimum. Thus, it becomes vital to fine-tune hyperparameters like learning rate.

A more straightforward implementation of the Gradient Descent algorithm can be used to carry out the algorithm's operations in Python.

```python
import numpy as np
import matplotlib.pyplot as plt


# Generate example data
X = 2 * np.random.rand(100, 1)
y = 4 + 3 * X + np.random.randn(100, 1)


# Add intercept term to independent variables
X_b = np.c_[np.ones((100, 1)), X]


# Gradient Descent parameters
eta = 0.1 # Learning rate
n_iterations = 1,000
m = 100 # Number of data points


# Random initialization of coefficients
theta = np.random.randn(2, 1)


# Gradient Descent
for iteration in range(n_iterations):
  gradients = 2/m * X_b.T.dot(X_b.dot(theta) - y)
  theta -= eta * gradients


# Plot data points
plt.scatter(X, y, color='blue', label='Data Points')
```

```
# Plot regression line
X_new = np.array([[0], [2]])
X_new_b = np.c_[np.ones((2, 1)), X_new]
y_predict = X_new_b.dot(theta)
plt.plot(X_new, y_predict, color='red', label='Regression Line')

plt.xlabel('X')
plt.ylabel('y')
plt.title('Gradient Descent Linear Regression')
plt.legend()
plt.show()

# Print final coefficients
print("Intercept:", theta[0][0])
print("Slope:", theta[1][0])
```

–   Create a sample set of data called X and Y, where X represents a feature and Y the desired variable.
–   np.c_[np.ones((100, 1)), X] to add an intercept term to the independent variables.
–   Establish the settings for Gradient Descent, including the number of data points (m), the number of iterations (n_iterations), and the learning rate (eta).
–   Randomly initialize the coefficients theta.
–   Update the coefficients theta using the gradient of the cost function with respect to the coefficients and perform Gradient Descent for a predetermined number of iterations.
–   Use Matplotlib to plot the regression line and the data points.
–   Print the regression line's final coefficients at the end.

Program output is a plot with data points and the regression line fitted with gradient descent. Furthermore, the final regression line coefficients, which reflect the slope and intercept, are printed.

Matrix Inversion Method

By directly solving the normal equation, the matrix inversion approach is a mechanism used to find the coefficients of a multiple linear regression model. The optimization problem of reducing the sum of squared discrepancies between the dependent variable's predicted and observed values yields the normal equation. We can find the regression model's ideal coefficients by resolving this equation.

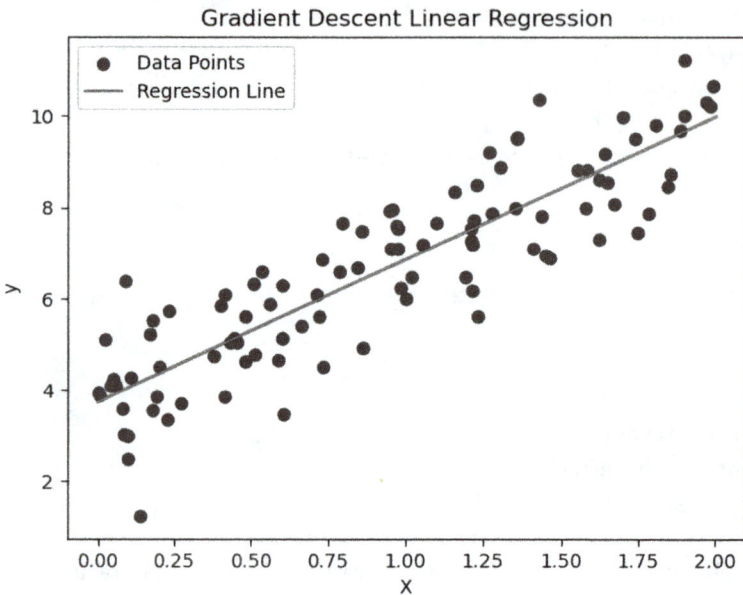

Fig. 5.5: Gradient descent linear regression.

Fig. 5.5 illustrates the concept of gradient descent, a widely used optimization algorithm in the context of linear regression.

- This method involves solving the normal equation $(X^T X)^{-1} X^T y$, where X is the matrix of independent variables, y is the vector of the dependent variable, and $(X^T X)^{-1}$ is the inverse of the matrix $X^T X$.
- The multiple linear regression model's coefficients can be solved using matrix inversion in the form of an algebraic statement.
- This operation can be resource-intensive when applied to extensive datasets, owing to the requirement of calculating the inverse of a matrix. This is particularly true when the matrix is not well conditioned.
- Nevertheless, matrix inversion ensures precise solutions without the necessity for iterative optimization, rendering it advantageous for datasets of smaller proportions.

```
import numpy as np
import matplotlib.pyplot as plt


# Generate synthetic dataset
X = 2 * np.random.rand(100, 1)
y = 4 + 3 * X + np.random.randn(100, 1)
```

```
# Add intercept term to feature matrix
X_b = np.c_[np.ones((100, 1)), X]
# Compute coefficients using matrix inversion method
theta_best = np.linalg.inv(X_b.T.dot(X_b)).dot(X_b.T).dot(y)

# Plot data points
plt.scatter(X, y, color='blue', label='Data Points')

# Plot regression line
X_new = np.array([[0], [2]])
X_new_b = np.c_[np.ones((2, 1)), X_new]
y_predict = X_new_b.dot(theta_best)
plt.plot(X_new, y_predict, color='red', label='Regression Line')

plt.xlabel('X')
plt.ylabel('y')
plt.title('Multiple Linear Regression with Matrix Inversion Method')
plt.legend()
plt.show()

# Print final coefficients
print("Intercept:", theta_best[0][0])
print("Slope:", theta_best[1][0])
```

Selection of Method

- The selection of methodology is contingent upon various factors, including the extent of the dataset, the availability of computational resources, and the necessity for interpretability.
- Ordinary least squares (OLS) is the preferred approach for datasets of a smaller scale and when interpretability is of utmost importance.
- Gradient Descent is well-suited for extensive datasets and environments that facilitate parallel processing.
- Matrix Inversion is a suitable technique for datasets ranging from small to moderately sized, provided that computational resources are sufficient.

5.1.3 Polynomial Regression

The process of using an 'n-th degree' polynomial function to analyze regression data in order to determine the relationship between the independent variable (represented by 'x') and the dependent variable (represented by 'y') is known as polynomial regres-

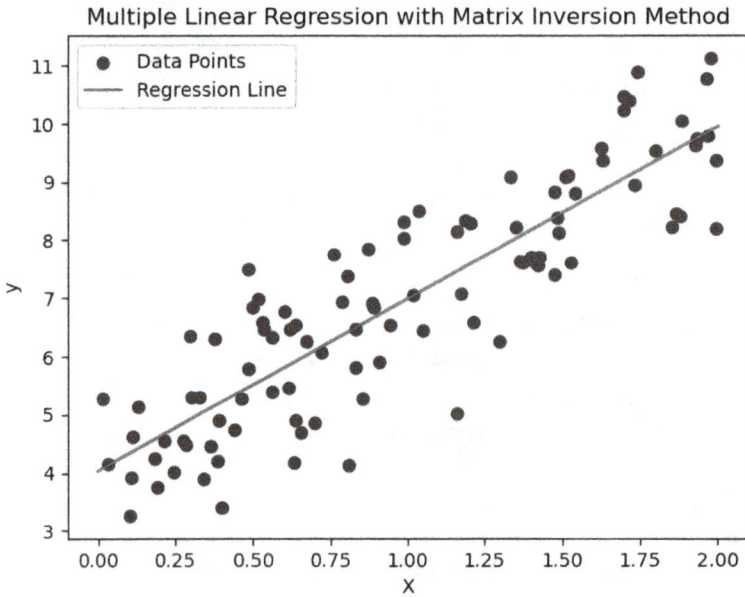

Intercept: 4.028910964982237
Slope: 2.9589962022044998

Fig. 5.6: Multi-linear regression with Matrix Inversion method.

sion. Unlike simple linear regression, which assumes a linear relationship between the variables, polynomial regression allows complex and non-linear relationships to be represented in an efficient manner.

Fig. 5.6 presents a visual representation of a multi-linear regression model, which involves more than one independent variable, fitted using the Matrix Inversion method.

Working Principle

1. Model Representation: $y = \theta_0 + \theta_1 x + \theta_2 x_2 + \cdots + \theta_n x_n + \varepsilon$ is the polynomial function of degree n that polynomial regression uses to represent the relationship between x and y. The coefficients are $\theta_0, \theta_1, \ldots$, and θ_n, and the error term is denoted by 0.
2. Degree of Polynomial: The model's complexity is based on the degree of the polynomial. Greater degrees have the potential to overfit but can also capture more complex interactions.
3. Model Fitting: In polynomial regression, the model is fitted to the training set of data using methods such as matrix inversion, gradient descent, or ordinary least squares (OLS).
4. Evaluation: Metrics like as cross-validation, R2 score, and MSE are used to assess the model's performance.
5. Prediction: The model can be taught to generate predictions on fresh data points.

For instance, consider a scenario where we have data on the relationship between the temperature (x) and the rate of ice cream sales (y). Simple linear regression may not capture the non-linear relationship adequately. In such cases, polynomial regression, such as quadratic or cubic regression, can be used to better model the curvature in the relationship, potentially improving predictive accuracy.

Applications

- **Curve fitting**: Polynomial regression is commonly used in curve fitting applications where the relationship between variables is non-linear.
- **Engineering and physics**: It is widely used in engineering and physics to model relationships between variables in physical systems.
- **Economics**: In economics, polynomial regression can model relationships between economic variables that exhibit non-linear behavior.

With Python, we can utilize libraries like NumPy and scikit-learn to conduct polynomial regression. NumPy will be utilized for numerical operations, and scikit-learn offers useful methods for regression modeling and polynomial features. We'll visualize the data using Matplotlib.

```python
import numpy as np
import matplotlib.pyplot as plt
from sklearn.preprocessing import PolynomialFeatures
from sklearn.linear_model import LinearRegression


# Generate example data
X = np.linspace(-3, 3, 100).reshape(-1, 1)
y = 2 * X + np.random.normal(0, 1, size=X.shape)


# Polynomial features
poly_features = PolynomialFeatures(degree=2) # Quadratic regression
X_poly = poly_features.fit_transform(X)


# Fit polynomial regression model
poly_reg = LinearRegression()
poly_reg.fit(X_poly, y)


# Predictions
y_pred = poly_reg.predict(X_poly)


# Plot data points
plt.scatter(X, y, color='blue', label='Data Points')
```

```
# Plot regression line

plt.plot(X, y_pred, color='red', label='Polynomial Regression')
plt.xlabel('X')
plt.ylabel('y')
plt.title('Polynomial Regression Example')
plt.legend()
plt.show()

# Print coefficients
print("Intercept:", poly_reg.intercept_)
print("Coefficients:", poly_reg.coef_)
```

- Import NumPy for numerical computations and Matplotlib for data visualization.
- Generate example data with a linear relationship ($y = 2x$) with some added noise.
- Use PolynomialFeatures from scikit-learn to generate polynomial features up to degree 2 (quadratic regression).
- Utilizing the polynomial characteristics, fit a linear regression model.
- Based on the fitted model, make predictions.
- Matplotlib can be used to plot the regression line and the data points.
- The polynomial regression model's coefficients should then be printed.

The resulting output of the program depicts a graphical representation that exhibits both the data points as well as the regression line, which has been fitted utilizing polynomial regression, more specifically quadratic regression for this particular instance. Furthermore, it also provides a printed representation of the coefficients associated with the polynomial regression model, encompassing both the intercept and the coefficients pertaining to the polynomial features.

5.2 Logistic Regression

Logistic regression, a well-received algorithm in supervised learning, is commonly employed in binary classification tasks wherein the target variable exhibits two potential outcomes. Contrary to its nomenclature, logistic regression is categorized as a classification algorithm as opposed to a regression algorithm.

Fig. 5.7 depicts a polynomial regression model, which is a form of regression analysis that fits a non-linear relationship between the independent variable(s) and the dependent variable.

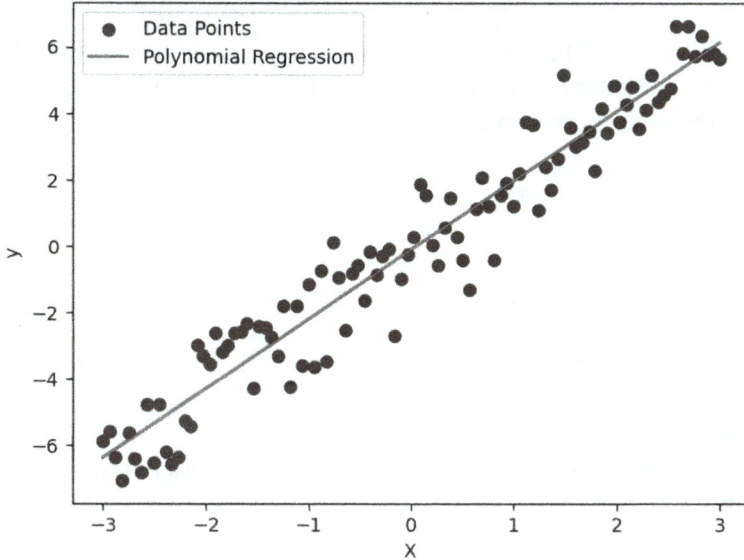

Intercept: [-0.12211726]
Coefficients: [[0.00000000e+00 2.08372128e+00 1.31488961e-03]]

Fig. 5.7: Polynomial regression.

Working Principle

1. **Model representation**: Logistic regression is a statistical model that estimates the likelihood of an input being a member of a specific category. It employs a logistic function, also known as a sigmoid function, to transform the result of a linear combination of features into a probability value ranging from 0 to 1.

$$P(y=1\,|x) = \frac{1}{1+e^{-z}}$$

The linear combination of feature values, denoted as z, can be expressed as $\theta 0 + \theta 1 x1 + \theta 2 x2 + \cdots + \theta nxn$, where θ represents the coefficients.

2. **Decision boundary**: Logistic regression makes predictions about class labels by determining if the predicted probability exceeds a specified threshold, usually set at 0.5. The decision boundary is the hypersurface that distinguishes the different classes within the feature space.

3. **Training**: The model undergoes training through the utilization of optimization algorithms such as gradient descent or Newton's method, with the purpose of identifying the most favorable coefficients that lead to the minimization of the logistic loss function.

4. **Evaluation**: The evaluation of the model's performance is conducted by employing metrics such as accuracy, precision, recall, F1-score, and ROC-AUC.
5. **Prediction**: Once the model has undergone training, it is capable of estimating the likelihood of a new instance being a member of each class, subsequently assigning the appropriate class label in accordance with the predetermined threshold.

Advantages

–   **Simple and efficient**: Logistic regression is computationally efficient and easy to implement.
–   **Interpretability**: The logistic regression coefficients offer valuable insights into the significance of individual features as well as the direction in which they influence the target variable.
–   **Probabilistic interpretation**: Logistic regression outputs probabilities, allowing for uncertainty estimation.

Limitations

–   **Linear decision boundary**: Logistic regression postulates a linear association between the characteristics and the logarithm of the odds of the dependent variable, which might fail to encompass intricate non-linear connections.
–   **Binary classification**: Logistic regression is limited to binary classification tasks and cannot be directly applied to multi-class problems without modifications.

Applications

–   **Medical diagnosis**: Logistic regression is used in medical diagnosis, such as predicting the likelihood of a disease based on patient characteristics.
–   **Credit scoring**: It is employed in credit scoring models to predict the likelihood of default based on financial attributes.
–   **Marketing analytics**: Logistic regression is used in marketing analytics for customer segmentation and predicting customer churn.

Example

Consider a situation in which we aim to forecast whether an electronic mail is classified as spam or not, utilizing the characteristics of its content such as word frequency and the presence of specific keywords. Logistic regression has the ability to be educated on a labeled collection of electronic mails (spam or non-spam) to categorize new electronic mails as either spam or not spam based on the attributes of their content.

Let's go through a numerical example of simple logistic regression step by step:

Step 1: Data Preparation

Suppose we possess a dataset encompassing two characteristics, namely x and y, alongside a binary target variable y which signifies whether a student triumphs (1) or falters (0) an examination. Here is a condensed rendition of our dataset:

x	y	Pass/Fail
2.5	3.5	1
3.0	4.0	1
2.0	3.0	0
2.5	3.0	1
3.5	4.0	0

Step 2: Model Representation

We depict the association between the characteristics and the likelihood of achieving success in the examination by employing logistic regression:

$$P(y=1|x) = \frac{1}{1+e^{-z}}$$

where $z = \theta 0 + \theta 1 x1 + \theta 2 x2$ is the linear combination of features and coefficients.

Step 3: Training

We employ optimization algorithms such as gradient descent to identify the most favorable coefficients ($\theta 0$, $\theta 1$, $\theta 2$) that minimize the logistic loss function. The logistic loss function gauges the disparity between the anticipated probabilities and the factual categories.

Step 4: Prediction

Once the logistic regression model has undergone training, it becomes capable of forecasting the likelihood of success in the examination for incoming students, taking into consideration their respective characteristic values. To illustrate, if a fresh student possesses x = 2.8 and y = 3.7, we are able to anticipate the probability of success by employing the acquired coefficients.

Step 5: Evaluation

We assess the model's performance by employing various metrics such as accuracy, precision, recall, and F1-score on a distinct validation or test dataset. These metrics serve as indicators of the model's ability to accurately predict the true classes.

Example

Let us consider a scenario in which we have successfully trained a logistic regression model. The model is characterized by the coefficients $\theta 0 = -1$, $\theta 1 = 2$, and $\theta 2 = 3$.

For a new student with $x = 2.8$ and $y = 3.7$, we compute:

$$z = -1 + 2 \times 2.8 + 3 \times 3.7 = 8.4$$

$$P(y = 1 \,|\, x) = \frac{1}{1 + e^{-8.4}} \approx 0.9997$$

So, the logistic regression model predicts with high probability that the new student will pass the exam.

5.2.1 Binary Classification

Binary classification is an essential undertaking in the realm of machine learning, where the primary aim revolves around categorizing input data into one of two potential categories or classes. This encompasses the determination of whether an email is deemed as spam or not, as well as whether a tumor is classified as malignant or benign, or whether a transaction is characterized as fraudulent or legitimate. Let us now proceed to comprehensively explore the intricate realm of binary classification:

Working Principle
-   The aim of binary classification is to acquire knowledge about the relationship between input features and discrete binary labels, commonly represented as 00 or 11, which signify the two classes.
-   Dataset Preparation: The dataset is segregated into independent variables (features) and their corresponding dependent variable (binary labels). Each data point comprises feature values and the associated class label.
-   Model Selection: Multiple algorithms, including but not limited to Logistic Regression, Decision Trees, Support Vector Machines (SVM), Random Forests, and Neural Networks, have the potential to be utilized for the purpose of binary classification.
-   Model Training: The selected algorithm is subjected to training with the aid of a labeled dataset, enabling it to grasp the intricate patterns and interconnections between various features and class labels. During the duration of the training procedure, the algorithm modifies its internal parameters with the objective of minimizing a pre-established loss or error function.
-   Model Evaluation: The evaluation of the trained model is conducted by employing assessment metrics such as accuracy, precision, recall, F1-score, and receiver operating characteristic (ROC) curve. These metrics are utilized to measure the mod-

el's capacity to make accurate predictions of the true class labels on data that has not been previously observed.

– Prediction: After the completion of the training and evaluation process, the model can be employed for the purpose of making predictions on fresh data instances. This is achieved by classifying each instance into one of the two classes, which is based on the feature values associated with that particular instance.

Evaluation Metrics

– The accuracy metric denotes the proportion of accurately classified instances out of the total number of instances.
– Precision, on the other hand, signifies the ratio of true positive predictions to all positive predictions, which highlights the model's efficacy in minimizing false positives.
– Recall, also referred to as sensitivity, measures the proportion of true positive predictions to all actual positive instances, thus demonstrating the model's capability to detect all positive instances.
– The F1-score, as the harmonic mean of precision and recall, provides a balanced evaluation of these two measures.
– ROC-AUC evaluates the area under the Receiver Operating Characteristic curve, thereby evaluating the model's capability to distinguish between positive and negative classes at different thresholds.

Applications

Binary classification is applied in diverse domains, encompassing a wide array of applications:

– Medical Diagnosis: Identifying diseases based on symptoms or medical test results.
– Email Spam Detection: Classifying emails as spam or legitimate.
– Credit Risk Assessment: Predicting whether a loan applicant is likely to default.
– Fraud Detection: Identifying fraudulent transactions in financial systems.
– Sentiment Analysis: Determining the sentiment of a text, whether it conveys a positive or negative tone, is a significant task.

Example

Suppose we have a dataset containing information about customer transactions, including transaction amount, time of transaction, and whether the transaction is fraudulent (1) or legitimate (0). By training a binary classification model on this dataset, we can predict whether future transactions are likely to be fraudulent, enabling proactive measures to prevent fraudulent activities.

Let's consider a Python code to perform binary classification using logistic regression, along with plots and evaluation metrics. We'll use the famous Iris dataset available in scikit-learn, where we'll classify whether a given iris flower is of the "setosa" species or not.

- Load the Iris dataset and retrieve solely the characteristics and target labels linked to the "setosa" species.
- Divide the dataset into two sets for the purpose of training and testing.
- Employ a logistic regression model to train the data for classification.
- Generate predictions using the test data and assess the model's performance by considering accuracy, precision, recall, F1-score, and the confusion matrix.
- Represent the data points together with the decision boundary in a visual manner to facilitate classification visualization.

```python
import numpy as np
import matplotlib.pyplot as plt
import seaborn as sns
from sklearn.datasets import load_iris
from sklearn.model_selection import train_test_split
from sklearn.linear_model import LogisticRegression
from sklearn.metrics import accuracy_score, precision_score,
recall_score, f1_score, confusion_matrix

# Load the Iris dataset
iris = load_iris()
X = iris.data[:, :2] # Take only first two features for simplicity
y = (iris.target == 0).astype(int) # Binary classification: Setosa or not

# Split the dataset into training and testing sets
X_train, X_test, y_train, y_test = train_test_split(X, y, test_size=0.2,
random_state=42)

# Train a logistic regression model
model = LogisticRegression()
model.fit(X_train, y_train)

# Make predictions on the test set
y_pred = model.predict(X_test)

# Evaluate the model
accuracy = accuracy_score(y_test, y_pred)
precision = precision_score(y_test, y_pred)
recall = recall_score(y_test, y_pred)
f1 = f1_score(y_test, y_pred)
conf_matrix = confusion_matrix(y_test, y_pred)
print("Accuracy:", accuracy)
print("Precision:", precision)
```

```
print("Recall:", recall)
print("F1-score:", f1)
print("Confusion Matrix:\n", conf_matrix)
# Plot decision boundary
x_min, x_max = X[:, 0].min() - 1, X[:, 0].max() + 1
y_min, y_max = X[:, 1].min() - 1, X[:, 1].max() + 1
xx, yy = np.meshgrid(np.arange(x_min, x_max, 0.01), np.arange(y_min,
y_max, 0.01))
Z = model.predict(np.c_[xx.ravel(), yy.ravel()])
Z = Z.reshape(xx.shape)
plt.contourf(xx, yy, Z, alpha=0.3)
sns.scatterplot(x=X_test[:, 0], y=X_test[:, 1], hue=y_test)
plt.xlabel('Sepal Length')
plt.ylabel('Sepal Width')
plt.title('Binary Classification (Setosa vs. Not Setosa)')
plt.show()
```

```
Accuracy: 1.0
Precision: 1.0
Recall: 1.0
F1-score: 1.0
Confusion Matrix:
 [[20  0]
  [ 0 10]]
```

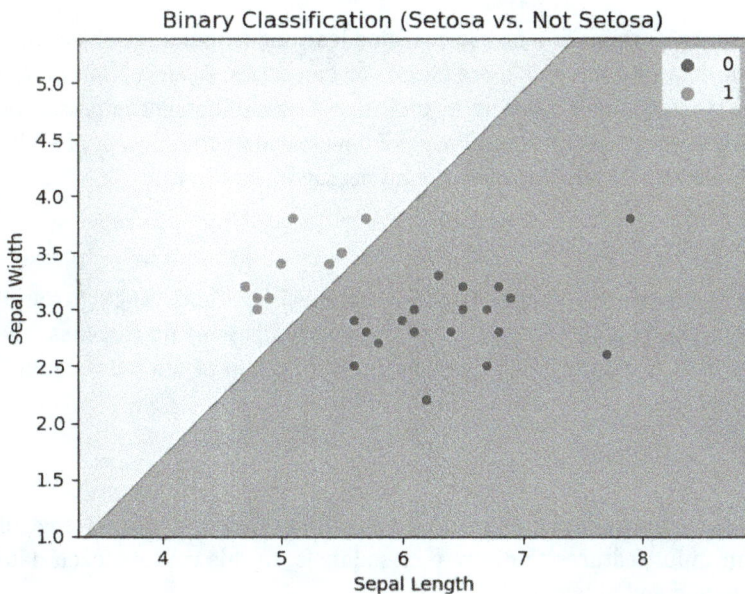

Fig. 5.8: Binary classification (Setosa vs. Not Setosa).

Fig. 5.8 presents a visual representation of a binary classification problem, specifically distinguishing between the Setosa species of iris flowers and all other non-Setosa species. The plot displays a scatter of data points, where each point represents an individual iris flower sample.

– The outcomes of the code encompass a variety of evaluation metrics including accuracy, precision, recall, F1-score, and the confusion matrix.

– Accuracy represents the proportion of instances that are correctly classified out of the total number of instances.

– Precision indicates the proportion of true positive predictions to all positive predictions, while recall measures the proportion of true positive predictions to all actual positive instances.

– The F1-score is a measure of balance between precision and recall, calculated as the harmonic mean of the two metrics. The confusion matrix displays the frequencies of true positive, true negative, false positive, and false negative predictions.

– Moreover, the code generates a visual representation of the decision boundary in conjunction with the test data points, which aids in understanding the classification. Data points classified as "setosa" are depicted in one color, while those classified as "not setosa" are represented in a different color.

5.2.2 Multiclass Classification

Multiclass classification pertains to a task in machine learning wherein the objective is to categorize input data into three or more classes or categories. Distinct from binary classification, which entails solely two classes, multiclass classification encompasses the prediction of multiple potential outcomes. We shall now elucidate the concept of multiclass classification through the employment of a numerical illustration.

Example

Consider a dataset consisting of images depicting handwritten digits ranging from 0 to 9. Each individual image is represented as a matrix encompassing pixel values. The primary objective is to accurately classify each image into one of ten possible digit classes, specifically 0, 1, 2, . . ., 9.

Working Principle

The fundamental principle behind multiclass classification is to acquire knowledge of the mapping from input features to discrete class labels. In this context, each data point is assigned to one and only one class.

- **Dataset preparation:** The dataset is divided into distinct features, which represent the input data, and their corresponding class labels. It should be noted that each data point is characterized by multiple features and is assigned to one of several classes.
- **Model selection:** There are numerous algorithms that can be utilized for multiclass classification, such as Logistic Regression, Decision Trees, Random Forests, Support Vector Machines (SVM), and Neural Networks. Some algorithms inherently support multiclass classification, while others can be extended using techniques like One-vs-Rest (OvR) or One-vs-One (OvO).
- **Model training:** The selected algorithm undergoes training using a labeled dataset, where it learns the underlying patterns and relationships between the features and class labels. Throughout the training process, the algorithm adjusts its internal parameters to minimize a predefined loss or error function.
- **Model evaluation:** The performance of the trained model is assessed using various metrics, including accuracy, precision, recall, F1-score, and confusion matrix. These metrics provide an evaluation of how effectively the model predicts the true class labels for unseen data.
- **Prediction:** Once the model has been trained and evaluated, it can be utilized to make predictions on new data instances. This involves assigning each instance to one of the multiple classes based on its feature values.

Evaluation Metrics

- **Accuracy:** Accuracy is defined as the ratio of correctly classified instances to the total number of instances.
- **Precision:** Precision, on the other hand, is the ratio of true positive predictions for each class to all positive predictions for that class.
- **Recall (sensitivity):** Recall, also known as sensitivity, is the ratio of true positive predictions for each class to all actual positive instances for that class.
- **F1-score:** The F1-score, which is the harmonic mean of precision and recall, serves as a means of striking a balance between the two.
- **Confusion matrix:** A confusion matrix is a table that displays the counts of true positive, true negative, false positive, and false negative predictions for each class.

Applications

Multiclass classification has numerous real-world applications across various domains, including:
- Handwritten digit recognition
- Speech recognition
- Image classification
- Natural language processing (e.g., sentiment analysis, topic classification)
- Medical diagnosis (e.g., disease classification)

Multiclass classification is a critical task in machine learning, providing valuable insights and predictions for decision-making in diverse applications.

Below is an illustrative Python code instance that executes multiclass categorization by utilizing the widely recognized Iris dataset, which is accessible in scikit-learn. Our objective is to categorize iris flowers into one of three species, namely Setosa, Versicolor, or Virginica. To accomplish this objective, we will employ a basic logistic regression model.

- Load the dataset of Iris and extract the features and target labels.
- Divide the dataset into sets for training and testing.
- Educate a model of logistic regression on the data meant for training.
- Formulate predictions on the data meant for testing.
- Assess the model by means of accuracy, precision, recall, F1-score, and the matrix of confusion.
- Create a visualization of the performance of the model by means of a plot of the matrix of confusion.

```python
import numpy as np
import matplotlib.pyplot as plt
import seaborn as sns
from sklearn.datasets import load_iris
from sklearn.model_selection import train_test_split
from sklearn.linear_model import LogisticRegression
from sklearn.metrics import accuracy_score, precision_score,
recall_score, f1_score, confusion_matrix

# Load the Iris dataset
iris = load_iris()
X = iris.data
y = iris.target

# Split the dataset into training and testing sets
X_train, X_test, y_train, y_test = train_test_split(X, y, test_size=0.2,
random_state=42)

# Train a logistic regression model
model = LogisticRegression(max_iter=1,000)
model.fit(X_train, y_train)

# Make predictions on the test set
y_pred = model.predict(X_test)
```

```
# Evaluate the model
accuracy = accuracy_score(y_test, y_pred)
precision = precision_score(y_test, y_pred, average='weighted')
recall = recall_score(y_test, y_pred, average='weighted')
f1 = f1_score(y_test, y_pred, average='weighted')
conf_matrix = confusion_matrix(y_test, y_pred)

print("Accuracy:", accuracy)
print("Precision:", precision)
print("Recall:", recall)
print("F1-score:", f1)
print("Confusion Matrix:\n", conf_matrix)

# Plot confusion matrix
plt.figure(figsize=(8, 6))
sns.heatmap(conf_matrix, annot=True, fmt='d', cmap='Blues',
xticklabels=iris.target_names, yticklabels=iris.target_names)
plt.xlabel('Predicted Label')
plt.ylabel('True Label')
plt.title('Confusion Matrix')
plt.show()
```

- The outcomes produced by the code encompass a range of metrics, which include accuracy, precision, recall, F1-score, as well as the confusion matrix.
- Accuracy serves as a measurement of the proportion of instances that are correctly classified out of the total number of instances.
- Precision, recall, and F1-score provide valuable insights into the effectiveness of the model in classifying each individual class.
- The confusion matrix offers a comprehensive breakdown of the number of true positive, true negative, false positive, and false negative predictions for each class.
- Additionally, the code generates a heatmap of the confusion matrix to visually depict the performance of the model. The diagonal elements of the matrix correspond to accurate classifications, while the off-diagonal elements indicate misclassifications.

5.2.3 Regularization in Logistic Regression

Regularization is a technique used in machine learning to address the issue of overfitting by integrating an extra term into the loss function. In logistic regression, regularization plays a crucial role in controlling the complexity of the model by imposing penalties on large coefficient values. This prevents the model from overly relying on the training data, resulting in improved generalization and performance on unseen data.

```
Accuracy: 1.0
Precision: 1.0
Recall: 1.0
F1-score: 1.0
Confusion Matrix:
  [[10  0  0]
   [ 0  9  0]
   [ 0  0 11]]
```

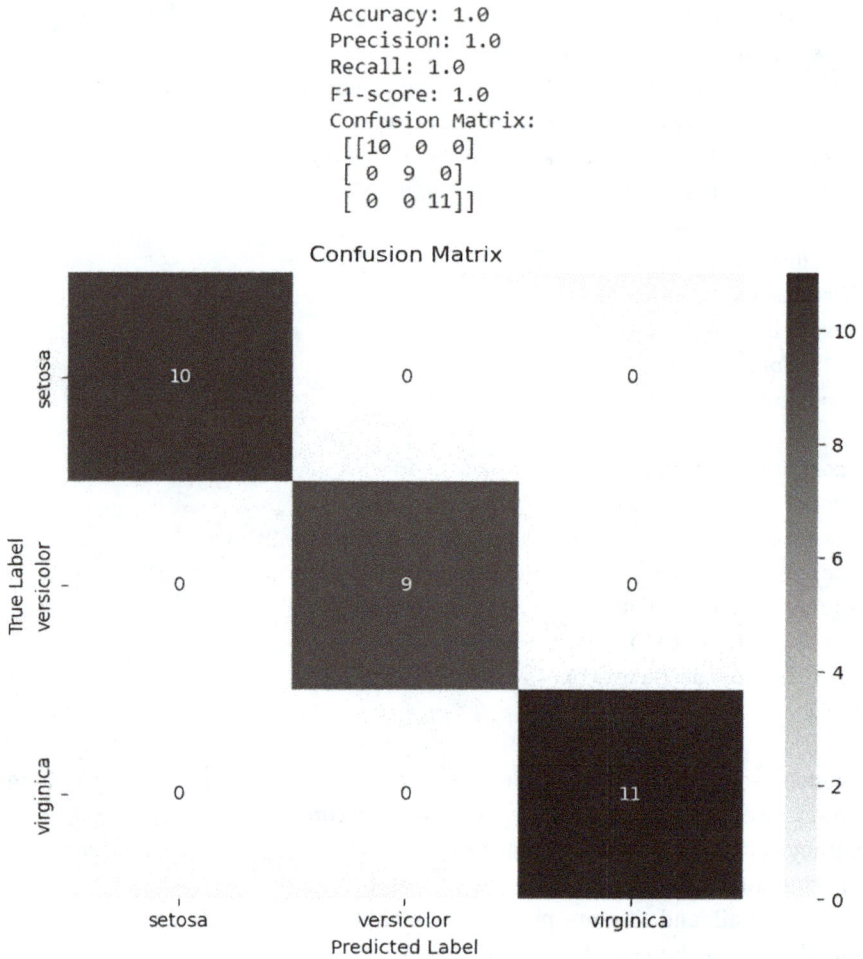

Fig. 5.9: Multiclass classification.

Figure 5.9 presents a comprehensive visual representation of a multiclass classification problem, encompassing various evaluation metrics and a confusion matrix.

Working Principle
- The primary objective of logistic regression is to ascertain the optimal coefficients that minimize the logistic loss function and effectively classify instances into their corresponding classes.
- **Regularization term:** Regularization incorporates a penalty component into the loss function, which in turn discourages the existence of coefficients with large values. When it comes to logistic regression, the two prevalent methods of regu-

larization are L1 regularization (also known as Lasso) and L2 regularization (frequently referred to as Ridge).

- **L1 regularization (Lasso):** L1 regularization incorporates the absolute values of the coefficients into the loss function. This mechanism promotes sparsity in the model by driving certain coefficients to zero, effectively performing feature selection.
- **L2 regularization (Ridge):** L2 regularization includes the squared values of the coefficients in the loss function. It penalizes the presence of large coefficient values, leading to their reduction and preventing overfitting.
- **Regularization parameter (λ):** The strength of regularization is determined by a hyperparameter denoted as λ (lambda). Higher values of λ correspond to more intense regularization, resulting in smaller coefficient values and simpler models.

Example

Suppose a logistic regression model is constructed with two features, namely x1 and x2, alongside a binary target variable denoted as y, which signifies whether a customer will engage in purchasing a product (1) or not (0). In the absence of regularization, the model may exhibit impeccable fitting to the training data, yet its ability to generalize to novel data may be limited.

By implementing L1 or L2 regularization, a penalty term is incorporated into the loss function, taking into account the magnitude of the coefficients. For instance, when utilizing L2 regularization, the loss function is modified.

$$Loss = -\frac{1}{N}\sum_{i=1}^{N}[y_i \log(\hat{y}_i) + (1-y_i)\log(1-\hat{y}_i)] + \lambda\sum_{j=1}^{p}\theta_j^2$$

the regularization parameter λ, the number of instances N, the number of features p, and the coefficients θ_j are all important factors in this context.

Regularization confers several advantages. Firstly, it serves as a preventative measure against overfitting. By effectively managing the complexity of the model, regularization ensures that the model does not become excessively sensitive to noise present in the training data. Moreover, regularization enhances the generalization abilities of the model. The inclusion of regularization techniques often results in models that are more adept at extrapolating to unseen data, as it helps to minimize variance.

Below, an example of Python code is presented, which demonstrates the implementation of L2 regularization (also known as Ridge) in logistic regression. This example includes the usage of plots and evaluation metrics. In order to apply regularization and prevent overfitting, the Iris dataset from scikit-learn is utilized.

- Load the Iris dataset and obtain the features as well as target labels.
- Partition the dataset into separate training and testing sets.
- Employ a logistic regression model with L2 regularization (Ridge) to train the data.

–   Generate predictions on the test data.
–   Assess the model's performance using accuracy, precision, recall, F1-score, and
     the confusion matrix.
–   Illustrate the impact of regularization on the model's decision boundary by plot-
     ting it.

```python
import numpy as np
import matplotlib.pyplot as plt
import seaborn as sns
from sklearn.datasets import load_iris
from sklearn.model_selection import train_test_split
from sklearn.linear_model import LogisticRegression
from sklearn.metrics import accuracy_score, precision_score,
recall_score, f1_score, confusion_matrix

# Load the Iris dataset
iris = load_iris()
X = iris.data[:, :2] # Take only first two features for simplicity
y = (iris.target == 0).astype(int) # Binary classification: Setosa or not

# Split the dataset into training and testing sets
X_train, X_test, y_train, y_test = train_test_split(X, y, test_size=0.2,
random_state=42)

# Train a logistic regression model with L2 regularization (Ridge)
model = LogisticRegression(penalty='l2', max_iter=1,000, C=1) # C is the
inverse of regularization strength
model.fit(X_train, y_train)

# Make predictions on the test set
y_pred = model.predict(X_test)

# Evaluate the model
accuracy = accuracy_score(y_test, y_pred)
precision = precision_score(y_test, y_pred)
recall = recall_score(y_test, y_pred)
f1 = f1_score(y_test, y_pred)
conf_matrix = confusion_matrix(y_test, y_pred)

print("Accuracy:", accuracy)
print("Precision:", precision)
print("Recall:", recall)
```

```
print("F1-score:", f1)
print("Confusion Matrix:\n", conf_matrix)

# Plot decision boundary
x_min, x_max = X[:, 0].min() - 1, X[:, 0].max() + 1
y_min, y_max = X[:, 1].min() - 1, X[:, 1].max() + 1
xx, yy = np.meshgrid(np.arange(x_min, x_max, 0.01), np.arange(y_min,
y_max, 0.01))
Z = model.predict(np.c_[xx.ravel(), yy.ravel()])
Z = Z.reshape(xx.shape)
plt.contourf(xx, yy, Z, alpha=0.3)
sns.scatterplot(x=X_test[:, 0], y=X_test[:, 1], hue=y_test)
plt.xlabel('Sepal Length')
plt.ylabel('Sepal Width')
plt.title('Regularization in Logistic Regression (L2)')
plt.show()
```

```
Accuracy: 1.0
Precision: 1.0
Recall: 1.0
F1-score: 1.0
Confusion Matrix:
 [[20  0]
  [ 0 10]]
```

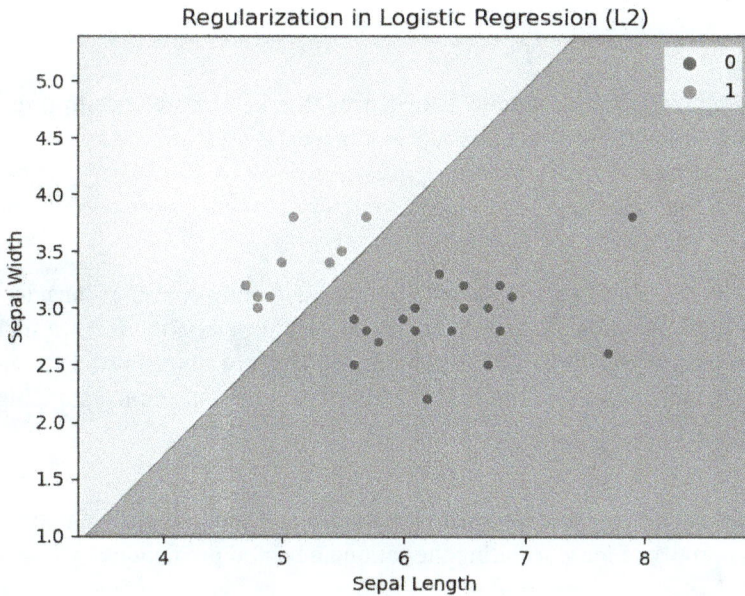

Fig. 5.10: Regularization in Logistic Regression (L2).

Fig. 5.10 illustrates the effects of applying L2 regularization to a logistic regression model.

- The results of the code encompass several evaluation metrics, namely accuracy, precision, recall, F1-score, and the confusion matrix.
- The accuracy metric gauges the ratio of correctly classified instances to the total number of instances.
- Precision, recall, and F1-score offer valuable insights into the model's performance when classifying the positive class.
- The confusion matrix provides a breakdown of the true positive, true negative, false positive, and false negative predictions.
- Moreover, the code generates a visual representation that illustrates the decision boundary alongside the test data points.
- The utilization of regularization techniques aids in smoothing the decision boundary, thereby mitigating the risk of overfitting to the training data and enhancing the model's ability to generalize to new data.

5.3 Decision Trees and Random Forests

Decision Trees and Random Forests have gained considerable popularity as machine learning algorithms employed in the domains of classification and regression tasks.

Decision Trees

Definition: Decision Trees are hierarchical structures that bear semblance to trees. Each internal node within these structures represents a decision predicated on a specific characteristic. Meanwhile, each branch signifies the resulting outcome of said decision. Finally, each leaf node serves as a representation of the ultimate decision or prediction.

Working principle: Decision Trees repeatedly divide the feature space by considering the values of input features. At each node, the algorithm selects the feature that most effectively separates the data into similar subsets. This process persists until either all data points are assigned to the same category or a predetermined stopping criterion is met.

Advantages:
Interpretability: Decision Trees possess a straightforward and comprehensible nature, rendering them appropriate for elucidating the rationale behind predictions.

Non-parametric: They refrain from making presumptions about the underlying distribution of data. Accommodate both numerical and categorical data.

Disadvantages:
Prone to overfitting: Decision Trees possess the inclination to produce excessively complex models that excessively adhere to the training data, hence leading to insufficient generalization on unseen data.

Instability: Minor fluctuations in the data can give rise to dissimilar tree structures, thus rendering them susceptible to noise.

Random Forests

Definition: Random Forests are a type of ensemble learning methodology that consists of a group of Decision Trees. Every individual tree in the forest is trained on a randomly chosen subset of the training data along with a randomized subset of features. The predictions made by each tree are then combined to formulate the ultimate prediction.

Working principle: Random Forests combine the predictive power of multiple Decision Trees to improve generalization performance and mitigate overfitting. In the training phase, each tree is grown independently using a random subset of the training data and features. The final prediction is obtained by averaging the predictions made by all the trees (for regression) or by majority voting (for classification).

Advantages:
Enhanced generalization: Random Forests alleviate the problem of overfitting by aggregating the predictions of numerous individual trees.

Robustness: They adeptly handle noisy data and outliers due to the amalgamation effect. Feature importance: They furnish a metric of feature importance, affording users the ability to discern the most pertinent features for prediction.

Disadvantages:
Complexity: Random Forests exhibit greater intricacy compared to individual Decision Trees, rendering them more arduous to interpret.

Computational cost: Training and predicting with Random Forests can incur considerable computational expenses, particularly when confronted with voluminous datasets.

Applications

Decision Trees and Random Forests are extensively utilized in diverse domains, encompassing but not limited to:
–   Finance: The assessment of creditworthiness and the identification of fraudulent activities. Healthcare: The determination of diseases and the prognostic evaluation.

- Marketing: The segregation of customers and the prediction of churn.
- Environmental science: The categorization of species and the classification of land cover.

Decision Trees and Random Forests are formidable machine learning algorithms with their individual merits and demerits. While Decision Trees proffer transparency and simplicity, Random Forests furnish enhanced generalization aptitude and resilience via ensemble learning.

5.3.1 Building Decision Trees

The process of constructing Decision Trees entails iteratively dividing the dataset according to the input feature values, resulting in the formation of a hierarchical structure resembling a tree. In this structure, internal nodes signify decisions, while leaf nodes indicate the ultimate prediction.

Example: Predicting Loan Approval
Suppose we have a dataset of loan applicants containing features such as income, credit score, and employment status, and the target variable indicates whether the loan was approved (Yes or No).

- The process of constructing decision trees begins with the selection of the optimal split, which involves identifying the feature that can most effectively divide the dataset into separate, homogeneous subsets. An example of this could be the credit score feature, which has the ability to create groups with the highest level of purity. In other words, each group primarily consists of instances belonging to a single class label, such as "Yes" or "No" for loan approval.
- Once the most advantageous division has been ascertained, a decision node is established at the apex of the tree to symbolize the selected attribute and its associated partition. This acts as a crucial juncture in the process of making decisions.
- After the decision node is established, the dataset is partitioned into subgroups according to the values of the chosen characteristic. Each subgroup corresponds to a branch emerging from the decision node, facilitating additional examination and investigation.
- The procedure of recursive division subsequently occurs, in which the previously mentioned measures are reiterated for each subset. This iterative strategy persists until one of the termination conditions is satisfied. These criteria include the following:
  - All data points within a subset belong to the same class, indicating a high level of homogeneity.
  - The maximum depth of the tree has been reached, indicating that further splits would not yield significant improvements.
  - The minimum number of data points within a node has been reached, suggesting that further division would not provide meaningful insights.

–   Upon the satisfaction of the stopping criteria, the initiation of the construction of leaf nodes takes place. These leaf nodes encapsulate the label of the majority class that is found within the subset. As a result, the tree is empowered to generate precise predictions by leveraging the provided data.

In summary, the process of building decision trees involves a series of carefully executed steps, including the selection of an optimal split, the creation of decision nodes and leaf nodes, and the iterative process of recursive splitting. These steps ultimately result in the creation of a powerful and interpretable model for making data-driven decisions.

Fig. 5.11: Decision tree: credit card.

Fig. 5.11 shows the decision tree for credit card approval.

In this example, the decision tree splits the dataset based on the credit score feature. If an applicant's credit score is 700 or higher, they are approved for the loan; otherwise, they are denied.

Let us examine a more intricate numerical illustration of constructing a decision tree to anticipate whether consumers will procure a product, relying on demographic and behavioral attributes.

Example: Predicting Purchase Decision

Suppose we have a dataset of customers containing the following features:

–   Age (numeric)
–   Gender (categorical: Male, Female)
–   Income (numeric)
–   Website Visit Duration (numeric)
–   Product Reviews (numeric)

And the target variable indicates whether the customer made a purchase (Yes or No).

–   Selecting the Optimal Division: Our initial step involves the selection of the characteristic that yields the most homogeneous subsets within the dataset. As an illustration, we may discover that segmenting the data based on age leads to subsets exhibiting the highest degree of purity.

–   Generation of Decision Nodes: At the apex of the tree, we establish a decision node that represents the chosen characteristic and its division point. For example, if the optimal division is age < 30, we generate a decision node labeled "Age < 30?"

- Subdivision of the Data: The dataset is partitioned into subgroups based on the values of the chosen attribute. Each subgroup represents a branch originating from the decision node.
- Recursive Division: We perform the aforementioned process recursively for each subset until one of the specified stopping conditions is fulfilled:
  - All data points within a subset pertain to the same class (homogeneous).
  - The maximum depth of the tree has been reached.
  - The minimum number of data points within a node has been reached. No significant enhancement in the reduction of impurity is observed.
- Generation of Terminal Nodes: Upon fulfillment of the stopping conditions, we generate terminal nodes that contain the majority class label found within the respective subset.

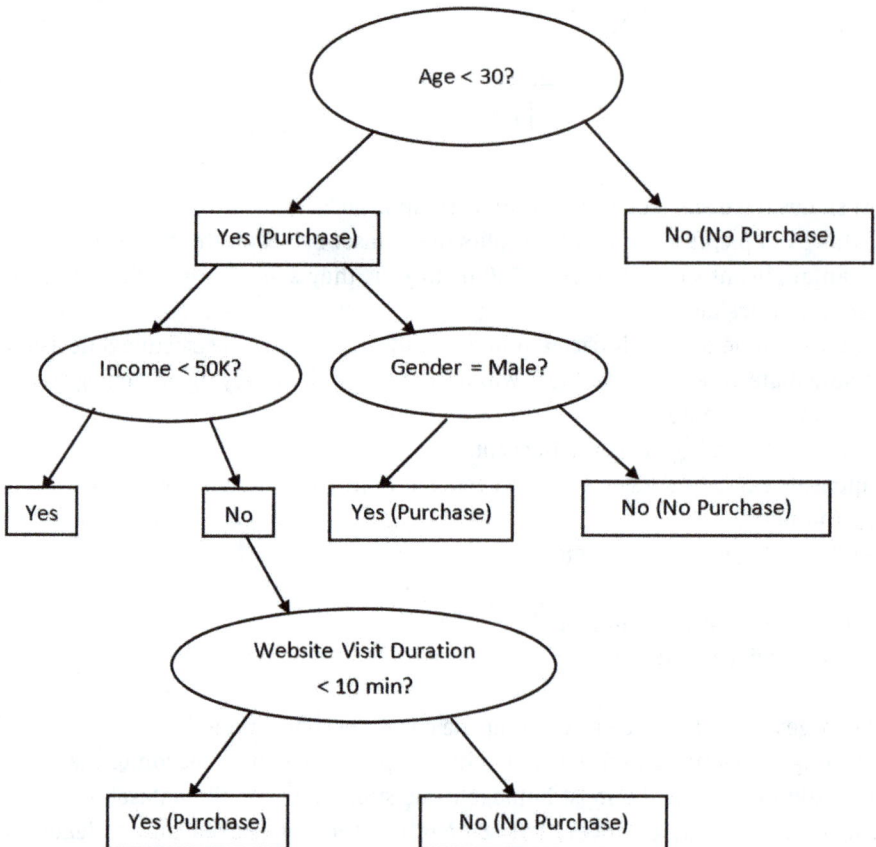

Fig. 5.12: Decision tree: consumers will procure a product.

Fig. 5.12 depicts a decision tree model that predicts whether a consumer will procure a specific product or not.

In this particular illustration, the decision tree forecasts a transaction in the event that the patron is below 30 years of age and possesses an income that falls below 50 K, or if they are of the male gender. In any other case, the decision tree proceeds to divide based on the duration of the visit to the website, projecting a transaction if the duration of the visit falls below 10 min.

The scikit-learn library, often employed for Decision Trees, is widely utilized in the field. This library is a robust tool for machine learning, offering a range of algorithms, such as Decision Trees, to construct models that can make accurate predictions. A comprehensive elucidation of scikit-learn's DecisionTreeClassifier can be found below:

- The DecisionTreeClassifier is a class implemented in the scikit-learn library, which serves as an implementation of the Decision Tree algorithm specifically designed for classification tasks.
- The DecisionTreeClassifier exhibits a prominent characteristic in its ability to accommodate multiple splitting criteria, namely Gini impurity and entropy (information gain). By specifying the criterion parameter as either "gini" or "entropy," users possess the flexibility to employ the most appropriate criterion for their classification requirements.
- In order to mitigate the issue of overfitting and improve the overall ability to make accurate predictions on unseen data, the DecisionTreeClassifier implementation in scikit-learn provides various pruning techniques. These techniques involve the application of constraints, such as the maximum depth of the tree, the minimum number of samples allowed in each leaf, and the minimum number of samples required for a split.
- In terms of handling categorical features, the DecisionTreeClassifier automatically deals with them by executing either one-hot encoding or integer encoding.
- Furthermore, the DecisionTreeClassifier possesses the capability to handle missing values. It does so by creating splits in the nodes based on whether the feature is present or absent.
- After training, the DecisionTreeClassifier provides a feature_importances_ attribute, which allows users to assess the significance of each feature in the prediction process.
- The training procedure for a DecisionTreeClassifier model encompasses the instantiation of an object from the DecisionTreeClassifier class and the subsequent invocation of the fit method. This particular method necessitates the feature matrix (X_train) and target vector (y_train) as its input parameters.
- Once the DecisionTreeClassifier model has been trained, it can be utilized to make predictions on fresh data by making use of the predict method and providing the feature matrix of the new data.

- When considering the visualization of decision trees, one can employ tools like graphviz and matplotlib. In order to simplify the process of visualization, scikit-learn provides the plot_tree function, which enables the direct visualization of the decision tree.
- Users have the ability to assess the effectiveness of a DecisionTreeClassifier model by utilizing different evaluation metrics, including accuracy, precision, recall, F1-score, and the confusion matrix. These metrics can be accessed through the metrics module in the sklearn library.

Example:

```
from sklearn.tree import DecisionTreeClassifier
from sklearn.datasets import load_iris
from sklearn.model_selection import train_test_split
from sklearn.metrics import accuracy_score

# Load the Iris dataset
iris = load_iris()
X = iris.data
y = iris.target

# Split the dataset into training and testing sets
X_train, X_test, y_train, y_test = train_test_split(X, y, test_size=0.2,
random_state=42)

# Train a DecisionTreeClassifier model
model = DecisionTreeClassifier()
model.fit(X_train, y_train)

# Make predictions on the test set
y_pred = model.predict(X_test)

# Evaluate the model
accuracy = accuracy_score(y_test, y_pred)
print("Accuracy:", accuracy)
```

Output:
Accuracy: 1.0

Below is an illustrative Python code snippet showcasing the implementation of Decision Trees for regression on the Diabetes dataset from the scikit-learn library. The code encompasses various steps such as dataset loading, model training using DecisionTreeRegressor, prediction generation, model evaluation, and visualization of the decision tree.

```python
import numpy as np
import matplotlib.pyplot as plt
from sklearn.datasets import load_diabetes
from sklearn.model_selection import train_test_split
from sklearn.tree import DecisionTreeRegressor, plot_tree
from sklearn.metrics import mean_squared_error

# Load the Diabetes dataset
diabetes = load_diabetes()
X = diabetes.data
y = diabetes.target

# Split the dataset into training and testing sets
X_train, X_test, y_train, y_test = train_test_split(X, y, test_size=0.2,
random_state=42)

# Train a DecisionTreeRegressor model
model = DecisionTreeRegressor(random_state=42)
model.fit(X_train, y_train)

# Make predictions on the test set
y_pred = model.predict(X_test)

# Evaluate the model
mse = mean_squared_error(y_test, y_pred)
print("Mean Squared Error:", mse)

# Visualize the decision tree
plt.figure(figsize=(15, 10))
plot_tree(model, filled=True, feature_names=diabetes.feature_names)
plt.show()
```

Output:

  Mean Squared Error: 4976.797752808989

  The MSE computation is executed by the code in order to determine the disparity between the target values (y_test) and the predicted values (y_pred) on the test set. MSE represents the average squared deviation between the actual and predicted values, thus providing an indication of the model's precision.

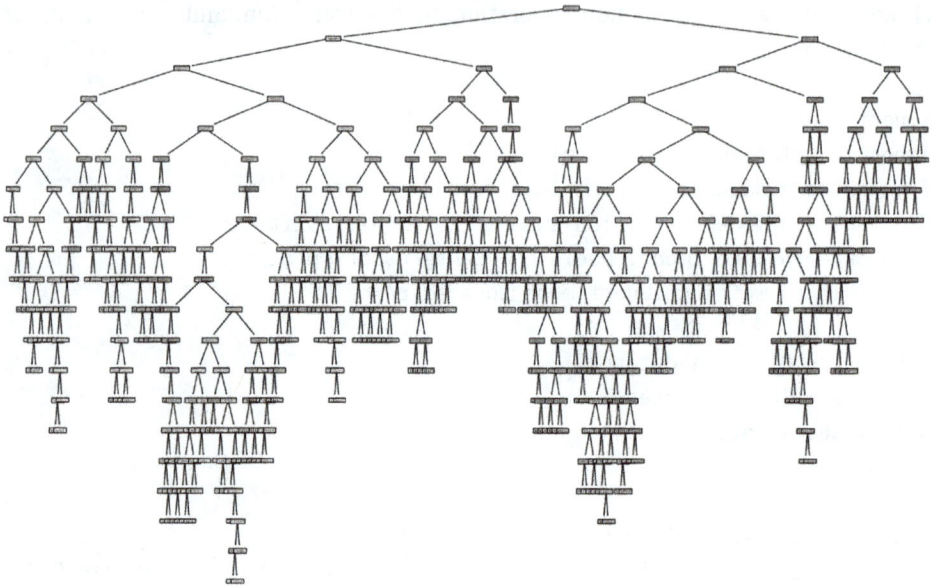

Fig. 5.13: Decision tree of diabetes dataset.

Fig. 5.13 presents a decision tree model trained on a diabetes dataset. The tree structure consists of internal nodes representing tests or decisions based on various features or attributes.

The act of visualizing the decision tree is facilitated by the plot_tree function from scikit-learn. It portrays the structure of the decision tree through the utilization of nodes and branches. Each node corresponds to a decision based on a specific feature, while each leaf node corresponds to the predicted target value.

The data's output and visualization provide valuable insights into the performance and decision-making process of the Decision Tree Regression model, which has been trained on the Diabetes dataset. Understanding the organization of the decision tree and interpreting its nodes and branches is essential for gaining insights into the relationships between characteristics and the target variable. Furthermore, evaluating the model's performance by utilizing metrics such as MSE assists in assessing its accuracy and effectiveness in generating predictions.

5.3.2 Entropy and Information Gain

Entropy and Information Gain are principles utilized in Decision Trees for the purpose of ascertaining the most optimal attribute to divide the data at each node.

Entropy

Entropy quantifies the degree of impurity or uncertainty within a given dataset, and it is determined through the analysis of the dataset's distribution in terms of various classes or categories.

Formula: For a dataset with K classes and proportion p_i of class i:

$$Entropy(S) = - \sum_{i=1}^{K} p_i log_2(p_i)$$

Consider a dataset comprising 10 instances, wherein 6 instances are categorized under class A, while the remaining 4 instances fall under class B.

Proportion of class A:

$$p_A = \frac{6}{10} = 0.6$$

Proportion of class B:

$$p_B = \frac{4}{10} = 0.4$$

$$Entropy(S) = -0.6 \ log_2(0.6) + 0.4 \ log_2(0.4)$$

$$Entropy(S) = -0.6 * (-0.737) + 0.4 * (-1.322)$$

$$Entropy(S) = -(-0.4422 - 0.5288)$$

$$Entropy(S) = 0.971$$

Information Gain

Information Gain assesses the decrease in entropy or uncertainty obtained by dividing the dataset according to a specific characteristic. It quantifies the extent to which a characteristic imparts knowledge about the class labels.

For a dataset S with N instances, and m subsets after splitting based on feature A:

$$IG(S, \ A) = Entropy(S) - \sum_{j=1}^{m} \frac{N_j}{N} * Entropy(S_j)$$

Suppose that we are interested in partitioning the dataset according to a specific feature, denoted as X, thereby yielding two subsets, S1 and S2, which consist of 7 and 3 instances, respectively.

Entropy before split: $Entropy(S) = 0.971$

Entropy of subset S_1: $Entropy(S_1) = -(0.7 * log_2(0.7) + 0.3 * log_2(0.3))$

Entropy of subset S_2: $\quad Entropy(S_2) = -\,(0.3 * \log_2(0.3) + 0.7 * \log_2(0.7))$

$$IG(S,\ X) = 0.971 - \left(\frac{7}{10} * Entropy(S_1) + \frac{3}{10} * Entropy(S_2)\right)$$

Outlook	Temperature	Play football
Sunny	Hot	No
Sunny	Hot	No
Overcast	Hot	Yes
Rainy	Mild	Yes
Rainy	Cool	Yes
Rainy	Cool	No
Overcast	Cool	Yes
Sunny	Mild	No
Sunny	Cool	Yes
Rainy	Mild	Yes
Sunny	Mild	Yes
Overcast	Mild	Yes
Overcast	Hot	Yes
Rainy	Mild	No

let us examine an archetypal instance of making a decision regarding participation in football contingent on meteorological circumstances. We will compute the entropy and information gain for every characteristic in order to ascertain the most suitable characteristic for dividing the dataset.

Suppose we possess a dataset comprising fourteen instances, characterized by two distinct features namely Outlook (Sunny, Overcast, Rainy) and Temperature (Hot, Mild, Cool), with the target variable denoting the decision of playing football (Yes or No).

Step 1: Calculate Entropy for Target Variable (Play Football)

– Total instances $N = 14$
– Number of instances with Play = Yes $P_{Yes} = 9$
– Number of instances with Play = No $P_{No} = 5$

$$Entropy(S) = -\left(\frac{9}{14}\ log_2\left(\frac{9}{14}\right) + \frac{5}{14}\ log_2\left(\frac{5}{14}\right)\right)$$

$$Entropy(S) = -\left(\frac{9}{14} * -0.764 + \frac{5}{14} * -1\right)$$

$$Entropy(S) = -\,(-0.439 + -0.357)$$

$$Entropy(S) = 0.796$$

Step 2: Calculate Information Gain for each Feature

For Outlook:
- Split the dataset based on Outlook (Sunny, Overcast, Rainy)
- Calculate the proportion of instances in each subset and the corresponding entropy.
- Weighted average of entropies to calculate Information Gain.

$$IG(S, Outlook) = Entropy(S) - \left(\frac{5}{14} \times Entropy(S_{sunny}) + \frac{4}{14} \times Entropy(S_{Overcast}) \right.$$
$$\left. + \frac{5}{14} \times Entropy(S_{Rainy}) \right)$$

$$= 0.796 - \left(\frac{5}{14} \times 0.971 + \frac{4}{14} \times 0 + \frac{5}{14} 0.971 \right)$$

$$= 0.796 - (0.347 + 0 + 0.347)$$

$$= 0.796 - 0.694$$

$$IG(S, Outlook) = 0.102$$

For Temperature:
- Split the dataset based on Temperature (Hot, Mild, Cool)
- Calculate the proportion of instances in each subset and the corresponding entropy.
- Weighted average of entropies to calculate Information Gain.

$$IG(S, Temperature) = Entropy(S) - \left(\frac{4}{14} \times Entropy(S_{Hot}) + \frac{6}{14} \times Entropy(S_{Mild}) \right.$$
$$\left. + \frac{4}{14} \times Entropy(S_{Cool}) \right)$$

$$= 0.796 - \left(\frac{4}{14} \times 0.811 + \frac{6}{14} \times 0.918 + \frac{4}{14} \times 0.811 \right)$$

$$= 0.796 - (0.23 + 0.405 + 0.23)$$

$$= 0.796 - 0.865$$

$$IG(S, Temperature) = -0.069$$

- The entropy of the target variable (Play Football) is 0.796.
- The Information Gain for Outlook is 0.102, and for Temperature is −0.069.
- The attribute possessing the greatest Information Gain (Outlook) is selected for partitioning the dataset in a Decision Tree, as it offers the greatest decrease in uncertainty.

5.3.3 Random Forests and Bagging

Random Forests and Bagging, specifically ensemble learning techniques, are utilized in order to augment the effectiveness and robustness of machine learning models by merging numerous individual models.

Bagging, also known as Bootstrap Aggregating, is a methodology in which numerous foundational models, often in the form of decision trees, are independently trained on randomly selected subsets of the training data. This selection process involves replacement, resulting in each base model acquiring unique insights into the underlying data due to the inherent randomness. The predictions generated by these models are subsequently combined through averaging or aggregation techniques to formulate the final prediction.

For instance, consider a dataset comprising 1,000 instances, where the objective is to train a decision tree. In the context of bagging, the following steps are undertaken:
1. A random sample, consisting of 70% of the instances, is selected (with replacement) to train the initial decision tree.
2. This process is repeated multiple times to train several decision trees, with each model utilizing a distinct subset of the data.
3. To formulate a prediction, the predictions derived from all decision trees are aggregated, employing methods such as averaging in the case of regression or voting for classification.

By adhering to the principles of bagging, the aforementioned steps facilitate the creation of an ensemble model capable of leveraging the diverse perspectives acquired by the individual base models.

Random Forests is a method that builds on the idea of bagging by introducing an additional element of randomness. This is accomplished by choosing a random subset of features at each decision tree node. The aim of this random feature selection is to decrease the correlation between the trees, thus reducing the risk of overfitting and improving the overall generalization capability.

Example
Continuing with the previous example, in Random Forests:
1. When training each decision tree, instead of using all features, we randomly select a subset of features.
2. The subset of characteristics is employed to ascertain the optimal division at every node within the tree.
3. The variability in the process of selecting features guarantees that every decision tree within the collection acquires distinct characteristics of the dataset, thereby resulting in a more heterogeneous assortment of models.
4. Predictions are aggregated as in bagging.

Advantages
–   The phenomenon of overfitting can be effectively mitigated through the utiliza-
     tion of Bagging and Random Forests, as these methods employ a strategy of aver-
     aging predictions obtained from numerous models, each of which is trained on
     distinct subsets of the available data.
–   Random Forests are particularly proficient at enhancing the generalization capa-
     bilities of models by introducing an additional element of randomness, thereby
     fostering the development of more diverse models that exhibit superior perfor-
     mance in terms of generalization.
–   Ensembling techniques possess a significant advantage in their capacity to tackle
     the problem of noise within the data. Through the aggregation of predictions
     from various models, ensembling aids in mitigating the influence of noisy data
     points and outliers, thereby enhancing the resilience of the approach.

The Python libraries commonly employed for Random Forests and Bagging are primarily implemented by scikit-learn, a well-known Python library for machine learning. Within this context, we find the main libraries utilized to carry out Random
Forests and Bagging:

scikit-learn (sklearn)
–   **ensemble**: The **ensemble** module in scikit-learn provides classes for implement-
     ing ensemble learning techniques, including Random Forests and Bagging.
–   **RandomForestClassifier**: This class implements the Random Forest algorithm
     for classification tasks.
–   **RandomForestRegressor**: This class implements the Random Forest algorithm
     for regression tasks.
–   **BaggingClassifier**: This class implements the Bagging ensemble method for clas-
     sification tasks.
–   **BaggingRegressor**: This class implements the Bagging ensemble method for re-
     gression tasks.
–   These classes provide easy-to-use interfaces for training ensemble models and
     making predictions.

numpy (np)
–   numPy is an essential module for conducting scientific computations in the Py-
     thon programming language.
–   It offers comprehensive assistance for dealing with multi-dimensional arrays and
     matrices, which are crucial for effectively managing data in various machine
     learning algorithms.
–   In the context of Random Forests and Bagging, numpy is often used for data ma-
     nipulation and numerical computations.

matplotlib.pyplot (plt)

- matplotlib.pyplot is a plotting library used for creating visualizations in Python.
- It provides functions for creating various types of plots, such as line plots, scatter plots, and histograms.
- In the context of Random Forests and Bagging, matplotlib.pyplot is used to visualize decision boundaries and other relevant plots for model evaluation.

These libraries present a comprehensive array of tools for the implementation and assessment of Random Forests and Bagging algorithms in the Python programming language. They offer proficient implementations of these ensemble techniques and provide supplementary functionalities for data preprocessing, evaluation, and visualization, rendering them indispensable for the construction of resilient machine learning models.

Below is a Python code example demonstrating the use of Random Forests and Bagging with the Iris dataset from scikit-learn. It includes loading the dataset, training Random Forest and Bagging classifiers, making predictions, evaluating the models, and visualizing the decision boundaries.

```
import numpy as np
import matplotlib.pyplot as plt
from sklearn.datasets import load_iris
from sklearn.model_selection import train_test_split
from sklearn.ensemble import RandomForestClassifier, BaggingClassifier
from sklearn.tree import DecisionTreeClassifier
from sklearn.metrics import accuracy_score
from itertools import product


# Load the Iris dataset
iris = load_iris()
X = iris.data[:, :2] # Using only the first two features for
visualization purposes
y = iris.target


# Split the dataset into training and testing sets
X_train, X_test, y_train, y_test = train_test_split(X, y, test_size=0.2,
random_state=42)


# Create Decision Tree, Random Forest, and Bagging classifiers
dt = DecisionTreeClassifier(random_state=42)
rf = RandomForestClassifier(n_estimators=10, random_state=42)
```

```
bagging = BaggingClassifier(base_estimator=dt, n_estimators=10,
random_state=42)

# Train classifiers
dt.fit(X_train, y_train)
rf.fit(X_train, y_train)
bagging.fit(X_train, y_train)

# Make predictions
y_pred_dt = dt.predict(X_test)
y_pred_rf = rf.predict(X_test)
y_pred_bagging = bagging.predict(X_test)

# Evaluate classifiers
accuracy_dt = accuracy_score(y_test, y_pred_dt)
accuracy_rf = accuracy_score(y_test, y_pred_rf)
accuracy_bagging = accuracy_score(y_test, y_pred_bagging)

print("Decision Tree Accuracy:", accuracy_dt)
print("Random Forest Accuracy:", accuracy_rf)
print("Bagging Accuracy:", accuracy_bagging)

# Plot decision boundaries
plt.figure(figsize=(15, 5))
for i, clf in enumerate([dt, rf, bagging]):
 plt.subplot(1, 3, i + 1)
 # Plot decision boundaries
 x_min, x_max = X[:, 0].min() - 1, X[:, 0].max() + 1
 y_min, y_max = X[:, 1].min() - 1, X[:, 1].max() + 1
 xx, yy = np.meshgrid(np.arange(x_min, x_max, 0.1),
 np.arange(y_min, y_max, 0.1))
 Z = clf.predict(np.c_[xx.ravel(), yy.ravel()])
 Z = Z.reshape(xx.shape)
 plt.contourf(xx, yy, Z, alpha=0.4)

 # Plot data points
 plt.scatter(X[:, 0], X[:, 1], c=y, s=20, edgecolor='k')
 plt.title(['Decision Tree', 'Random Forest', 'Bagging'][i])
plt.show()
```

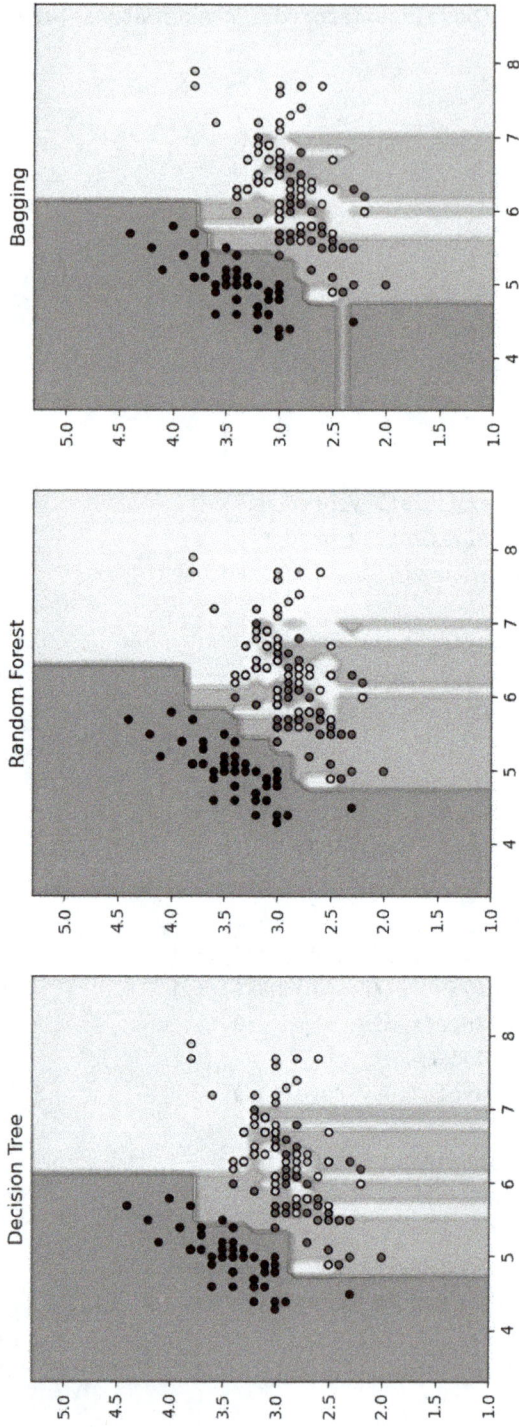

Decision Tree Accuracy: 0.6333333333333333
Random Forest Accuracy: 0.7666666666666667
Bagging Accuracy: 0.7

Fig. 5.14: Comparisons of accuracy in Decision Tree, Random Forest, and Bagging.

Fig. 5.14 shows the plots for comparisons of accuracy in Decision Tree, Random Forest, and Bagging.

The code uses the Iris dataset, which contains 150 samples with 4 features each (sepal length, sepal width, petal length, and petal width). For visualization purposes, only the first two features are used.

Output

– The precision of the Decision Tree, Random Forest, and Bagging classifiers when applied to the test data is displayed.
– Decision boundaries of each classifier are plotted to visualize their performance in separating different classes.

Explanation

– The dataset is initially divided into training and testing sets.
– Subsequently, Decision Tree, Random Forest, and Bagging classifiers are instantiated. By employing the fit method, each classifier is trained on the training data.
– Predictions are generated on the test data through the utilization of the predict method.
– Using the accuracy_score function from scikit-learn, accuracy scores are computed for each classifier.
– Eventually, decision boundaries are plotted to visually represent how each classifier separates the classes within the feature space.

Visualization

Decision boundaries are plotted for each classifier, showing regions where each class is predicted. Different colors represent different classes, and data points are plotted as markers. Decision boundaries help visualize the classification performance of each classifier in the feature space.

5.4 Support Vector Machines

The support vector machine (SVM) is a supervised learning algorithm utilized for classification and regression purposes. It demonstrates notable effectiveness in high-dimensional spaces and possesses the ability to effectively capture intricate relationships within data. SVMs function by identifying the optimal hyperplane that separates classes within the feature space. This process maximizes the margin between classes while simultaneously minimizing classification errors.

The essential principles of SVM comprise support vectors, which are the data points closest to the hyperplane, and the margin, which denotes the distance between the hyperplane and the support vectors.

The objective of SVMs is to maximize this margin, thereby endowing the decision boundary with resilience against noise and outliers. In situations where classes are not able to be linearly separated, SVMs can employ kernel functions to map input features into a space of higher dimensionality. This allows for the establishment of non-linear decision boundaries.

The versatility of SVMs is underscored by their manifold applications, including text classification, image recognition, and bioinformatics. Due to their effectiveness and scalability, SVMs are prevalently utilized in both binary and multiclass classification problems. Nevertheless, it should be noted that SVMs can impose a notable computational burden and necessitate the judicious selection of hyperparameters in order to achieve optimal performance. All in all, SVMs are a potent tool for classification tasks, as they offer flexibility, accuracy, and robustness in their treatment of diverse datasets.

Types of Support Vector Machines

Linear support vector machines: Linear Support Vector Machines classify data by detecting the optimal hyperplane that efficiently separates classes in the feature space. It demonstrates impressive performance when the data demonstrates linear separability.

Kernel support vector machines: Kernel Support Vector Machines augment the capabilities of linear Support Vector Machines through the application of kernel functions (such as polynomial and radial basis functions) to convert the input features into a higher-dimensional space, thereby establishing non-linear decision boundaries. In an efficient manner, Kernel Support Vector Machines effectively manage data that is not linearly separable.

Working Principle

- Support vector machines (SVMs) strive to discover the hyperplane that maximizes the margin, which refers to the distance between the hyperplane and the closest data points (known as support vectors) from each class.
- In the case of linearly separable data, the equation for the hyperplane can be expressed as $w \cdot x + b = 0$, where w represents the weight vector, x denotes the feature vector, and b signifies the bias term.

- The margin is computed as $\frac{2}{\|w\|}$, and the objective is to maximize this margin while minimizing classification errors.

Steps to Perform SVM

Data Preparation: We start by preparing our dataset, consisting of features (x1 and x2) and corresponding class labels.

Model Training:
- Next, the SVM model is trained on the dataset.
- The SVM algorithm aims to identify the optimal hyperplane that effectively separates the two classes in the feature space.
- The linear SVM hyperplane equation is denoted as w·x + b = 0, where w represents the weight vector, x denotes the feature vector, and b signifies the bias term.
- The objective is to determine the w and b parameters that maximize the margin between the hyperplane and the nearest support vectors, which are the data points of each class.

Model Evaluation:
- Once the training process of the model is completed, we proceed to assess its performance by utilizing a range of metrics including accuracy, precision, recall, and F1-score.
- Additionally, we employ the technique of visualizing the decision boundary to gain insights into the effectiveness of the Support Vector Machine (SVM) in segregating the classes within the feature space.

The execution of Support Vector Machine (SVM) commonly involves the utilization of Python libraries, which are predominantly provided by scikit-learn (sklearn), a popular machine learning library in the Python programming language. In the subsequent discussion, we will introduce the main libraries employed in the implementation of SVM.

scikit-learn (sklearn)

- scikit-learn is an extensive Python library that encompasses the field of machine learning, offering optimized implementations of diverse algorithms, among them Support Vector Machines (SVM).
- The **svm** module in scikit-learn contains classes and functions related to SVMs.
- **SVC** (Support Vector Classifier): This class implements the SVM algorithm for classification tasks.

–   **SVR** (Support Vector Regressor): This class implements the SVM algorithm for re-
    gression tasks.
–   These classes provide flexible and easy-to-use interfaces for training SVM models,
    making predictions, and tuning hyperparameters.

numpy (np)

–   numPy serves as a fundamental package for scientific computing in the Python
    programming language.
–   The provision of support for multi-dimensional arrays and matrices is integral to
    effectively managing data in SVM algorithms.
–   numpy arrays are often used to represent feature vectors and labels in SVM train-
    ing and prediction processes.

matplotlib.pyplot (plt)

–   matplotlib.pyplot is a plotting library used for creating visualizations in Python.
–   The library offers a range of capabilities for generating diverse plot types, includ-
    ing line plots, scatter plots, and histograms.
–   In SVM, the utilization of matplotlib.pyplot is frequently employed for the pur-
    pose of illustrating decision boundaries, support vectors, and other pertinent
    graphical representations to assess the model.

These libraries offer a comprehensive set of tools for implementing and evaluating
SVM algorithms in Python. They provide efficient implementations of SVM models,
support for data manipulation and numerical computations, and functionalities for
visualization and model evaluation. By leveraging these libraries, users can easily
build, train, and evaluate SVM models for various classification and regression tasks.

5.4.1 Linear SVM

The Linear Support Vector Machine (SVM) is a supervised learning technique utilized
for the purpose of binary classification tasks. Its main objective is to ascertain the
most suitable hyperplane that efficiently partitions the classes within the feature
space. A comprehensive explanation of the Linear SVM is provided hereafter:

Objective: The aim of the Linear Support Vector Machine (SVM) is to identify the hyperplane possessing the utmost margin, thereby distinguishing the classes within the feature space.

Hyperplane: The equation $w \cdot x + b = 0$ serves as a mathematical representation of the hyperplane, in which the weight vector w is orthogonal to the hyperplane, the feature vector x is representative of the features, and the bias term b has a significant role.

Margin: The margin is defined as the separation between the hyperplane and the closest support vectors of each class, in terms of distance. The objective of the linear SVM is to optimize this margin, aiming to maximize it.

Optimization: The formulation of Linear SVM involves an optimization problem that aims to minimize the norm of the weight vector w, while ensuring that the constraint $y_i(w \cdot x_i + b) \geq 1$ holds for all training instances (x_i, y_i).

Classification: Upon completion of training, Linear SVM assigns new data points to classes based on their position in relation to the hyperplane. Data points falling on one side are assigned to one class, while those on the other side are assigned to the other class.

Kernel trick: While the performance of Linear SVM is commendable in the case of linearly separable data, the utilization of kernel functions allows for the transformation of data into a higher-dimensional space. This transformation effectively renders the data linearly separable, thereby facilitating the classification of data that is not linearly separable.

Regularization: Linear SVM encompasses regularization parameters to handle outliers and achieve a trade-off between maximizing the margin and minimizing classification errors.

Scalability: Linear SVM is characterized by its efficiency and scalability, making it a suitable choice for handling large datasets that have high-dimensional feature spaces.

The Linear Support Vector Machine (SVM) algorithm exhibits remarkable efficacy in executing binary classification tasks, demonstrating robust resilience to errors, substantial computational efficiency, and the capability to manage voluminous datasets. It discerns the most suitable hyperplane that effectively discriminates between distinct classes within the feature space, thereby contributing to its extensive utilization in various machine learning tasks.

Let us contemplate a binary classification problem which entails two distinct features, denoted as x1 and x2. In the scenario at hand, we are presented with a dataset that can be described as follows:

x1	x2	Class
1	2	0
2	3	0
3	4	1
4	5	1

We aim to conduct training on a Linear Support Vector Machine (SVM) in order to categorize data points into two distinct classes: Class 0 and Class 1.

Steps:

Data Preparation:

The dataset is prepared by incorporating features (x1 and x2) alongside their corresponding class labels (0 or 1).

Model Training:
- The provided dataset is used to train the Linear SVM model.
- The optimal hyperplane, which maximizes the margin between the different classes, is calculated by the SVM algorithm.
- The equation of the hyperplane is denoted as w·x + b = 0 in which w represents the weight vector perpendicular to the hyperplane and b represents the bias term.
- Assuming the weight vector w = [1,1] and the bias term b = − 5, the equation of the hyperplane can be expressed as x1 + x2 − 5 = 0.

Model Evaluation:

The evaluation of the Linear Support Vector Machine (SVM) model is conducted by making predictions on the test data and comparing them with the actual labels. To measure the performance of the model, different metrics such as accuracy, precision, recall, and F1-score are computed. Additionally, the decision boundary, which represents the hyperplane that effectively separates the two classes, is presented visually. Let's consider a Python code to perform Linear SVM:

```
import numpy as np
import matplotlib.pyplot as plt
from sklearn import svm


# Generate synthetic data
np.random.seed(0)
X = np.r_[np.random.randn(20, 2) - [2, 2], np.random.randn(20, 2) + [2, 2]]
y = [-1] * 20 + [1] * 20


# Plot data before SVM
plt.figure(figsize=(10, 5))
plt.scatter(X[:, 0], X[:, 1], c=y, cmap=plt.cm.Paired)
plt.title('Data Before SVM')
plt.xlabel('X1')
plt.ylabel('X2')
```

```
# Train Linear SVM
clf = svm.SVC(kernel='linear')
clf.fit(X, y)

# Plot decision boundary and support vectors
w = clf.coef_[0]
b = clf.intercept_[0]
x0_min, x0_max = X[:, 0].min() - 1, X[:, 0].max() + 1
x1_min, x1_max = X[:, 1].min() - 1, X[:, 1].max() + 1
xx0, xx1 = np.meshgrid(np.arange(x0_min, x0_max, 0.1),
 np.arange(x1_min, x1_max, 0.1))
Z = clf.predict(np.c_[xx0.ravel(), xx1.ravel()])
Z = Z.reshape(xx0.shape)

# Plot data after SVM
plt.figure(figsize=(10, 5))
plt.contourf(xx0, xx1, Z, alpha=0.3, cmap=plt.cm.Paired)
plt.scatter(X[:, 0], X[:, 1], c=y, cmap=plt.cm.Paired)
plt.title('Data After SVM with Hyperplane')
plt.xlabel('X1')
plt.ylabel('X2')

# Plot support vectors
plt.scatter(clf.support_vectors_[:, 0], clf.support_vectors_[:, 1],
 s=100, edgecolors='k', facecolors='none', linewidths=1)

# Plot hyperplane
plt.plot([x0_min, x0_max], [-(w[0]*x0_min + b)/w[1], -(w[0]*x0_max +
b)/w[1]], 'k--')
plt.xlim(x0_min, x0_max)
plt.ylim(x1_min, x1_max)
plt.show()
```

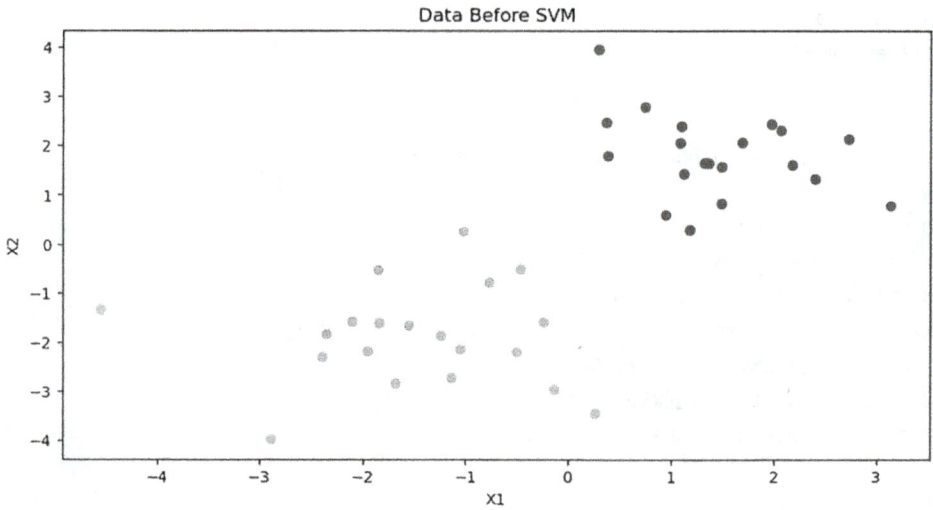

Fig. 5.15: Data before SVM.

Fig. 5.15 presents a scatter plot visualization of the dataset prior to applying the Support Vector Machine (SVM) algorithm. The plot displays the data points, each representing an individual observation or instance, distributed across two dimensions or features. These features are represented by the x-axis and y-axis, respectively.

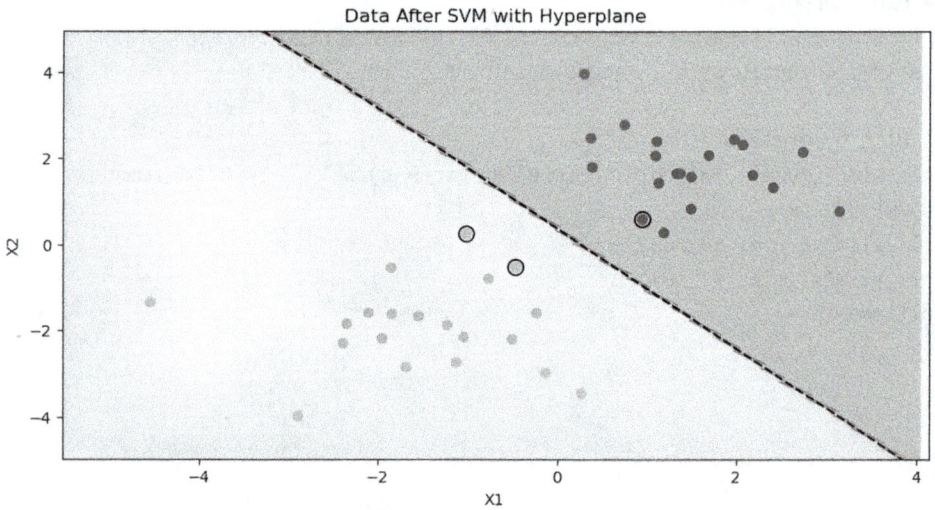

Fig. 5.16: Data after SVM with hyperplane.

Fig. 5.16 presents a scatter plot visualization of the dataset after applying the Support Vector Machine (SVM) algorithm. Similar to the previous scatter plot (Fig. 5.15), the data points are plotted in the feature space, with the x-axis and y-axis representing two chosen features or dimensions.

However, in this figure, an additional component is superimposed onto the scatter plot: the decision boundary or separating hyperplane learned by the SVM model. This decision boundary is a line (or a higher-dimensional hyperplane in case of more features) that optimally separates the different classes or categories present in the dataset.

This piece of code produces artificial data, visualizes it prior to employing Support Vector Machine (SVM), subsequently trains a model of Linear SVM, and visualizes the data after utilizing SVM with the decision boundary (hyperplane) and support vectors.

Explanation of Code:

– Import the requisite libraries: numpy for numerical calculations, matplotlib.pyplot for visualization, and the svm module from sklearn for the Support Vector Machine.
– Generate Synthetic Data:
  – Synthetic data is generated using the np.r_ function to concatenate two sets of randomly generated 2D points.
  – The initial collection of data points is generated from a standard distribution with a center at (–2, –2), denoted as class –1.
  – A subsequent collection of data points is generated from a standard distribution with a center at (2, 2), denoted as class 1.
  – The acquired data is stored in the variable X, with the corresponding labels being stored in the variable y.
– Train Linear SVM:
  – We create an SVM classifier object using svm.SVC with kernel = 'linear', indicating a linear kernel.
  – The classifier undergoes training on the synthetic data with the utilization of the fit method.
– Plot Data After SVM:
  – We create a contour plot to visualize the decision boundary (hyperplane) obtained after applying SVM.
  – The decision boundary is plotted along with the support vectors and data points.
  – Support vectors are marked with circles, and the hyperplane is plotted as a dashed line.
  – The title and axis labels are added to the plot for clarity.

This code exemplifies the utilization of scikit-learn in order to execute Linear SVM classification on fabricated data. Initially, it generates fabricated data and graphs it prior to the application of SVM. Subsequently, it proceeds to train a Linear SVM model and graphically illustrates the data post SVM application, showcasing the decision boundary and support vectors.

Let us examine an alternative Python code that executes Linear SVM on a dataset obtained from scikit-learn, specifically the load_iris dataset.

```python
import numpy as np
import matplotlib.pyplot as plt
from sklearn import datasets
from sklearn.pipeline import Pipeline
from sklearn.preprocessing import StandardScaler
from sklearn.svm import LinearSVC

# Load the iris dataset
iris = datasets.load_iris()
X = iris.data[:, :2] # We only take the first two features
y = iris.target

# Create a pipeline to scale the data and apply SVM
clf = Pipeline([
 ('scaler', StandardScaler()),
 ('linear_svc', LinearSVC(C=1, loss='hinge', random_state=42))
])

# Fit the pipeline
clf.fit(X, y)

# Plot the data before applying SVM
x0_min, x0_max = X[:, 0].min() - 1, X[:, 0].max() + 1
x1_min, x1_max = X[:, 1].min() - 1, X[:, 1].max() + 1
xx, yy = np.meshgrid(np.arange(x0_min, x0_max, 0.1),
 np.arange(x1_min, x1_max, 0.1))

plt.figure(figsize=(10, 6))
plt.subplot(1, 2, 1)
plt.title('Data before SVM')
plt.scatter(X[:, 0], X[:, 1], c=y, cmap=plt.cm.Set1, edgecolor='k')

# Plot the data after applying SVM
plt.subplot(1, 2, 2)
plt.title('Data after SVM')
Z = clf.predict(np.c_[xx.ravel(), yy.ravel()])
Z = Z.reshape(xx.shape)
plt.contourf(xx, yy, Z, cmap=plt.cm.Set1, alpha=0.8)
plt.scatter(X[:, 0], X[:, 1], c=y, cmap=plt.cm.Set1, edgecolor='k')
plt.xlim(xx.min(), xx.max())
plt.ylim(yy.min(), yy.max())
```

```
plt.xticks(())
plt.yticks(())

plt.show()
```

Steps for above code:
- Loads the iris dataset from the scikit-learn library and proceeds to exclusively choose the initial two characteristics.
- Creates a pipeline that first scales the data using StandardScaler and then applies a linear SVM using LinearSVC.
- Fits the pipeline to the data.
- Creates a mesh grid to plot the data before and after applying SVM.
- Plots the original data (before SVM) in the first subplot.
- Plots the data after applying SVM in the second subplot, including the decision boundary (hyperplane) using plt.contourf.
- Displays the plots.

The above code displays two subplots. The first subplot shows the original data points before applying SVM, colored according to their class labels. The second subplot shows the data points after applying linear SVM, along with the decision boundary (hyperplane) separating the classes as shown below.

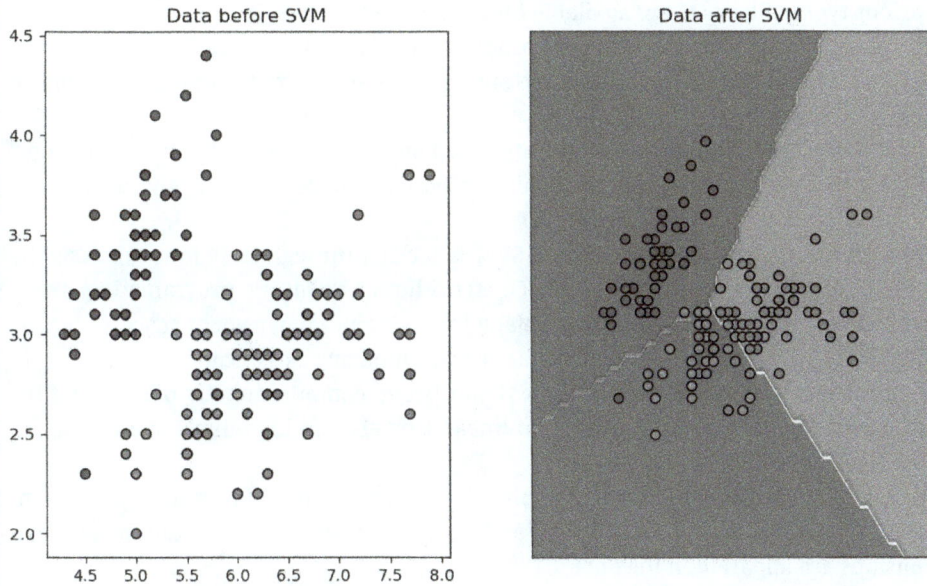

Fig. 5.17: IRIS data before and after SVM.

Fig. 5.17 presents a comparative visualization of the Iris dataset before and after applying the Support Vector Machine (SVM) algorithm.

5.4.2 Kernel SVM

The Kernel Support Vector Machine (SVM) is known for its significant advancement over the conventional SVM algorithm. This allows the SVM to classify data that cannot be separated linearly. This is accomplished by implicitly mapping the data into a feature space with a higher dimensionality.

The primary objective of Kernel SVM is to identify the most optimal hyperplane in the feature space, capable of separating the classes. This is achieved by non-linearly transforming the data using kernel functions.

The technique known as the kernel trick plays a crucial role in allowing the computation of dot products in the feature space of higher dimensionality, all the while avoiding the explicit transformation of the data. Various kernel functions, such as the linear, polynomial, radial basis function (RBF), and sigmoid functions, are employed to gauge the similarity between different data points.

By transforming the data into a space of higher dimensionality, kernel SVM enables the establishment of decision boundaries that are non-linear in nature within the original feature space. This allows for the linear separation of classes.

Various types of kernels are available for Kernel SVM:
– Linear Kernel: Computes the dot product between input features.
– Polynomial Kernel: Computes the similarity based on polynomial expansion of input features.
– RBF Kernel: Computes the similarity based on the Gaussian radial basis function.
– Sigmoid Kernel: Computes the similarity based on hyperbolic tangent function.

The optimization problem for Kernel SVM is tackled through techniques such as the Sequential Minimal Optimization (SMO) algorithm or quadratic programming. These methods ascertain the optimal hyperplane in the higher-dimensional space, either by maximizing the margin between classes or by minimizing classification errors.

In terms of scalability, Kernel SVM can prove computationally demanding for large datasets, particularly when non-linear kernels and high-dimensional feature spaces are involved.

Kernel SVM finds widespread application in diverse machine learning tasks, encompassing classification, regression, and anomaly detection, where non-linear relationships are apparent in the data.

To conclude, Kernel SVM stands as a versatile and effective algorithm for handling non-linear relationships in data, enabling the construction of intricate decision boundaries in the feature space. Its capacity to implicitly transform data using kernel functions renders it suitable for a vast array of machine learning applications.

Below is a Python code that demonstrates the implementation of Kernel SVM.
Steps:

- First generate synthetic data using the make_circles function from scikit-learn, creating circular clusters with some noise.
- Plot the generated data before applying SVM using plt.scatter.
- Train a model with Radial Basis Function (RBF) kernel using Support Vector Classifier (SVC) from the scikit-learn library in order to conduct Kernel Support Vector Machine (SVM) training.
- Following the completion of SVM model training, it is necessary to visually represent the data through a plot and superimpose the decision boundary derived from the SVM model using the contourf method.

```python
import numpy as np
import matplotlib.pyplot as plt
from sklearn.datasets import make_circles
from sklearn.svm import SVC


# Generate synthetic data
X, y = make_circles(n_samples=100, noise=0.1, factor=0.4,
random_state=42)


# Plot data before SVM
plt.figure(figsize=(10, 5))
plt.scatter(X[:, 0], X[:, 1], c=y, cmap='coolwarm', edgecolors='k')
plt.title('Data Before SVM')
plt.xlabel('Feature 1')
plt.ylabel('Feature 2')


# Train Kernel SVM
svm_model = SVC(kernel='rbf', gamma='auto')
svm_model.fit(X, y)


# Plot data after SVM
plt.figure(figsize=(10, 5))
plt.scatter(X[:, 0], X[:, 1], c=y, cmap='coolwarm', edgecolors='k')


# Plot decision boundary
ax = plt.gca()
xlim = ax.get_xlim()
ylim = ax.get_ylim()
```

```
xx, yy = np.meshgrid(np.linspace(xlim[0], xlim[1], 50),
  np.linspace(ylim[0], ylim[1], 50))
Z = svm_model.decision_function(np.c_[xx.ravel(), yy.ravel()])
Z = Z.reshape(xx.shape)
plt.contourf(xx, yy, Z, cmap='coolwarm', alpha=0.3)
plt.title('Data After SVM with Hyperplane')
plt.xlabel('Feature 1')
plt.ylabel('Feature 2')

plt.show()
```

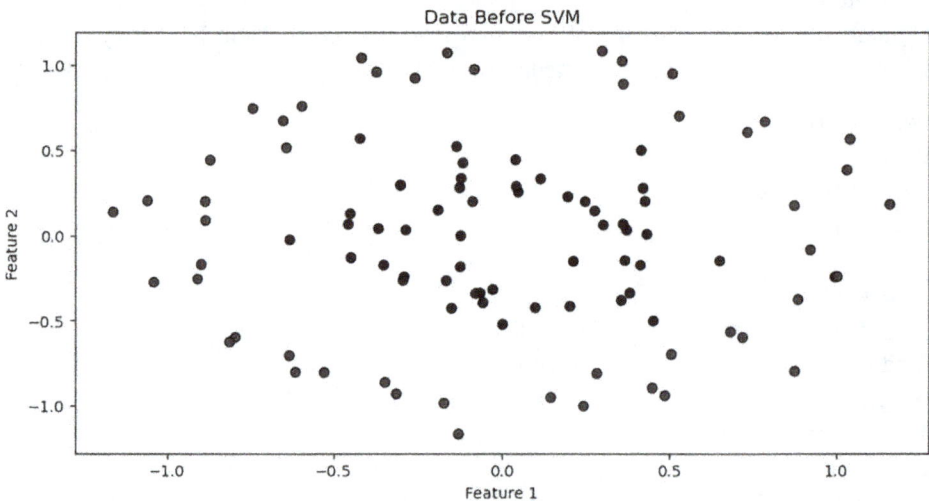

Fig. 5.18: Data before Kernel SVM.

Fig. 5.18 presents a scatter plot visualization of the dataset prior to applying the kernel Support Vector Machine (SVM) algorithm. The plot displays the data points, each representing an individual observation or instance, distributed across two dimensions or features. These features are represented by the x-axis and y-axis, respectively.

However, in this figure, an additional component is superimposed onto the scatter plot: the decision boundary or separating hyperplane learned by the kernel SVM model in the transformed higher-dimensional feature space.

– The first plot displays the synthetic data generated using the **make_circles** function.
– Data points belonging to different classes are represented by different colors.
– The original feature space does not allow for linear separation due to its circular distribution.

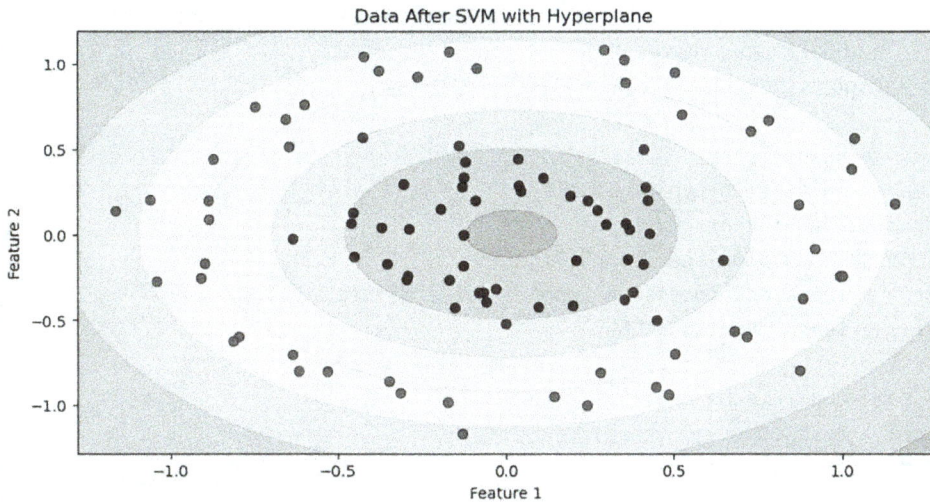

Fig. 5.19: Data after Kernel SVM with hyperplane.

Fig. 5.19 presents a scatter plot visualization of the dataset after applying the kernel Support Vector Machine (SVM) algorithm. Similar to the previous scatter plot (Fig. 5.18), the data points are plotted in the feature space, with the x-axis and y-axis representing two chosen features or dimensions.

- The second plot shows the same synthetic data after applying Kernel SVM.
- The data points are once again depicted using distinct colors to indicate varying classes.
- Furthermore, the SVM model's learned decision boundary is illustrated as a contour plot.
- The decision boundary effectively separates the circular clusters into different regions, demonstrating the non-linear separation capability of Kernel SVM.

Let us now examine an alternative Python code that executes the kernel Support Vector Machine (SVM) algorithm, utilizing the Radial Basis Function (RBF) kernel, on a dataset known as Iris, sourced from the scikit-learn library.

Steps:
- Loads the iris dataset from the scikit-learn library and specifically chooses solely the initial two characteristics.
- Creates a pipeline that first scales the data using StandardScaler and then applies a kernel SVM with an RBF kernel using SVC(kernel = 'rbf').
- Fits the pipeline to the data.
- Creates a mesh grid to plot the data before and after applying SVM.
- Plots the original data (before SVM) in the first subplot.

- Plots the data after applying SVM in the second subplot, including the decision boundary using plt.contourf.
- Displays the plots.

```python
import numpy as np
import matplotlib.pyplot as plt
from sklearn import datasets
from sklearn.pipeline import Pipeline
from sklearn.preprocessing import StandardScaler
from sklearn.svm import SVC

# Load the iris dataset
iris = datasets.load_iris()
X = iris.data[:, :2] # We only take the first two features
y = iris.target

# Create a pipeline to scale the data and apply SVM
clf = Pipeline([
  ('scaler', StandardScaler()),
  ('svc', SVC(kernel='rbf', C=10, gamma=0.1, random_state=42))
])

# Fit the pipeline
clf.fit(X, y)

# Plot the data before applying SVM
x0_min, x0_max = X[:, 0].min() - 1, X[:, 0].max() + 1
x1_min, x1_max = X[:, 1].min() - 1, X[:, 1].max() + 1
xx, yy = np.meshgrid(np.arange(x0_min, x0_max, 0.1),
  np.arange(x1_min, x1_max, 0.1))

plt.figure(figsize=(10, 6))
plt.subplot(1, 2, 1)
plt.title('Data before SVM')
plt.scatter(X[:, 0], X[:, 1], c=y, cmap=plt.cm.Set1, edgecolor='k')

# Plot the data after applying SVM
plt.subplot(1, 2, 2)
plt.title('Data after SVM')
Z = clf.predict(np.c_[xx.ravel(), yy.ravel()])
Z = Z.reshape(xx.shape)
plt.contourf(xx, yy, Z, cmap=plt.cm.Set1, alpha=0.8)
```

```
plt.scatter(X[:, 0], X[:, 1], c=y, cmap=plt.cm.Set1, edgecolor='k')
plt.xlim(xx.min(), xx.max())
plt.ylim(yy.min(), yy.max())
plt.xticks(())
plt.yticks(())

plt.show()
```

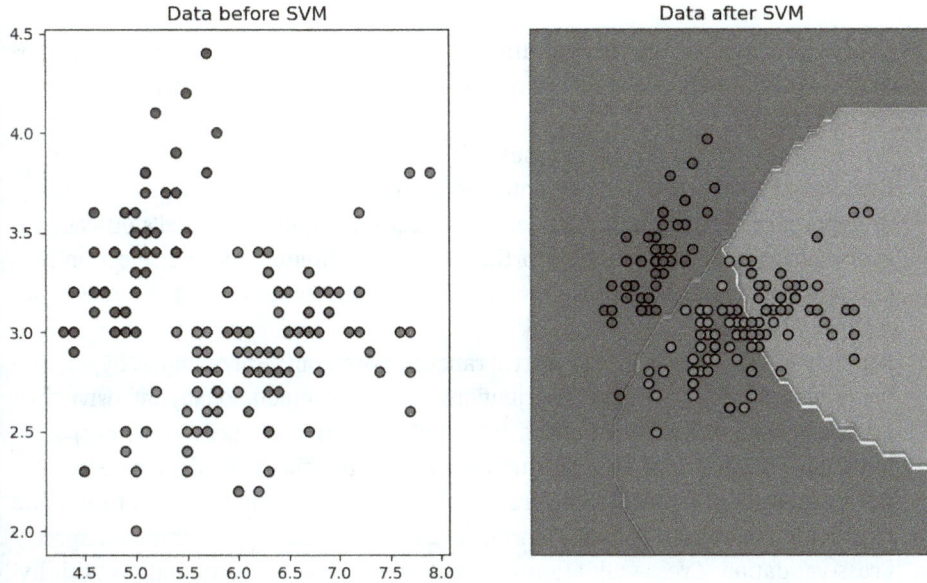

Fig. 5.20: IRIS Data before and after Kernel SVM.

Fig. 5.20 presents a comparative visualization of the Iris dataset before and after applying the Kernel Support Vector Machine (SVM) algorithm. The code displays two subplots. The first subplot shows the original data points before applying SVM, colored according to their class labels. The second subplot shows the data points after applying kernel SVM with an RBF kernel, along with the decision boundary separating the classes.

5.4.3 Hyperparameter Tuning in SVM

The process of hyperparameter tuning in Support Vector Machines (SVM) involves the selection of a set of hyperparameters that will optimize the performance of the SVM model. These hyperparameters are predetermined before the training process and cannot be directly estimated from the data.

SVM encompasses several hyperparameters, including:
- The kernel type refers to the specific type of kernel function utilized, such as linear, polynomial, or radial basis function (RBF).
- The regularization parameter (C) plays a crucial role in balancing the optimization of margin maximization and classification error minimization.
- Additionally, kernel-specific parameters, such as the degree of the polynomial kernel or the gamma parameter for the RBF kernel, further contribute to the customization and fine-tuning of the kernel function.

The choice of hyperparameters significantly impacts the performance of the SVM model. Suboptimal hyperparameters can lead to inadequate generalization, overfitting, or underfitting.

Hyperparameter Tuning Techniques:
- Grid Search: This methodology entails establishing a grid encompassing a range of hyperparameter values, followed by an assessment of the model's efficacy for every conceivable combination of these values. Subsequently, the selection process involves identifying those sets of hyperparameters that yield the most optimal performance.
- Random Search: Similar to grid search, random search randomly samples hyperparameter values from predefined distributions. It is less computationally intensive than grid search and may be more effective for high-dimensional hyperparameter spaces.
- Bayesian Optimization: This technique utilizes probabilistic models to search for the optimal set of hyperparameters. It strikes a balance between exploration and exploitation to efficiently identify promising regions of the hyperparameter space.
- Cross-validation: Cross-validation is frequently utilized in combination with hyperparameter optimization in order to evaluate the overall performance of various hyperparameter configurations. It serves as a valuable tool to mitigate the risk of overfitting to the validation set.

Various assessment measures can be employed to evaluate the performance of different hyperparameter configurations, such as accuracy, precision, recall, F1-score, or area under the ROC curve (AUC).

Hyperparameter optimization can be implemented using libraries such as scikit-learn, which provide in-built functions for grid search (GridSearchCV) and random search (RandomizedSearchCV). The selected evaluation metric, such as accuracy, is maximized over a predefined range of hyperparameters using cross-validation.

Hyperparameter tuning often involves an iterative process, where different combinations of hyperparameters are experimented with, and the model's performance is evaluated until satisfactory results are achieved.

Hyperparameter tuning in SVM involves the process of selecting the most suitable set of hyperparameters to enhance the performance of the model. This step is crucial as it contributes to improving the generalization capability of the SVM models and achieving higher predictive accuracy. To efficiently explore the hyperparameter space and identify the optimal configuration, various techniques such as grid search, random search, and Bayesian optimization can be employed.

The following Python code exemplifies the process of hyperparameter tuning for SVM using grid search. Additionally, it includes plots that depict the performance of the SVM model before and after the hyperparameter tuning stage. For this demonstration, synthetic data will be used, which is generated through the implementation of the make_classification function from the scikit-learn library.

```python
import numpy as np
import matplotlib.pyplot as plt
from sklearn.datasets import make_classification
from sklearn.model_selection import train_test_split, GridSearchCV
from sklearn.svm import SVC

# Step 1: Generate Synthetic Data
X, y = make_classification(n_samples=100, n_features=2, n_classes=2,
 n_clusters_per_class=1, n_redundant=0, random_state=42)

# Step 2: Split Data into Train and Test Sets
X_train, X_test, y_train, y_test = train_test_split(X, y, test_size=0.2,
random_state=42)

# Step 3: Define Parameter Grid for Grid Search
param_grid = {'C': [0.1, 1, 10], 'gamma': [0.1, 1, 10], 'kernel':
['rbf', 'poly', 'sigmoid']}

# Step 4: Perform Grid Search with Cross-Validation
svm_model = GridSearchCV(SVC(), param_grid, cv=5)
svm_model.fit(X_train, y_train)

# Step 5: Plot Data Before SVM
plt.figure(figsize=(10, 5))
plt.scatter(X[:, 0], X[:, 1], c=y, cmap='coolwarm', edgecolors='k')
plt.title('Data Before SVM')
plt.xlabel('Feature 1')
plt.ylabel('Feature 2')

# Step 6: Plot Data After SVM with Hyperplane
plt.figure(figsize=(10, 5))
plt.scatter(X[:, 0], X[:, 1], c=y, cmap='coolwarm', edgecolors='k')
```

```
# Plot decision boundary
ax = plt.gca()
xlim = ax.get_xlim()
ylim = ax.get_ylim()
xx, yy = np.meshgrid(np.linspace(xlim[0], xlim[1], 50),
 np.linspace(ylim[0], ylim[1], 50))
Z = svm_model.predict(np.c_[xx.ravel(), yy.ravel()])
Z = Z.reshape(xx.shape)
plt.contourf(xx, yy, Z, cmap='coolwarm', alpha=0.3)
plt.title('Data After SVM with Hyperplane')
plt.xlabel('Feature 1')
plt.ylabel('Feature 2')

plt.show()

# Step 7: Display Best Hyperparameters
print("Best Hyperparameters:", svm_model.best_params_)

# Step 8: Evaluate Model Performance
accuracy = svm_model.score(X_test, y_test)
print("Accuracy:", accuracy)
```

Steps:
1. Generate artificial data with two characteristics using the make_classification function.
2. Split the data into training and testing sets using the train_test_split function.
3. Define a grid of parameters that specifies the hyperparameters to be tuned and their potential values.
4. Conduct a grid search with cross-validation (cv = 5) to identify the optimal combination of hyperparameters using the GridSearchCV function.
5. Visualize the artificial data prior to applying SVM. Subsequently, plot the data again after implementing SVM.
6. Additionally, depict the decision boundary derived from the SVM model.
7. Present the Best Hyperparameters: We present the hyperparameters chosen as the best through the grid search.
8. Evaluate Model Performance: We assess the model's performance on the test set by employing the accuracy score.

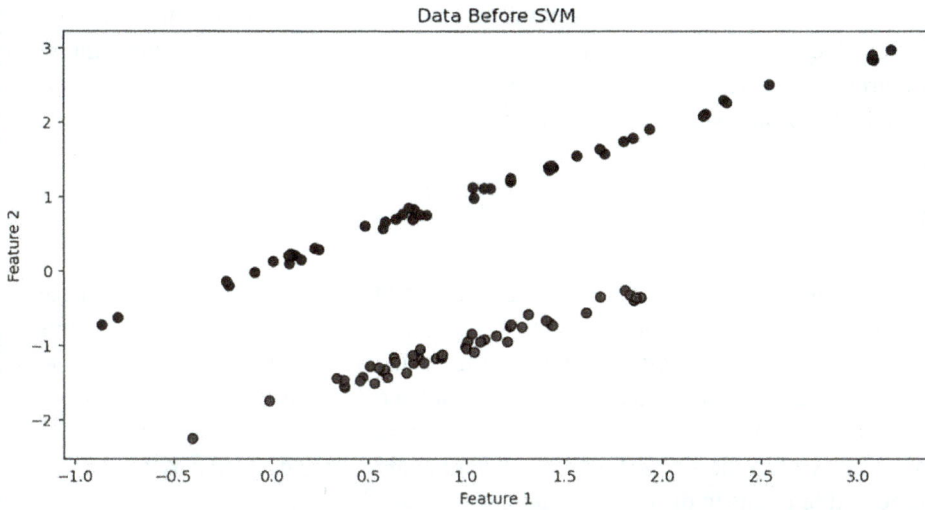

Fig. 5.21: Data before SVM and Hypertuning.

Fig. 5.21 presents a scatter plot visualization of the dataset prior to applying the Support Vector Machine (SVM) algorithm and performing hyperparameter tuning. The plot displays the data points, each representing an individual observation or instance, distributed across two dimensions or features. These features are represented by the x-axis and y-axis, respectively.

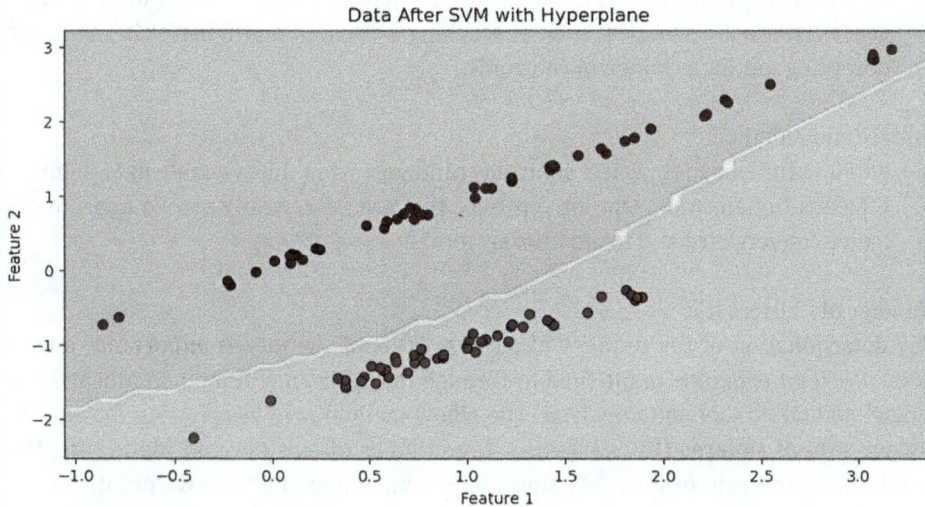

Fig. 5.22: Data after SVM and Hypertuning.

Fig. 5.22 presents a scatter plot visualization of the dataset after applying the Support Vector Machine (SVM) algorithm and performing hyperparameter tuning. Similar to the previous scatter plot (Fig. 5.21), the data points are plotted in the feature space, with the x-axis and y-axis representing two chosen features or dimensions.

5.5 K-Means Clustering

K-Means clustering is a technique in the field of machine learning that is utilized to divide a dataset into distinct clusters. The process involves assigning data points to the nearest cluster centroid and updating the centroids based on the mean of the assigned data points. This article provides a detailed explanation of K-Means clustering:

The main goal of K-Means clustering is to group data points into clusters, where the points within the same cluster display a higher degree of similarity to each other compared to points in different clusters.

Algorithm Steps:
–   Initialization: The first step is to determine the number of clusters (k) and randomly initialize the centroids of these clusters.
–   Assignment Step: Next, we allocate each data point to the nearest centroid by utilizing a distance metric, commonly the Euclidean distance.
–   Update Step: We then proceed to recalculate the centroids of the clusters by computing the mean of all data points assigned to each cluster.
–   Convergence: Finally, we repeat the assignment and update steps until convergence criteria are satisfied, such as reaching a maximum number of iterations or observing minimal change in centroids.

Initialization Methods:
–   Random Initialization: Select centroids randomly from the available data points.
–   K-Means Initialization: Opt for centroids that are strategically spaced apart to enhance convergence and avoid inferior local optima.

Number of Clusters (k):
The determination of the number of clusters (k) is of significant importance and is often based on expertise in the field or through the utilization of methods such as the elbow method or silhouette analysis. The elbow method involves plotting the within-cluster sum of squares (WCSS) against the number of clusters and identifying the point where the rate of decrease slows down, known as the "elbow" point. On the other hand, silhouette analysis entails calculating the silhouette score for different values of k and selecting the value that produces the highest silhouette score.

Scalability:
K-Means is computationally efficient and capable of handling large datasets with numerous features.

Assumptions:
K-Means assumes that clusters are spherical and possess similar sizes. Furthermore, it assumes that the variance of the distribution of each feature is equal across all clusters.

Applications:
K-Means clustering finds extensive application in diverse domains such as customer segmentation, image segmentation, anomaly detection, and recommendation systems.

Limitations:
Depending on the initial centroids, K-Means may converge to local optima. It is highly sensitive to the choice of k and may produce suboptimal outcomes if the true number of clusters is unknown or if clusters exhibit irregular shapes or varying sizes.

To summarize, K-Means clustering is a versatile and widely employed algorithm for partitioning data into clusters. Despite its simplicity and efficiency, careful attention must be given to initialization methods, the choice of k, and the interpretation of results to ensure meaningful clustering.

5.5.1 Clustering Basics

Clustering, as an unsupervised learning method, is employed for the purpose of detecting inherent structures or patterns in a given dataset. The main aim of this technique is to categorize data points into groups on the basis of similarity, eliminating the requirement of labeled instances.

In clustering, data points are partitioned into clusters, with the aim of maximizing intra-cluster similarity and minimizing inter-cluster similarity. Common clustering algorithms include K-Means, Hierarchical Clustering, and DBSCAN, each with its approach to defining clusters.

- K-Means iteratively assigns data points to the nearest cluster centroid and updates centroids until convergence.
- Hierarchical Clustering constructs a hierarchical structure of clusters through the repeated process of merging or dividing according to a linkage criterion.
- DBSCAN identifies clusters based on density, grouping points in high-density regions while considering low-density regions as noise.

Clustering has diverse applications, including customer segmentation, image segmentation, anomaly detection, and recommendation systems. Challenges in clustering include determining the optimal number of clusters, handling high-dimensional data, dealing with noise and outliers, and interpreting cluster assignments effectively. Understanding clustering basics is crucial for selecting the appropriate algorithm, interpreting results, and extracting meaningful insights from unlabeled data.

5.5.2 Selecting the Number of Clusters

Selecting the suitable number of clusters is an essential stage in clustering analysis as it directly impacts the quality of the clustering results. In this section, we present a comprehensive elucidation of the procedure for choosing the number of clusters:

Domain Knowledge:

Previous knowledge or expertise in the field can provide insights into the anticipated quantity of clusters in the dataset. Understanding the fundamental structure of the data and its context can guide the choice of an appropriate quantity of clusters.

Elbow Method: The Elbow Method, a heuristic technique, is utilized to determine the optimal number of clusters by analyzing the within-cluster sum of squares (WCSS) as a function of the number of clusters (k). The WCSS serves as a measure of the proximity among the clusters, and a reduction in WCSS signifies an enhancement in clustering. Generally, plotting the WCSS against the number of clusters yields a curve resembling an "elbow." The point at which the rate of decrease in WCSS slows down is often considered the optimal number of clusters.

Silhouette Analysis: Silhouette analysis is an evaluative technique used to gauge the quality of clustering by measuring the degree of separation between clusters. The silhouette coefficient serves as a quantitative measure of similarity between a data point and its own cluster relative to other clusters. A higher silhouette score is indicative of superior clustering performance. Silhouette scores can be calculated for various values of k, and the optimal number of clusters is determined by selecting the value of k that maximizes the average silhouette score across all data points.

Gap Statistics: Gap statistics are utilized to compare the dispersion present within clusters with that of a reference null distribution in order to ascertain the optimal quantity of clusters. This process entails generating reference datasets that possess random uniform distributions and subsequently calculating the gap statistic for every value of k. The value of k that maximizes the gap statistic signifies the optimal quantity of clusters.

Expert Review and Iteration: It is crucial to review the results obtained from various methods and consider additional factors such as interpretability, practicality, and the specific objectives of the analysis. The selection process may involve iterating through different values of k and evaluating the clustering results until a satisfactory solution is achieved.

Visual Inspection: Visualizing the data and clustering results can provide insights into the underlying structure and assist in selecting the optimal quantity of clusters. Techniques such as scatter plots, heatmaps, or dendrograms can be employed to visualize clusters and assess their quality.

Cross-Validation: Cross-validation methodologies, including k-fold cross-validation, can be employed to assess the robustness and efficacy of clustering algorithms across various k values in terms of stability and generalizability.

In conclusion, the process of selecting the quantity of clusters involves a combination of statistical methods, domain knowledge, and expert judgment. It is an iterative process that requires careful consideration of various factors to determine the optimal quantity of clusters for meaningful and interpretable results.

Consider a numerical illustration in which a dataset of two-dimensional points is available, and the objective is to ascertain the optimal number of clusters through the utilization of the elbow method.

Suppose we have the following dataset:

```
X = [(2, 4), (3, 5), (4, 6), (10, 12), (11, 13), (12, 14), (20, 22),
(21, 23), (22, 24)]
```

We can visualize the dataset and observe its structure:

```
import numpy as np
import matplotlib.pyplot as plt

X = np.array([(2, 4), (3, 5), (4, 6), (10, 12), (11, 13), (12, 14), (20,
22), (21, 23), (22, 24)])

plt.scatter(X[:, 0], X[:, 1])
plt.xlabel('Feature 1')
plt.ylabel('Feature 2')
plt.title('Dataset Visualization')
plt.show()
```

The scatter plot illustrates that the dataset encompasses points that have the potential to develop clusters. Subsequently, we shall employ the K-Means clustering algorithm for various values of k and employ the elbow method to ascertain the most optimal number of clusters.

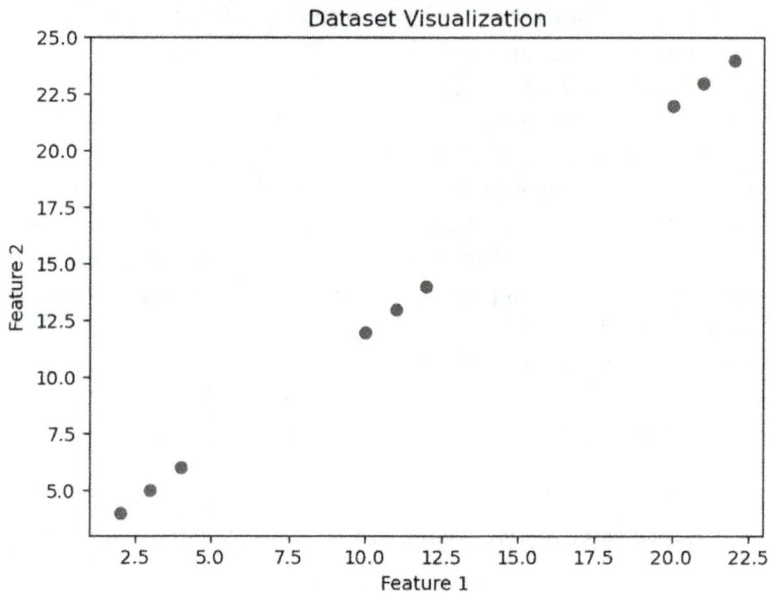

Fig. 5.23: Dataset visualization.

Fig. 5.23 presents scatter plot of data set used for selecting number of clusters.

```
from sklearn.cluster import KMeans
# Define a range of k values
k_values = range(1, 6)
inertia = []

# Apply K-Means for each k value and compute inertia
for k in k_values:
  kmeans = KMeans(n_clusters=k, random_state=42)
  kmeans.fit(X)
  inertia.append(kmeans.inertia_)

# Plot the elbow curve
plt.plot(k_values, inertia, marker='o')
plt.xlabel('Number of Clusters (k)')
plt.ylabel('Within-Cluster Sum of Squares (WCSS)')
plt.title('Elbow Method for Optimal k')
plt.xticks(k_values)
plt.show()
```

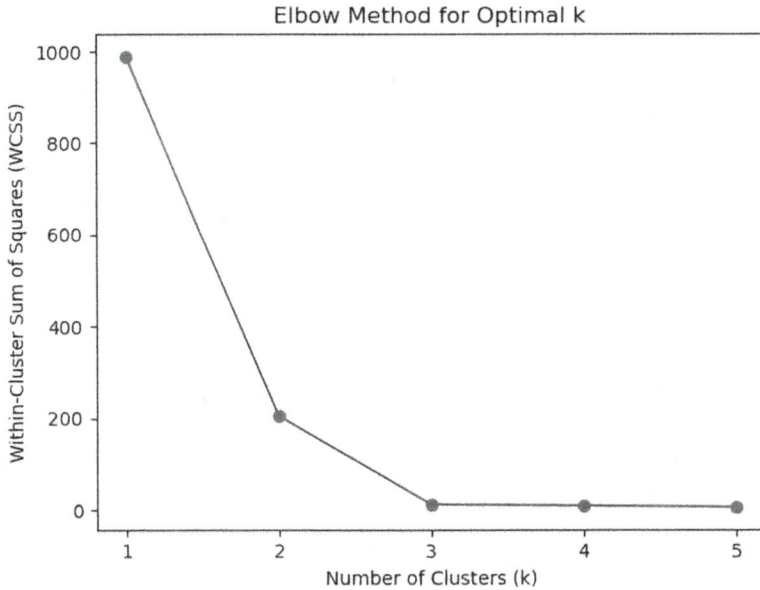

Fig. 5.24: Elbow method for optimal k.

Fig. 5.24 illustrates the application of the Elbow method, a widely used technique for determining the optimal number of clusters (k) in k-means clustering. The figure likely consists of two subplots or panels. The elbow method aids us in discerning the juncture at which the pace of decline in within-cluster sum of squares (WCSS) decelerates. In the present scenario, we discern an elbow juncture at k = 3. Consequently, we can deduce that the most suitable number of clusters for this dataset is 3.

Below is a Python script that facilitates the execution of K-Means clustering methodology, encompassing visual representations both pre and post K-Means, in conjunction with a comprehensive elucidation of every procedural stage and corresponding outcome.

Steps:

1. Create synthetic data by utilizing the make_blobs function from scikit-learn. This particular dataset comprises 300 samples, encompassing 2 features and 4 clusters.
2. Before applying the K-Means clustering technique, visualize the generated data.
3. Commence by initializing and fitting the K-Means clustering algorithm to the data. In order to ensure reproducibility, we set the random state and specify the number of clusters as 4.
4. Upon completion of fitting the K-Means model, we obtain the cluster centers as well as the labels assigned to each data point.
5. Proceed to plot the data following K-Means clustering, where each data point is color-coded based on its assigned cluster, and the cluster centers are denoted by red crosses.

```python
import numpy as np
import matplotlib.pyplot as plt
from sklearn.datasets import make_blobs
from sklearn.cluster import KMeans

# Step 1: Generate Synthetic Data
X, _ = make_blobs(n_samples=300, centers=4, cluster_std=0.60,
random_state=0)

# Step 2: Plot Data Before K-Means
plt.figure(figsize=(10, 5))
plt.scatter(X[:, 0], X[:, 1], s=50)
plt.title('Data Before K-Means Clustering')
plt.xlabel('Feature 1')
plt.ylabel('Feature 2')

# Step 3: Apply K-Means Clustering
kmeans = KMeans(n_clusters=4, random_state=0)
kmeans.fit(X)

# Step 4: Get Cluster Centers and Labels
cluster_centers = kmeans.cluster_centers_
cluster_labels = kmeans.labels_

# Step 5: Plot Data After K-Means
plt.figure(figsize=(10, 5))
plt.scatter(X[:, 0], X[:, 1], c=cluster_labels, s=50, cmap='viridis')
plt.scatter(cluster_centers[:, 0], cluster_centers[:, 1], c='red',
s=200, alpha=0.75)
plt.title('Data After K-Means Clustering')
plt.xlabel('Feature 1')
plt.ylabel('Feature 2')
plt.show()
```

Data Before K-Means Clustering

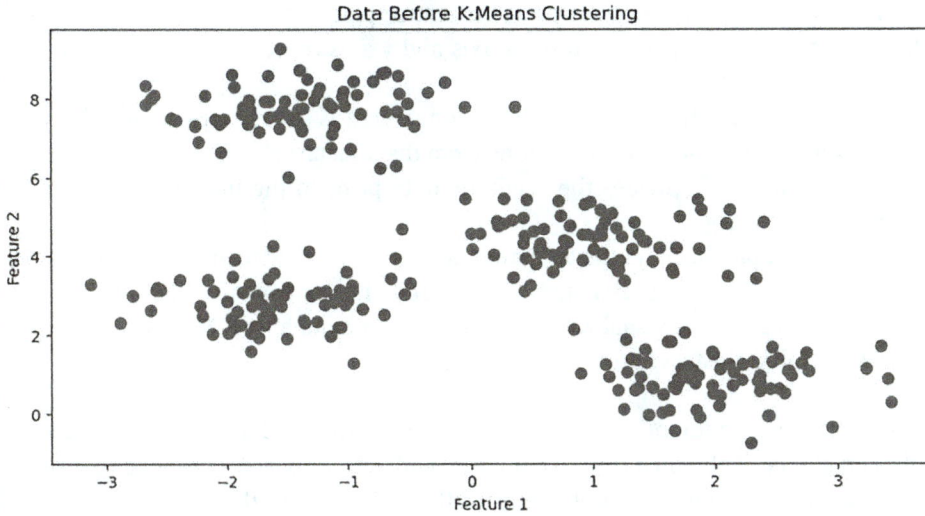

Fig. 5.25: Data before K-Means clustering.

Fig. 5.25 presents a scatter plot visualization of the dataset prior to applying the k-means clustering algorithm. The plot displays the data points, each representing an individual observation or instance, distributed across two dimensions or features. These features are represented by the x-axis and y-axis, respectively.

Data After K-Means Clustering

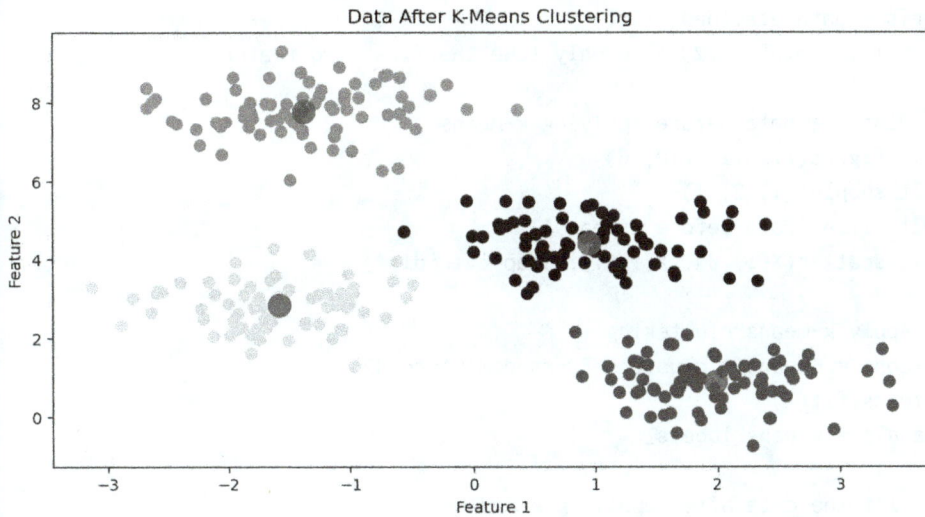

Fig. 5.26: Data after K-Means clustering.

Fig. 5.26 algorithm. Similar to the previous scatter plot (Fig. 5.25), the data points are plotted in the feature space, with the x-axis and y-axis representing two chosen features or dimensions.

However, in this figure, an additional component is superimposed onto the scatter plot: the cluster assignments resulting from the k-means algorithm.

- The initial plot illustrates the synthetic data prior to the implementation of K-Means clustering.
- The second plot displays the data after clustering with K-Means. Each point is colored according to its assigned cluster, and the centroids of the clusters are marked in red. This visualization helps us understand how K-Means has grouped the data into clusters based on similarity.

Let us examine an additional Python script that performs the k-means clustering algorithm on a dataset obtained from scikit-learn, while simultaneously producing graphical depictions of the data before and after the utilization of the k-means clustering algorithm.

```python
import numpy as np
import matplotlib.pyplot as plt
from sklearn import datasets
from sklearn.cluster import KMeans

# Load the iris dataset
iris = datasets.load_iris()
X = iris.data[:, :2] # We only take the first two features

# Plot the data before applying k-means
plt.figure(figsize=(10, 6))
plt.subplot(1, 2, 1)
plt.title('Data before K-Means')
plt.scatter(X[:, 0], X[:, 1], cmap='viridis')

# Apply k-means clustering
kmeans = KMeans(n_clusters=3, random_state=42)
kmeans.fit(X)
labels = kmeans.labels_

# Plot the data after applying k-means
plt.subplot(1, 2, 2)
plt.title('Data after K-Means')
plt.scatter(X[:, 0], X[:, 1], c=labels, cmap='viridis')
```

```
# Plot the cluster centers
centers = kmeans.cluster_centers_
plt.scatter(centers[:, 0], centers[:, 1], c='red', s=100, alpha=0.5)

plt.show()
```

Steps:

1. Importing the required libraries is essential for conducting various operations. The libraries that need to be imported include numpy for performing numerical operations, matplotlib.pyplot for visualization purposes, and datasets and cluster from sklearn for working with datasets and clustering algorithms respectively.
2. Load the iris dataset from the scikit-learn library and opt to exclusively utilize the initial two attributes for the objective of visualization.
3. Create a figure with two subplots using plt.figure and plt.subplot.
4. In the first subplot, plot the original data points using plt.scatter with the cmap = 'viridis' colormap (you can choose any colormap you prefer).
5. Instantiate a KMeans instance with n_clusters = 3 (as the iris dataset possesses 3 categories) and specify a random_state to ensure reproducibility.
6. Train the KMeans model on the dataset by invoking the fit method on the kmeans object.
7. Obtain the cluster labels for every individual data point by utilizing the kmeans labels_ attribute.
8. In the second subplot, plot the data points using plt.scatter, but this time color them according to their cluster labels using c = labels and the cmap = 'viridis' colormap.
9. Get the coordinates of the cluster centers using kmeans.cluster_centers_.
10. Plot the cluster centers using plt.scatter with c = 'red' (red color), s = 100 (larger size), and alpha = 0.5 (semi-transparent).
11. Display the plots using plt.show().

- The first subplot shows the original data points before applying k-means clustering, colored with a continuous colormap (viridis in this case).
- The second subplot shows the data points after applying k-means clustering, where each point is colored according to its assigned cluster. Additionally, the cluster centers are plotted as larger red dots.

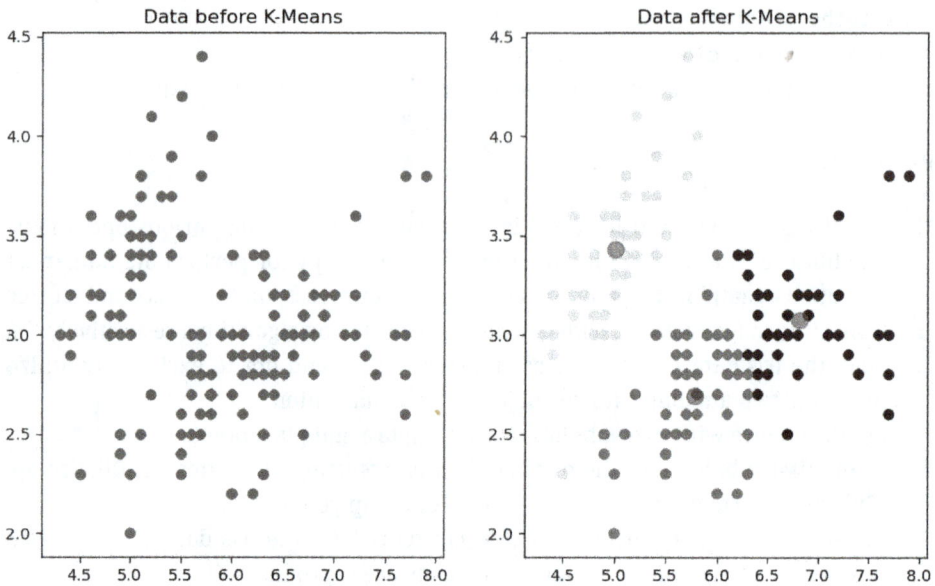

Fig. 5.27: IRIS Data before and after K-Means Clustering.

Fig. 5.27 presents a visual comparison of the IRIS dataset before and after applying the k-means clustering algorithm.

5.6 Principal Component Analysis

PCA, commonly known as Principal Component Analysis, is a highly prevalent method employed for the purpose of reducing dimensionality in various domains such as machine learning, data mining, and signal processing. It is an empirical procedure that converts a dataset with a high number of dimensions into a subspace with fewer dimensions, while retaining a significant portion of the original data's variability. Especially when confronted with datasets with a high number of dimensions, PCA proves to be highly beneficial as it aids in simplifying computational complexity, eliminating noise, and facilitating data visualization within a lower-dimensional space.

Mathematical Concepts Employed in PCA

Covariance matrix: PCA commences by standardizing the data in order to achieve a mean of zero and a standard deviation of one for each feature. Subsequently, the covariance matrix is calculated to capture the associations between pairs of features.

The computation of the covariance between two features xi and xj is performed as follows:

$$cov(x_i, y_i) = \frac{1}{n-1} \sum_{k=1}^{n}(x_{ki} - \bar{x}_i)\,(x_{kj} - \bar{x}_j)$$

where n represents the total number of samples, xki and xkj denote the values of the ith and jth features of the kth sample, and μi and μj correspond to the means of features xi and xj, respectively.

Eigendecomposition

PCA employs eigendecomposition on the covariance matrix to ascertain the principal components. The eigenvectors of said matrix encapsulate the directions of maximal variance, commonly identified as the principal components. Moreover, the corresponding eigenvalues offer vital information regarding the proportion of variance elucidated by each distinct component.

Covariance Matrix × Eigenvector = Eigenvalue × Eigenvector

Moreover, the eigenvectors are mutually orthogonal and collectively establish a fresh foundation for the data.

Selecting Principal Components

- The principal components are ranked in a descending order based on the eigenvalues, with the first component capturing the highest amount of variance, followed by the second component capturing the second highest amount of variance, and so on.
- It is a widely accepted convention to choose a particular percentage of the total variance, such as 90%, as a threshold for determining the number of principal components to retain.

Projection

Finally, the data is projected onto the designated principal components in order to acquire the representation with reduced dimensions. This projection is accomplished by performing the multiplication of the original data matrix with the matrix consisting of the chosen eigenvectors (principal components).

Mathematical Representation

- Let X denote the standardized data matrix, which possesses $n \times m$ dimensions, with n representing the number of samples and m representing the number of features.
- PCA identifies k principal components, whereby k is less than or equal to m, which are characterized by the eigenvectors V originating from the covariance matrix of X. The initial k principal components are selected with respect to their associated eigenvalues.
- The reduced-dimensional representation Y of the data is obtained by projecting X onto the selected principal components:

$$Y = X \cdot Vk$$

where Vk is the matrix of the first k eigenvectors.

PCA is an influential instrument utilized for the pre-processing of data, visualization, and the extraction of features. Its extensive employment can be witnessed across diverse domains, such as machine learning, signal processing, and image analysis. Through its mathematical underpinnings, PCA affords valuable perspectives into the inherent structure of data with high dimensions, consequently facilitating the computation of reduced-dimensional representations in an efficient manner.

PCA finds multiple applications, such as the visual representation of data, reduction of noise, extraction of features, and compression of data. It is extensively utilized as a preliminary step in machine learning pipelines, particularly when handling high-dimensional data, for example, images, signals, or textual data.

Below are the steps to perform PCA:

1. **Data preprocessing**:
   - Standardization of the data is achieved by subtracting the mean value from each feature and subsequently dividing by the standard deviation. This crucial step guarantees that all features are uniformly scaled and possess equal significance in the subsequent analysis.
2. **Calculate the covariance matrix:**
   - Compute the covariance matrix of the standardized data, whereby the covariance matrix denotes the measure of the variance and covariance among the features.
3. **Calculate eigenvectors and eigenvalues:**
   - Compute the eigenvectors and associated eigenvalues of the covariance matrix.
   - The eigenvectors depict the principal components, while the eigenvalues indicate the extent to which each principal component captures the variance.

4. **Sort eigenvectors by eigenvalues**:
   - Sort the eigenvectors in descending order based on their corresponding eigenvalues.
   - The principal component that captures the maximum variance in the data is the eigenvector associated with the highest eigenvalue.
5. **Select principal components**:
   - Decide the number of principal components to retain by considering the extent of variance you wish to preserve or the intended reduction in dimensionality.
   - One common approach is to choose the top k principal components that capture a certain percentage (e.g., 95%) of the total variance in the data.
6. **Project data onto principal components**:
   - Project the original data onto the selected principal components by multiplying the original data with the chosen eigenvectors.
   - This procedure converts the data from the initial feature space to the subsequent subspace specified by the principal components.
7. **Dimensionality reduction**:
   - The transformed data now exists in the lower-dimensional subspace defined by the selected principal components.
   - If one were to select k principal components, the dimensionality of the data would be diminished from the initial number of features to k dimensions.
8. **Optional: reconstruction or visualization**:
   - Optionally, it is possible to restore the initial data from the diminished representation by performing the multiplication of the transformed data with the transposed chosen eigenvectors.
   - Visualize the transformed data in the lower-dimensional subspace for exploration or interpretation purposes.

It is important to highlight that PCA is a type of unsupervised technique, indicating that it does not take into account any class labels or target variables. It solely concentrates on capturing the maximum variance in the data, which may or may not be significant for a specific supervised learning task.

5.6.1 Dimensionality Reduction

Dimensionality reduction is a crucial technique in the realm of machine learning and data analysis, especially when dealing with data that contains a large number of dimensions. The main objective of dimensionality reduction is to reduce the number of features or dimensions in a dataset while retaining as much relevant information as possible.

The ultimate goal of dimensionality reduction is to transform data with a high number of dimensions into a space with fewer dimensions, making it more manageable and computationally efficient. By doing so, it helps overcome the challenges posed by the "curse of dimensionality," which occurs when the complexity of the data increases exponentially with the number of dimensions. This, in turn, leads to issues like overfitting, increased computational costs, and data sparsity.

There are two primary approaches to dimensionality reduction: feature selection and feature extraction. Feature selection involves choosing a subset of the original features, while feature extraction involves creating new features by combining or transforming the original ones.

PCA is a commonly used technique for feature extraction. It identifies the directions of maximum variance in the data and projects the data onto a lower-dimensional subspace defined by these directions, known as principal components.

Other notable techniques for dimensionality reduction include Linear Discriminant Analysis (LDA), which aims to maximize the separability between classes, and t-Distributed Stochastic Neighbor Embedding (t-SNE), a non-linear technique suitable for visualizing high-dimensional data in a lower-dimensional space.

Dimensionality reduction has the potential to improve the performance of machine learning models by eliminating irrelevant or redundant features, reducing noise, and enhancing the interpretability of the data. However, it is important to strike a balance between reducing dimensions and preserving essential information for the specific task at hand. Dimensionality reduction techniques find extensive use in diverse domains such as image and signal processing, text mining, bioinformatics, and recommendation systems, among others. They play a fundamental role in data preprocessing, visualization, and feature engineering pipelines within the context of machine learning workflows.

Feature selection and feature extraction are two frequently utilized methodologies within the domains of machine learning and data analysis, which aim to reduce the dimensionality of datasets and amplify the efficacy of models. Herein lies an extensive elucidation of each approach:

Feature Selection

Feature selection involves the careful selection of a subset of the original features from the dataset, with the exclusion of any features that are deemed irrelevant or redundant. The primary objective is to ameliorate model performance by curbing overfitting, diminishing computational complexity, and augmenting interpretability. The techniques employed for feature selection can be classified into three distinct types:

– Filter Methods: Filter methods assess the relevance of features independently of the chosen learning algorithm. Standard techniques encompass correlation analysis, information gain, and statistical tests such as ANOVA and chi-square.
– Wrapper Methods: Wrapper methods appraise feature subsets by iteratively training the model using different combinations of features and evaluating their performance. Techniques such as forward selection, backward elimination, and recursive feature elimination (RFE) correspond to this category.

– Embedded Methods: Embedded methods incorporate feature selection into the process of training the model. Illustrations of embedded feature selection techniques encompass algorithms such as LASSO (Least Absolute Shrinkage and Selection Operator) and decision trees that make use of feature importance scores.

Advantages: Preserves the explicability of features, diminishes computational intricacy, and enhances model performance by eliminating irrelevant features.

Disadvantages: Might neglect interactions among features and struggle to encompass intricate relationships.

Feature Extraction

Feature extraction is the process of converting the initial features into a fresh collection of features through the act of combining or altering them, all the while preserving the crucial information. The primary objective is to decrease the dimensionality of the dataset while maintaining the utmost amount of pertinent information possible. There are two main classifications for feature extraction methods: linear and non-linear techniques:

– Linear Methods: Linear techniques, including PCA and Linear Discriminant Analysis (LDA), generate fresh characteristics by forming linear combinations of the initial characteristics. PCA detects the orientations that exhibit the highest variance, whereas LDA concentrates on enhancing the distinction between classes.
– Non-linear Methods: Non-linear techniques, such as t-distributed Stochastic Neighbor Embedding (t-SNE) and Isomap, produce novel characteristics by capturing non-linear associations within the data. These approaches prove to be especially advantageous when it comes to representing high-dimensional data in lower-dimensional spaces while simultaneously conserving local structures.

Advantages: Efficiently diminishes dimensionality, captures fundamental structures in the data, and enriches visualization and explicability.

Disadvantages: Sacrifices explicability as the novel features may not directly correspond to the original features, and non-linear approaches may demand significant computational resources.

5.6.2 Eigenvectors and Eigenvalues

Eigenvectors and eigenvalues represent pivotal principles within the realm of linear algebra, possessing extensive utility across diverse domains, encompassing machine learning and data analysis.

Eigenvectors

- Eigenvectors are vectors of particular significance that pertain to linear transformations, serving to denote the directions in which the transformation solely imparts elongation or compression upon the vector, while leaving its orientation unaltered.
- From a mathematical standpoint, a vector v is classified as an eigenvector of a square matrix A if it satisfies the equation:

$$A \cdot v = \lambda \cdot v$$

where λ denotes a scalar referred to as the eigenvalue corresponding to v.
- To maintain consistency, eigenvectors are typically adjusted to possess a unit length, thereby adhering to the condition that $\| v \| = 1$.

Eigenvalues

- Eigenvalues are the scalars that represent the factor by which the corresponding eigenvector is stretched or compressed during a linear transformation.
- Each eigenvector of a matrix A corresponds to a unique eigenvalue.
- Eigenvalues have a significant impact on the determination of the characteristics of linear transformations, such as the process of diagonalizing matrices, analyzing stability, and finding solutions to differential equations.

The computation of eigenvectors and eigenvalues can be accomplished by solving the characteristic equation $\det(A - \lambda I) = 0$, where I represents the identity matrix.

Upon obtaining the eigenvalues, one can derive the corresponding eigenvectors by solving the equation $(A - \lambda I)v = 0$ for each individual eigenvalue.

Applications

- Image and signal processing: Eigenvectors are used for image compression and noise reduction.
- Structural analysis: Eigenvalues determine the stability and natural frequencies of structures.
- Machine learning: Eigenvectors and eigenvalues are used in dimensionality reduction, feature extraction, and clustering algorithms.

The subsequent Python code demonstrates the implementation of PCA for dimensionality reduction.

```python
import numpy as np

# Original data
X = np.array([[2.5, 2.4, 0.5, 0.7],
 [2.1, 1.9, 1.8, 1.3],
 [1.6, 1.6, 1.5, 1.1],
 [1.0, 0.9, 1.0, 0.7],
 [0.5, 0.6, 0.7, 0.5]])

# Step 1: Calculate the mean of each feature (dimension)
mean = np.mean(X, axis=0)
print("Mean:", mean)

# Step 2: Subtract the mean from each observation to center the data
X_centered = X - mean

# Step 3: Calculate the covariance matrix
covariance_matrix = np.cov(X_centered.T)
print("\nCovariance Matrix:")
print(covariance_matrix)

# Step 4: Calculate the eigenvalues and eigenvectors of the covariance
matrix
eigenvalues, eigenvectors = np.linalg.eig(covariance_matrix)
print("\nEigenvalues:", eigenvalues)

# Step 5: Sort the eigenvectors in descending order of their
corresponding eigenvalues
sorted_indices = np.argsort(eigenvalues)[::-1]
sorted_eigenvectors = eigenvectors[:, sorted_indices]
sorted_eigenvalues = eigenvalues[sorted_indices]

print("\nSorted Eigenvectors:")
for i, eigenvector in enumerate(sorted_eigenvectors.T):
 print(f"PC{i+1}: {eigenvector}")

# Step 6: Project the centered data onto the new subspace defined by the
principal components
X_projected = X_centered @ sorted_eigenvectors
print("\nProjected Data:")
print(X_projected)
```

This code follows the steps you outlined for dimensionality reduction using PCA. Here's a breakdown of what the code does:

1. The original data X is defined as a NumPy array.
2. The mean of each feature is calculated and subtracted from the data to center it (Steps 1 and 2).
3. The covariance matrix is calculated using np.cov (Step 3).
4. The eigenvalues and eigenvectors of the covariance matrix are calculated through the utilization of the np.linalg.eig function, as outlined in Step 4.
5. The eigenvectors are sorted in descending order based on their corresponding eigenvalues (Step 5).
6. The centered data X_centered is projected onto the new subspace defined by the sorted eigenvectors using matrix multiplication (Step 6).

```
Mean: [1.54 1.48 1.1  0.86]

Covariance Matrix:
[[0.653  0.5885 0.0775 0.142 ]
 [0.5885 0.537  0.05   0.119 ]
 [0.0775 0.05   0.295  0.165 ]
 [0.142  0.119  0.165  0.108 ]]

Eigenvalues: [1.23214566e+00 3.57843561e-01 3.01078173e-03 4.32153957e-18]

Sorted Eigenvectors:
PC1: [-0.7246738  -0.65326858 -0.12634088 -0.17923735]
PC2: [-0.11283679 -0.16433601  0.87715334  0.43687934]
PC3: [-0.67701497  0.70717358 -0.05268396  0.19692806]
PC4: [ 0.06137164 -0.21480074 -0.46028731  0.85920298]

Projected Data:
[[-1.19221144e+00 -8.55705150e-01  7.67212816e-04  1.11022302e-16]
 [-8.47493183e-01  6.74024515e-01 -3.23459052e-02  2.22044605e-16]
 [-2.15425975e-01  4.29221847e-01  7.04290811e-02 -2.49800181e-16]
 [ 8.11531693e-01 -1.36927178e-03 -7.08126875e-02  3.60822483e-16]
 [ 1.44359890e+00 -2.46171940e-01  3.19622988e-02 -5.55111512e-17]]
```

Fig. 5.28: Principal component analysis (PCA) for dimensionality reduction.

Fig. 5.28 displays the results of Principal Component Analysis (PCA), a technique used for dimensionality reduction, showcasing the transformed dataset where data points are represented in a lower-dimensional space while preserving the most significant variance across the original features.

The code prints out the mean, covariance matrix, eigenvalues, sorted eigenvectors (labeled as PC1, PC2, etc.), and the projected data X_projected.

Below is an exemplification of a Python code that showcases the implementation of PCA on an IRIS dataset. Additionally, it demonstrates the visualization of the outcomes both pre- and post-PCA.

```python
import numpy as np
import matplotlib.pyplot as plt
from sklearn.datasets import load_iris
from sklearn.preprocessing import StandardScaler
from sklearn.decomposition import PCA

# Load the Iris dataset
iris = load_iris()
X = iris.data
y = iris.target

# Standardize the features
scaler = StandardScaler()
X_scaled = scaler.fit_transform(X)

# Instantiate PCA and fit the data
pca = PCA(n_components=2)
X_pca = pca.fit_transform(X_scaled)

# Plot original data
plt.figure(figsize=(10, 5))
plt.subplot(1, 2, 1)
plt.scatter(X[:, 0], X[:, 1], c=y, cmap='viridis', edgecolor='k')
plt.title('Original Data')
plt.xlabel('Feature 1')
plt.ylabel('Feature 2')
plt.colorbar()

# Plot data after PCA
plt.subplot(1, 2, 2)
plt.scatter(X_pca[:, 0], X_pca[:, 1], c=y, cmap='viridis',
edgecolor='k')
plt.title('Data After PCA')
plt.xlabel('Principal Component 1')
plt.ylabel('Principal Component 2')
plt.colorbar()

plt.tight_layout()
plt.show()
```

Steps:

1. Importing the required libraries includes numpy, matplotlib.pyplot, load_iris from sklearn datasets, StandardScaler from sklearn preprocessing, and PCA from sklearn.decomposition.
2. Load the Iris dataset.
3. Standardize the features utilizing the StandardScaler.
4. Instantiate **PCA** with the desired number of components (in this case, 2) and fit it to the standardized data.
5. Transform the initial dataset into a lower-dimensional space through the utilization of the properly adjusted PCA model.
6. Visualize the initial dataset as well as the dataset post-PCA by means of the matplotlib.pyplot.scatter function.
7. Set appropriate titles, labels, and colorbars for better visualization.
8. Display the plots using **plt.show()**.

This code generates two subplots: one showing the original data and another showing the data after PCA. The data points colored based on the target labels (species) to visualize any patterns or clusters before and after PCA.

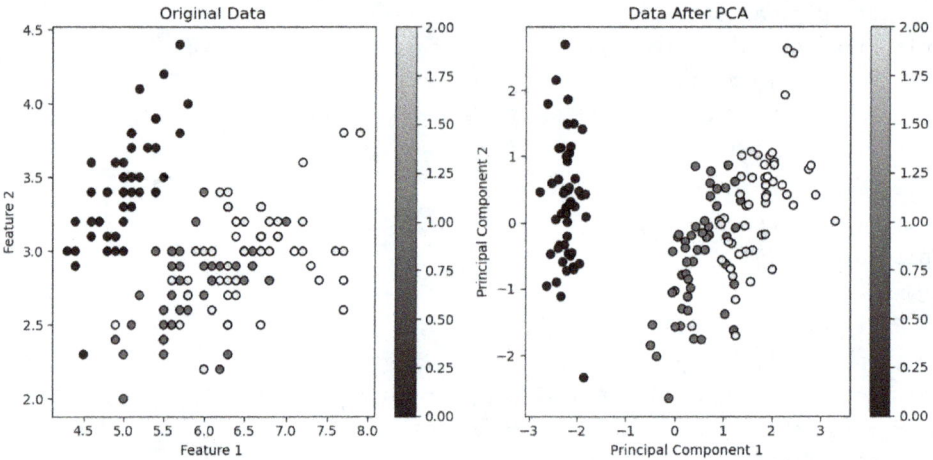

Fig. 5.29: Data before and after principal component analysis.

Fig. 5.29 illustrates the IRIS dataset both before and after Principal Component Analysis (PCA) transformation. The plot likely demonstrates how PCA reduces the dimensionality of the data while retaining the most important information, aiding in visualizing the dataset's structure and potential clustering patterns.

5.7 Naive Bayes

Naive Bayes, a classification algorithm that leverages Bayes' theorem and assumes independence between features, is both simple and effective. Despite its oversimplified assumptions, it often performs exceptionally well in practical scenarios, especially in the realm of text classification problems.

The core idea of Naive Bayes is to calculate the probability of each class based on the feature values of the instance being classified. Subsequently, predictions are made by selecting the class with the highest probability.

Naive Bayes, a powerful probabilistic classifier, relies on Bayes' theorem and assumes feature independence in a straightforward manner.

Bayes' Theorem

Naive Bayes is grounded on Bayes' theorem, an articulated principle that outlines the probability of a hypothesis when provided with the evidence:

$$P(class|data) = (P(data|class)*P(class))/P(data)$$

Where:
- $P(class|data)$ represents the likelihood of the class in relation to the given data, which is determined by the feature values.
- $P(data|class)$ signifies the conditional probability of the data based on the class.
- $P(class)$ denotes the prior probability associated with the class.
- $P(data)$ serves as the evidence and functions as a constant that scales the probabilities.

The "naive" assumption is derived from the notion that Naive Bayes assumes conditional independence among all features, given the class label. This simplification enables the calculation of $P(data|class)$ to be performed in the subsequent manner:

Mathematically, this is expressed as:

$$P(data|class) = P(feature1|class) * P(feature2|class) *...* P(featureN|class)$$

This assumption, although seldom valid in practical scenarios, renders the computations significantly more manageable and enables the application of Naive Bayes to problems with a high number of dimensions.

To conduct training for a Naive Bayes classifier, it is imperative to compute the prior probabilities $P(class)$ and the likelihood probabilities $P(feature|class)$ based on the available training data. In the case of numerical features, it is often assumed that they follow a Gaussian distribution, and consequently, the mean and variance for each class are estimated. As for categorical features, the frequency of each feature value for each class can be straightforwardly calculated.

During the prediction phase, the posterior probability P(class|data) is computed for each class, utilizing the prior and likelihood probabilities estimated during the training phase. The class that possesses the greatest posterior probability is subsequently chosen as the anticipated class for the given example.

Despite its straightforwardness, Naive Bayes frequently serves as a reliable benchmark classifier and can exhibit remarkable effectiveness, particularly when the assumption of feature independence is not flagrantly violated. Moreover, it is highly efficient for both training and prediction, rendering it well suited for real-time applications and large datasets.

There are different variants of Naive Bayes classifiers, including:

- Gaussian Naive Bayes: Assumes that continuous features adhere to a Gaussian (normal) distribution.
- Multinomial Naive Bayes: Suitable for discrete attributes, such as word frequencies in the task of categorizing text.
- Bernoulli Naive Bayes: Assumes binary features, often used for document classification tasks.

Let's consider a simple example of using Naive Bayes for email spam classification.

We consider a dataset consisting of emails, each classified as either "spam" or "not spam" (ham). Our objective is to construct a Naive Bayes classifier that can forecast whether a new email is spam or not by analyzing the presence or absence of specific words within the email's body.

Let's say we have the following training data:

```
Email 1 (ham): "You have won a free vacation!"
Email 2 (spam): "Make money fast with our secret system!"
Email 3 (ham): "Meeting at 3 pm to discuss project."
Email 4 (spam): "Earn $$$$ from home today!"
```

We can extract the unique words (features) from the dataset:

```
['you', 'have', 'won', 'free', 'vacation', 'make', 'money', 'fast',
'secret', 'system', 'meeting', 'pm', 'discuss', 'project', 'earn',
'from', 'home', 'today']
```

In order to educate the Naive Bayes classifier, it is necessary to compute the prior probabilities P(spam) and P(ham), as well as the likelihood probabilities P(word|spam) and P(word|ham) for each individual word.

Given that an equivalent amount of spam and ham emails are present in the training data, the prior probabilities would be as follows:

```
P(spam) = P(ham) = 0.5
```

For the likelihood probabilities, we can calculate the frequency of each word in the spam and ham emails. For example:

```
P(won|ham) = 1/2 (won appears once in 2 ham emails)
P(won|spam) = 0 (won does not appear in any spam email)
P(make|spam) = 1/2 (make appears once in 2 spam emails)
P(make|ham) = 0 (make does not appear in any ham email)
```

Once all the requisite probabilities have been estimated from the training data, a new email can be classified by computing the posterior probability P(spam|email) and P (ham|email) utilizing Bayes' theorem and the assumption of naive independence. The prediction is made by selecting the class with the highest posterior probability.

For example, let's say we have a new email with the text: "Get rich quickly with our system!" To classify this email, we would calculate P(spam|email) and P(ham| email) using the estimated probabilities from the training phase, and choose the class with the higher probability.

This particular example demonstrates the fundamental operations of Naive Bayes in the context of text classification. In practical applications, more sophisticated techniques such as feature selection, smoothing, and handling of non-occurring events are frequently employed to enhance the performance of Naive Bayes classifiers.

Let's consider a numerical example of using Naive Bayes for classification.

Suppose we possess a dataset comprising weather observations, wherein each instance is categorized as either "Play" or "Don't Play" contingent upon four characteristics: Outlook (Sunny, Overcast, Rain), Temperature (Hot, Mild, Cool), Humidity (High, Normal), and Wind (Strong, Weak).

Here's the training dataset:

Outlook	Temperature	Humidity	Wind	Play?
Sunny	Hot	High	Weak	No
Sunny	Hot	High	Strong	No
Overcast	Hot	High	Weak	Yes
Rain	Mild	High	Weak	Yes
Rain	Cool	Normal	Weak	Yes
Rain	Cool	Normal	Strong	No
Overcast	Cool	Normal	Strong	Yes
Sunny	Mild	High	Weak	No
Sunny	Cool	Normal	Weak	Yes
Rain	Mild	Normal	Weak	Yes
Sunny	Mild	Normal	Strong	Yes
Overcast	Mild	High	Strong	Yes
Overcast	Hot	Normal	Weak	Yes
Rain	Mild	High	Strong	No

We can calculate the prior probabilities from the training data:
- P(Play) = 9/14 = 0.643
- P(Don't Play) = 5/14 = 0.357

Next, we calculate the likelihood probabilities for each feature value given the class:

For example, let's calculate P(Outlook = Sunny | Play) and P(Outlook = Sunny | Don't Play):
- P(Outlook = Sunny | Play) = 2/9 = 0.222 (2 out of 9 instances with Play have Outlook = Sunny)
- P(Outlook = Sunny | Don't Play) = 3/5 = 0.6 (3 out of 5 instances with Don't Play have Outlook = Sunny)

We can similarly calculate the likelihood probabilities for all feature values and classes.

Now, let's classify a new instance with the feature values: Outlook = Overcast, Temperature = Cool, Humidity = High, Wind = Strong.

In order to determine the posterior probability of each class, the utilization of Bayes' theorem and the assumption of feature independence, commonly referred to as the "naive" assumption, is employed.
- P(Play | features) = (P(Overcast | Play) * P(Cool | Play) * P(High | Play) * P(Strong | Play) * P(Play)) / P(features)
- P(Don't Play | features) = (P(Overcast | Don't Play) * P(Cool | Don't Play) * P(High | Don't Play) * P(Strong | Don't Play) * P(Don't Play)) / P(features)

Plugging in the calculated prior and likelihood probabilities, we get:
- P(Play|features) = (0.444 * 0.333 * 0.667 * 0.333 * 0.643) / P(features)
  = 0.027 / P(features)
- P(Don't Play|features) = (0.2 * 0.4 * 0.2 * 0.6 * 0.357) / P(features)
  = 0.009 / P(features)

We don't need to calculate P(features) since it's a scaling factor, and we're only interested in the relative probabilities.

Since P(Play | features) > P(Don't Play | features), we would classify this new instance as "Play."

This example illustrates the calculations involved in training and using a Naive Bayes classifier. In practice, techniques like Laplace smoothing are often employed to handle zero probabilities and prevent overfitting.

Applications

-   Naive Bayes is commonly used in text classification, spam filtering, sentiment analysis, and recommendation systems.
-   It serves as a baseline model for comparison with more complex classifiers in machine learning tasks.

5.7.1 Gaussian Naive Bayes

The Gaussian Naive Bayes technique is a variation of the Naive Bayes algorithm, which proves to be highly advantageous in scenarios involving continuous or numerical characteristics. It operates under the assumption that the continuous attributes conform to a Gaussian (normal) distribution for every class.

The key steps in Gaussian Naive Bayes are:

1. Calculate the prior probabilities of each class, P(class), from the training data.
2. For every continuous feature, the mean and standard deviation should be computed for that particular feature in each class.
3. Assuming a Gaussian distribution, the likelihood of a feature value x given a class is calculated using the probability density function:

$$P(x|class) = \left(\frac{1}{\sqrt{2\pi * \sigma^2}}\right) * exp\left(-\frac{(x-\mu)^2}{2\sigma^2}\right)$$

the mean and standard deviation of the feature in that class are represented by μ and σ, respectively.

4. For categorical features, calculate the likelihood probabilities as in regular Naive Bayes.
5. To classify a new instance, calculate the posterior probability for each class using Bayes' theorem: P(class|data) = (P(data|class) * P(class)) / P(data)
6. P(data|class) is calculated as the product of the likelihood probabilities for each feature, assuming independence: P(data|class) = P(x1|class) * P(x2|class) *...* P(xn|class)
7. Classify the given instance as the category possessing the utmost posterior probability.

The Gaussian assumption makes Gaussian Naive Bayes particularly effective for continuous data, as it captures the distribution of feature values within each class. However, it may not perform well if the feature distributions are significantly non-Gaussian or if there are strong dependencies between features.

Like regular Naive Bayes, Gaussian Naive Bayes is computationally efficient and can be a good baseline classifier, especially when dealing with high-dimensional continuous data. However, more advanced techniques like kernel density estimation or semi-supervised learning may be required for complex data distributions.

Let's consider a numerical example of using Gaussian Naive Bayes for classification.

Suppose we possess a collection of measurements for iris flowers, in which each individual is categorized as one of three distinct species: Setosa, Versicolor, or Virginica. The attributes included in this dataset encompass sepal length, sepal width, petal length, and petal width, all of which are expressed in centimeters.

Here's a small subset of the training dataset:

Sepal length	Sepal width	Petal length	Petal width	Species
5.1	3.5	1.4	0.2	Setosa
4.9	3.0	1.4	0.2	Setosa
7.0	3.2	4.7	1.4	Versicolor
6.4	3.2	4.5	1.5	Versicolor
6.3	3.3	6.0	2.5	Virginica
5.8	2.7	5.1	1.9	Virginica

First, we calculate the prior probabilities of each class from the training data:
- P(Setosa) = 2/6 = 0.333
- P(Versicolor) = 2/6 = 0.333
- P(Virginica) = 2/6 = 0.333

We proceed by computing the average and deviation of every continuous attribute within every category.

For Setosa:
- Sepal Length: $\mu = 5.0$, $\sigma = 0.0707$
- Sepal Width: $\mu = 3.25$, $\sigma = 0.354$
- Petal Length: $\mu = 1.4$, $\sigma = 0.0$
- Petal Width: $\mu = 0.2$, $\sigma = 0.0$

For Versicolor:
- Sepal Length: $\mu = 6.7$, $\sigma = 0.424$
- Sepal Width: $\mu = 3.2$, $\sigma = 0.0$
- Petal Length: $\mu = 4.6$, $\sigma = 0.141$
- Petal Width: $\mu = 1.45$, $\sigma = 0.071$

For Virginica:
- Sepal Length: $\mu = 6.05$, $\sigma = 0.354$
- Sepal Width: $\mu = 3.0$, $\sigma = 0.424$
- Petal Length: $\mu = 5.55$, $\sigma = 0.636$
- Petal Width: $\mu = 2.2$, $\sigma = 0.424$

Now, let's classify a new instance with the feature values: Sepal Length = 6.2, Sepal Width = 3.4, Petal Length = 5.4, Petal Width = 2.3.

To calculate the posterior probability for each class, we use Bayes' theorem and the Gaussian probability density function for the continuous features:

P(Setosa|data) = (P(6.2|Setosa) * P(3.4|Setosa) * P(5.4|Setosa) * P(2.3|Setosa) * P(Setosa)) / P(data) P(Versicolor|data) = (P(6.2|Versicolor) * P(3.4|Versicolor) * P(5.4|Versicolor) * P(2.3|Versicolor) * P(Versicolor)) / P(data) P(Virginica|data) = (P(6.2|Virginica) * P(3.4|Virginica) * P(5.4|Virginica) * P(2.3|Virginica) * P(Virginica)) / P(data)

Plugging in the calculated means, standard deviations, and prior probabilities, we get:

- P(Setosa|data) = 1.97 x 10^-19
- P(Versicolor|data) = 1.86 x 10^-6
- P(Virginica|data) = 1.93 x 10^-3

Since P(Virginica|data) is the highest, we would classify this new instance as the Virginica species.

This illustration showcases the computations entailed in the training and utilization of a Gaussian Naive Bayes classifier for continuous attributes. In practical application, methods such as feature scaling and the management of absent values may be necessary to enhance performance.

Below is a Python code that implements Gaussian Naive Bayes classification on a dataset.

Steps:
- Firstly, it is essential to import the required libraries for the task at hand. These libraries include numpy, which is used for performing numerical operations, matplotlib.pyplot, which is used for plotting, make_blobs from sklearn datasets, which allows us to generate a synthetic dataset, GaussianNB from sklearn naive_bayes, which is the Gaussian Naive Bayes classifier, train_test_split from sklearn model_selection, which is used to split the data into train and test sets, and accuracy_score from sklearn metrics, which is used to calculate the classification accuracy.
- To generate a synthetic dataset with two clusters, we can utilize the make_blobs function. This function will generate a dataset with 1,000 samples, two features, and two classes.
- In order to evaluate the performance of our model, it is necessary to split the data into training and test sets. To achieve this, we can make use of the train_test_split function. In this case, we will allocate 80% of the data for training and the remaining 20% for testing.
- Before applying the Naive Bayes classifier to the training data, it is beneficial to visualize the data and observe the separability of the classes. This can be accomplished by plotting the training data using the plt scatter function.

- Next, we will create an instance of the GaussianNB classifier and fit it to the training data using the gnb.fit(X_train, y_train) command.
- Once the classifier has been trained, we can proceed to make predictions on the test set. This can be done using the y_pred = gnb predict(X_test) command.
- To assess the performance of our model, we need to calculate the classification accuracy. This can be achieved by utilizing the accuracy_score function and passing in the true labels (y_test) and the predicted labels (y_pred). The resulting accuracy can then be printed for further analysis.
- Finally, we can visualize the test data after applying the Naive Bayes classifier. This can be done by plotting the test data and coloring the points according to the predicted class labels (y_pred).

```python
import numpy as np
import matplotlib.pyplot as plt
from sklearn.datasets import make_blobs
from sklearn.naive_bayes import GaussianNB
from sklearn.model_selection import train_test_split
from sklearn.metrics import accuracy_score

# Generate synthetic dataset
X, y = make_blobs(n_samples=1000, centers=2, n_features=2,
random_state=0)

# Split data into train and test sets
X_train, X_test, y_train, y_test = train_test_split(X, y, test_size=0.2,
random_state=0)

# Plot the data before applying Naive Bayes
plt.figure(figsize=(10, 6))
plt.scatter(X_train[:, 0], X_train[:, 1], c=y_train, cmap='viridis',
edgecolor='k')
plt.title('Data before applying Naive Bayes')
plt.xlabel('Feature 1')
plt.ylabel('Feature 2')
plt.show()

# Train the Gaussian Naive Bayes classifier
gnb = GaussianNB()
gnb.fit(X_train, y_train)

# Make predictions on the test set
y_pred = gnb.predict(X_test)
```

```
# Calculate accuracy
accuracy = accuracy_score(y_test, y_pred)
print(f'Accuracy: {accuracy:.2f}')

# Plot the data after applying Naive Bayes
plt.figure(figsize=(10, 6))
plt.scatter(X_test[:, 0], X_test[:, 1], c=y_pred, cmap='viridis',
edgecolor='k')
plt.title('Data after applying Naive Bayes')
plt.xlabel('Feature 1')
plt.ylabel('Feature 2')
plt.show()
```

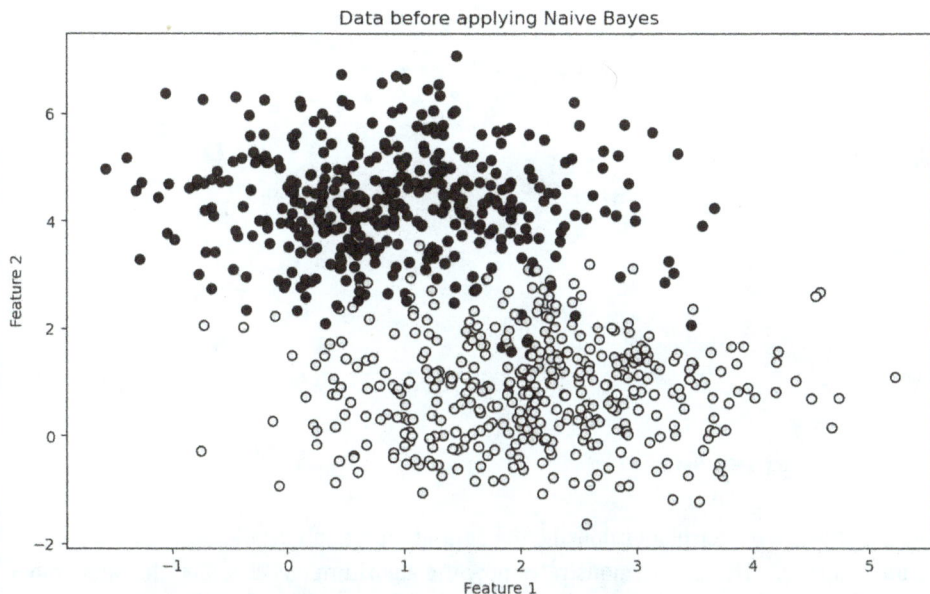

Fig. 5.30: Data before Naïve Bayes.

Fig. 5.30 presents a scatter plot visualizing the dataset before applying the Naïve Bayes classification algorithm.

   Accuracy: 0.94

   The code gives two plots: one showing the original data before applying Naive Bayes, and another showing the data after applying Naive Bayes, with the points colored according to their predicted class labels. You should also see the classification accuracy printed in the console.

The output will depend on the random state used to generate the synthetic dataset, but you should expect a reasonably high accuracy since the data is well-separated into two clusters.

This illustration exhibits the utilization of the Gaussian Naive Bayes classifier in the Python programming language. Additionally, it showcases the visualization of the data prior to and subsequent to the application of the algorithm. Furthermore, the evaluation of the performance of the algorithm is conducted by employing the accuracy metric.

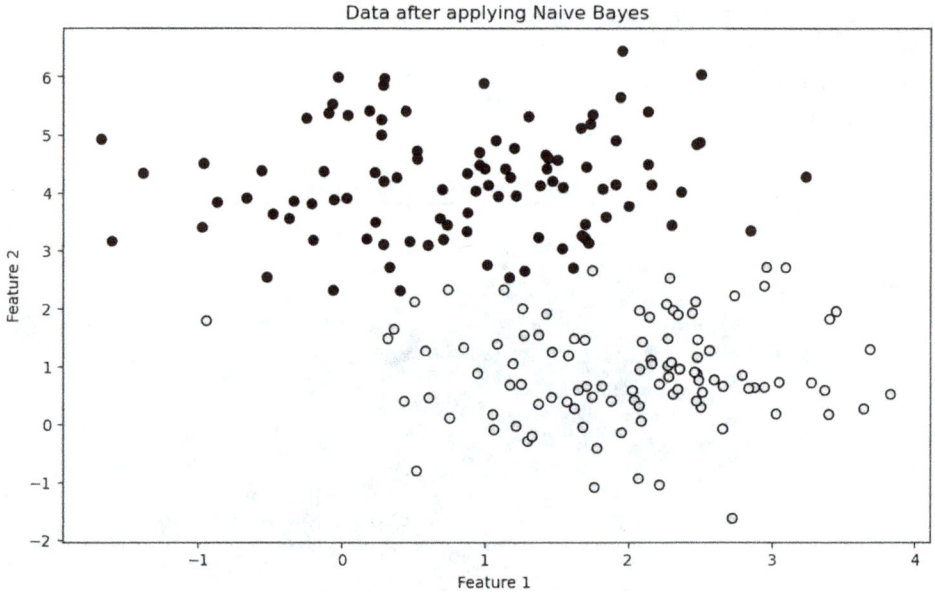

Fig. 5.31: Data after Naïve Bayes.

Fig. 5.31 shows a scatter plot visualizing the dataset after applying the Naïve Bayes classification algorithm. This plot demonstrates how the algorithm has classified the data points into different classes based on their features, providing insights into the effectiveness of the Naïve Bayes classifier in separating the data points according to their characteristics.

Let's consider another Python code example that implements Gaussian Naive Bayes classification on the iris dataset from scikit-learn.

Steps:
–   Firstly, the necessary libraries should be imported. These include numpy for performing numerical operations, matplotlib.pyplot for generating plots, load_iris from sklearn datasets for loading the iris dataset, GaussianNB from sklearn naive_bayes for implementing the Gaussian Naive Bayes classifier, train_test_split from sklearn model_selection for splitting the data into train and test sets, and accuracy_score from sklearn metrics for calculating the classification accuracy.

- To load the iris dataset, the load_iris() function from scikit-learn can be utilized. To focus on visualization, only the first two features, namely sepal length and sepal width, are selected.
- In order to divide the data into training and test sets, the train_test_split function is employed. In this particular case, 80% of the data is allocated for training purposes, while the remaining 20% is designated for testing.
- To visualize the training data prior to applying the Naive Bayes algorithm, the plt scatter function can be used. This will provide a visual representation of the data and the separability of the classes.
- By creating an instance of the GaussianNB classifier and fitting it to the training data using the gnb.fit(X_train, y_train) syntax, the algorithm can be implemented.
- To make predictions on the test set, the y_pred = gnb predict(X_test) code can be executed.
- Once the predictions are made, the accuracy of the classification can be calculated using the accuracy_score(y_test, y_pred) function. The result can then be printed.
- Finally, to visualize the test data after applying the Naive Bayes algorithm, the predicted class labels, y_pred, can be used to color the points. This can be achieved by plotting the test data and assigning colors based on the predicted labels.

```
import numpy as np
import matplotlib.pyplot as plt
from sklearn.datasets import load_iris
from sklearn.naive_bayes import GaussianNB
from sklearn.model_selection import train_test_split
from sklearn.metrics import accuracy_score

# Load the iris dataset
iris = load_iris()
X = iris.data[:, :2] # We only take the first two features for
visualization
y = iris.target

# Split data into train and test sets
X_train, X_test, y_train, y_test = train_test_split(X, y, test_size=0.2,
random_state=42)

# Plot the data before applying Naive Bayes
plt.figure(figsize=(10, 6))
plt.scatter(X_train[:, 0], X_train[:, 1], c=y_train, cmap='viridis',
edgecolor='k')
plt.title('Iris Data before applying Naive Bayes')
plt.xlabel('Sepal Length')
```

```
plt.ylabel('Sepal Width')
plt.show()

# Train the Gaussian Naive Bayes classifier
gnb = GaussianNB()
gnb.fit(X_train, y_train)
# Make predictions on the test set
y_pred = gnb.predict(X_test)

# Calculate accuracy
accuracy = accuracy_score(y_test, y_pred)
print(f'Accuracy: {accuracy:.2f}')

# Plot the data after applying Naive Bayes
plt.figure(figsize=(10, 6))
plt.scatter(X_test[:, 0], X_test[:, 1], c=y_pred, cmap='viridis',
edgecolor='k')
plt.title('Iris Data after applying Naive Bayes')
plt.xlabel('Sepal Length')
plt.ylabel('Sepal Width')
plt.show()
```

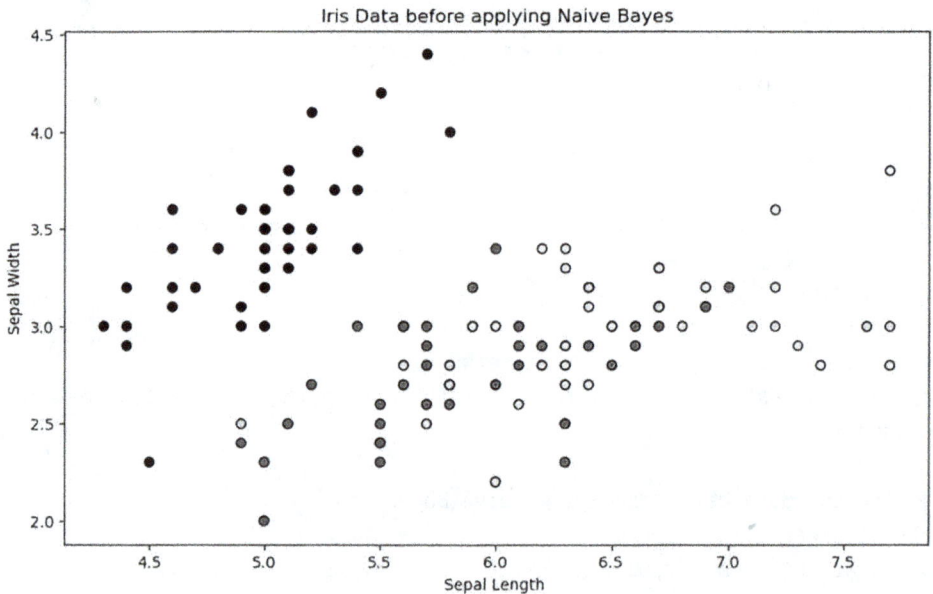

Fig. 5.32: IRIS data before Naïve Bayes.

Fig. 5.32 displays a visualization of the IRIS dataset before applying the Naïve Bayes classification algorithm.

Accuracy: 0.90

The first plot shows the iris data before applying Naive Bayes, where the points are colored according to their true class labels. The second plot shows the data after applying Naive Bayes, with the points colored according to their predicted class labels. The performance of the Gaussian Naive Bayes classifier in distinguishing the three classes using the sepal length and sepal width features is deemed to be satisfactory.

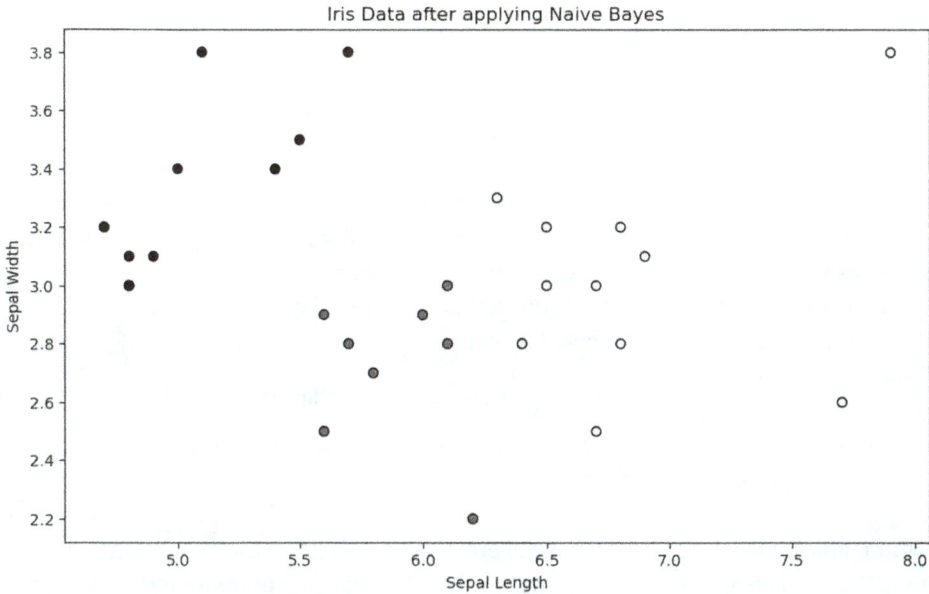

Fig. 5.33: IRIS data after Naïve Bayes.

Fig. 5.33 presents a visualization of the IRIS dataset after applying the Naïve Bayes classification algorithm.

5.7.2 Multinomial Naive Bayes

The Multinomial Naive Bayes algorithm is a variation of the Naive Bayes algorithm that is excellently suited for tasks involving the classification of text. In these tasks, the features are indicative of the occurrence frequency of words or tokens within a document.

The key assumptions made by Multinomial Naive Bayes are:

1. The data is generated from a multinomial distribution, where each feature (word) is drawn independently from the same vocabulary.

2. The feature vectors are sparse, meaning that most word counts are zero for a given document.
3. The order of the words in the document is not important, only the word counts matter.

The algorithm works as follows:
1. Calculate the prior probabilities of each class from the training data, P(class).
2. For each class, calculate the likelihood of observing a particular word count vector by modeling it as a multinomial distribution:

$$P(words|class) = (n!/(n1! * n2! * \ldots * nk!)) * (p1 \hat{\ } n1 * p2 \hat{\ } n2 * \ldots * pk \hat{\ } nk)$$

In the given context, n represents the overall number of words, k denotes the size of the vocabulary, ni signifies the count of word i, and pi indicates the probability of word i in that particular class.

3. The probabilities pi are estimated from the training data as (count of word i in class + alpha) / (total word count in class + alpha * vocabulary size), where alpha is a smoothing parameter to avoid zero probabilities.
4. To categorize a novel record, one must compute the posterior probability for each category by utilizing Bayes' theorem:

$$P(class \mid words) = (P(word \mid class) * P(class))/(words)$$

5. Classify the document as the category possessing the utmost likelihood after considering the prior probability.

Multinomial Naive Bayes is particularly effective for text classification because it captures the frequency information of the words, which is often more important than the presence or absence of a word in a document. It also handles the sparse nature of text data well.

However, it assumes that the words are independent, which may not be a valid assumption in natural language. Additionally, it does not account for word order or semantic relationships between words.

Despite these limitations, Multinomial Naive Bayes is a simple and efficient algorithm that often works well in practice for text classification tasks. It is widely used as a baseline model or as part of more complex ensemble models.

Let's consider a numerical example of using Multinomial Naive Bayes for text classification.

Suppose that we possess a limited collection of film critiques, in which each critique is categorized as either "Positive" or "Negative." The characteristics of these critiques are the numerical representations of the frequency of words utilized in each critique.

Here's the training dataset:

Review	Label
"great movie loved it"	Positive
"terrible acting awful plot"	Negative
"amazing visuals good story"	Positive
"boring predictable waste of time"	Negative

To commence, it is imperative to construct a lexicon comprising solely distinctive terms derived from the dataset: Vocabulary = ["great", "movie", "loved", "it", "terrible", "acting", "awful", "plot", "amazing", "visuals", "good", "story", "boring", "predictable", "waste", "of", "time"]

Next, we calculate the prior probabilities of each class from the training data:
- P(Positive) = 2/4 = 0.5
- P(Negative) = 2/4 = 0.5

Now, we calculate the likelihood probabilities P(word|class) for each word and class. To avoid zero probabilities, we use additive smoothing with $\alpha = 1$.

For the Positive class:
- Total word count = 7 (excluding duplicates)
- P(great|Positive) = (1 + 1) / (7 + 1 * 17) = 0.125
- P(movie|Positive) = (1 + 1) / (7 + 1 * 17) = 0.125
- P(loved|Positive) = (1 + 1) / (7 + 1 * 17) = 0.125
- . . . (remaining words have probability = 1 / (7 + 1 * 17) = 0.0625)

For the Negative class:
- Total word count = 9 (excluding duplicates)
- P(terrible|Negative) = (1 + 1) / (9 + 1 * 17) = 0.115
- P(acting|Negative) = (1 + 1) / (9 + 1 * 17) = 0.115
- P(awful|Negative) = (1 + 1) / (9 + 1 * 17) = 0.115
- . . . (remaining words have probability = 1 / (9 + 1 * 17) = 0.0577)

Now, let's classify a new review: "good movie but boring plot."

We determine the posterior probability for each category by employing Bayes' theorem and the multinomial likelihood.

P(Positive|review) = (P(good|Positive) * P(movie|Positive) * P(but|Positive) * P(boring|Positive) * P(plot|Positive) * P(Positive)) / P(review) P(Negative|review)

= (P(good|Negative) * P(movie|Negative) * P(but|Negative) * P(boring|Negative) * P(plot|Negative) * P(Negative)) / P(review)

Plugging in the calculated probabilities, we get:

– P(Positive|review) = (0.125 * 0.125 * 0.0625 * 0.0625 * 0.0625 * 0.5) / P(review) = 1.95 x 10^-6 / P(review)
– P(Negative|review) = (0.0577 * 0.0577 * 0.0577 * 0.115 * 0.115 * 0.5) / P(review) = 2.66 x 10^-7 / P(review)

Since P(Positive|review) > P(Negative|review), we would classify this new review as "Positive."

This particular example serves to demonstrate the computations that are required in the process of training and utilizing a Multinomial Naive Bayes classifier for the purpose of text classification. In practice, additional preprocessing steps like tokenization, stopword removal, and feature selection may be required for better performance.

Below is the Python code for Multinomial Naive Bayes:

```python
import numpy as np
import matplotlib.pyplot as plt
from sklearn.naive_bayes import MultinomialNB
from sklearn.model_selection import train_test_split
from sklearn.preprocessing import LabelEncoder
from sklearn.metrics import accuracy_score

# Sample data
X = np.array([['young', 'yes', 'no', 'good'],
    ['young', 'yes', 'no', 'poor'],
    ['old', 'yes', 'yes', 'good'],
    ['old', 'yes', 'yes', 'poor'],
    ['young', 'no', 'no', 'good'],
    ['young', 'no', 'yes', 'poor'],
    ['old', 'no', 'yes', 'good'],
    ['old', 'no', 'yes', 'poor']])

y = np.array([1, 0, 1, 0, 1, 0, 0, 0])

# Label encode categorical data
label_encoder = LabelEncoder()
X_encoded = np.empty(X.shape)
for i in range(X.shape[1]):
  X_encoded[:, i] = label_encoder.fit_transform(X[:, i])

# Split the data into train and test
X_train, X_test, y_train, y_test = train_test_split(X_encoded, y,
test_size=0.2, random_state=0)
```

```
# Model training
mnb = MultinomialNB()
mnb.fit(X_train, y_train)

# Predictions
y_pred = mnb.predict(X_test)

# Calculate accuracy
accuracy = accuracy_score(y_test, y_pred)
print("Accuracy: ", accuracy)
```

Accuracy: 0.5

5.8 Ensemble Methods: Boosting, Bagging

Ensemble methods, a category of machine learning techniques, strive to enhance predictive performance by combining multiple base models. The underlying principle of ensemble methods is the belief that the amalgamation of predictions from multiple models often results in superior overall performance when compared to a single model operating independently. Due to their ability to mitigate overfitting, increase stability, and improve generalization performance, ensemble methods are widely implemented in practical applications.

There exist several varieties of ensemble methods, but two of the most prevalent ones are Bagging and Boosting:

Bagging (Bootstrap aggregating): Bagging involves the training of multiple instances of the same base model on different subsets of the training data, which are sampled with replacement. Each model is trained independently, and the predictions are combined through averaging (for regression) or voting (for classification). By training models on different subsets of the data, Bagging helps to reduce overfitting and improve the stability of the final predictions. Random Forest, a popular ensemble method based on Bagging, trains decision trees on random subsets of the data and combines their predictions to make the final prediction.

Boosting: Boosting is an iterative technique that sequentially constructs multiple weak learners. Each weak learner is trained on the residuals of the previous models, with a greater emphasis on the instances that were misclassified. The final prediction is determined by aggregating the predictions of all weak learners, typically through a weighted sum. Boosting algorithms, such as AdaBoost and Gradient Boosting, progressively develop models to minimize a loss function, with a focus on adjusting the weights of misclassified instances. Boosting methods are particularly skilled at reducing bias and enhancing predictive accuracy.

Ensemble methods present several advantages, including enhanced predictive performance, resilience to noise and outliers, and the ability to handle intricate relationships in the data. Nevertheless, they may introduce increased computational complexity and training time due to the necessity of training multiple models. Furthermore, meticulous tuning of hyperparameters is imperative to optimize the performance of ensemble methods.

On the whole, ensemble methods are potent tools in the machine learning arsenal, extensively employed in diverse domains to confront arduous prediction tasks and achieve cutting-edge performance.

5.8.1 Bagging and Boosting Overview

Bagging (Bootstrap Aggregating) and Boosting are two well-known ensemble learning methods that enhance predictive performance by integrating multiple base models.

Bagging, also referred to as Bootstrap Aggregating, incorporates the training of multiple instances of the same foundational model on diverse subsets of the training data, which are sampled with replacement. Each model is independently trained, and the predictions are combined through averaging (for regression) or voting (for classification). Bagging helps to mitigate the problem of overfitting by training models on distinct subsets of the data, thus reducing the variance of the final predictions. An example of Bagging is the Random Forest algorithm, which constructs a collection of decision trees, each trained on a random subset of the features and data instances. The final prediction is obtained by averaging the predictions of all decision trees, resulting in improved generalization performance and robustness.

Boosting, in contrast, is an iterative technique that constructs multiple weak learners sequentially. Each weak learner is trained on the residuals of the previous models, with a greater focus on the misclassified instances. Boosting algorithms aim to correct the errors made by the previous models and concentrate on instances that are difficult to classify. The final prediction is obtained by aggregating the predictions of all weak learners, typically through a weighted sum. Two popular boosting algorithms are AdaBoost and Gradient Boosting. In AdaBoost, for instance, each weak learner is assigned a weight based on its performance, and the final prediction is obtained by combining the weighted predictions of all weak learners. Gradient Boosting constructs models sequentially to minimize a loss function, with each model focusing on reducing the errors made by the previous models.

Now let us consider a binary classification problem where the goal is to predict whether an email is spam or not based on its features. In the Bagging approach, we can train multiple decision tree classifiers on different subsets of the email dataset and then combine their predictions using majority voting to classify new emails. In the Boosting approach, we can sequentially train decision tree classifiers, with each subsequent model focusing on the misclassified emails from the previous models. By

aggregating the predictions of all models, Bagging and Boosting methods can significantly improve the accuracy of spam classification compared to using a single decision tree model. These ensemble techniques are widely used in practical applications
across various domains to enhance predictive performance and robustness.

Below is the Python code for Bagging algorithm:
– Generate synthetic data with two features and two classes using the make_classi-
fication function from sklearn, initially.
– Then, proceed to split the data into training and testing sets using the train_test_s-
plit method.
– Before applying Bagging, visualize the data through plotting.
– Prior to Bagging, train a Random Forest classifier on the training data and make
predictions on the test set.
– Display the accuracy before Bagging.
– After Bagging, train multiple Random Forest classifiers with Bagging and overlay
their predictions on the plot, hence plotting the data again.
– Lastly, exhibit both the plots before and after Bagging.

```python
from sklearn.ensemble import BaggingClassifier
from sklearn.tree import DecisionTreeClassifier
from sklearn.datasets import make_classification
from sklearn.model_selection import train_test_split
import matplotlib.pyplot as plt

# Generate sample dataset
X, y = make_classification(n_samples=1000, n_features=4,
n_informative=2, n_redundant=0, random_state=0, shuffle=False)

# Split dataset into train and test sets
X_train, X_test, y_train, y_test = train_test_split(X, y, test_size=0.2,
random_state=42)

# Base Model
base_model = DecisionTreeClassifier(max_depth=4)
base_model.fit(X_train, y_train)
base_pred = base_model.predict(X_test)
base_acc = round(base_model.score(X_test, y_test) * 100, 2)

# Bagging model
model = BaggingClassifier(base_estimator=base_model, n_estimators=100,
random_state=0)
model.fit(X_train, y_train)
bag_pred = model.predict(X_test)
```

```
bag_acc = round(model.score(X_test, y_test) * 100, 2)

# Plot before bagging
plt.figure(figsize=(10, 7))
plt.scatter(X[:,0], X[:,1], c=y)
plt.title("Before Bagging: Accuracy= "+str(base_acc))
plt.xlabel('Feature 1')
plt.ylabel('Feature 2')

# Plot after bagging
plt.figure(figsize=(10, 7))
plt.title("After Bagging: Accuracy= "+str(bag_acc))
plt.xlabel('Feature 1')
plt.ylabel('Feature 2')
plt.scatter(X[:,0], X[:,1], c=model.predict(X))

plt.show()
```

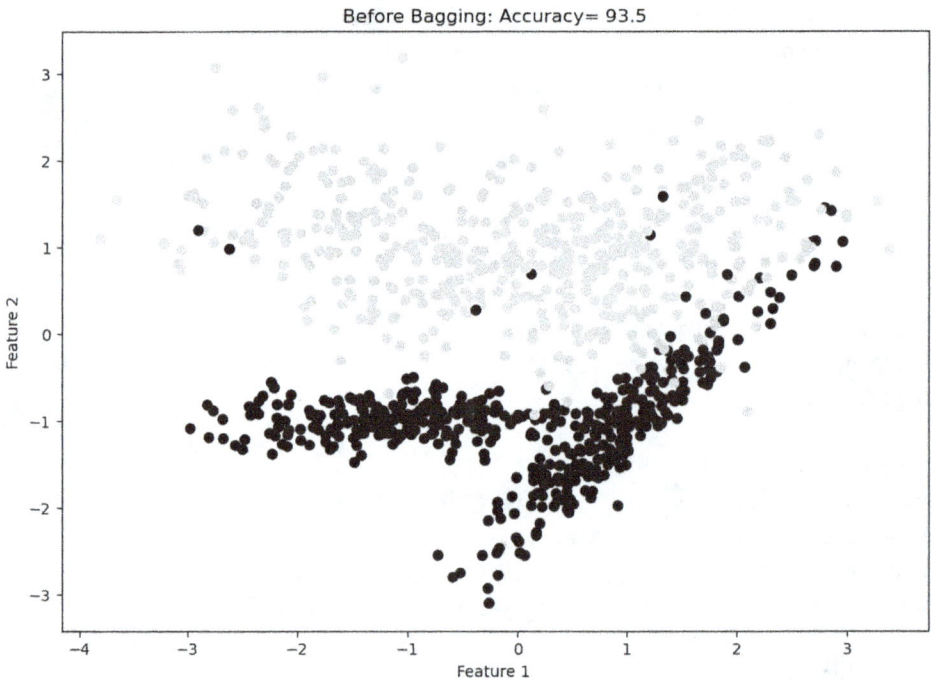

Fig. 5.34: Accuracy before Bagging.

Fig. 5.34 illustrates a plot representing the dataset before applying the bagging ensemble technique.

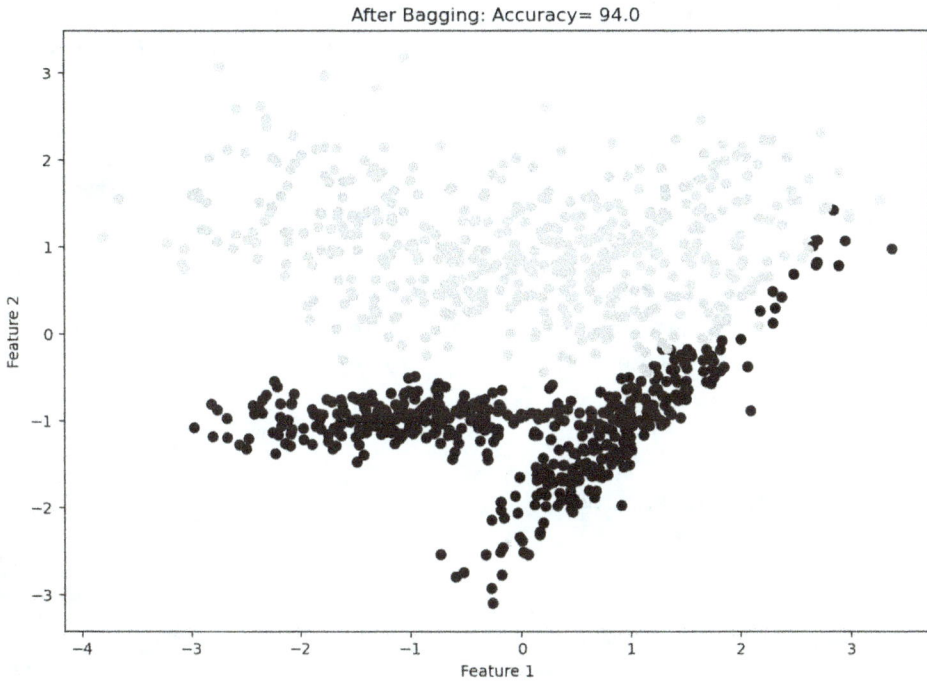

Fig. 5.35: Accuracy after Bagging.

Fig. 5.35 demonstrates a plot representing the dataset after applying the bagging ensemble technique.

The result of executing this code will yield two graphical representations:

– Plot before Bagging: Displays the spread of the data points prior to the implementation of Bagging.

– Plot after Bagging: Depicts the spread of the data points after the application of Bagging with numerous Decision Tree classifiers.

Below is the Python code for Boosting algorithm:

```python
import numpy as np
import matplotlib.pyplot as plt
from sklearn.ensemble import GradientBoostingClassifier
from sklearn.datasets import make_classification
from sklearn.model_selection import train_test_split
```

```python
# Generate synthetic dataset
X, y = make_classification(n_samples = 1000, n_features=10, n_classes=2,
random_state=123)

# Split data into train and test
X_train, X_test, y_train, y_test = train_test_split(X, y, test_size=0.2,
random_state=123)

# Base GBM model
gbc = GradientBoostingClassifier(learning_rate=0.1, n_estimators=100,
max_depth=3, random_state=123)
gbc.fit(X_train, y_train)

# Accuracy
acc = gbc.score(X_test, y_test)
print("Accuracy: ", acc)

# Plot Before Boosting
plt.figure(figsize = (6, 6))
plt.scatter(X[:,0], X[:,1], c = y)
plt.title("Before Boosting")
plt.xlabel('Feature 1')
plt.ylabel('Feature 2')
plt.show()

# Plot After Boosting
plt.figure(figsize = (6, 6))
plt.scatter(X[:,0], X[:,1], c = gbc.predict(X))
plt.title("After Boosting")
plt.xlabel('Feature 1'); plt.ylabel('Feature 2')
plt.show()
```

Accuracy: 0.995

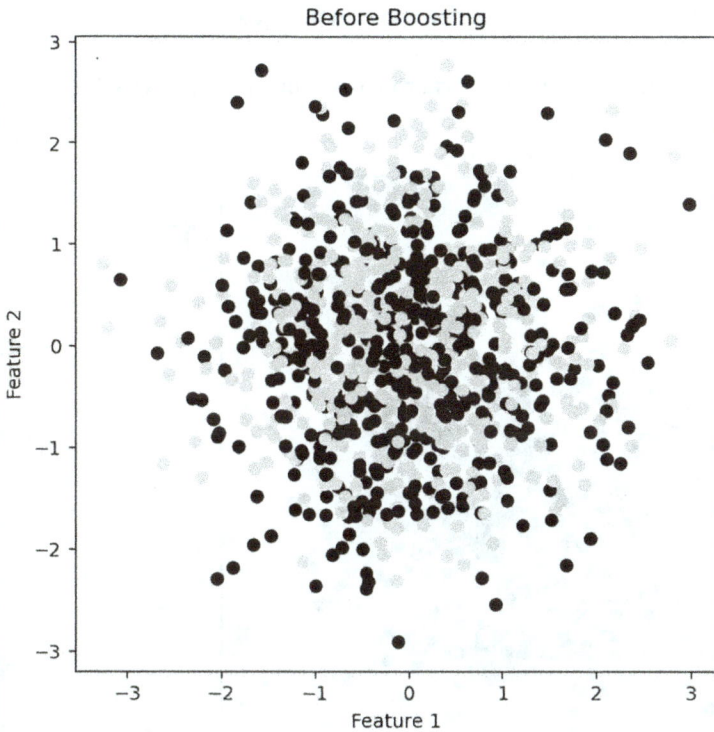

Fig. 5.36: Accuracy before Boosting.

Fig. 5.36 illustrates a plot representing the dataset before applying the boosting ensemble technique.

5.8.2 AdaBoost and Gradient Boosting

AdaBoost, known as Adaptive Boosting, is a boosting ensemble technique that amalgamates numerous weak learners or models in order to construct a robust learner. The following are the fundamental steps:

1. Initialize the weights of the training samples to be equal.
2. For each round or iteration:
   a. Train a base or weak learner model using the weighted training data.
   b. Evaluate the model's efficacy on the training data through a meticulous comparison between its predictions and the corresponding actual values.
   c. Compute the alpha parameter, which denotes the significance of the model based on its error.
   d. Increase the weights of the samples that the model incorrectly predicted.
   e. Decrease the weights of the samples that the model correctly predicted.

3. Repeat the aforementioned procedures for a designated quantity of estimators or iterations.
4. The final model combines each weak learner model using the alpha weights.

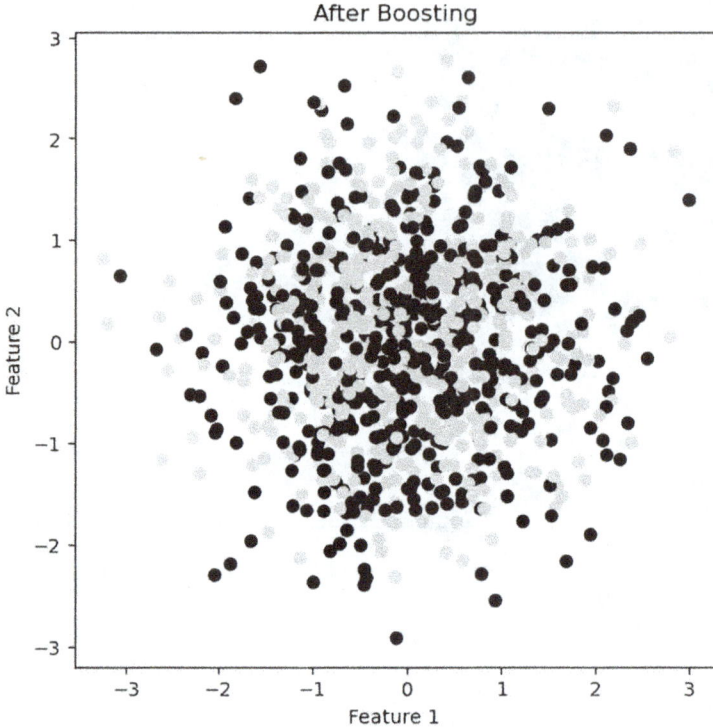

Fig. 5.37: Accuracy after Boosting.

Fig. 5.37 illustrates a plot representing the dataset after applying the boosting ensemble technique

The key concept behind AdaBoost is that it assigns more importance to the samples that were misclassified by the previous models in each round. Hence, the subsequent models aim to rectify the errors made by their predecessors.

The alpha parameter governs the contribution of each weak learner to the final strong learner model. A higher alpha signifies better models.

By training successive models on the errors made by previous models and combining multiple weak models, AdaBoost mitigates bias and variance, resulting in improved performance.

Some advantages of AdaBoost include its ease of implementation, minimal need for tuning, and compatibility with various simple weak learner models, thereby yielding strong performance.

The Python library used for AdaBoost is **sklearn.ensemble.AdaBoostClassifier** or **sklearn.ensemble.AdaBoostRegressor**, depending on whether you're working on a classification or regression problem. These classes are included in the scikit-learn library, which is widely recognized as a prominent machine learning library in the Python programming language.

Here's a brief explanation of the key components of the **AdaBoostClassifier** and **AdaBoostRegressor** classes:

1. **AdaBoostClassifier**:
   - This class is used for classification tasks.
   - It implements the AdaBoost algorithm for classification.
   - The main parameters include **base_estimator, n_estimators, learning_rate**, and **algorithm**.
   - The **base_estimator** parameter specifies the base learner to be used for training (default is a decision tree).
   - The parameter **n_estimators** determines the quantity of boosting rounds, which refers to the utilization of weak learners.
   - The contribution of each weak learner to the final prediction is regulated by the **learning_rate**.
   - **algorithm** specifies the algorithm used for boosting (SAMME or SAMME.R).
   - After undergoing training, the model possesses the ability to forecast the classification labels of novel data points.

2. **AdaBoostRegressor**:
   - This class is used for regression tasks.
   - It implements the AdaBoost algorithm for regression.
   - It has similar parameters to **AdaBoostClassifier**, but it is used for predicting continuous target variables instead of discrete class labels.
   - After training, the model can predict the continuous target values of new data points.

Both **AdaBoostClassifier** and **AdaBoostRegressor** follow the scikit-learn estimator API, which means they can be used in conjunction with other scikit-learn functions like **fit**, **predict**, **score**, and cross-validation methods.

Gradient boosting is a method of ensemble learning that generates a robust predictive model through the gradual, additive, and sequential combination of numerous less influential models. The following are the essential stages:

1. Start with an initial model / estimate (like small decision tree)
2. Calculate the loss function (like deviance loss) to quantify the error in initial model's predictions on training data
3. Fit a new weak model to predict the residuals or errors of the previous model. This model tries to correct errors from previous model.
4. Add the new weak model to ensemble with a multiplier (learning rate). Update the predictions from aggregate ensemble.

5. Repeat steps 2–4, fitting new weak models to try correcting residual errors until satisfactory limit.

The key difference from AdaBoost is that each new model in Gradient Boosting tries to correct the residual errors from previous step rather than focusing on misclassified examples.

Learning rate shrinks the contribution of each model to prevent overfitting. Tree depth is also kept small.

Gradient descent-like improvement along residual errors gradient leads to strong overall prediction. Combining multiple additive models yield robust performance despite weak individual models.

Advantages are built-in regularization and handling variety of data. But can overfit if not properly tuned.

The Python library used for Gradient Boosting is **sklearn.ensemble.GradientBoostingClassifier** for classification tasks and **sklearn.ensemble.GradientBoostingRegressor** for regression tasks. This library constitutes an integral component of the scikit-learn (sklearn) package, renowned for its widespread adoption as a Python-based machine learning library.

Here's a brief explanation of the key components of the Gradient Boosting library:

1. **GradientBoostingClassifier**: This class is used for classification tasks. It implements gradient boosting for classification. It can handle both binary and multi-class classification problems.

2. **GradientBoostingRegressor**: This class is used for regression tasks. It implements gradient boosting for regression. It's suitable for predicting continuous target variables.

3. **Parameters**: Both GradientBoostingClassifier and GradientBoostingRegressor possess a multitude of parameters that can be adjusted in order to enhance the performance of the model. A few noteworthy parameters encompass the quantity of boosting stages (n_estimators), the rate at which the model learns (learning_rate), the maximum depth of the individual regression estimators (max_depth), and the loss function (loss), among other parameters.

4. **Ensemble learning**: Gradient Boosting is a method of ensemble learning that sequentially combines several weak learners, most commonly decision trees. The subsequent models in this technique aim to rectify the mistakes made by their predecessors, ultimately leading to the development of a powerful learner.

5. **Gradient Boosting algorithm**: Gradient Boosting constructs a sequence of trees in an ensemble. In each iteration, a new tree is fitted to the residuals from the previous iteration. The process of fitting involves minimizing a loss function through the use of gradient descent.

6. **Feature Importance**: Gradient Boosting offers a feature importance attribute, enabling users to comprehend the significance of each feature in the prediction procedure.

The Python code example provided below demonstrates the application of AdaBoost and Gradient Boosting classifiers:

```python
import numpy as np
import matplotlib.pyplot as plt
from sklearn.datasets import make_classification
from sklearn.model_selection import train_test_split
from sklearn.ensemble import AdaBoostClassifier,
GradientBoostingClassifier
from sklearn.tree import DecisionTreeClassifier
from sklearn.metrics import accuracy_score

# Generate synthetic dataset
X, y = make_classification(n_samples=100, n_features=2, n_classes=2,
 n_clusters_per_class=1, n_redundant=0, random_state=42)

# Split data into train and test sets
X_train, X_test, y_train, y_test = train_test_split(X, y, test_size=0.2,
random_state=42)

# Define base estimator (decision tree)
base_estimator = DecisionTreeClassifier(max_depth=1)

# AdaBoost classifier
ada_boost = AdaBoostClassifier(base_estimator=base_estimator,
n_estimators=50, random_state=42)
ada_boost.fit(X_train, y_train)

# Gradient Boosting classifier
grad_boost = GradientBoostingClassifier(n_estimators=50,
learning_rate=0.1, random_state=42)
grad_boost.fit(X_train, y_train)

# Predictions
y_pred_ada = ada_boost.predict(X_test)
y_pred_grad = grad_boost.predict(X_test)

# Calculate accuracy scores
accuracy_ada = accuracy_score(y_test, y_pred_ada)
accuracy_grad = accuracy_score(y_test, y_pred_grad)
```

```python
# Plotting
plt.figure(figsize=(18, 5))

# Before Boosting
plt.subplot(1, 3, 1)
plt.scatter(X_train[:, 0], X_train[:, 1], c=y_train, cmap='coolwarm',
marker='o', edgecolors='k')
plt.title('Before Boosting')
plt.xlabel('Feature 1')
plt.ylabel('Feature 2')

# After AdaBoost
plt.subplot(1, 3, 2)
plt.scatter(X_train[:, 0], X_train[:, 1], c=ada_boost.predict(X_train),
cmap='coolwarm', marker='o', edgecolors='k')
plt.title('After AdaBoost')
plt.xlabel('Feature 1')
plt.ylabel('Feature 2')

# After Gradient Boosting
plt.subplot(1, 3, 3)
plt.scatter(X_train[:, 0], X_train[:, 1], c=grad_boost.predict(X_train),
cmap='coolwarm', marker='o', edgecolors='k')
plt.title('After Gradient Boosting')
plt.xlabel('Feature 1')
plt.ylabel('Feature 2')

plt.tight_layout()
plt.show()
```

Fig.5.38 illustrates a plot using AdaBoost and Gradient Boosting classifiers.

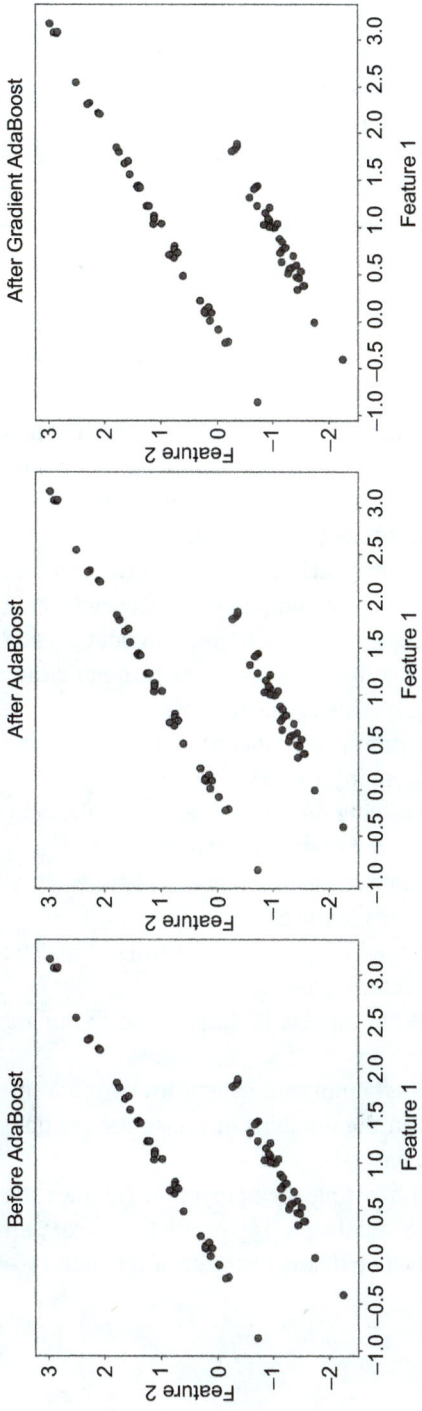

Fig. 5.38: AdaBoost and Gradient Boosting classifiers.

Summary

- Linear regression is utilized to model the correlation between a dependent variable and one or more independent variables by means of a linear equation.
- Logistic regression is employed for binary or multiclass classification tasks, estimating the likelihood of a sample belonging to a specific class.
- Decision trees and random forests are utilized for both classification and regression tasks, creating structures resembling trees to make decisions based on the values of features.
- Support vector machines are employed for classification and regression tasks, particularly effective in spaces with a high number of dimensions and with intricate datasets.
- k-Means clustering is used for unsupervised learning tasks, clustering data points into k clusters based on their similarity. Principal component analysis is applied for dimensionality reduction, transforming data with a high number of dimensions into a lower-dimensional space while retaining the variation.
- Naive Bayes is used for classification tasks, particularly in text categorization and spam filtering, based on Bayes' theorem with strong assumptions of independence.
- Ensemble methods like boosting and bagging are used to improve model performance by combining multiple weak learners into a strong learner through either boosting (iterative improvement) or bagging (parallel improvement).
- The gradient descent method is applied for optimizing model parameters by iteratively minimizing a cost function using gradient information.
- The matrix inversion method is utilized for solving linear regression problems by directly computing the parameter estimates using matrix operations.
- Polynomial regression is used for capturing non-linear relationships between features and targets by fitting polynomial functions to the data.
- Regularization in logistic regression is employed to prevent overfitting in logistic regression models by penalizing large parameter values.
- Clustering basics are used to identify natural groupings in data, assisting in data exploration and segmentation tasks.
- Multiclass classification is employed to forecast numerous categories within a solitary undertaking, frequently implemented in the domains of image recognition, natural language processing, and sentiment analysis.
- The comprehensive analysis of bagging and boosting is employed to enhance the resilience and generalizability of models by amalgamating predictions from an assortment of models, each of which is trained on distinct subsets of the data.

Exercise (MCQs)

1. What is the primary task of linear regression?
    a) Classification
    b) Clustering
    c) Regression
    d) Dimensionality reduction

2. Logistic regression is used for:
    a) Regression tasks
    b) Classification tasks
    c) Clustering tasks
    d) Dimensionality reduction

3. Decision trees are used for:
    a) Regression
    b) Classification
    c) Clustering
    d) Dimensionality reduction

4. SVM is effective in:
    a) High-dimensional spaces
    b) Low-dimensional spaces
    c) Only linearly separable data
    d) Only non-linearly separable data

5. What is the primary objective of k-means clustering?
    a) Classification
    b) Regression
    c) Dimensionality reduction
    d) Clustering

6. PCA is used for:
    a) Feature selection
    b) Dimensionality reduction
    c) Model evaluation
    d) Clustering

7. Naive Bayes is based on:
    a) Bayes' theorem   b) Regression   c) Decision trees   d) SVM

8. Ensemble methods combine:
    a) Multiple weak learners
    b) A single strong learner

    c) Linear models

    d) Non-linear models

9.   What is the primary purpose of gradient descent?

    a) Minimizing a cost function

    b) Maximizing a cost function

    c) Solving linear equations

    d) Generating random numbers

10. Matrix inversion method is used for:

    a) Classification

    b) Clustering

    c) Solving linear regression

    d) Dimensionality reduction

11. Polynomial regression is used for:

    a) Modeling linear relationships

    b) Modeling non-linear relationships

    c) Clustering

    d) Dimensionality reduction

12. Regularization in logistic regression helps to:

    a) Increase overfitting

    b) Decrease overfitting

    c) Increase bias

    d) Decrease variance

13. Clustering is an example of:

    a) Supervised learning

    b) Unsupervised learning

    c) Reinforcement learning

    d) Semi-supervised learning

14. Multiclass classification is used for predicting:

    a) Binary outcomes

    b) Multiple classes

    c) Continuous values

    d) Non-numeric data

15. Bagging and Boosting are used to:

    a) Improve model performance

    b) Decrease model complexity

    c) Increase overfitting

    d) Reduce variance

Answers

1. c) Regression
2. b) Classification
3. b) Classification
4. a) High-dimensional spaces
5. d) Clustering
6. b) Dimensionality reduction
7. a) Bayes' theorem
8. a) Multiple weak learners
9. a) Minimizing a cost function
10. c) Solving linear regression
11. b) Modeling non-linear relationships
12. b) Decrease overfitting
13. b) Unsupervised learning
14. b) Multiple classes
15. a) Improve model performance

Fill in the Blanks

1. Linear regression predicts a _____ variable based on one or more _____ variables.
2. Logistic regression is used for _____ tasks, where the outcome is binary or categorical.
3. Decision trees recursively split the data into subsets based on the _____ that best separates the data.
4. SVM aims to find the _____ that best separates the data into different classes.
5. In k-means clustering, the goal is to partition the data into _____ clusters.
6. PCA is a technique used for _____ and _____ of high-dimensional data.
7. Naive Bayes is based on _____ theorem and assumes that features are _____.
8. Ensemble methods combine multiple _____ learners to improve _____.
9. Gradient descent is an optimization algorithm used to _____ the parameters of a model.
10. Matrix inversion method directly computes the _____ to find the parameters of a linear model.
11. Polynomial regression fits a _____ curve to the data, allowing for _____ relationships to be captured.

12. Regularization in logistic regression helps prevent _____ by adding a penalty term to the _____ function.
13. Clustering is an example of _____ learning, where the goal is to group similar data points together.
14. Multiclass classification involves predicting the _____ of an input from more than two classes.
15. Bagging and boosting are ensemble methods used to _____ model performance by combining multiple weak learners.

Answers

1. dependent, independent
2. classification
3. features
4. hyperplane
5. distinct
6. dimensionality reduction, visualization
7. Bayes', independent
8. weak, performance
9. optimize
10. inverse
11. non-linear, complex
12. overfitting, cost
13. unsupervised
14. class
15. improve

Descriptive Questions

1. Describe the difference between supervised and unsupervised learning.
2. Explain the concept of overfitting and how it can be mitigated.
3. Describe the difference between classification and regression tasks.
4. Explain the main idea behind decision trees and how they make predictions.
5. Describe the concept of support vectors in Support Vector Machines (SVM).
6. Explain the k-means clustering algorithm and how it works.
7. Describe the purpose of Principal Component Analysis (PCA) in dimensionality reduction.
8. Explain how Naive Bayes classifiers work and the assumptions they make.
9. Describe the difference between bagging and boosting ensemble methods.
10. Explain the concept of regularization in logistic regression and its purpose.

11. Use the Boston house prices dataset (from sklearn.datasets import load_boston) to predict house prices based on features like average number of rooms and crime rate.
12. Use the Iris dataset (from sklearn.datasets import load_iris) to classify iris flowers into different species based on sepal and petal measurements.
13. Use the Iris dataset to build a decision tree classifier to predict the species of an iris flower.
14. Generate a synthetic dataset using make_blobs from sklearn.datasets and apply k-means clustering to identify clusters.
15. Apply PCA to the Iris dataset to reduce the dimensionality of the data and visualize the transformed data.

Chapter 6
Advanced Machine Learning Techniques

6.1 Gradient Boosted Trees: XGBoost and LightGBM

In the 1990s, Robert Schapire and Yoav Freund developed a very popular algorithm called AdaBoost, where underfitting and reducing bias were introduced for the first time. AdaBoost is known as a parent of all gradient boosted decision trees. In the same series of algorithm development, the gradient boosted trees (GBTs) are a powerful and versatile machine learning technique that can be used for both regression and classification tasks. GBT is another popular model ensembling method which works by combining multiple weak learners, such as decision trees, with a single strong learner. Each weak learner is trained to improve the predictions of the previous learner, and the final prediction is made by combining the predictions of all weak learners. Various advantages of GBTs were described further.

High Accuracy

GBTs can often achieve high accuracy on a variety of tasks, even with complex datasets.

Flexibility

GBTs can be adapted to a wide range of tasks by changing the type of weak learner, the loss function, and other hyperparameters.

Faster Interpretability

Unlike some other machine learning models, GBTs can be relatively easy to interpret, which can be helpful for understanding why the model is making certain predictions.

Quick Response

XGBoost is well known for slow learning and quick response.

https://doi.org/10.1515/9783110697186-006

Preprocessing Not Required

If we work with XGBoost, there is no need for data preprocessing.

Any Data Accepted

With XGBoost, any type of data is accepted for training and testing the model.

Faster Prediction

Algorithms are very complex to build sequentially, that is a very time-consuming process, but when it comes to prediction, it is quite fast. That is why we can say "Faster prediction over the slow training."

Any way there is no doubt on the GBTs that are very good in the field of deep learning still it has some of the disadvantages like a coin. In further development boosting can be optimized by adequate loss function. This works on the concept of "A big set of weak learner can create one strong learner". XGBoost is coming from Gradient Boosted decision tree algorithm. Decision tree is always known as weak learner that why many experiments happened with it. Still we can say that there are still some drawbacks in algorithms.

1. **Computational cost:** Training a GBT model can be computationally expensive, especially for large datasets.
2. **Overfitting:** GBTs can be prone to overfitting if they are not carefully regularized.

Overfitting is a big challenge in any machine learning techniques, where we found different outputs in the testing and production environment. This problem leads to the performance and accuracy of the model training. In other words, we can say GBT is a powerful and versatile machine learning technique that can be used for a wide range of tasks. They are particularly well-suited for tasks where high accuracy and interpretability are important. Let's have a look on the following code:

The Drawing 6.1 shows the Decision Tree to buy a smart phone based on age.

```
import seaborn as sns
import pandas as pd
import numpy as np
import matplotlib.pyplot as plt
import warnings

warnings.filterwarnings("ignore")
```

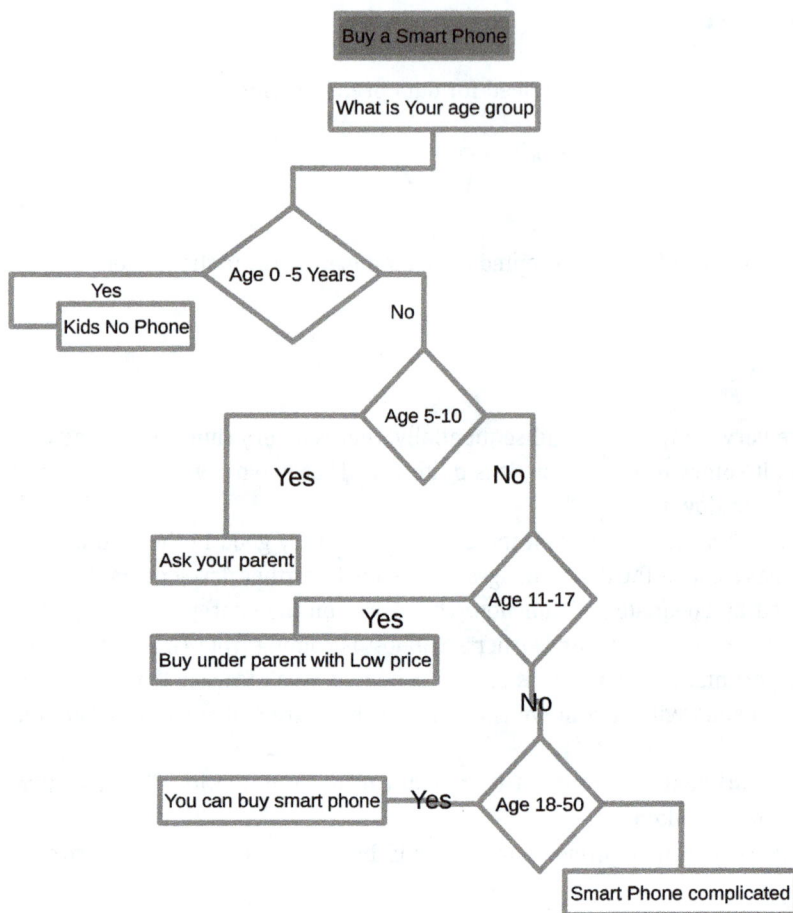

Drawing 6.1: Decision tree.

```
diamonds = sns.load_dataset("diamonds")
diamonds.head()
diamonds.shape
diamonds.describe()
diamonds.describe(exclude=np.number)
from sklearn.model_selection import train_test_split

# Extract feature and target arrays
X, y = diamonds.drop('price', axis=1), diamonds[['price']]
# Extract text features
cats = X.select_dtypes(exclude=np.number).columns.tolist()
# Convert to Pandas category
for col in cats:
```

```
X[col] = X[col].astype('category')
```

```
X.dtypes
# Split the data
X_train, X_test, y_train, y_test = train_test_split(X, y,
random_state=1)
import xgboost as xgb
```

```
# Create regression matrices
dtrain_reg = xgb.DMatrix(X_train, y_train, enable_categorical=True)
dtest_reg = xgb.DMatrix(X_test, y_test, enable_categorical=True)
```

In the above code, we have seen step-by-step preparation of the dataset and getting ready for training and testing data. The percentage of the dataset for training and testing may be changed according to the application. But in many of the cases, we are keeping 20% for testing and 80% for training purpose. In gradient boosting, at each step, a new weak model is trained to predict the "error" of the current strong model and we know that the error is a difference between the predicted value and the expected value. The low error model is known better than the higher error rate:

$$F|_{i+1} = F|_i - f|_i$$

where F_{i+1} is the final error calculated, F_i is the strong model at step i, and f_i is the weak model at step I. This operation keeps repeating until it meets the given maximum accuracy. Some of the points are given below, which will help us to understand the internal working mechanism of GBTs:

1. GBT works by iteratively building the decision trees. Each tree is trained to improve upon the predictions of the previous tree, and the final prediction is made by combining the predictions of all the trees.
2. The loss function is a measure of how well the model's predictions fit the data. The loss function is used to train each tree, and it is also used to determine when to stop training the model.
3. GBTs have a number of hyperparameters that can be tuned to improve the model's performance. These hyperparameters include the number of trees, the learning rate, and the maximum depth of the trees.

6.1.1 XGBoost Algorithm

XGBoost, short for *eXtreme Gradient Boosting*, is a specific and very popular implementation of GBTs. In the previous code, we have seen that data collection and sampling by specified percentage for training and testing datasets. Now let's have a look at how to calculate mean squared error (MSE) for better accuracy of the trained model.

```python
import numpy as np

mse = np.mean((actual - predicted) ** 2)
rmse = np.sqrt(mse)
# Define hyperparameters
params = {"objective": "reg:squarederror", "tree_method": "gpu_hist"}
n = 100
model = xgb.train(
    params=params,
    dtrain=dtrain_reg,
    num_boost_round=n,
)
from sklearn.metrics import mean_squared_error

preds = model.predict(dtest_reg)
rmse = mean_squared_error(y_test, preds, squared=False)

print(f"RMSE of the base model: {rmse:.3f}")
```

In general, we can say that all these boosting algorithms share a common principle, use boosting to create an ensemble of learners, and not only inherit the strengths of GBTs like high accuracy, flexibility, and interpretability, but also boast several improvements and unique features:

1. **Scalability:** XGBoost is optimized for speed and efficiency, making it capable of handling large datasets much faster than traditional GBT implementations.
2. **Regularization:** XGBoost incorporates various regularization techniques to prevent overfitting, a common issue with GBTs. This allows it to achieve better performance on unseen data.
3. **Parallelization:** XGBoost can be easily parallelized across multiple cores or machines, further enhancing its training speed.
4. **Second-order optimization:** XGBoost utilizes a second-order Taylor approximation in its loss function, leading to faster convergence and potentially better accuracy compared to standard GBTs.
5. **Sparse data handling:** XGBoost efficiently handles sparse data, where most features have missing values for most observations. This is crucial for many real-world datasets.
6. **Customization:** XGBoost offers numerous hyperparameters to fine-tune the model for specific tasks and data characteristics.

Due to its impressive performance and flexibility, XGBoost has become widely adopted across various domains, including:

1. **Finance:** Predicting loan defaults, credit risk, and stock prices
2. **E-commerce:** Recommending products, predicting customer churn, and detecting fraudulent transactions
3. **Manufacturing:** Predicting machine failures, optimizing production processes, and improving quality control
4. **Healthcare:** Predicting disease diagnoses, analyzing medical images, and personalizing treatment plans

XGBoost is a powerful tool for machine learning practitioners, offering a robust and adaptable solution for various prediction and classification tasks. Let's have a look on the following code:

```python
import xgboost as xgb
from sklearn.datasets import load_iris
from sklearn.model_selection import train_test_split
from sklearn.metrics import accuracy_score

# Load the Iris dataset
iris = load_iris()
X = iris.data
y = iris.target

# Split the data into training and testing sets
X_train, X_test, y_train, y_test = train_test_split(X, y, test_size=0.2,
random_state=42)

# Create an XGBoost classifier
xgb_model = xgb.XGBClassifier(objective='multi:softmax', # For multi-
class classification
        num_class=3, # Number of classes in the dataset
        n_estimators=100, # Number of trees
        learning_rate=0.1, # Step size shrinkage
        max_depth=5, # Maximum depth of each tree
        gamma=0.2, # Minimum loss reduction required to make a further
        partition
                )

# Train the model
xgb_model.fit(X_train, y_train)
# Make predictions on the test set
```

```
y_pred = xgb_model.predict(X_test)

# Evaluate the model's accuracy
accuracy = accuracy_score(y_test, y_pred)
print("Accuracy:", accuracy)
```

Gradient boosting techniques deal with a biggest problem called bias. Usually, we get one issue with the decision tree that underfits the data. It splits the dataset only few of times in an attempt to separate the data but technically we can divide into small two pieces. This is how we can improve the performance of the model. Random forest is a good example here, where it prunes and grows tree based on the required data. Bagging is the technique here to reduce overall variance of the algorithm implementation:

$$H(x) = \sum_{j=1}^{m} a_j h_j(x)$$

where a_j is the rate of learning, $h_j(x)$ is a weak learner, and if we make it a sum of all this, then it becomes more powerful than an ensemble of weak learners. Let's see another code for extreme gradient boost code in production environment that will produce a better accuracy in comparing with the previous example. Here, we have given the complete code that starts from the beginning to end:

```
import seaborn as sns
import pandas as pd
import numpy as np
import matplotlib.pyplot as plt
import warnings

warnings.filterwarnings("ignore")

diamonds = sns.load_dataset("diamonds")
diamonds.head()

diamonds.shape
diamonds.describe()
diamonds.describe(exclude=np.number)
from sklearn.model_selection import train_test_split

# Extract feature and target arrays
X, y = diamonds.drop('price', axis=1), diamonds[['price']]
# Extract text features
```

```python
cats = X.select_dtypes(exclude=np.number).columns.tolist()

# Convert to Pandas category
for col in cats:
    X[col] = X[col].astype('category')

X.dtypes
# Split the data
X_train, X_test, y_train, y_test = train_test_split(X, y,
random_state=1)
import xgboost as xgb

# Create regression matrices
dtrain_reg = xgb.DMatrix(X_train, y_train, enable_categorical=True)
dtest_reg = xgb.DMatrix(X_test, y_test, enable_categorical=True)

import numpy as np

mse = np.mean((actual - predicted) ** 2)
rmse = np.sqrt(mse)
# Define hyperparameters
params = {"objective": "reg:squarederror", "tree_method": "gpu_hist"}
n = 100
model = xgb.train(
    params=params,
    dtrain=dtrain_reg,
    num_boost_round=n,
)
from sklearn.metrics import mean_squared_error

preds = model.predict(dtest_reg)
rmse = mean_squared_error(y_test, preds, squared=False)

print(f"RMSE of the base model: {rmse:.3f}")


params = {"objective": "multi:softprob", "tree_method": "gpu_hist",
"num_class": 5}
n = 1000

results = xgb.cv(
    params, dtrain_clf,
```

```
    num_boost_round=n,
    nfold=5,
    metrics=["mlogloss", "auc", "merror"],
)
results.keys()

Index(['train-mlogloss-mean', 'train-mlogloss-std', 'train-auc-mean',

       'train-auc-std', 'train-merror-mean', 'train-merror-std',

       'test-mlogloss-mean', 'test-mlogloss-std', 'test-auc-mean',

       'test-auc-std', 'test-merror-mean', 'test-merror-std'],

       dtype='object')
results['test-auc-mean'].max()
import xgboost as xgb

# Train a model using the scikit-learn API
xgb_classifier = xgb.XGBClassifier(n_estimators=100, objective='binary:
logistic', tree_method='hist', eta=0.1, max_depth=3,
enable_categorical=True)
xgb_classifier.fit(X_train, y_train)

# Convert the model to a native API model
model = xgb_classifier.get_booster()
```

6.1.1.1 Ensemble Learning

Ensemble learning is a model that makes prediction based on a number of different models. By combining a number of different models, ensemble learning tends to be more flexible with less bias and less variance or data sensitivity. In this segment, begging and boosting is the most common approach, where bagging is a training bunch of models in a parallel way and learns from a random subset of the data. Let's have a look on the following code that shows the actual implementation of a gradient boosting classifier on 5,000 random numbers:

```
from sklearn.ensemble import HistGradientBoostingClassifier
from sklearn.datasets import make_hastie_10_2

X, y = make_hastie_10_2(random_state=0)
X_train, X_test = X[:5000], X[5000:]
```

```
y_train, y_test = y[:5000], y[5000:]

clf = HistGradientBoostingClassifier(max_iter=100).fit(X_train, y_train)
score = clf.score(X_test, y_test)
print(score)
```

The above code will gives us the score *0.9274285714285714*, which is best in the system in the initial stage. If we will train this model again, then the accuracy will improve because of the begging and boosting technique.

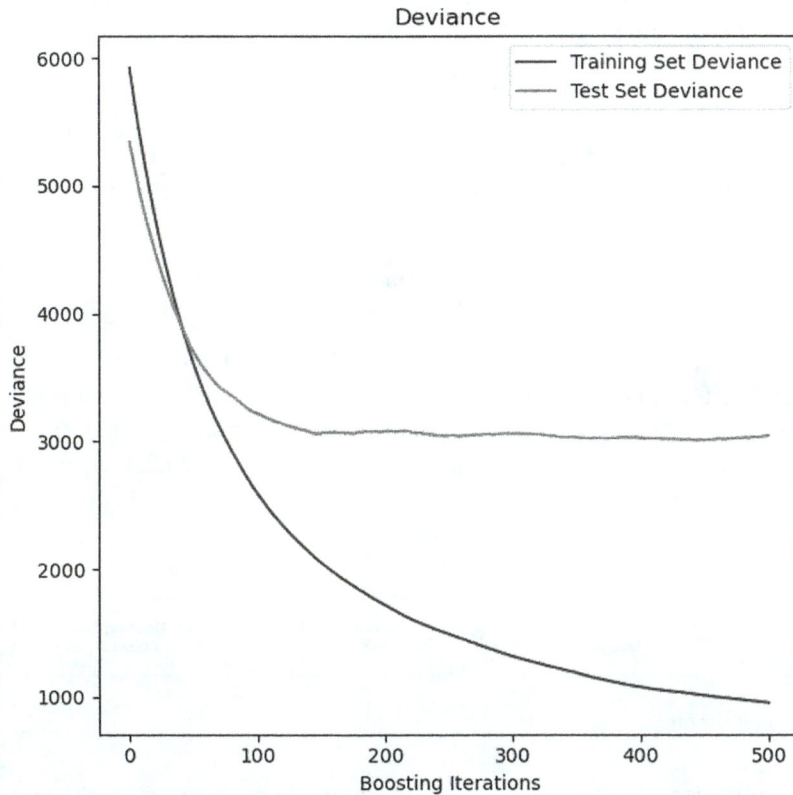

Fig. 6.1: Boosting iterations and deviation in training model.

The Fig 6.1 shows plot of the Boosting iterations and deviation in training model.

The best example of bagging is random forest. On the other hand, boosting means training a bunch of models sequentially, where every model learns from previous mistakes. The best example for the boosting is gradient boosting tree. Let's have a look in the picture given below

| Decision Tree-1 Accuracy - 95 | Decision Tree-2 Accuracy - 99 | Decision Tree-3 Accuracy - 92 | Decision Tree-n Accuracy - 96 |

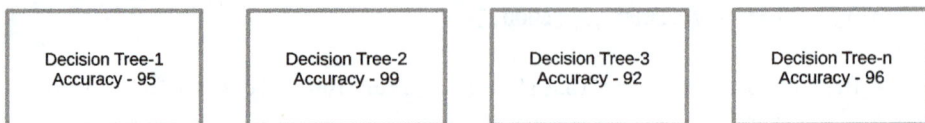

Drawing 6.2: Bagging method.

The Drawing 6.2 shows the Bagging method. The boosting technique combines weak learners sequentially so that every new tree corrects the error of the previous one. There are several different loss functions but for multiclass classification, cross-entropy is a very popular option. The cross-entropy of the distribution q relative to a distribution p over a given set is defined in the cross-entropy formula:

$$H(p,q) = -E_p[\log(q)]$$

where $E_p[\cdot]$ is the expected value operator with respect to the distribution p.

The discrete probability distributions p and q with the same support x are as follows:

$$H(p,q) = -\sum_{x \in X} p(x)\log q(x)$$

Finally, we can say that boosting is a core concept in XGBoost and plays a crucial role in its impressive performance and capabilities. It is completely different from traditional gradient boosting line. It builds an ensemble of weak learners (often decision trees) sequentially. Each new learner focuses on correcting the errors made by previous learners and uses the gradient of the loss function to guide the learning process. Some of the key components of XGBoost are given below:

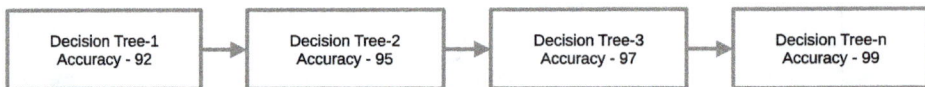

| Decision Tree-1 Accuracy - 92 | → | Decision Tree-2 Accuracy - 95 | → | Decision Tree-3 Accuracy - 97 | → | Decision Tree-n Accuracy - 99 |

Drawing 6.3: Boosting algorithm.

Second-order optimization: Employs Taylor approximations to optimize the loss function, leading to faster convergence and potentially better accuracy.

Regularization: Incorporates various techniques like L1/L2 regularization and shrinkage to prevent overfitting and improve generalization.

Parallelization: Leverages parallelization across cores and machines, significantly speeding up training for large datasets.

Sparse data handling: Efficiently handles data with many missing values, making it suitable for real-world scenarios.

There are few steps to boost the performance of the XGBoost, and some of them are given below:

Initialize: Begin with a constant prediction (e.g., mean of target variable).

The Drawing 6.3 shows the Boosting algorithm.

Iteration
a) Calculate the residual (difference between actual and predicted values) for each data point.
b) Build a new decision tree on the residuals, focusing on reducing errors.
c) Update the final prediction by weighting the new tree's predictions based on the learning rate.
d) Repeat: Iterate steps a-c until a stopping criterion is met (e.g., maximum iterations, minimal progress).

6.1.2 LightGBM Versus XGBoost

LightGBM, short for "light gradient boosting machine," is a powerful open-source machine learning library that leverages gradient boosting to tackle both regression and classification tasks. LightGBM is well known for its blazing-fast training speed. It outperforms many gradient boosting alternatives, making it ideal for large datasets. It consumes significantly less memory in all other algorithms even after bigger datasets on machines with limited resources. It supports the multiple machine execution in the same time. This is how we can reduce the training and execution time. It can handle more set of hyperparameters with fine grain control over the learning process. LightGBM is a compelling choice for machine learning tasks, where speed, efficiency, and memory usage are critical. Its impressive performance and ease of use make it a valuable tool for both beginners and experts. This algorithm can be used in multiple sectors like:
1. **Finance:** Fraud detection, credit risk assessment, and stock price prediction
2. **E-commerce:** Product recommendation, customer churn prediction, and anomaly detection
3. **Natural language processing (NLP):** Text classification, sentiment analysis, and machine translation
4. **Computer vision:** Image classification, object detection, and image segmentation

Both algorithms are widely used in the different sectors still we have some comparisons below:

Tab. 6.1: Comparison of LightGBM and XGBoost algorithms.

Features	LightGBM	XGBoost
Speed	Faster	Slower
Memory usage	Low	Higher
Accuracy	Equal	Equal
Ease of use	Easier	Complex

The Tab. 6.1 shows the Comparison of LightGBM and XGBoost algorithms with respect to speed, memory usage, accuracy and ease of use. Let's have a look by hands-on coding, and a sample dataset snapshot is given below. Before execution of this code, do not forget to install "*lightbgm*" library by using the following command:

pip install lightbgm

Below code will display as training accuracy 0.9647 and testing accuracy 0.8163. It may change in your computer according to the dataset size:

PassengerId	Survived	Pclass	Sex	Age	SibSp	Parch	Fare	Embarked
1	0	3	Male	22	1	0	7.25	3
2	1	1	female	38	1	0	71.2833	1
3	1	3	female	26	0	0	7.925	3
4	1	1	female	35	1	0	53.1	3
5	0	3	Male	35	0	0	8.05	3
6	0	3	Male	60	0	0	8.4583	2
7	0	1	Male	54	0	0	51.8625	3
8	0	3	Male	2	3	1	21.075	3
9	1	3	female	27	0	2	11.1333	3
10	1	2	female	14	1	0	30.0708	1
11	1	3	female	4	1	1	16.7	3
12	1	1	female	58	0	0	26.55	3
13	0	3	Male	20	0	0	8.05	3
14	0	3	Male	39	1	5	31.275	3
15	0	3	female	14	0	0	7.8542	3
16	1	2	female	55	0	0	16	3
17	0	3	Male	2	4	1	29.125	2
18	1	2	Male	60	0	0	13	3
19	0	3	female	31	1	0	18	3

Fig. 6.2: Dataset for model training with LightBGM.

The Fig 6.2 shows the Dataset for model training with LightBGM.

```
import pandas as pd
from sklearn.model_selection import train_test_split
import lightbgm as lgb

data = pd.read_csv("SVMtrain.csv")
# To define the input and output feature
x = data.drop(['Embarked', 'PassengerId'], axis=1)
y = data.Embarked
# train and test split
x_train, x_test, y_train, y_test = train_test_split(x, y,
test_size=0.33, random_state=42)
model = lgb.LGBMClassifier(learning_rate=0.09, max_depth=-5,
random_state=42)
model.fit(x_train, y_train, eval_set=[(x_test, y_test), (x_train,
y_train)],
          verbose=20, eval_metric='logloss')
print('Training accuracy {:.4f}'.format(model.score(x_train, y_train)))
print('Testing accuracy {:.4f}'.format(model.score(x_test, y_test)))
```

Components of LightGBM

There are two major components:

1. **Gradient-based one-side sampling (GOSS):** This technique intelligently samples data instances based on their gradients, focusing on informative examples that contribute more to improving the model. It is a method for efficiently selecting a subset of the training data during each iteration of the boosting process.

2. **Exclusive feature bundling (EFB):** Bundles similar features together during tree construction, reducing memory usage and potentially improving efficiency. EFB aims to reduce the number of features involved in the learning process, while minimizing information loss. It focuses on "mutually exclusive" features, meaning features that rarely take nonzero values simultaneously. Let's assume features representing different colors (red, blue, and green). They are mutually exclusive because an object cannot be red and blue at the same time.

3. **Gradient centralized (GC) algorithm:** It optimizes calculations around gradients, leading to faster training times and aims to improve training efficiency and potentially even the final model's performance by modifying the gradients used in the optimization process. Here, gradients tell the optimizer how much to update the weights of the neural network in each step. GC centralizes these gradients, meaning it subtracts the mean value from each column of the gradient matrix. This essentially forces the gradients to have an average of zero. GC differs

from gradient clipping, which limits the magnitude of individual gradients. While clipping prevents exploding gradients, GC focuses on overall gradient direction. Overall, we can say GC algorithm is a promising technique for improving the training of DNNs. It is relatively simple to implement and has shown positive results in various applications. However, it is important to consider its limitations and evaluate its effectiveness on a case-by-case basis.

Steps to Implement GOSS Works

GOSS is a powerful technique that contributes to the efficiency and accuracy of LightGBM models. It is specifically designed for gradient boosting algorithms and might not be directly applicable to other machine learning models.

1. **Calculate gradients:** For each data point, the algorithm calculates the gradient of the loss function with respect to the current model's predictions. Imagine a landscape where the loss function represents the valleys and hills, and the gradient points you in the direction of steepest descent.
2. **Sort by gradients:** Data points are then sorted based on the absolute magnitude of their gradients. Points with larger gradients (meaning they are farther away from the ideal prediction) are considered more "important" for training.

Selective Sampling

1. **Large gradients:** All data points with large gradients are **retained** for training. These points contain valuable information for improvement.
2. **Small gradients:** Points with small gradients are **randomly sampled with a certain probability**. This maintains diversity in the training set while focusing on more informative points.

Steps to Work with EFB

EFB is a valuable technique for improving the efficiency and potentially the accuracy of LightGBM models, especially when dealing with large datasets and high-dimensional feature spaces. However, it is important to consider its limitations and evaluate its effectiveness in your specific context. Steps are given below:

1. **Identify exclusive features:** Algorithms search for features with minimal overlap in nonzero values.
2. **Bundle creation:** These identified features are grouped into a single "bundle." This bundled feature acts as a combined representation of the individual features.
3. **Decision tree splitting:** During tree building, the algorithm considers these bundles instead of individual features for splitting decisions. This reduces the search space and overall computation.
4. **Unbundling (optional):** If needed, predictions can be "unbundled" back to the original features for interpretability.

6.2 Kernel Methods

Kernel methods are a powerful technique used in various machine learning tasks like classification, regression, and clustering. They offer a way to effectively handle nonlinear data by implicitly transforming it into a higher dimensional space where complex relationships become more apparent. Imagine trying to separate different colored dots on a two-dimensional plane. Let's have a look on the code below:

```python
# Importing Image and ImageFilter module from PIL package
from PIL import Image, ImageFilter

# creating a image object
im1 = Image.open(r"author.jpg")

# applying the Kernel filter
im2 = im1.filter(ImageFilter.Kernel((3, 3),
                        (-1, -1, -1, -1, 9, -1, -1, -1, -1), 1, 0))

im2 = im2.show()
```

By just applying the image classifier as a kernel method, update the pixels in the memory-loaded photograph. If we apply the following changes, then we will some black image that is the way of extracting important and required features from image. This image will look like the below snapshot:

```python
im2 = im1.filter(ImageFilter.Kernel((3, 3),
                        (-1, -1, -1, -1, 9, -1, -1, -1, -1), 1, 0))
```

Fig. 6.3: Author's original image.

The Fig 6.3 shows the Author's original image before applying the kernel method.

If the dots are linearly separable (e.g., a straight line can divide them), traditional linear algorithms like linear regression or linear support vector machines (SVMs) work well. However, what if the dots form a more complex pattern, like a circle or a spiral? Linear algorithms would not be able to effectively separate them.

Fig. 6.4: Author's image after applying the kernel method.

The Fig 6.4 shows the Author's image after applying the kernel method.

Kernel methods come to the rescue! They implicitly map the data to a higher dimensional space where the separation becomes linear. This mapping is done using a mathematical function called a kernel.

How the Kernel Method Works?

1. **Kernel function:** This function takes two data points as input and calculates a similarity measure between them. Different kernels exist for different data types and problems (e.g., linear kernel, Gaussian kernel, and polynomial kernel).
2. **Feature space:** The kernel function essentially represents an inner product in a high-dimensional feature space, even though we never explicitly compute the coordinates of the data points in that space.
3. **Linear algorithm:** A standard linear algorithm, like a linear SVM or linear regression, operates in this high-dimensional space using the similarity measure provided by the kernel.

6.2.1 Kernel Tricks

The "kernel trick" is a key aspect of using kernel methods effectively in machine learning. It refers to the clever way that kernel methods work with data without explicitly transforming it into high-dimensional space, saving both computational time and memory. Imagine you have data points that are not linearly separable in their original lower dimensional space. To use a linear algorithm for classification or regression, you would need to explicitly map the data into a higher dimensional space, where it becomes linearly separable. However, this transformation can be computationally expensive and memory-intensive for large datasets.

Instead of explicitly performing the transformation, the kernel trick leverages a special function called a kernel. This kernel function takes two data points as input and computes a measure of their similarity based on their inner product in the high-dimensional space.

Important Points to Remember About Kernel Tricks

1. The kernel never explicitly calculates the high-dimensional coordinates of the data points. It only computes the similarity measure, which essentially captures the relevant information for the learning algorithm.
2. This avoids the computational burden of high-dimensional representations while still enabling the use of linear algorithms in nonlinear scenarios.
3. Different kernel functions exist, each capturing different types of relationships between data points. Choosing the right kernel is crucial for the performance of the model.

The kernel tricks will help us by selecting the right kernel, and its hyperparameters are crucial for good performance. We can use it to understand the model behavior in the high-dimensional space, which can be challenging. Kernel methods can be prone to overfitting if not regularized properly. The kernel trick is a powerful technique that unlocks the potential of kernel methods in machine learning. By efficiently capturing data similarity in a high-dimensional space without explicit computations, it enables flexible and powerful solutions for nonlinear problems.

6.2.2 Radial Basis Function (RBF) Kernel

The radial basis function (RBF) kernel, also known as the Gaussian kernel, is one of the most popular and versatile kernels used in machine learning, particularly with SVMs and other kernel methods. It excels at handling nonlinear data, making it a valuable tool for various tasks like classification, regression, and clustering. Imagine data points scattered in a two-dimensional plane. If the data forms a straight line, a linear kernel can separate them easily. But what if the data forms a circle or a more complex shape? That's where RBF comes in. It implicitly maps the data points to a higher dimensional space, where the separation becomes more linear. This mapping is done by calculating the similarity between each pair of data points based on their

Euclidean distance. Points closer in the original space have a higher similarity in the high-dimensional space, represented by a larger kernel value. The interpolant that takes the form of a weighted sum of RBF interpolation is a mesh-free method, meaning the nodes (points in the domain) need not lie on a structured grid, and does not require the formation of a mesh. It is often spectrally accurate and stable for large numbers of nodes even in high dimensions.

The Fig 6.5 shows the Different stages of RBF optimization.

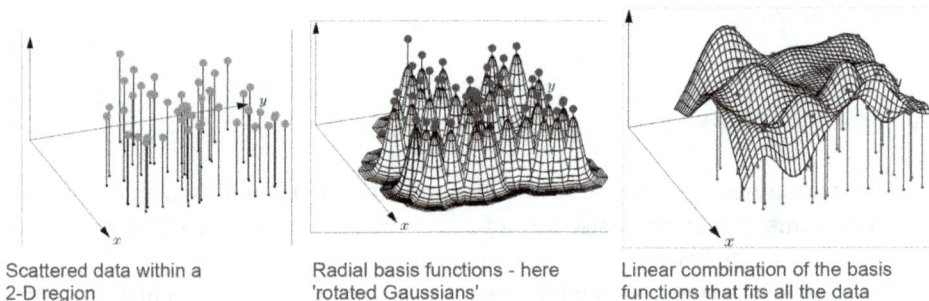

Scattered data within a 2-D region   Radial basis functions - here 'rotated Gaussians'   Linear combination of the basis functions that fits all the data

Fig. 6.5: Different stages of RBF optimization.

There are many types of RBFs available and some of them are given below.
1. **Gaussian:** Gaussian RBF is a powerful tool used in various machine learning algorithms, particularly for handling nonlinear data. It is a general class of functions that measure the similarity between two data points based on their distance. A specific type of RBF is shaped like a bell curve, where closer points have higher similarity scores than farther ones.
2. **Multiquadratic:** The multiquadratic RBF (MQ-RBF) is another type of RBF used in machine learning, particularly for interpolation and approximation tasks. It shares some similarities with the Gaussian RBF. Some of the functions are given below:
    (i) Unlike the bell-shaped Gaussian, the MQ-RBF takes the form: $\varphi(r) = \sqrt{(r^2 + c^2)}$, where r is the distance between two data points and c is a shape parameter.
    (ii) It combines the aspects of the linear and inverse MQ-RBFs, making it more flexible than either alone.
3. **Inverse quadratic:** The inverse of a function is another function that "undoes" the original function. When applied to a quadratic function, finding the inverse isn't always straightforward. Quadratic functions typically don't pass the horizontal line test, meaning one input can have multiple outputs, which isn't a property of a function and its inverse:
    1. However, if we restrict the domain of the quadratic function to a specific range where it only has one output for each input (passes the horizontal line test), then we can find its inverse. This restricted function is called a bijection.

2. Finding the inverse of a quadratic function in this case involves:
    (i)   Replacing the function's output (usually denoted by y) with a new variable (often x').
    (ii) Swapping the roles of x and x' in the equation.
    (iii) Solving the equation for x' in terms of y (which now represents the input).
3. This process can result in various solutions depending on the original quadratic function. You might need to choose the appropriate solution based on the restricted domain you defined.

Let's have a look on the code given below:

```python
import pandas as pd
import numpy as np
from keras.layers import Layer
from keras import backend as K


class RBFLayer(Layer):
    def __init__(self, units, gamma, **kwargs):
        super(RBFLayer, self).__init__(**kwargs)
        self.units = units
        self.gamma = K.cast_to_floatx(gamma)

    def build(self, input_shape):
        #           print(input_shape)
        #           print(self.units)
        self.mu = self.add_weight(name='mu',
                                  shape=(int(input_shape[1]), self.units),
                                  initializer='uniform',
                                  trainable=True)
        super(RBFLayer, self).build(input_shape)

    def call(self, inputs):
        diff = K.expand_dims(inputs) - self.mu
        l2 = K.sum(K.pow(diff, 2), axis=1)
        res = K.exp(-1 * self.gamma * l2)
        return res

    def compute_output_shape(self, input_shape):
        return (input_shape[0], self.units)
```

```python
# following dataset can be download from the URL
# https://www.kaggle.com/datasets/anokas/kuzushiji?resource=download&se
lect=k49-train-imgs.npz
# https://www.kaggle.com/datasets/anokas/kuzushiji?resource=download&se
lect=k49-train-labels.npz
X = np.load('k49-train-imgs.npz')['arr_0']
y = np.load('k49-train-labels.npz')['arr_0']
y = (y <= 25).astype(int)

from keras.layers import Dense, Flatten
from keras.models import Sequential
from keras.losses import binary_crossentropy

model = Sequential()
model.add(Flatten(input_shape=(28, 28)))
model.add(RBFLayer(10, 0.5))
model.add(Dense(1, activation='sigmoid', name='foo'))

model.compile(optimizer='rmsprop', loss=binary_crossentropy)

model.fit(X, y, batch_size=256, epochs=3)
```

```
=================================Output=================================
Epoch 1/3
WARNING:tensorflow:From C:\Users\23188\PycharmProjects\workshop\.venv\Lib\site-
packages\keras\src\utils\tf_utils.py:492: The name tf.ragged.RaggedTensorValue is dep-
recated. Please use tf.compat.v1.ragged.RaggedTensorValue instead.

908/908 [==============================] - 7s 7ms/step - loss: 0.6821
Epoch 2/3
908/908 [==============================] - 7s 8ms/step - loss: 0.6805
Epoch 3/3
908/908 [==============================] - 10s 11ms/step - loss: 0.6805
=======================================================================
```

6.2.3 Clustering Techniques Beyond k-Means

k-Means is a popular and straightforward clustering algorithm, but it does have some limitations. So, venturing beyond k-means opens up a diverse toolbox for tackling more complex data structures and clustering needs. This is an experiment with different techniques, evaluates their performance using appropriate metrics, and chooses the one that best suits your needs. Remember that there's no "one-size-fits-all" solution, and exploring beyond k-means opens up a world of possibilities for effective data clustering! Some of the important techniques are given below:

Hierarchical clustering: This approach builds a hierarchy of clusters, either agglomerative (bottom-up) or divisive (top-down), grouping points based on their proximity. It's flexible but lacks clear guidelines for choosing the "best" level of granularity.

Ward's method: This approach minimizes the variance within each cluster, aiming for compact and spherical clusters. However, it might struggle with elongated or irregular shapes.

Average linkage: This method joins clusters based on the average distance between all pairs of points in the clusters, leading to more balanced clusters but potentially sacrificing compactness.

Density-based spatial clustering of applications with noise (DBSCAN): This method identifies clusters based on core points (high density) and their connected neighbors, allowing for irregular-shaped clusters and handling noise effectively. It is a powerful clustering algorithm that goes beyond the limitations of k-means. We can use DBSCAN in anomaly detection (noise identification), image segmentation, customer segmentation, market research, and scientific data analysis. DBSCAN is a valuable tool in your data analysis toolkit, but understanding its strengths and limitations is crucial for effective application.

DBSCAN have some advantages too:
- **Density-based:** Identifies clusters based on **density**, focusing on areas with many nearby points and leaving out sparse regions considered noise.
- **No predefined number of clusters:** Unlike k-means, you don't need to specify the number of clusters beforehand. DBSCAN finds them automatically based on the data's inherent density.
- **Handles noise effectively:** Can identify and exclude outliers or points in low-density regions, making it robust to noisy data.
- **Finds arbitrarily shaped clusters:** Unlike k-means which assumes spherical clusters, DBSCAN can discover clusters of any shape, including elongated or irregular forms.

How DBSCAN Works?

- **Define the following two parameters:**
  - **ε (epsilon):** Maximum distance between points to be considered neighbors.
  - **MinPts (minimum points):** Minimum number of neighbors required for a point to be a core point (high density).
- **Identify core points:** Points with at least MinPts neighbors within ε distance.
- **Expand clusters:** Starting from core points, iteratively add their neighbors that also have MinPts neighbors, forming clusters.
- **Mark remaining points:** Points not part of any cluster expansion are considered noise.

The Fig 6.6 shows plot of Sorted observation versus k-NN distance.

Let's have a look on the code below, which is implementing DBSCN algorithm:

```python
import pandas as pd
from numpy import array


df = pd.read_csv("https://reneshbedre.github.io/assets/posts/tsne/tsne_
scores.csv")
df.head(2)
# check the shape of dataset
print(df.shape)


import numpy as np
from sklearn.neighbors import NearestNeighbors
# n_neighbors = 5 as kneighbors function returns distance of point to
# itself (i.e. first column will be zeros)
nbrs = NearestNeighbors(n_neighbors = 5).fit(df)
# Find the k-neighbors of a point
neigh_dist, neigh_ind = nbrs.kneighbors(df)
# sort the neighbor distances (lengths to points) in ascending order #
# axis = 0 represents sort along first axis i.e. sort along row
sort_neigh_dist = np.sort(neigh_dist, axis = 0)


import matplotlib.pyplot as plt
k_dist = sort_neigh_dist[:, 4]
plt.plot(k_dist)
plt.ylabel("k-NN distance")
plt.xlabel("Sorted observations (4th NN)")
plt.show()
```

```
from kneed import KneeLocator
kneedle = KneeLocator(x = range(1, len(neigh_dist)+1), y = k_dist, S =
1.0,
                  curve = "concave", direction = "increasing", online=True)
```

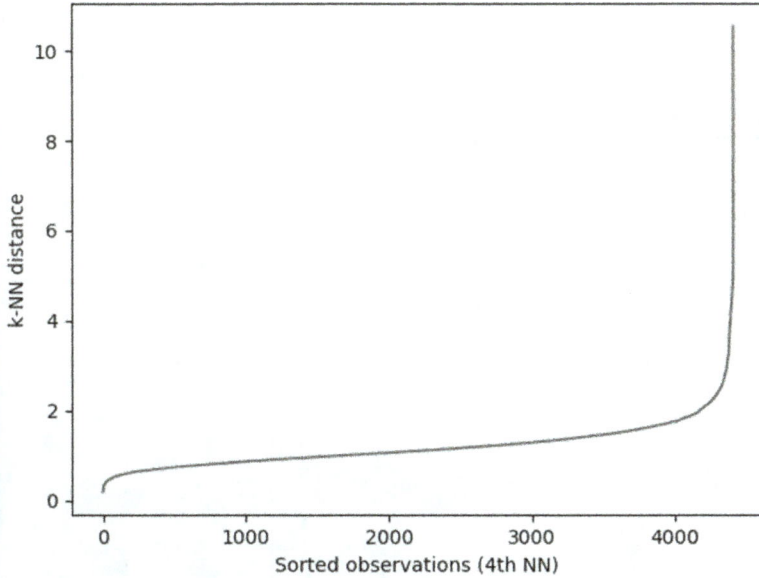

Fig. 6.6: Sorted observation versus k-NN distance.

```
# get the estimate of knee point
print(kneedle.knee_y)

kneedle.plot_knee()
plt.show()

from sklearn.cluster import DBSCAN
clusters = DBSCAN(eps = 4.54, min_samples = 4).fit(df)
# get cluster labels
clusters.labels_

# check unique clusters
set(clusters.labels_)

from collections import Counter
Counter(clusters.labels_)
```

```
import seaborn as sns
import matplotlib.pyplot as plt
p = sns.scatterplot(data = df, x = "t-SNE-1", y = "t-SNE-2", hue =
clusters.labels_, legend = "full", palette = "deep")
sns.move_legend(p, "upper right", bbox_to_anchor = (1.17, 1.), title =
'Clusters')
plt.show()
```

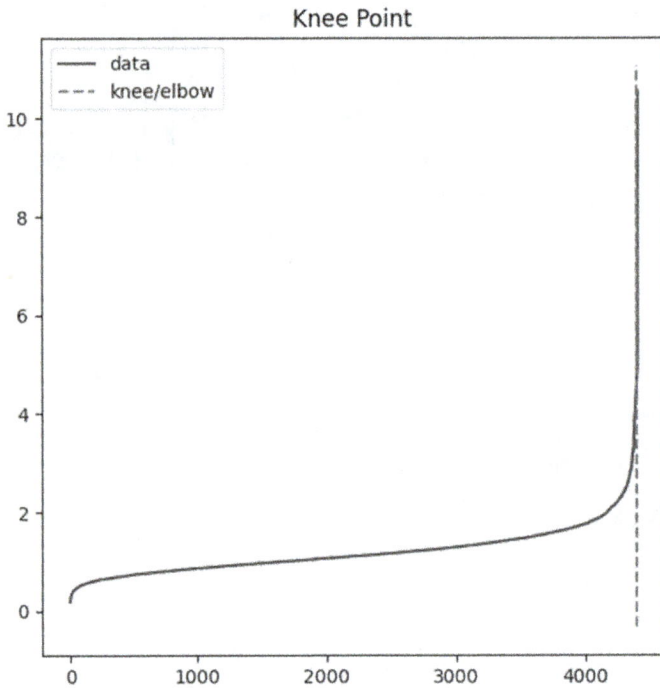

Fig. 6.7: Find knee point.

The Fig 6.7 shows plot to Find knee point.

Where Not to Use DBSCAN?

- **Parameter sensitivity:** Choosing optimal values for ε and MinPts can impact results and require some experimentation.
- **Curse of dimensionality:** Can be less effective in high-dimensional data due to the influence of distance calculations.

– **Clustering by fast search and ordering points (CLARA):** This algorithm partitions data into k clusters while minimizing the cost of moving points between clusters, leading to compact and well-separated clusters. This is a density-based clustering algorithm known for its efficiency and ability to identify clusters without a predetermined number. CLARA can be used in anomaly detection (noise identification), image segmentation, customer segmentation, market research, and scientific data analysis.

The Fig 6.8 shows plot of Final clustering after implementation of DBSCAN.

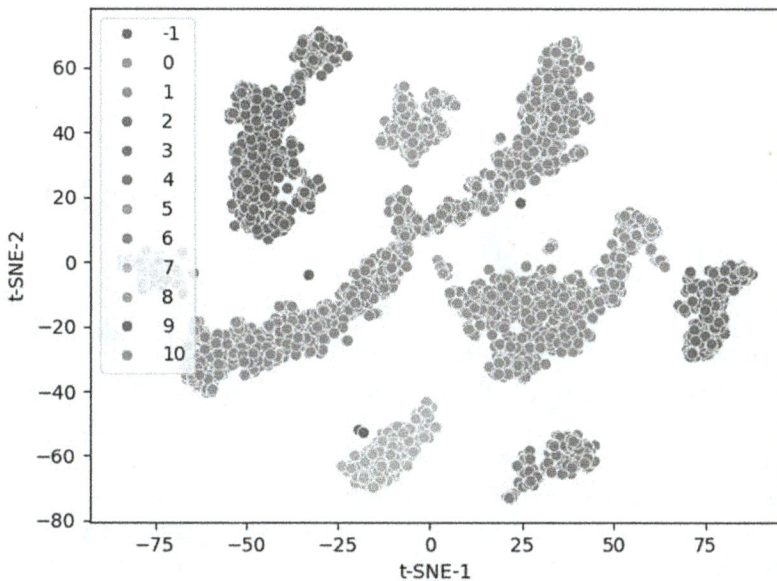

Fig. 6.8: Final clustering after implementation of DBSCAN.

Some of the important features of CLARA are given below:
– **Density-based:** Similar to DBSCAN, it identifies clusters based on **density**, focusing on areas with many neighboring points and leaving out sparse regions.
– **Fast search:** Utilizes a decision graph to efficiently identify core points and their potential cluster membership.
– **No predefined number of clusters:** Like DBSCAN, you don't need to specify the number of clusters beforehand. CFSFDP finds them based on the data's inherent density.
– **Handles noise effectively:** Can identify and exclude outliers or points in low-density regions.
– **Finds arbitrarily shaped clusters:** Similar to DBSCAN, it can discover clusters of any shape, including elongated or irregular forms.

How CLARA Works?

1. Calculate local density and reachability distance:
   1. **Local density (ρ):** Number of neighbors within a specific distance.
   2. **Reachability distance (δ):** Distance to the farthest neighbor with higher density.
2. **Identify core points:** Points with both high density and large reachability distance.
3. **Build decision graph:** Connect core points based on their reachability distances.
4. **Order points:** Traverse the decision graph from higher to lower density, assigning points to clusters based on their connections.
5. **Refine clusters:** Optionally adjust cluster boundaries based on additional criteria.

Where Not to Use CLARA?

- **Parameter sensitivity:** Like DBSCAN, choosing optimal parameters (distance threshold and density ratio) can impact results.
- **Curse of dimensionality:** Similar to DBSCAN, performance can decrease in high-dimensional data.

Mixture models: These models assume that the data arises from a mixture of probability distributions, where each distribution represents a cluster. Popular examples include Gaussian mixture models (GMMs) and latent Dirichlet allocation (LDA). GMMs are a powerful tool for data clustering and density estimation, particularly when dealing with data that can be represented as a mixture of multiple overlapping Gaussian distributions while LDA is a powerful and versatile probabilistic topic modeling technique widely used in text analysis and NLP tasks. We can use them in *document categorization and organization, text summarization and topic extraction, information retrieval and recommendation systems, anomaly detection and plagiarism detection, sentiment analysis and opinion mining,* and *language modeling and dialogue systems.* Mixture model is not recommended in:

1. **Choosing the number of topics:** Requires careful consideration and evaluation.
2. **Sensitivity to hyperparameters:** Tuning these parameters can impact results.
3. **Black box nature:** While topics are identified, their semantic meaning might require further interpretation.

- **Spectral clustering:** This method leverages the spectral properties of a similarity matrix to group data points. It is often effective for high-dimensional data and uncovering nonlinear relationships. Spectral clustering is a powerful unsupervised learning technique that leverages the power of linear algebra to partition data into meaningful clusters. We can use it in image segmentation (grouping pixels into regions), social network analysis (identifying communities), anomaly detection (finding unusual data points), document clustering (grouping documents based on similarity), and computer vision (object recognition and image classification). Let's have a look on the following code for CLARA internal workings. Don't forget to install library pyclustering using *pip install pyclustering*:

```python
from pyclustering.cluster.clarans import clarans;
from pyclustering.utils import timedcall;
from sklearn import datasets

# import iris dataset from sklearn library
iris = datasets.load_iris();

# get the iris data. It has 4 features, 3 classes and 150 data points.
data = iris.data

"""!
The pyclustering library clarans implementation requires list of lists
as its input dataset.
Thus we convert the data from numpy array to list.
"""
data = data.tolist()

# get a glimpse of dataset
print("A peek into the dataset : ", data[:4])

"""!
@brief Constructor of clustering algorithm CLARANS.
@details The higher the value of maxneighbor, the closer is CLARANS to
K-Medoids, and the longer is each search of a local minima.
@param[in] data: Input data that is presented as list of points
(objects), each point should be represented by list or tuple.
@param[in] number_clusters: amount of clusters that should be allocated.
@param[in] numlocal: the number of local minima obtained (amount of
iterations for solving the problem).
@param[in] maxneighbor: the maximum number of neighbors examined.
"""
clarans_instance = clarans(data, 3, 6, 4);

# calls the clarans method 'process' to implement the algortihm
(ticks, result) = timedcall(clarans_instance.process);
print("Execution time : ", ticks, "\n");
```

```
# returns the clusters
clusters = clarans_instance.get_clusters();

# returns the mediods
medoids = clarans_instance.get_medoids();
print("Index of the points that are in a cluster : ", clusters)
print("The target class of each datapoint : ", iris.target)
print("The index of medoids that algorithm found to be best : ",
medoids)
```

=================================Output===================================
A peek into the dataset : [[5.1, 3.5, 1.4, 0.2], [4.9, 3.0, 1.4, 0.2], [4.7, 3.2, 1.3, 0.2], [4.6, 3.1, 1.5, 0.2]]
Execution time : 1.2831659999792464

Index of the points that are in a cluster : [[50, 51, 52, 53, 54, 55, 56, 57, 58, 59, 60, 61, 62, 63, 64, 65, 66, 67, 68, 69, 70, 71, 72, 73, 74, 75, 76, 78, 79, 80, 81, 82, 83, 84, 85, 86, 87, 88, 89, 90, 91, 92, 93, 94, 95, 96, 97, 98, 99, 101, 106, 113, 119, 121, 123, 126, 127, 133, 138, 142, 149], [77, 100, 102, 103, 104, 105, 107, 108, 109, 110, 111, 112, 114, 115, 116, 117, 118, 120, 122, 124, 125, 128, 129, 130, 131, 132, 134, 135, 136, 137, 139, 140, 141, 143, 144, 145, 146, 147, 148], [0, 1, 2, 3, 4, 5, 6, 7, 8, 9, 10, 11, 12, 13, 14, 15, 16, 17, 18, 19, 20, 21, 22, 23, 24, 25, 26, 27, 28, 29, 30, 31, 32, 33, 34, 35, 36, 37, 38, 39, 40, 41, 42, 43, 44, 45, 46, 47, 48, 49]]
The target class of each datapoint : [0 0 0 0 0 0 0 0 0 0 0 0 0 0 0 0 0 0 0 0 0 0 0 0 0 0 0 0 0 0 0 0 0 0 0 0 0 0 0 0 0 0 0 0 0 0 0 0 0 0 1 1 1 1 1 1 1 1 1 1 1 1 1 1 1 1 1 1 1 1 1 1 1 1 1 1 1 1 1 1 1 1 1 1 1 1 1 1 1 1 1 1 1 1 1 1 1 1 1 1 2 2 2 2 2 2 2 2 2 2 2 2 2 2 2 2 2 2 2 2 2 2 2 2 2 2 2 2 2 2 2 2 2 2 2 2 2 2 2 2 2 2 2 2 2 2 2 2 2 2]
The index of medoids that algorithm found to be best : [78, 128, 2]
===

How Spectral Clustering Works?

1. **Construct a similarity graph:** Represent data points as nodes and connect similar points with edges (weighted based on similarity).
2. **Calculate the Laplacian matrix:** This matrix encodes the connections between nodes and reflects the similarity graph's structure.
3. **Extract eigenvectors and eigenvalues:** Compute the eigenvectors and eigenvalues of the Laplacian matrix.
4. **Project data onto lower dimensions:** Use the eigenvectors associated with the smallest eigenvalues to project data points into a lower dimensional space.

5. **Perform clustering in the projected space:** Apply traditional clustering algorithms (e.g., k-means) to the projected data to identify clusters.

Where Should Spectral Clustering Not Be Used?

1. **Computationally expensive:** Calculating eigenvalues and eigenvectors can be computationally demanding for large datasets.
2. **Choosing the number of clusters:** While it avoids specifying clusters beforehand, determining the appropriate number of clusters still requires evaluation.
3. **Interpretability challenges:** Understanding the meaning of eigenvectors and the resulting clusters can be challenging.

Mean shift: This nonparametric technique iteratively moves points toward denser regions until convergence, identifying clusters of arbitrary shapes. Mean shift is a density-based clustering algorithm that excels at discovering clusters of arbitrary shapes in your data. It can be used in *anomaly detection (noise identification), image segmentation, customer segmentation, market research*, and *scientific data analysis*.

How Mean Shift Works?

1. **Define a kernel function:** This function determines how the influence of neighboring points decreases with distance. (The commonly used kernels include flat and Gaussian.)
2. **Start at each data point:**
   (i) Calculate the average (mean) of its neighboring points within the kernel bandwidth.
   (ii) Shift the point toward this calculated mean.
3. **Repeat steps 1 and 2:** Iteratively shift each point toward the mean of its neighbors until convergence (meaning points stop moving significantly).
4. **Identify clusters:** Points that converge to the same location form a cluster.

Where Should Mean Shift Not Be Used?

1. **Parameter sensitivity:** Choosing optimal values for the kernel and bandwidth can impact results and require some experimentation.
2. **Curse of dimensionality:** Can be less effective in high-dimensional data due to the influence of distance calculations.
3. **Computationally expensive:** Iterative nature and dependence on distance calculations can lead to higher computational cost compared to some other methods.

– **Self-organizing maps (SOMs):** These artificial neural networks project high-dimensional data onto a lower dimensional grid, preserving topological relationships and revealing clusters visually. They are also known as the *Kohonen map*, a type of artificial neural network used for dimensionality reduction and data visualization. They excel at representing high-dimensional data in a lower dimensional space while preserving topological relationships. We can use it in customer segmentation, image and document clustering, fraud detection, market research, and anomaly detection. Some of the advantages are:
  1. **Unsupervised learning:** Discovers patterns and relationships in data without labeled examples.
  2. **Dimensionality reduction:** Projects high-dimensional data onto a lower dimensional grid (typically 2D), making it easier to visualize and analyze.
  3. **Topology preservation:** Maintains the relative distances between data points in the original high-dimensional space as much as possible in the lower dimensional map.
  4. **Visual interpretation:** The map visually represents the structure and relationships present in the data.

How Do SOMs Work?

1. **Initialize the map:** Create a grid of neurons in the lower dimensional space, each with randomly assigned weights.
2. **Present a data point:** Randomly select a data point from the high-dimensional space.
3. **Find the winning neuron:** Calculate the distance between the data point and each neuron using a similarity measure (e.g., Euclidean distance). Identify the neuron closest to the data point as the "winner."
4. **Update weights:** Adjust the weights of the winning neuron and its neighbors toward the data point, making them more responsive to similar data points in the future.
5. **Repeat steps 2–4:** Iterate through the data points multiple times, refining the map based on the data distribution.

Where Should SOMs Not Be Used?

1. **Parameter selection:** Choosing the right grid size and learning rate can impact the results.
2. **Interpretability:** While visually informative, understanding the meaning of specific regions on the map might require further analysis.
3. **Performance in high dimensions:** Effectiveness can decrease with increasing dimensionality of the input data.

Choosing the Right Technique

The best clustering technique depends on your specific data and goals. Consider factors like:

1. **Data type:** Numerical, categorical, text, etc.
2. **Number of clusters:** Known or unknown beforehand?
3. **Cluster shape:** Spherical, elongated, or irregular?
4. **Presence of noise:** Does the data contain outliers?
5. **Interpretability:** How important is understanding the reasons behind clusters?

6.3 Anomaly Detection

Anomaly detection stands for *identifying the Unusual*, also known as outlier detection, which involves identifying data points that deviate significantly from the expected pattern in a dataset. This is an important task in various fields, from fraud detection to system health monitoring. Some of the important anomaly detection techniques are based on their type to detect anomalies are described below.

6.3.1 Statistical Methods

6.3.1.1 Z-Score

Z-score, also known as the standard score, is a simple yet powerful statistical method for anomaly detection. It tells you how many standard deviations a particular data point is away from the mean of the dataset, providing a standardized measure of deviation from the average. It measures how many standard deviations a data point is away from the mean. Points with high Z-scores are potential anomalies:

$$Z - score = \frac{x - mean}{standard\ deviation}$$

where mean is the average of all data points in the dataset and standard deviation measures the spread of the data around the mean.

A Z-score of 0 means the data point is exactly equal to the mean. Positive Z-scores indicate points above the mean, with higher values representing larger deviations. Negative Z-scores indicate points below the mean, with absolute values signifying the degree of deviation. Typically, data points with absolute Z-scores greater than 2 or 3 are considered potential anomalies, as they fall outside the expected range of the majority of data points. However, this threshold can be adjusted based on your specific data and desired sensitivity. Let's have a look on the code:

```
import pandas as pd
import numpy as np

# Generate some sample data (replace with your dataset)
data = np.random.normal(loc=0, scale=1, size=100)

# Calculate the z-score for each data point
z_scores = (data - np.mean(data)) / np.std(data)

# Set a threshold for anomaly detection (e.g., z-score > 2 or < -2)
threshold = 2

# Identify anomalies
anomalies = np.where(np.abs(z_scores) > threshold)[0]

print(f"Anomalous data points: {anomalies}")
```

Where to Use Z-Score?

-   **Anomaly detection:** Z-score is widely used for identifying unusual data points, such as fraudulent transactions, system errors, or outliers in scientific experiments.
-   **Feature scaling:** In machine learning, Z-score is often used to standardize features before processing by algorithms, ensuring all features have similar scales and preventing one feature from dominating the analysis.
-   **Quality control:** Monitoring process variables in manufacturing or other industries often involves using Z-scores to detect deviations from normal operating ranges.

Where Should Z-Score Not Be Used?

1. Can be sensitive to outliers itself, as they affect the mean and standard deviation used for normalization.
2. Less effective for skewed or heavy-tailed data distributions.

6.3.1.2 Interquartile range (IQR)

Interquartile range (IQR) is a robust measure of variability in statistics, focusing on the middle 50% of your data. It helps you understand how spread out your data is without being overly influenced by extreme values, unlike the range. It identifies points outside the range between $Q1$ (25th percentile) and $Q3$ (75th percentile).

Steps to Calculate IQR

-   Order all data points from smallest to largest (ascending order).
-   Identify the first quartile ($Q1$): the median of the lower half of the data.
-   Identify the third quartile ($Q3$): the median of the upper half of the data.
-   Calculate the IQR: $Q3-Q1$.

Where to Use IQR?

1. **Outlier detection:** Points falling outside the range $Q1 - 1.5$ IQR and $Q3 + 1.5$ IQR can be considered potential outliers.
2. **Data exploration:** IQR provides a quick grasp of the central tendency and spread of your data, complementing the median.
3. **Comparing data distributions:** You can compare the IQRs of different groups or datasets to understand their relative variability.
4. **Robust measure of variability:** IQR is less sensitive to outliers compared to the range, making it more reliable for skewed or noisy data.

Where Should IQR Not Be Used?

-   Doesn't provide information about the entire data range.
-   Sensitive to the presence of a few very large or small values within the middle 50%.

6.3.1.3 One-Class SVMs (OCSVM)

One-class SVM (OCSVM) is also known as learning normalcy for anomaly detection. OCSVM is a powerful and versatile tool for anomaly detection, leveraging the principles of SVMs to learn the *normal* behavior of your data and identify points that deviate significantly. Let's imagine you have a training dataset containing only examples of "normal" data. An OCSVM analyzes this data and constructs a boundary around it, capturing the essential characteristics of normalcy. It learns a boundary around the normal data and flags points outside as anomalies. Data points falling outside this boundary are then flagged as potential anomalies. Some of the famous applications are *fraud detection, anomaly detection in sensor data, network intrusion detection,* and *industrial process monitoring.*

How Does OCSVM Work?

1. **Choose a kernel:** Similar to SVMs, OCSVMs use a kernel function to convert data points into higher dimensional space, potentially enabling better separation of normal and abnormal regions.
2. **Optimize the boundary:** The algorithm seeks to find the maximum-margin hyperplane (decision boundary) in the high-dimensional space that encloses most of the training data with the largest possible margin.
3. **Identify anomalies:** New data points are projected onto the same high-dimensional space. Points falling outside the learned boundary or exceeding a distance threshold are considered anomalies.

Where Should OCSVM Not Be Used?

– **Parameter tuning:** Choosing the optimal kernel and regularization parameters can impact performance.
– **High-dimensional data challenges:** Performance might decrease in extremely high-dimensional settings.
– **One-class limitation:** Requires only normal data for training, limiting its use to scenarios where abnormal examples are scarce.

6.3.2 Distance-Based Methods

6.3.2.1 Nearest Neighbors

Nearest neighbor (NN) is a versatile technique for anomaly detection. Points with very few or many neighbors compared to others might be anomalies. The assumption is that normal data points tend to cluster together, while anomalies deviate from these clusters, having fewer (or more) similar neighbors. By analyzing the number of NN for each data point, we can identify those significantly different and flag them as potential anomalies. We can use NN in *fraud detection, intrusion detection in networks,* and *anomaly detection in sensor data.*

Industrial process monitoring

Some of the very popular approaches are given below:

1. **k-Nearest neighbors (kNN):** Define a fixed number of neighbors (k) to consider. Points with significantly fewer or more neighbors than the typical number in their local area might be anomalies.

2. **Local outlier factor (LOF):** Calculate the ratio of a point's local density (number of close neighbors) to the density of its neighbors' neighbor. High LOF values indicate potential anomalies.
3. **Isolation forest:** Randomly partition the data and measure the isolation depth of each point, which reflects the number of splits needed to isolate it completely. Anomalies are easier to isolate and have lower depths.

Where Should NN Not Be Used?

– Performance can be sensitive to the choice of the "k" parameter in kNN.
– Can be computationally expensive for large datasets, especially with high-dimensional data.
– Might not be effective for complex anomaly shapes or overlapping clusters.

6.4 Clustering

Clustering in deep learning refers to using deep neural networks to automatically group data points into meaningful clusters based on their underlying similarities. Unlike traditional clustering algorithms, deep learning approaches can discover complex, nonlinear relationships between data points, making them particularly suitable for analyzing high-dimensional data making them particularly suitable for analyzing high-dimensional data. Data points not assigned to any cluster or belonging to small clusters could be anomalous. We can use it in the following fields:
– **Image segmentation:** Grouping pixels into regions based on their content (e.g., segmenting objects in an image)
– **Document clustering:** Categorizing documents based on their topics or themes
– **Customer segmentation:** Grouping customers based on their behavior or preferences
– **Anomaly detection:** Identifying data points that deviate significantly from the typical clusters
– **Scientific data analysis:** Discovering hidden patterns and relationships in complex datasets

Some of the advantages of clustering techniques are *automatic feature learning, handling complex data, identifying complex clusters,* and *scalability.* Some of the common approaches are given below:
– **Deep autoencoders:** These networks learn compressed representations of the data, with similar data points having similar code representations. Clustering can be performed on these encoded representations.

- **Clustering with generative models:** Generative models like variational autoencoders can learn to generate data similar to the input data. Clustering can be done based on the latent variables that control the generation process.
- **Graph-based approaches:** Deep learning techniques can be combined with graph-based clustering methods to leverage the network structure inherent in some data types.

6.4.1 Isolation Forest

Isolation forest is a powerful anomaly detection algorithm that utilizes isolation trees to identify anomalies in your data. This isolates anomalies by randomly partitioning the data space and measuring the isolation depth of each point. Its functions are given below:
1. Randomly select features and split points within their ranges.
2. Divide the data into two branches based on the chosen split.
3. Repeat steps 1 and 2 recursively until reaching isolation or a maximum depth.
4. Each data point has a path length representing the number of splits needed to isolate it.
5. Average the path lengths of a data point across all isolation trees in the forest.
6. Points with shorter path lengths (easier to isolate) are considered more anomalous.

6.4.2 Density-Based Methods

LOF: LOF is another powerful algorithm for anomaly detection, utilizing the concept of local density to identify data points deviating from their surroundings. It is used to calculate the ratio of the local density of a point to the density of its neighbors. High LOF values indicate potential anomalies. LOF compares the local density of a data point (its neighborhood) to the local densities of its neighbors. Anomalies are considered points with significantly lower local density, indicating they reside in sparse regions compared to their neighbors. The working mechanism and steps involved in smooth working are given below:
1. **Define the neighborhood:** Choose a parameter "k" representing the number of NN to consider for each data point.
2. **Calculate reachability distance:** Measure the reachability distance from each point to its neighbors, considering both their distance and the density of their neighborhoods.
3. **Compute local density:** Estimate the local density of each point by inverting the average reachability distance of its kNN.
4. **Calculate LOF:** Divide the local density of a point by the average local density of its kNN.

5. **Identify anomalies:** Points with significantly higher LOF values (higher than a predefined threshold) are considered potential anomalies, residing in sparser regions compared to their surroundings.

DBSCAN: Already discussed in this chapter.

6.4.3 Other Techniques

1. **Time series analysis:** The time series analysis is a powerful tool for studying and understanding sequences of data points collected over time. It detects anomalies in time-dependent data by deviating from expected patterns or trends. Time series analysis focuses on extracting meaningful information and patterns from data points ordered chronologically. Some of the key points about time series analysis are given below:
   – **Decomposition:** Breaks down the time series into trend, seasonality, and residual components to analyze each aspect separately.
   – **Autocorrelation and partial autocorrelation:** Examine the relationship between data points at different time lags to identify patterns and dependencies.
   – **Statistical modeling:** Fit various statistical models (e.g., ARIMA and SARIMA) to the data to capture seasonality, trends, and random components.
   – **Machine learning:** Utilize techniques like recurrent neural networks or long short-term memory networks to automatically learn complex patterns and make predictions.
   This could involve anything from stock prices to website traffic, and sensor readings to weather data. It helps to answer questions like:
   1. *Are there any trends or seasonalities in the data?*
   2. *What are the underlying patterns driving the data's behavior?*
   3. *Can we predict future values based on the historical data?*
2. **Spectral analysis:** Spectral analysis is also known as delving into the frequency domain. Spectral analysis is a powerful technique for decomposing signals into their constituent frequencies, revealing hidden patterns and insights that might be obscured in the time domain. It analyzes the frequency domain of data to identify unusual patterns. Imagine a complex signal like music, speech, or an EEG recording. We can use the following sectors:
   – **Audio analysis:** Identifying musical notes, analyzing speech patterns, and detecting audio anomalies
   – **Image processing:** Identifying textures, edges, and objects based on their frequency content
   – **Signal processing:** Filtering noise, extracting specific frequency components, and analyzing vibrations in mechanical systems

- **Economics and finance:** Studying trends and periodicities in financial time series
- **Geophysics and meteorology:** Analyzing weather patterns, understanding ocean waves, and studying earthquakes

While it appears as a single waveform over time, it is actually composed of various frequencies contributing to its overall sound or behavior. Spectral analysis breaks down this signal into its component frequencies, just like a prism separates white light into its constituent colors. Some of the key methods are used in:

1. **Fourier transform (FT):** The fundamental tool, decomposing the signal into a sum of sine and cosine waves of different frequencies and amplitudes.
2. **Fast FT:** A computationally efficient algorithm for calculating the FT, making it practical for large datasets.
3. **Power spectral density (PSD):** This represents the distribution of power (or energy) across different frequencies, providing insights into the dominant frequencies and their relative importance.
4. **Spectrogram:** A visual representation of the PSD over time, showing how the frequency content changes over the signal's duration.

Summary

GBTs are a powerful machine learning technique used for both regression and classification tasks. They work by combining multiple weak learners, typically decision trees, into a single strong learner: XGBoost versus LightGBM, two gradient boosting powerhouses.

Both XGBoost and LightGBM are popular implementations of GBTs known for their high accuracy and efficiency. They are powerful algorithms for gradient boosting, combining weak learners (decision trees) for improved accuracy and performance.

Ensemble learning is a powerful machine learning technique that combines the predictions of multiple models to achieve better performance than any single model. It is like getting multiple experts to weigh in on a problem and then taking the best guess based on their combined insights.

Kernel methods are a powerful class of algorithms in machine learning, particularly known for their ability to handle **nonlinear relationships** in data. While traditional linear models are limited to linear relationships, kernel methods can learn complex patterns by implicitly mapping data into a higher dimensional space where these relationships become linear. The "kernel trick" is a crucial aspect of kernel methods, often referred to as the key to their magic. It allows them to handle nonlinear data while maintaining computational efficiency. In other words, we can say that they transform data into higher dimensions for linear separation, enabling complex relationships between features.

The RBF kernel is a popular and powerful kernel function widely used in various machine learning algorithms, particularly SVMs. It supports only nonlinear data.

While k-means is a popular and widely used clustering technique, it does have its limitations. Here are some alternative clustering techniques you can consider depending on your specific needs and data characteristics:

DBSCAN is a powerful clustering algorithm that groups data points based on their density and connectivity. It is particularly useful for:

- **Identifying clusters of arbitrary shapes and sizes:** Unlike k-means, which requires predefining spherical clusters, DBSCAN can handle clusters with complex shapes, making it suitable for various data types.
- **Detecting outliers:** DBSCAN can identify and separate outliers from the main clusters, making it ideal for noisy datasets.
- **Handling data without predefined number of clusters:** You do not need to specify the number of clusters beforehand, which can be helpful when the number of clusters is unknown or varies across different datasets.

NN is a fundamental concept in machine learning that has applications in both classification and regression tasks. It is a simple yet powerful technique that leverages the **similarity** between data points for making predictions.

Clustering is a fundamental technique in unsupervised machine learning that involves grouping similar data points together. It is a powerful tool for discovering hidden patterns and structures within unlabeled data, offering valuable insights across various domains.

Distance-based methods refer to a broad range of techniques in machine learning that leverage the concept of **distance** between data points for various tasks. These methods have applications in both **classification** and **regression**, making them valuable tools across different domains.

One-class SVMs are a powerful anomaly detection technique that leverages the principles of SVMs for unsupervised learning tasks. It learns a boundary around normal data, flagging points outside as anomalies.

The IQR is a robust measure of variability in statistics. It tells you how spread out the middle 50% of your data is, excluding the potential outliers at the very top and bottom.

Z-score identifies outliers based on standard deviations from the mean, sensitive to outliers itself. Anomaly detection is a crucial aspect of data analysis, focusing on identifying data points that deviate significantly from the expected patterns or norms. It plays a vital role in various domains, from fraud detection in finance to equipment failure prediction in manufacturing.

SOMs, also known as Kohonen maps, are a type of artificial neural network used for **dimensionality reduction** and **visualization** of high-dimensional data. They excel at preserving the **topological structure** of the data while mapping it onto a lower dimensional space, typically a 2D grid.

Mean shift is a powerful and versatile technique in machine learning and data analysis, particularly useful for **unsupervised learning** tasks like **clustering** and **density estimation**. It operates by iteratively shifting data points toward the "densest" region in their vicinity, ultimately converging to the **modes** or **peaks** in the underlying data distribution.

Spectral clustering is a powerful technique in machine learning often used for **unsupervised learning** tasks like **clustering** and **graph partitioning**. It leverages the **spectral properties** of a similarity matrix to group data points based on their underlying structure. This makes it particularly useful for **identifying nonconvex clusters** and **handling data with complex shapes**, where other clustering algorithms like k-means might struggle.

Exercise (MCQs)

1. **What is GBT?**
   A) A regression technique that iteratively builds trees to improve predictions
   B) A classification technique that uses decision trees to classify data points
   C) A dimensionality reduction technique that projects data onto lower-dimensional subspaces
   D) A clustering algorithm that groups data points based on their similarity

2. **What are the main advantages of XGBoost?**
   A) Faster training speed and memory efficiency compared to LightGBM
   B) Built-in feature importance analysis tools
   C) Both (A) and (B)
   D) None of the above

3. **What is the key difference between XGBoost and LightGBM in terms of optimization?**
   A) XGBoost uses second-order derivatives, while LightGBM uses first-order derivatives
   B) XGBoost focuses on minimizing the L1 loss, while LightGBM minimizes the L2 loss
   C) XGBoost is more parallelized, while LightGBM leverages GOSS
   D) XGBoost relies on tree-level pruning, while LightGBM uses leaf-level pruning

4. **Which scenario is best suited for using XGBoost?**
   A) Large-scale datasets with high dimensionality
   B) Tasks requiring interpretability
   C) Both (A) and (B)
   D) Small datasets with few features

5. **When might LightGBM be a better choice than XGBoost?**
   A) If speed and memory efficiency are paramount
   B) If interpretability is essential and interpretable models are comparable in performance
   C) Both (A) and (B)
   D) None of the above

6. **Which of the following is NOT a characteristic of DBSCAN?**
   A) It requires specifying the number of clusters in advance.
   B) It can identify clusters of arbitrary shapes.
   C) It is sensitive to outliers.
   D) It is computationally efficient.

7. **What is the role of the eps parameter in DBSCAN?**
   A) It defines the minimum number of neighbors a point needs to be considered a core point
   B) It defines the maximum distance between two points to be considered neighbors
   C) It determines the density threshold for clustering
   D) All of the above

8. **What is the role of the min_samples parameter in DBSCAN?**
   A) It defines the minimum number of neighbors a point needs to be considered a core point
   B) It defines the maximum distance between two points to be considered neighbors
   C) It determines the density threshold for clustering
   D) It is not used in DBSCAN

9. **What is the time complexity of DBSCAN?**
   A) $O(n^2)$
   B) $O(n \log n)$
   C) $O(n)$
   D) It depends on the number of clusters

10. **What are some of the limitations of DBSCAN?**
    A) It is sensitive to outliers
    B) It cannot handle clusters of varying densities
    C) It requires careful parameter tuning
    D) All of the above

11. **How can DBSCAN be used for outlier detection?**
    A) Points that are not assigned to any cluster are considered outliers
    B) Points that are classified as noise are considered outliers
    C) Both (A) and (B)
    D) Neither (A) nor (B)

12. **What are some of the real-world applications of DBSCAN?**
    A) Image segmentation
    B) Anomaly detection
    C) Customer segmentation
    D) All of the above

13. **How DBSCAN can be compared with other clustering algorithms like k-means?**
    A) DBSCAN is more efficient for high-dimensional data
    B) k-Means requires specifying the number of clusters in advance, while DBSCAN does not
    C) k-Means is more sensitive to outliers
    D) All of the above

14. **What is the difference between DBSCAN and OPTICS?**
    A) OPTICS can find clusters of varying densities, while DBSCAN cannot
    B) OPTICS is more efficient than DBSCAN
    C) OPTICS requires specifying the number of clusters in advance, while DBSCAN does not
    D) None of the above

15. **What are some of the challenges in using DBSCAN in practice?**
    A) Choosing the appropriate values for eps and `min_samples`
    B) Dealing with high-dimensional data
    C) Handling large datasets
    D) All of the above

Descriptive Type Questions

1. What is the role of learning rate in GBTs?
2. How does early stopping help prevent overfitting in GBTs?
3. What are the different regularization techniques available in XGBoost and LightGBM?
4. How can you compare the performance of XGBoost and LightGBM on a specific dataset?
5. What are some limitations of GBTs?
6. Explain how GBTs can be used for both regression and classification tasks.
7. When might other ensemble methods like random forests be preferable to GBTs?
8. How can GBTs be tuned for optimal performance?
9. Discuss the importance of feature engineering for GBTs.
10. What are some emerging developments in the field of gradient boosting?
11. Explain how DBSCAN works in detail.

12. What are the steps involved in using DBSCAN for clustering a dataset?
13. How can you choose the appropriate values for eps and min_samples?
14. How can you evaluate the performance of DBSCAN on a clustering task?
15. What are some of the alternative clustering algorithms to DBSCAN?

Fill in the Blanks

1. _____is known as parent of all the gradient boosted decision trees.
2. GBTs can be prone to_____ if they are not carefully regularized.
3. XGBoost is optimized for_____, making it capable of handling large datasets much faster than traditional GBT implementations.
4. _____ is a model that makes prediction based on a number of different models.
5. _____ is a compelling choice for machine learning tasks, where speed, efficiency, and memory usage are critical.

Answers

1. AdaBoost
2. overfitting
3. speed and efficiency
4. Ensemble learning
5. LightGBM

True and False

1. DBSCAN is a hierarchical clustering algorithm. (False)
2. DBSCAN is a density-based clustering algorithm. (True)
3. DBSCAN can handle clusters of arbitrary shapes. (True)
4. DBSCAN is always the best choice for clustering data. (False)
5. DBSCAN requires a distance metric to be defined. (True)

Chapter 7
Neural Networks and Deep Learning

7.1 Introduction to Neural Networks

Neural networks are a type of artificial intelligence inspired by the human brain. They consist of interconnected nodes called neurons, which process information in a similar way to biological neurons. It is inspired by the biological neural networks that constitute in human brain. The trained system can learn and make decision like human. This whole thing is based upon given prior data and its training. It learns from its mistakes and improves system according to time. Fundamentally mimics human brains to develop algorithms to build predictive models and complex patterns. The human brain consists of fundamental cells known as neurons to store and process information. In the form of electronic signals these neural neurons will process the input data. The signals are passed to other neurons. The component stimuli receive the signal by dendrites of neuron. Resulting, processed information in the neuron cells and covered as an output. The resultant generated after processing, which is passed through the Axon to the next available neuron. It is depending upon the strength of the signal. Then finally it depends upon neuron which can accept or reject produced output until output accuracy not reaches to the maximum level as we can see in Fig. 7.1.

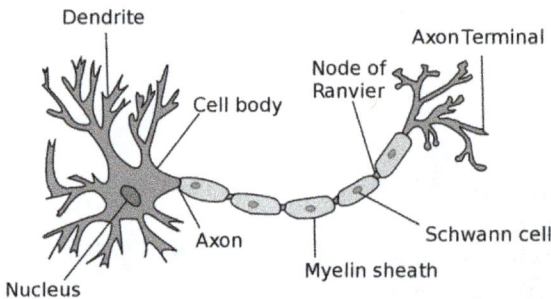

Fig. 7.1: Biological neuron in the human brain.

The Fig. 7.1 shows the Biological neuron in the human brain.

These networks learn by adjusting the connections between neurons based on data, enabling them to perform complex tasks like:

- **Image recognition:** Classifying objects in images (e.g., cats, dogs, and cars)
- **Natural language processing:** Understanding and generating text (e.g., machine translation and chatbots)
- **Recommendation systems:** Suggesting products or content users might like
- **Fraud detection:** Identifying suspicious financial transactions

https://doi.org/10.1515/9783110697186-007

Here are some key concepts to understand neural networks:
1. **Neurons:** The basic unit of a neural network. Each neuron receives input from other neurons, applies an activation function to process it, and sends its output to other neurons.
2. **Layers:** Neurons are organized into layers: input layer (receives raw data), hidden layer (process information), and output layer (generates final output).
3. **Activation function:** Determines how a neuron transforms its input. Common types include sigmoid, ReLU, and tanh.
4. **Learning:** Neural networks learn by adjusting the weights of connections between neurons. This is done through algorithms like backpropagation, which minimizes the error between the network's output and the desired output. In the world of neural networks, activation functions play a crucial role, acting as the gatekeepers that determine what information gets passed on to the next layer. They take the weighted sum of inputs from a neuron and transform it into an output value, introducing nonlinearity and allowing the network to learn complex patterns.
5. **Training data:** Large amounts of data are needed to train neural networks effectively. The quality and quantity of data significantly impact performance.

The Fig. 7.2 shows the Artificial neural network.

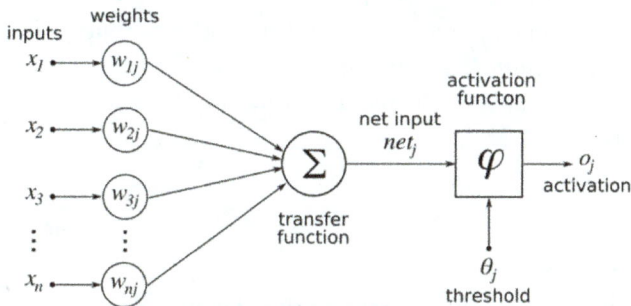

Fig. 7.2: Artificial neural network.

Types of Neural Networks
-   **Feedforward:** Information flows in one direction, from input to output. Common examples include multilayer perceptrons (MLPs) and convolutional neural networks (CNNs).
-   **Recurrent:** Information can flow in loops, allowing them to handle sequential data like text or time series. Examples include long short-term memory (LSTM) networks.

Benefits of Neural Networks
- **High accuracy:** Can achieve state-of-the-art performance on many tasks:

$$\text{Accuracy} = \frac{\text{True positive} + \text{true negative}}{\text{True positive} + \text{true negative} + \text{false positive} + \text{false negative}}$$

- **Flexibility:** Can be adapted to various tasks by changing architecture and training data.
- **Learning from data:** Can learn complex patterns from large amounts of data without explicit programming.

Challenges of Neural Networks
- **Data requirements:** Need large amounts of data for training, which can be expensive and time-consuming.
- **Black box problem:** Can be difficult to understand how they make decisions.
- **Computational cost:** Training large networks can require significant computing power.

7.2 Perceptron

Perceptrons are the fundamental building blocks of neural networks, serving as the basic unit of computation. While seemingly simple, they hold immense power when combined and trained, allowing complex learning and problem-solving. Here's a breakdown of their key features:

7.2.1 Structure of Perceptron

- **Inputs:** Perceptrons receive multiple inputs, representing features or attributes of the data.
- **Weights:** Each input is associated with a weight, determining its importance in influencing the output. These weights are initially random and adjusted during training.
- **Summation:** The weighted sum of all inputs is calculated.
- **Activation function:** This function transforms the sum into an output value. Common ones include the step function (binary output) and sigmoid function (continuous output).
- **Output:** The final result, representing the perceptron's classification or prediction.

7.2.2 Function of Perceptron

Perceptrons act as linear classifiers, meaning they can only learn and represent linearly separable patterns. This limitation led to the development of more complex architectures like MLPs with multiple layers and nonlinear activation functions. Despite their limitations, perceptrons are powerful tools for understanding the basic principles of neural networks and learning algorithms like perceptron learning rule.

7.2.3 Where to Use Perceptron

- While not used in complex tasks anymore, perceptrons still find application in:
- Simple classification problems like spam filtering
- Feature extraction and dimensionality reduction
- Understanding the theoretical foundations of neural networks
- To delve deeper, consider exploring concepts like
- MLPs and their ability to learn nonlinear relationships
- Different activation functions and their impact on learning
- Perceptron learning rule and its limitations
- Advanced neural network architectures like CNNs and recurrent neural networks (RNNs) built upon the foundation of perceptrons

7.2.4 Where to Use Activation Function

Nonlinearity: Without activation functions, neural networks would be limited to learning only linear relationships, which wouldn't be enough for real-world problems. Activation functions introduce nonlinearity, allowing the network to model complex curves and interactions between features.

- **Gradient propagation:** Activation functions are essential for backpropagation, the training algorithm used to adjust weights and biases in the network. They provide the necessary gradients (slopes) for these adjustments to occur, enabling the network to learn from its mistakes. The backpropagation is displayed in the next figure.
- **Sparsity and efficiency:** Some activation functions, like ReLU, encourage sparsity, where most neurons have zero outputs. This can improve efficiency and reduce the number of parameters to train.

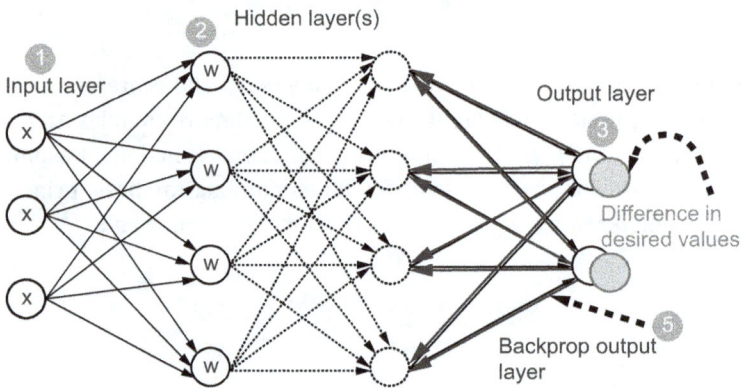

Fig. 7.3: Backpropagation.

The Fig. 7.3 shows the Backpropagation method.

While we are selecting the correct activation function then we need to take care of few things like:

Type of problem: Classification, regression, or other tasks?
- **Network architecture:** Deep or shallow network?
- **Computational efficiency:** How fast does it need to run?
- **Sparsity:** Is encouraging sparsity desired?

Some of the common activation functions are given below

Sigmoid: Outputs a value between 0 and 1, resembling a smooth S-shaped curve. Versatile but can suffer from vanishing gradients in deep networks.
- **Tanh:** Similar to Sigmoid but with an output range of −1 to 1. Less susceptible to vanishing gradients but can saturate at the extremes.
- **ReLU (rectified linear unit):** Simple and computationally efficient, outputs the input directly if positive, otherwise outputs zero. Popular choice due to its speed and sparsity.
- **Leaky ReLU:** Similar to ReLU but allows a small nonzero gradient for negative inputs, preventing neurons from dying completely.
- **ELU (exponential linear unit):** Smoothly transitions between linear and nonlinear behavior, addressing some issues of ReLU.

Let's have a look on python code implementation

```
import numpy as np
from sklearn.preprocessing import MinMaxScaler
import matplotlib.pyplot as plt
```

```python
# Create a Training and Test Data Set
input_train = np.array([[0, 1, 0], [0, 1, 1], [0, 0, 0],
                [10, 0, 0], [10, 1, 1], [10, 0, 1]])
output_train = np.array([[0], [0], [0], [1], [1], [1]])
input_pred = np.array([1, 1, 0])

input_test = np.array([[1, 1, 1], [10, 0, 1], [0, 1, 10],
              [10, 1, 10], [0, 0, 0], [0, 1, 1]])
output_test = np.array([[0], [1], [0], [1], [0], [0]])

# Scale the Data
scaler = MinMaxScaler()
input_train_scaled = scaler.fit_transform(input_train)
output_train_scaled = scaler.fit_transform(output_train)
input_test_scaled = scaler.fit_transform(input_test)
output_test_scaled = scaler.fit_transform(output_test)

# Create a Neural Network Class
class NeuralNetwork():
  # Create an Initialize Function
  def __init__(self, ):
    self.inputSize = 3
    self.outputSize = 1
    self.hiddenSize = 3

    self.W1 = np.random.rand(self.inputSize, self.hiddenSize)
    self.W2 = np.random.rand(self.hiddenSize, self.outputSize)

    self.error_list = []
    self.limit = 0.5
    self.true_positives = 0
    self.false_positives = 0
    self.true_negatives = 0
    self.false_negatives = 0

  # Create a Forward Propagation Function
  def forward(self, X):
    self.z = np.matmul(X, self.W1)
    self.z2 = self.sigmoid(self.z)
    self.z3 = np.matmul(self.z2, self.W2)
    o = self.sigmoid(self.z3)
    return o
```

```python
def sigmoid(self, s):
  return 1 / (1 + np.exp(-s))

def sigmoidPrime(self, s):
  return s * (1 - s)

# Create a Backward Propagation Function
  def backward(self, X, y, o):
  self.o_error = y - o
  self.o_delta = self.o_error * self.sigmoidPrime(o)
  self.z2_error = np.matmul(self.o_delta,
                  np.matrix.transpose(self.W2))
  self.z2_delta = self.z2_error * self.sigmoidPrime(self.z2)
  self.W1 += np.matmul(np.matrix.transpose(X), self.z2_delta)
  self.W2 += np.matmul(np.matrix.transpose(self.z2),
            self.o_delta)

# Create a Training Function
def train(self, X, y, epochs):
  for epoch in range(epochs):
    o = self.forward(X)
    self.backward(X, y, o)
    self.error_list.append(np.abs(self.o_error).mean())

# Create a Prediction Function
def predict(self, x_predicted):
  return self.forward(x_predicted).item()

# Plot the Mean Absolute Error Development
def view_error_development(self):
  plt.plot(range(len(self.error_list)), self.error_list)
  plt.title('Mean Sum Squared Loss')
  plt.xlabel('Epoch')
  plt.ylabel('Loss')

# Calculate the Accuracy and its Components
def test_evaluation(self, input_test, output_test):
  for i, test_element in enumerate(input_test):
    if self.predict(test_element) > self.limit and \
        output_test[i] == 1:
    self.true_positives += 1
    if self.predict(test_element) < self.limit and \
```

```
        output_test[i] == 1:
      self.false_negatives += 1
    if self.predict(test_element) > self.limit and \
        output_test[i] == 0:
      self.false_positives += 1
    if self.predict(test_element) < self.limit and \
        output_test[i] == 0:
      self.true_negatives += 1
  print('True positives: ', self.true_positives,
      '\nTrue negatives: ', self.true_negatives,
      '\nFalse positives: ', self.false_positives,
      '\nFalse negatives: ', self.false_negatives,
      '\nAccuracy: ',
      (self.true_positives + self.true_negatives) /
      (self.true_positives + self.true_negatives +
      self.false_positives +  self.false_negatives))

# Run a Script That Trains and Evaluate the Neural Network Model
NN = NeuralNetwork()
NN.train(input_train_scaled, output_train_scaled, 200)
NN.predict(input_pred)
NN.view_error_development()
NN.test_evaluation(input_test_scaled, output_test_scaled)
```

7.3 TensorFlow

TensorFlow is a powerful and popular open-source library for building and training machine learning models, particularly in the realm of deep learning. The fundamental data structure in TensorFlow. It represents multidimensional arrays of numerical values, similar to matrices in linear algebra. Tensors have a specific data type (integers, floats, etc.) and shape (number of dimensions and elements in each dimension). Operations in TensorFlow are performed on tensors, allowing for calculations and manipulations.

7.3.1 Computational Graph

- TensorFlow represents computations as a graph, where nodes are operations and edges are data dependencies.
- This graph defines the flow of data through the model.
- TensorFlow can automatically differentiate (calculate gradients) through this graph, enabling training via backpropagation.

7.3.2 Eager Execution

- TensorFlow 2.0 introduced eager execution, allowing you to see the results of operations immediately, line by line, similar to traditional scripting languages.
- This makes learning and debugging easier compared to the older symbolic execution mode.

Let's have a look on Python code to execute TensorFlow eager execution

```python
import tensorflow as tf

print("TensorFlow version:", tf.__version__)
mnist = tf.keras.datasets.mnist

(x_train, y_train), (x_test, y_test) = mnist.load_data()
x_train, x_test = x_train / 255.0, x_test / 255.0
model = tf.keras.models.Sequential([
 tf.keras.layers.Flatten(input_shape=(28, 28)),
 tf.keras.layers.Dense(128, activation='relu'),
 tf.keras.layers.Dropout(0.2),
 tf.keras.layers.Dense(10)
])
predictions = model(x_train[:1]).numpy()
predictions
tf.nn.softmax(predictions).numpy()

loss_fn = tf.keras.losses.SparseCategoricalCrossentropy
(from_logits=True)
loss_fn(y_train[:1], predictions).numpy()

model.compile(optimizer='adam',
 loss=loss_fn,
 metrics=['accuracy'])
model.fit(x_train, y_train, epochs=5)
model.evaluate(x_test, y_test, verbose=2)
probability_model = tf.keras.Sequential([
 model,
 tf.keras.layers.Softmax()
])

probability_model(x_test[:5])
```

=================================Output==

Epoch 1/5

– WARNING:tensorflow:From C:\Users\23188\PycharmProjects\workshop\.venv\Lib \site-packages\keras\src\utils\tf_utils.py:492: The name tf.ragged.RaggedTensor-Value is deprecated. Please use tf.compat.v1.ragged.RaggedTensorValue instead.

– WARNING:tensorflow:From C:\Users\23188\PycharmProjects\workshop\.venv\Lib \site-packages\keras\src\engine\base_layer_utils.py:384: The name tf.executing_ea-gerly_outside_functions is deprecated. Please use tf.compat.v1.executing_eager-ly_outside_functions instead.

– 1875/1875 [==============================] - 6s 2ms/step - loss: 0.2924 - accu-racy: 0.9146

– Epoch 2/5

– 1875/1875 [==============================] - 4s 2ms/step - loss: 0.1407 - accu-racy: 0.9585

– Epoch 3/5

– 1875/1875 [==============================] - 5s 3ms/step - loss: 0.1039 - accu-racy: 0.9687

– Epoch 4/5

– 1875/1875 [==============================] - 6s 3ms/step - loss: 0.0874 - accu-racy: 0.9734

– Epoch 5/5

– 1875/1875 [==============================] - 9s 5ms/step - loss: 0.0734 - accu-racy: 0.9770

– 313/313 - 2s - loss: 0.0697 - accuracy: 0.9786 - 2s/epoch – 5ms/step

===

7.3.3 Keras

– Keras is a high-level API built on top of TensorFlow, providing a user-friendly interface for building neural networks.

– It offers prebuilt layers, optimizers, and loss functions, simplifying the model creation process.

– Keras is a great way to get started with TensorFlow and experiment with different architectures.

7.3.4 Sessions

- In TensorFlow 1.x, sessions were used to manage the execution of the computational graph.
- With eager execution, sessions are no longer required, making the code cleaner and more intuitive.

7.3.5 Common Operations

- TensorFlow provides various built-in operations for mathematical calculations, linear algebra, data manipulation, and machine learning specific tasks.
- Examples include addition, matrix multiplication, convolutions, and activation functions. Let's have a look on the code given below:

```
import tensorflow as tf

# Create two tensors
a = tf.constant([1, 2, 2])
b = tf.constant([4, 5, 6])

# Add the tensors
c = tf.add(a, b)

# Print the result print(c) # Output: tf.Tensor([5 7 9], shape=(3,),
dtype=int32)
```

Above code demonstrates creating tensors, performing simple mathematical operations, and printing the result

7.4 Implementing Neural Network Using TensorFlow

Implementing neural networks with TensorFlow and Keras can be a rewarding experience, allowing you to build powerful machine learning models from scratch. Start with simple tasks and gradually increase complexity as you gain experience. Utilize tutorials and online resources for specific examples and code implementations. Experiment with different architectures and hyperparameters to find the best performing model for your task. Consider using tools like TensorBoard for visualizing training progress and model behavior. Here's a breakdown of the key steps involved:

1. **Define your problem:**
    1. What kind of problem are you trying to solve? (e.g., classification, regression, and image recognition)
    2. What type of data do you have? (e.g., images, text, and numerical data)
2. **Choose your network architecture:**
    1. What type of neural network is suitable for your problem? (e.g., feedforward network, CNN, and RNN)
    2. How many layers and neurons should your network have?
3. **Set up TensorFlow and Keras:**
    1. Install TensorFlow and Keras libraries using *pip install tensorflow keras*.
    2. Import necessary libraries in your Python code.
4. **Build your neural network model:**
    1. Use Keras' Sequential API or Functional API to define your network structure.
    2. Specify layers like Dense, Conv2D, and LSTM, depending on your chosen architecture.
    3. Set activation functions for each layer (e.g., ReLU and sigmoid).
5. **Prepare your data:**
    1. Preprocess your data, including normalization, scaling, and one-hot encoding if needed.
    2. Split your data into training, validation, and testing sets.
6. **Compile your model:**
    1. Define the optimizer (e.g., Adam and SGD) and loss function (e.g., categorical cross-entropy, mean squared error) appropriate for your task.
    2. Set metrics to evaluate your model's performance (e.g., accuracy, precision, and recall).
7. **Train your model:**
    1. Use the fit method to train your model on the training data.
    2. Monitor training progress on validation data to prevent overfitting.
    3. Adjust hyperparameters (e.g., learning rate and number of epochs) if needed.
8. **Evaluate your model:**
    1. Use the evaluate method to assess performance on the testing data.
    2. Analyze metrics to understand your model's strengths and weaknesses.
9. **Save and load your model:** Use the save and load methods to save your trained model for future use

Let's have a look on the given code below which demonstrates simple linear regression model by using TensorFlow deep learning framework eager execution:

```python
import tensorflow as tf

# Define training data
x_train = tf.constant([1.0, 2.0, 3.0, 4.0])
y_train = tf.constant([2.0, 4.0, 6.0, 8.0])

# Initialize variables for weights and bias
w = tf.Variable(tf.random.normal([1]))
print("Weight : ", w)
b = tf.Variable(tf.random.normal([1]))
print("bias : ", b)

# Define the model function
def predict(x):
  return w * x + b

# Define the loss function
def loss(x, y):
  # print(x, " : ", y)
  return tf.reduce_mean(tf.square(predict(x) - y))

# Optimizer
optimizer = tf.keras.optimizers.SGD(learning_rate=0.1)

# Training loop
for epoch in range(100):
  # Calculate loss
  current_loss = loss(x_train, y_train)

  # Update weights and bias based on the loss
  optimizer.minimize(lambda: loss(x_train, y_train), var_list=[w, b])

  # Print the current loss
  print(f"Epoch {epoch + 1}, Loss: {current_loss}")

# Make a prediction
prediction = predict(5)
print(f"Prediction for x = 5: {prediction}")
```

7.5 Building a Neural Network Using Keras Framework

```python
import tensorflow as tf
from tensorflow.keras.models import Sequential
from tensorflow.keras.layers import Dense, Flatten

# Load the MNIST dataset
(x_train, y_train), (x_test, y_test) = tf.keras.datasets.mnist.load_data()

# Preprocess the data
x_train = x_train.reshape(60000, 28 * 28).astype("float32") / 255.0
x_test = x_test.reshape(10000, 28 * 28).astype("float32") / 255.0

# One-hot encode the labels
y_train = tf.keras.utils.to_categorical(y_train, 10)
y_test = tf.keras.utils.to_categorical(y_test, 10)

# Build the model
model = Sequential([
  Flatten(input_shape=(28, 28)),
  Dense(128, activation="relu"),
  Dense(10, activation="softmax")
])

# Compile the model
model.compile(optimizer="adam", loss="categorical_crossentropy",
metrics=["accuracy"])

# Train the model
model.fit(x_train, y_train, epochs=5, validation_data=(x_test, y_test))

# Evaluate the model
loss, accuracy = model.evaluate(x_test, y_test)
print(f"Test accuracy: {accuracy:.4f}")
```

7.5.1 Difference between Keras and Tensorflow

Keras is a high-level API built on top of TensorFlow, designed for ease of use and rapid prototyping. It offers prebuilt components like layers, optimizers, and loss functions, simplifying the process of building and experimenting with neural networks. Keras is known for its readability and Pythonic syntax, making it easier to learn and use compared to TensorFlow's low-level APIs. Keras is widely used for quick experimentation, building prototypes, and developing deep learning models where simplicity and speed are priorities. On the other hand TensorFlow is a comprehensive framework offering a wide range of functionalities for various machine learning tasks including data manipulation, numerical computations, and deep learning. It provides low-level APIs that give you fine-grained control over your model architecture and training process. This allows for flexibility and customization, but requires more coding effort and understanding of the underlying concepts. TensorFlow is often used for research, complex tasks, and production-grade models where fine-tuning and control are crucial.

If you're new to deep learning or want to quickly experiment with different architectures, Keras is a great starting point. As you gain experience and need more control or flexibility, you can gradually transition to using TensorFlow's low-level APIs. You can even combine Keras and TensorFlow by building your model with Keras' high-level API and then fine-tuning specific parts using TensorFlow's lower-level functionalities. We can classify the TensorFlow and Keras applications based upon the model requirements. The Tab. 7.1 shows the Difference between TensorFlow and Keras framework based on different features:

Tab. 7.1: Difference between TensorFlow and Keras framework.

Features	TensorFlow	Keras
Level	Framework	High-level API
Focus	Flexibility, control	Ease of use, prototyping
Learning curve	Steeper	Easier
Applications	Research, complex tasks, production	Experimentation, prototyping, simpler models

7.6 Convolutional Neural Network (CNN)

CNNs are a powerful type of deep learning architecture specifically designed for processing grid-like data, most notably images. Their ability to automatically extract and learn features from visual inputs has made them a cornerstone of various applications from image classification and object detection to self-driving cars and medical image analysis. CNN is well known for image processing. Unlike traditional methods requiring manual feature engineering, CNNs automatically learn relevant features directly from the data. This is crucial for complex datasets where manually identifying features is impractical. CNNs are less sensitive to small shifts in the input image due to the use of shared weights and pooling. This makes them robust to variations in object position and viewpoint. CNNs can be easily scaled to larger and more complex datasets by adding more layers and increasing the number of filters. Some of the key concepts are given below:

1. **Convolution:** The core operation of CNNs involves applying a filter (kernel) to an input image. This filter slides across the image, calculating the dot product between its elements and the corresponding elements of the image at each position. This process helps identify local features like edges, textures, and colors.

2. **Pooling:** After convolution, pooling layers reduce the dimensionality of the data, summarizing the information extracted by the filters. Common pooling methods include max pooling, which selects the maximum value from a region, and average pooling, which takes the average. Average pooling computes the average value within the window. This summarizes the overall information in the region and can be helpful for capturing smoother features like textures. The pooling layer is used to reduced computational cost while Smaller data size translates to less computation needed during training and inference, making the model run faster. Overfitting prevention is very important part in any AI model. The pooling layer helps us by reducing data complexity. Pooling helps control model capacity and prevent it from memorizing the training data too closely, leading to better generalization on unseen data. Pooling can sometimes lead to better feature extraction by highlighting the most important information and suppressing insignificant details.

3. **Activation functions:** As activation function has been already discussed in the section 7.2.4 CNNs use activation functions to introduce nonlinearity and improve the model's ability to learn complex patterns. Popular choices include ReLU and Leaky ReLU.

4. **Layers:** CNNs typically consist of multiple convolutional and pooling layers stacked together, followed by fully connected layers for classification or regression tasks. Each layer learns increasingly complex features from the previous layer's output.

CNN is best in the recognizing objects, scenes, and activities in images (e.g., classifying handwritten digits and detecting faces in photos). It performs well in Locating and classifying objects within an image (e.g., identifying cars, pedestrians, and traffic signs in self-driving car applications). Image segmentation is the very powerful feature of CNN which is helping us by dividing an image into different regions corresponding to objects or semantic categories (e.g., segmenting organs in medical images). CNN is good in applying the artistic style of one image to another (e.g., creating images that look like they were painted by Van Gogh). Some of the popular CNN architectures include *LeNet-5, AlexNet, VGGNet, ResNet,* and *Inception.* Frameworks like TensorFlow and PyTorch offer tools for building and training CNNs. Let's have a look on CNN model trained in python:

```python
import matplotlib.pyplot as plt
import numpy as np
import PIL
import tensorflow as tf

from tensorflow import keras
from tensorflow.keras import layers
from tensorflow.keras.models import Sequential

import pathlib

dataset_url = "https://storage.googleapis.com/download.tensorflow.org/ex
ample_images/flower_photos.tgz"
data_dir = tf.keras.utils.get_file('flower_photos.tar',
origin=dataset_url, extract=True)
data_dir = pathlib.Path(data_dir).with_suffix('')
image_count = len(list(data_dir.glob('*/*.jpg')))
print(image_count)

roses = list(data_dir.glob('roses/*'))
PIL.Image.open(str(roses[0]))
PIL.Image.open(str(roses[1]))
tulips = list(data_dir.glob('tulips/*'))
PIL.Image.open(str(tulips[0]))
PIL.Image.open(str(tulips[1]))

batch_size = 32
img_height = 180
img_width = 180

train_ds = tf.keras.utils.image_dataset_from_directory(
  data_dir,
  validation_split=0.2,
  subset="training",
  seed=123,
  image_size=(img_height, img_width),
  batch_size=batch_size)

val_ds = tf.keras.utils.image_dataset_from_directory(
  data_dir,
  validation_split=0.2,
  subset="validation",
```

```
  seed=123,
  image_size=(img_height, img_width),
  batch_size=batch_size)
class_names = train_ds.class_names
print(class_names)

import matplotlib.pyplot as plt

plt.figure(figsize=(10, 10))
for images, labels in train_ds.take(1):
  for i in range(9):
    ax = plt.subplot(3, 3, i + 1)
    plt.imshow(images[i].numpy().astype("uint8"))
    plt.title(class_names[labels[i]])
    plt.axis("off")

for image_batch, labels_batch in train_ds:
  print(image_batch.shape)
  print(labels_batch.shape)
  break

AUTOTUNE = tf.data.AUTOTUNE

train_ds = train_ds.cache().shuffle(1000).prefetch(buffer_size=AUTOTUNE)
val_ds = val_ds.cache().prefetch(buffer_size=AUTOTUNE)

normalization_layer = layers.Rescaling(1. / 255)
normalized_ds = train_ds.map(lambda x, y: (normalization_layer(x), y))
image_batch, labels_batch = next(iter(normalized_ds))
first_image = image_batch[0]
# Notice the pixel values are now in `[0,1]`.
print(np.min(first_image), np.max(first_image))

num_classes = len(class_names)

model = Sequential([
  layers.Rescaling(1. / 255, input_shape=(img_height, img_width, 3)),
  layers.Conv2D(16, 3, padding='same', activation='relu'),
  layers.MaxPooling2D(),
  layers.Conv2D(32, 3, padding='same', activation='relu'),
  layers.MaxPooling2D(),
  layers.Conv2D(64, 3, padding='same', activation='relu'),
```

```python
    layers.MaxPooling2D(),
    layers.Flatten(),
    layers.Dense(128, activation='relu'),
    layers.Dense(num_classes)
])

model.compile(optimizer='adam',
      loss=tf.keras.losses.SparseCategoricalCrossentropy
(from_logits=True),
      metrics=['accuracy'])
model.summary()

epochs = 10
history = model.fit(
  train_ds,
  validation_data=val_ds,
  epochs=epochs
)

acc = history.history['accuracy']
val_acc = history.history['val_accuracy']

loss = history.history['loss']
val_loss = history.history['val_loss']

epochs_range = range(epochs)
plt.figure(figsize=(8, 8))
plt.subplot(1, 2, 1)
plt.plot(epochs_range, acc, label='Training Accuracy')
plt.plot(epochs_range, val_acc, label='Validation Accuracy')
plt.legend(loc='lower right')
plt.title('Training and Validation Accuracy')

plt.subplot(1, 2, 2)
plt.plot(epochs_range, loss, label='Training Loss')
plt.plot(epochs_range, val_loss, label='Validation Loss')
plt.legend(loc='upper right')
plt.title('Training and Validation Loss')
plt.show()
```

```python
data_augmentation = keras.Sequential(
  [
    layers.RandomFlip("horizontal",
               input_shape=(img_height,
                     img_width,
                     3)),
    layers.RandomRotation(0.1),
    layers.RandomZoom(0.1),
  ]
)
plt.figure(figsize=(10, 10))
for images, _ in train_ds.take(1):
  for i in range(9):
    augmented_images = data_augmentation(images)
    ax = plt.subplot(3, 3, i + 1)
    plt.imshow(augmented_images[0].numpy().astype("uint8"))
    plt.axis("off")

model = Sequential([
  data_augmentation,
  layers.Rescaling(1. / 255),
  layers.Conv2D(16, 3, padding='same', activation='relu'),
  layers.MaxPooling2D(),
  layers.Conv2D(32, 3, padding='same', activation='relu'),
  layers.MaxPooling2D(),
  layers.Conv2D(64, 3, padding='same', activation='relu'),
  layers.MaxPooling2D(),
  layers.Dropout(0.2),
  layers.Flatten(),
  layers.Dense(128, activation='relu'),
  layers.Dense(num_classes, name="outputs")
])
model.compile(optimizer='adam',
     loss=tf.keras.losses.SparseCategoricalCrossentropy(
     from_logits=True),
     metrics=['accuracy'])

model.compile(optimizer='adam',
     loss=tf.keras.losses.SparseCategoricalCrossentropy
     (from_logits=True),
     metrics=['accuracy'])
model.summary()
```

```
epochs = 15
history = model.fit(
  train_ds,
  validation_data=val_ds,
  epochs=epochs
)

acc = history.history['accuracy']
val_acc = history.history['val_accuracy']

loss = history.history['loss']
val_loss = history.history['val_loss']

epochs_range = range(epochs)

plt.figure(figsize=(8, 8))
plt.subplot(1, 2, 1)
plt.plot(epochs_range, acc, label='Training Accuracy')
plt.plot(epochs_range, val_acc, label='Validation Accuracy')
plt.legend(loc='lower right')
plt.title('Training and Validation Accuracy')

plt.subplot(1, 2, 2)
plt.plot(epochs_range, loss, label='Training Loss')
plt.plot(epochs_range, val_loss, label='Validation Loss')
plt.legend(loc='upper right')
plt.title('Training and Validation Loss')
plt.show()

sunflower_url = "https://storage.googleapis.com/download.tensorflow.org/
example_images/592px-Red_sunflower.jpg"
sunflower_path = tf.keras.utils.get_file('Red_sunflower',
origin=sunflower_url)

img = tf.keras.utils.load_img(
  sunflower_path, target_size=(img_height, img_width)
)
img_array = tf.keras.utils.img_to_array(img)
img_array = tf.expand_dims(img_array, 0) # Create a batch

predictions = model.predict(img_array)
score = tf.nn.softmax(predictions[0])
```

```python
print(
    "This image most likely belongs to {} with a {:.2f} percent
    confidence."
    .format(class_names[np.argmax(score)], 100 * np.max(score))
)

# Convert the model.
converter = tf.lite.TFLiteConverter.from_keras_model(model)
tflite_model = converter.convert()

# Save the model. with open('model.tflite', 'wb') as f:
    f.write(tflite_model)

TF_MODEL_FILE_PATH = 'model.tflite' # The default path to the saved
TensorFlow Lite model

interpreter = tf.lite.Interpreter(model_path=TF_MODEL_FILE_PATH)
interpreter.get_signature_list()
classify_lite = interpreter.get_signature_runner('serving_default')
classify_lite
predictions_lite = classify_lite(sequential_1_input=img_array)
['outputs']
score_lite = tf.nn.softmax(predictions_lite)
print(
    "This image most likely belongs to {} with a {:.2f} percent
    confidence."
    .format(class_names[np.argmax(score_lite)], 100 * np.max(score_lite))
)
print(np.max(np.abs(predictions - predictions_lite)))
```

```
===========================Output===========================
3670
Found 3670 files belonging to 5 classes.
Using 2936 files for training.
2024-02-26 08:25:07.145531: I tensorflow/core/platform/cpu_feature_guard.cc:182] This
TensorFlow binary is optimized to use available CPU instructions in performance-
critical operations.
To enable the following instructions: SSE SSE2 SSE3 SSE4.1 SSE4.2 AVX2 AVX512F
AVX512_VNNI FMA, in other operations, rebuild TensorFlow with the appropriate
compiler flags.
```

The Fig. 7.4 shows the List of feature classification.

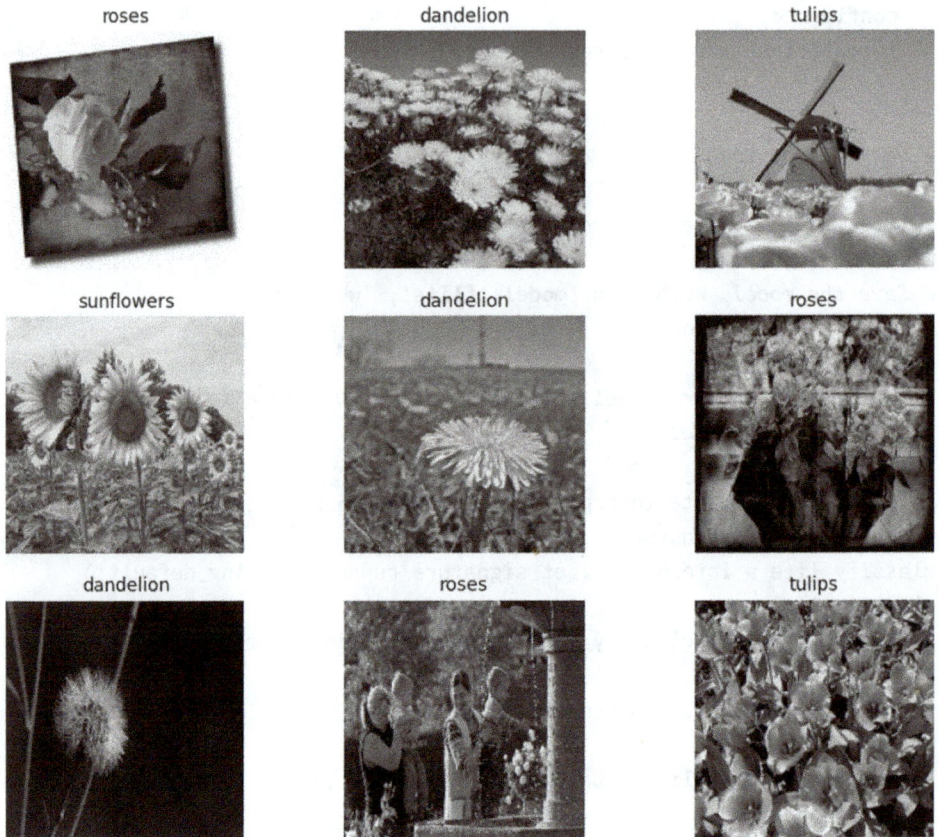

Fig. 7.4: List of feature classification.

Found 3670 files belonging to 5 classes.
Using 734 files for validation.
['daisy', 'dandelion', 'roses', 'sunflowers', 'tulips']
(32, 180, 180, 3)
(32,)
WARNING:tensorflow:From C:\Users\23188\PycharmProjects\workshop\.venv\Lib\site-packages\keras\src\backend.py:873: The name tf.get_default_graph is deprecated. Please use tf.compat.v1.get_default_graph instead.

0.0 1.0
WARNING:tensorflow:From C:\Users\23188\PycharmProjects\workshop\.venv\Lib\site-packages\keras\src\layers\pooling\max_pooling2d.py:161: The name tf.nn.max_pool is deprecated. Please use tf.nn.max_pool2d instead.

WARNING:tensorflow:From C:\Users\23188\PycharmProjects\workshop\.venv\Lib\site-packages\keras\src\optimizers_init_.py:309: The name tf.train.Optimizer is deprecated. Please use tf.compat.v1.train.Optimizer instead.

Model: "sequential"

Layer (type)	Output Shape	Param #
rescaling_1 (Rescaling)	(None, 180, 180, 3)	0
conv2d (Conv2D)	(None, 180, 180, 16)	448
max_pooling2d (MaxPooling2D)	(None, 90, 90, 16)	0
conv2d_1 (Conv2D)	(None, 90, 90, 32)	4640
max_pooling2d_1 (MaxPooling2D)	(None, 45, 45, 32)	0
conv2d_2 (Conv2D)	(None, 45, 45, 64)	18496
max_pooling2d_2 (MaxPooling2D)	(None, 22, 22, 64)	0
flatten (Flatten)	(None, 30976)	0
dense (Dense)	(None, 128)	3965056
dense_1 (Dense)	(None, 5)	645

Total params: 3989285 (15.22 MB)
Trainable params: 3989285 (15.22 MB)
Non-trainable params: 0 (0.00 Byte)

Epoch 1/10
WARNING:tensorflow:From C:\Users\23188\PycharmProjects\workshop\.venv\Lib\site-packages\keras\src\utils\tf_utils.py:492: The name tf.ragged.RaggedTensorValue is deprecated. Please use tf.compat.v1.ragged.RaggedTensorValue instead.

WARNING:tensorflow:From C:\Users\23188\PycharmProjects\workshop\.venv\Lib\site-packages\keras\src\engine\base_layer_utils.py:384: The name tf.executing_eagerly_outside_functions is deprecated. Please use tf.compat.v1.executing_eagerly_outside_functions instead.

92/92 [==============================] - 26s 234ms/step - loss: 1.2905 - accuracy: 0.4554 - val_loss: 1.0338 - val_accuracy: 0.5845
Epoch 2/10
92/92 [==============================] - 15s 164ms/step - loss: 0.9812 - accuracy: 0.6158 - val_loss: 0.9164 - val_accuracy: 0.6362
Epoch 3/10
92/92 [==============================] - 10s 105ms/step - loss: 0.7951 - accuracy: 0.7010 - val_loss: 0.8786 - val_accuracy: 0.6567
Epoch 4/10
92/92 [==============================] - 10s 104ms/step - loss: 0.6330 - accuracy: 0.7653 - val_loss: 1.0108 - val_accuracy: 0.6172

Epoch 5/10
92/92 [==============================] - 10s 106ms/step - loss: 0.4579 - accuracy: 0.8372 - val_loss: 0.8921 - val_accuracy: 0.6567
Epoch 6/10
92/92 [==============================] - 10s 108ms/step - loss: 0.2728 - accuracy: 0.9108 - val_loss: 1.0403 - val_accuracy: 0.6635
Epoch 7/10
92/92 [==============================] - 10s 110ms/step - loss: 0.1597 - accuracy: 0.9499 - val_loss: 1.2018 - val_accuracy: 0.6894
Epoch 8/10
92/92 [==============================] - 11s 115ms/step - loss: 0.0928 - accuracy: 0.9751 - val_loss: 1.4531 - val_accuracy: 0.6485
Epoch 9/10
92/92 [==============================] - 12s 126ms/step - loss: 0.0579 - accuracy: 0.9857 - val_loss: 1.4830 - val_accuracy: 0.6635
Epoch 10/10
92/92 [==============================] - 19s 201ms/step - loss: 0.0295 - accuracy: 0.9922 - val_loss: 1.7615 - val_accuracy: 0.6335
===

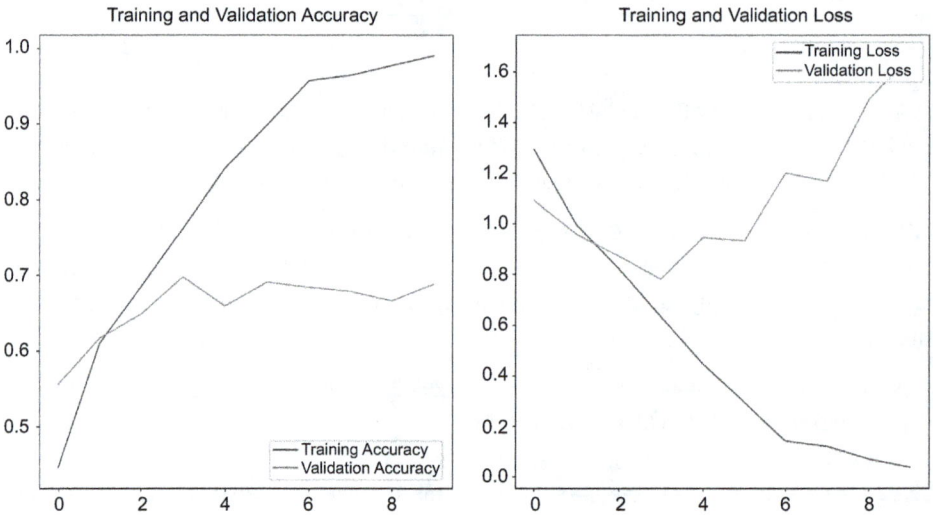

Fig. 7.5: Training and validation accuracy versus training and validation loss.

The Fig. 7.5 shows the Training and validation accuracy versus training and validation loss.

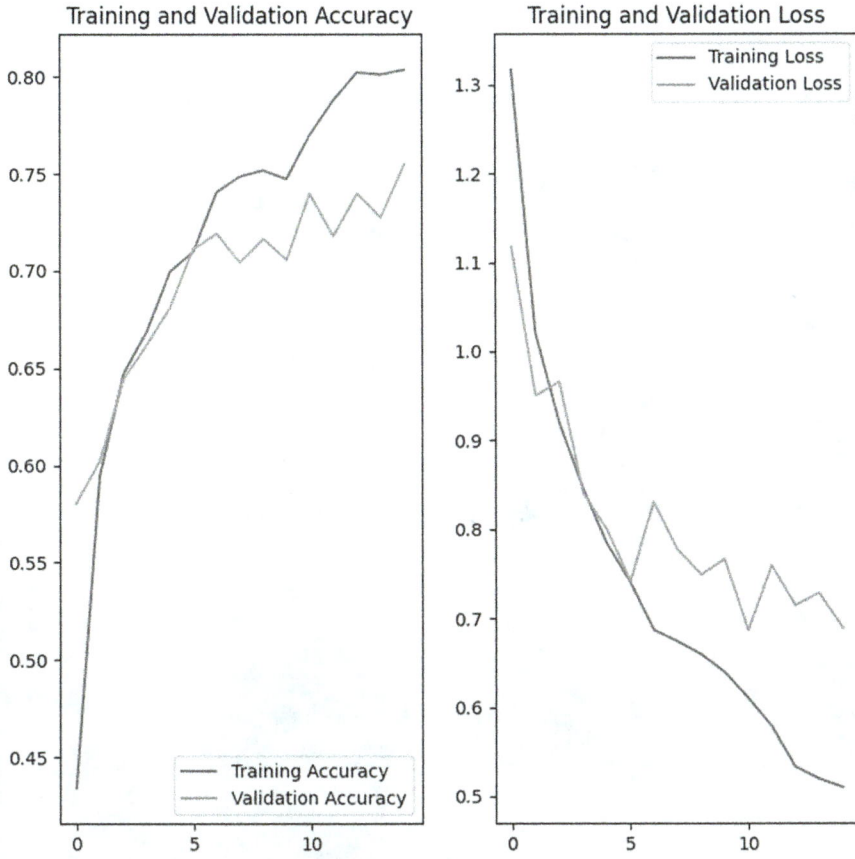

Fig. 7.6: Training and validation accuracy versus training and validation loss with 15 epochs.

The Fig. 7.6 shows the Training and validation accuracy versus training and validation loss with 15 epochs.

The same model is being trained on the 15 epochs and have look

7.6.1 Model: "sequential_2"

Fig. 7.7: Trained model with 15 epochs.

The Fig. 7.7 shows the Trained model with 15 epochs.

Layer (type)	Output shape	Param #
sequential_1 (Sequential)	(None, 180, 180, 3)	0
rescaling_2 (Rescaling)	(None, 180, 180, 3)	0
conv2d_3 (Conv2D)	(None, 180, 180, 16)	448
max_pooling2d_3 (MaxPooling2D)	(None, 90, 90, 16)	0
conv2d_4 (Conv2D)	(None, 90, 90, 32)	4640
max_pooling2d_4 (MaxPooling2D)	(None, 45, 45, 32)	0
conv2d_5 (Conv2D)	(None, 45, 45, 64)	18496
max_pooling2d_5 (MaxPooling2D)	(None, 22, 22, 64)	0
dropout (Dropout)	(None, 22, 22, 64)	0
flatten_1 (Flatten)	(None, 30976)	0
dense_2 (Dense)	(None, 128)	3965056
outputs (Dense)	(None, 5)	645

===
Total params: 3989285 (15.22 MB)
Trainable params: 3989285 (15.22 MB)
Nontrainable params: 0 (0.00 Byte)

Epoch 1/15
92/92 [==============================] - 17s 161ms/step - loss: 1.3169 - accuracy: 0.4343 - val_loss: 1.1176 - val_accuracy: 0.5804
Epoch 2/15
92/92 [==============================] - 15s 159ms/step - loss: 1.0208 - accuracy: 0.5947 - val_loss: 0.9498 - val_accuracy: 0.6022
Epoch 3/15
92/92 [==============================] - 16s 173ms/step - loss: 0.9197 - accuracy: 0.6471 - val_loss: 0.9662 - val_accuracy: 0.6444
Epoch 4/15
92/92 [==============================] - 16s 169ms/step - loss: 0.8458 - accuracy: 0.6689 - val_loss: 0.8407 - val_accuracy: 0.6621
Epoch 5/15
92/92 [==============================] - 15s 167ms/step - loss: 0.7843 - accuracy: 0.6996 - val_loss: 0.8002 - val_accuracy: 0.6812
Epoch 6/15
92/92 [==============================] - 15s 160ms/step - loss: 0.7400 - accuracy: 0.7098 - val_loss: 0.7416 - val_accuracy: 0.7112
Epoch 7/15
92/92 [==============================] - 15s 160ms/step - loss: 0.6869 - accuracy: 0.7405 - val_loss: 0.8310 - val_accuracy: 0.7193
Epoch 8/15
92/92 [==============================] - 15s 168ms/step - loss: 0.6741 - accuracy: 0.7486 - val_loss: 0.7771 - val_accuracy: 0.7044
Epoch 9/15
92/92 [==============================] - 15s 162ms/step - loss: 0.6595 - accuracy: 0.7517 - val_loss: 0.7488 - val_accuracy: 0.7166
Epoch 10/15
92/92 [==============================] - 14s 155ms/step - loss: 0.6391 - accuracy: 0.7473 - val_loss: 0.7664 - val_accuracy: 0.7057
Epoch 11/15
92/92 [==============================] - 15s 162ms/step - loss: 0.6100 - accuracy: 0.7698 - val_loss: 0.6865 - val_accuracy: 0.7398
Epoch 12/15
92/92 [==============================] - 17s 183ms/step - loss: 0.5785 - accuracy: 0.7878 - val_loss: 0.7593 - val_accuracy: 0.7180
Epoch 13/15

92/92 [==============================] - 15s 159ms/step - loss: 0.5330 - accuracy: 0.8021 - val_loss: 0.7144 - val_accuracy: 0.7398
Epoch 14/15
92/92 [==============================] - 16s 169ms/step - loss: 0.5198 - accuracy: 0.8011 - val_loss: 0.7283 - val_accuracy: 0.7275
Epoch 15/15
92/92 [==============================] - 14s 157ms/step - loss: 0.5101 - accuracy: 0.8035 - val_loss: 0.6892 - val_accuracy: 0.7548
Downloading data from https://storage.googleapis.com/download.tensorflow.org/exam ple_images/592px-Red_sunflower.jpg
117948/117948 [==============================] - 0s 3us/step
1/1 [==============================] - 0s 207ms/step
This image most likely belongs to sunflowers with a 99.46 percent confidence.
2024-02-26 08:38:03.604528: W tensorflow/compiler/mlir/lite/python/tf_tfl_flatbuffer_-helpers.cc:378] Ignored output_format.
2024-02-26 08:38:03.604626: W tensorflow/compiler/mlir/lite/python/tf_tfl_flatbuffer_-helpers.cc:381] Ignored drop_control_dependency.
2024-02-26 08:38:03.606292: I tensorflow/cc/saved_model/reader.cc:83] Reading Saved-Model from: C:\Users\23188\AppData\Local\Temp\tmp8t3deiwx
2024-02-26 08:38:03.611666: I tensorflow/cc/saved_model/reader.cc:51] Reading meta graph with tags { serve }
2024-02-26 08:38:03.611753: I tensorflow/cc/saved_model/reader.cc:146] Reading Saved-Model debug info (if present) from: C:\Users\23188\AppData\Local\Temp\tmp8t3deiwx
2024-02-26 08:38:03.624259: I tensorflow/compiler/mlir/mlir_graph_optimization_pass. cc:388] MLIR V1 optimization pass is not enabled
2024-02-26 08:38:03.626929: I tensorflow/cc/saved_model/loader.cc:233] Restoring Sa-vedModel bundle.
2024-02-26 08:38:03.803367: I tensorflow/cc/saved_model/loader.cc:217] Running initializa-tion op on SavedModel bundle at path: C:\Users\23188\AppData\Local\Temp\tmp8t3deiwx
2024-02-26 08:38:03.838746: I tensorflow/cc/saved_model/loader.cc:316] SavedModel load for tags { serve }; Status: success: OK. Took 232444 microseconds.
2024-02-26 08:38:03.924814: I tensorflow/compiler/mlir/tensorflow/utils/dump_mlir_util. cc:269] disabling MLIR crash reproducer, set env var `MLIR_CRASH_REPRODUCER_DIR-ECTORY` to enable.
Summary on the non-converted ops:
----
* Accepted dialects: tfl, builtin, func
* Non-Converted Ops: 11, Total Ops 23, % non-converted = 47.83 %
* 11 ARITH ops

- arith.constant: 11 occurrences (f32: 10, i32: 1)

(f32: 3)

(f32: 2)

(f32: 3)

(f32: 1)

This image most likely belongs to sunflowers with a 99.46 percent confidence.

9.536743e-07

===

7.6.2 CNN Architecture

CNN architecture, or the arrangement and configuration of layers within a CNN, plays a crucial role in its ability to learn and extract features from images. Some of the core building blocks of the CNN algorithm are given below:

1. **Convolutional layer:** The heart of a CNN, responsible for extracting features through the application of filters (kernels) across the image. Filters slide over the image, computing dot products to identify local patterns like edges and textures.
2. **Pooling layer:** Reduces the dimensionality of the data, summarizing the information captured by the convolutional layer. Common methods include max pooling and average pooling. Pooling layers play a crucial role in *reducing* the dimensionality of data while preserving important features. This compression helps manage computational costs, prevents overfitting, and can even strengthen the feature extraction process. Pooling layers reduce the spatial dimensions (width and height) of the data, typically by a factor of 2 or more. This results in a smaller output with fewer elements. By applying different pooling operations, the layer summarizes the information contained within a specific region of the input data. This region is often called a pooling window.
3. **Activation function:** Introduces nonlinearity, allowing the network to learn complex relationships between features. Popular choices include ReLU and Leaky ReLU.
4. **Fully connected layer:** Typically used in the final stages for tasks like classification or regression. Connects all neurons in one layer to all neurons in the next, integrating the learned features.

Common architecture in any CNN is

1. **LeNet-5:** A pioneering CNN architecture, used for handwritten digit recognition.
2. **AlexNet:** Introduced deeper architectures with stacked convolutional and pooling layers, achieving state-of-the-art performance on ImageNet classification.
3. **VGGNet:** Explored the use of smaller filters and deeper networks, demonstrating the benefits of increasing depth.
4. **ResNet:** Introduced skip connections, allowing gradients to flow directly through the network, addressing the vanishing gradient problem in deep architectures.

5. **Inception:** Used filter factorization and parallel processing for efficient feature extraction.

The optimal architecture depends on your specific problem, dataset size, and computational resources. Experimentation and exploration are key to finding the best configuration for your needs. Few points must have to be kept in mind before developing any CNN model:

- **Number of layers:** Deeper networks often learn more complex features, but require more data and computational resources.
- **Filter size and number:** Smaller filters capture local details, while larger ones capture larger features. More filters allow for learning a wider variety of patterns.
- **Pooling type and stride:** Max pooling identifies dominant features, while average pooling summarizes information. Stride controls the downsampling rate. Max pooling selects the maximum value within the pooling window. This emphasizes the strongest activations and can be useful for detecting dominant features like edges.
- **Activation function:** Choice depends on the task and desired properties (e.g., ReLU for efficiency and Leaky ReLU for avoiding dying neurons).
- **Batch normalization:** Helps stabilize training and improve generalization.
- **Regularization techniques:** Dropout and L1/L2 regularization prevent overfitting by reducing model complexity.
- **Transfer learning:** Utilize pretrained models on large datasets (e.g., ImageNet) as a starting point for fine-tuning on your specific task.
- **Data augmentation:** Artificially expand your dataset with variations (e.g., flips and rotations) to improve generalization.

7.7 Dropout Layers

The dropout layers act as powerful tools for preventing overfitting, a major challenge where models memorize training data too closely and fail to generalize well to unseen examples. During training, a dropout layer randomly drops out a certain proportion of neurons (units) in each layer, effectively turning them off for that training iteration. These dropped neurons don't contribute to the calculations or updates in that particular step. This process forces the remaining neurons to learn more robust and independent representations of the features, as they can't rely on the presence of any specific neuron every time. By preventing neurons from becoming overly reliant on each other, dropout encourages them to learn more diverse and generalizable features, improving the model's ability to perform well on new data. As different neurons are dropped out in each training iteration, the model effectively learns an ensemble of slightly different networks, making it less susceptible to specific noise or patterns in the training data. By effectively reducing the effective size of the network during training, dropout can sometimes lead to faster convergence and training time, especially for larger models.

7.8 Recurrent Neural Networks (RNNs)

Recurrent neural networks (RNNs) stand out for their ability to process and learn from sequential data, where elements are ordered and have dependencies. This makes them ideal for tasks like natural language processing (NLP), speech recognition, and time series analysis. Unlike traditional neural networks, RNNs have an internal memory that allows them to retain information from previous inputs and use it to process the current one. This memory enables them to capture the context and relationships within sequences as shown in Fig. 7.8.

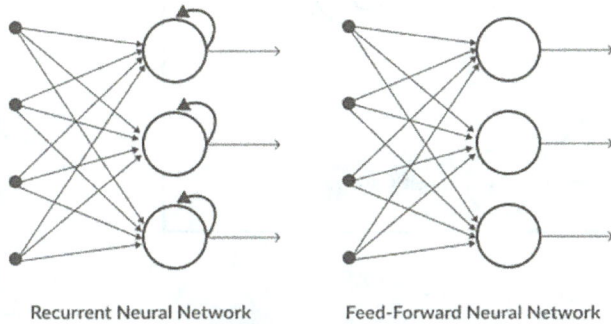

Recurrent Neural Network   Feed-Forward Neural Network

Fig. 7.8: Recurrent neural network.

The Fig. 7.8 shows the Recurrent neural network.

An RNN can be imagined as unfolding its layers over time, where each layer receives not only the current input but also the hidden state from the previous layer, effectively carrying information across time steps. We can use RNNs in NLP machine translation, sentiment analysis, text generation, chatbots, converting spoken language into text, predicting future values in a sequence (e.g., stock prices and weather patterns), and creating realistic and coherent musical pieces.

7.8.1 Types of RNNs

1. **Vanilla RNN:** The basic RNN architecture, but can suffer from vanishing and exploding gradients, limiting its ability to learn long-term dependencies. Vanilla RNNs struggle with vanishing and exploding gradients, making it difficult to learn dependencies over long sequences. LSTMs address this by introducing gating mechanisms that control the flow of information through the network.
2. **Long short-term memory (LSTM):** Introduces gating mechanisms to control the flow of information, addressing the gradient issues and enabling learning of lon-

ger dependencies. LSTM networks stand out for their ability to learn and exploit long-term dependencies within sequential data as shown in Fig. 7.9.

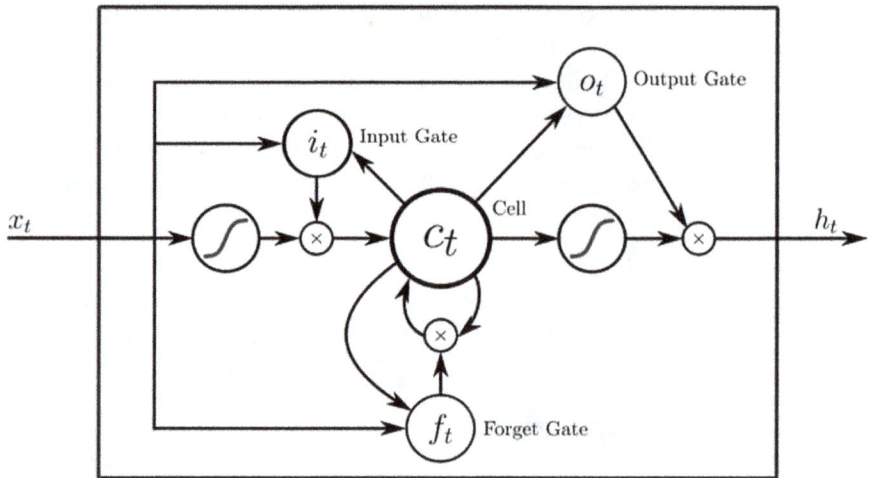

Fig. 7.9: Long-short term memory.

The Fig. 7.9 shows the Long-short term memory.

This makes them particularly well-suited for tasks like NLP, speech recognition, and time series forecasting, where understanding the context across extended periods is crucial. The three main important gates available are

A) **Forget gate:** Decides what information from the previous cell state (memory) to discard.

B) **Input gate:** Controls what information from the current input to integrate into the cell state.

C) **Output gate:** Determines what part of the cell state to expose as the output of the unit.

3. **Gated recurrent unit (GRU):** Similar to LSTM but with simpler architecture and fewer parameters, offering a balance between performance and efficiency. GRU emerges as a compelling alternative to LSTMs. While both excel at learning long-term dependencies within sequential data, GRUs offer a more streamlined architecture with certain advantages. GRUs aim to provide comparable performance to LSTMs while being simpler and potentially less computationally expensive. GRUs combine the Forget and Input gates of LSTMs into a single update gate and introduce a reset gate to control the flow of information. This reduces the number of parameters and operations compared to LSTMs.

Let's have a look on the RNN Python code:

```python
import numpy as np # linear algebra
import pandas as pd # data processing, CSV file I/O (e.g. pd.read_csv)
import matplotlib.pyplot as plt

# Input data files are available in the "../input/" directory.
# For example, running this (by clicking run or pressing Shift+Enter)
# will list the files in the input directory

import os
print(os.listdir("../input"))
dataset_train = pd.read_csv('../input/stockprice-
train/Stock_Price_Train.csv')
dataset_train.head()
train = dataset_train.loc[:, ['Open']].values #array'e çevirdik
train
from sklearn.preprocessing import MinMaxScaler #bununla, 0-1 arasına
scale ettik
scaler = MinMaxScaler(feature_range = (0, 1))
train_scaled = scaler.fit_transform(train)
train_scaled

plt.plot(train_scaled)

# ilk 1-50 yi alıp X_train'e, 51. data point'i de y_train'e,
# 2-51'i alıp X_train'e, 52'yi y_train'e ...olacak şekilde data frame i
oluşturuyoruz:
X_train = []
y_train = []
timesteps = 50

for i in range(timesteps, 1250):
  X_train.append(train_scaled[i - timesteps:i, 0])
  y_train.append(train_scaled[i, 0])

X_train, y_train = np.array(X_train), np.array(y_train)

#Reshaping:
X_train = np.reshape(X_train, (X_train.shape[0], X_train.shape[1], 1))
```

```python
#import libraries and packages:
from keras.models import Sequential
from keras.layers import Dense
from keras.layers import SimpleRNN
from keras.layers import Dropout

#Initialize RNN:
regressor = Sequential()

#Adding the first RNN layer and some Dropout regularization
regressor.add(SimpleRNN(units = 50, activation='tanh',
return_sequences=True, input_shape= (X_train.shape[1],1)))
regressor.add(Dropout(0.2))

#Adding the second RNN layer and some Dropout regularization
regressor.add(SimpleRNN(units = 50, activation='tanh',
return_sequences=True))
regressor.add(Dropout(0.2))

#Adding the third RNN layer and some Dropout regularization
regressor.add(SimpleRNN(units = 50, activation='tanh',
return_sequences=True))
regressor.add(Dropout(0.2))

#Adding the fourth RNN layer and some Dropout regularization
regressor.add(SimpleRNN(units = 50))
regressor.add(Dropout(0.2))

#Adding the output layer
regressor.add(Dense(units = 1))

#Compile the RNN
regressor.compile(optimizer='adam', loss='mean_squared_error')

#Fitting the RNN to the Training set
regressor.fit(X_train, y_train, epochs=100, batch_size=32)

dataset_test = pd.read_csv('../input/stockprice-test/Stock_Price_Test.
csv')
dataset_test.head()
```

```
real_stock_price = dataset_test.loc[:, ['Open']].values
real_stock_price

#Getting the predicted stock price
dataset_total = pd.concat((dataset_train['Open'], dataset_test['Open']),
axis=0)
inputs = dataset_total[len(dataset_total)-len(dataset_test) -
timesteps:].values.reshape(-1,1)
inputs = scaler.transform(inputs) #minmax scaler
inputs

X_test = []
for i in range(timesteps, 70):
  X_test.append(inputs[i-timesteps:i,0])
X_test = np.array(X_test)
X_test = np.reshape(X_test, (X_test.shape[0], X_test.shape[1], 1))
predicted_stock_price = regressor.predict(X_test)
predicted_stock_price = scaler.inverse_transform(predicted_stock_price)
#inverse_transform ile, scale edildikten sonra predict edilen değerleri
gerçek değer aralığına çekiyoruz

plt.plot(real_stock_price, color='red', label='Real Google Stock Price')
plt.plot(predicted_stock_price, color='blue', label='Predicted Google
Stock Price')
plt.title('Google Stock Price Prediction')
plt.xlabel('Time')
plt.ylabel('Google Stock Price')
plt.legend()
plt.show()

data = pd.read_csv('../input/international-airline-
passengers/international-airline-passengers.csv')
data.head()

dataset = data.iloc[:, 1].values
plt.plot(dataset)
plt.xlabel('time')
plt.ylabel('number of passengers (in thousands)')
plt.title('Passengers')
plt.show()
```

```
dataset = dataset.reshape(-1,1) #(145, ) iken (145,1)e çevirdik
dataset = dataset.astype('float32')
dataset.shape

scaler = MinMaxScaler(feature_range= (0,1))
dataset = scaler.fit_transform(dataset)

train_size = int(len(dataset)*0.5)
test_size = len(dataset)- train_size

train = dataset[0:train_size, :]
test = dataset[train_size:len(dataset), :]

print('train size: {}, test size: {}'.format(len(train), len(test)))

dataX = []
datay = []
timestemp = 10

for i in range(len(train) - timestemp - 1):
  a = train[i:(i + timestemp), 0]
  dataX.append(a)
  datay.append(train[i + timestemp, 0])

trainX, trainy = np.array(dataX), np.array(datay)

dataX = []
datay = []
for i in range(len(test) - timestemp - 1):
  a = test[i:(i + timestemp), 0]
  dataX.append(a)
  datay.append(test[i + timestemp, 0])

testX, testy = np.array(dataX), np.array(datay)

trainX.shape

trainX = np.reshape(trainX, (trainX.shape[0],1, trainX.shape[1]))
testX = np.reshape(testX, (testX.shape[0],1, testX.shape[1]))

trainX.shape
```

```python
# Creating LSTM Model
from keras.models import Sequential
from keras.layers import Dense
from keras.layers import LSTM
from sklearn.preprocessing import MinMaxScaler
from sklearn.metrics import mean_squared_error

# model
model = Sequential()
model.add(LSTM(10, input_shape=(1, timestemp))) # 10 lstm neuron(block)
model.add(Dense(1))
model.compile(loss='mean_squared_error', optimizer='adam')
model.fit(trainX, trainy, epochs=50, batch_size=1)

#make predictions
trainPredict = model.predict(trainX)
testPredict = model.predict(testX)

# invert predictions
trainPredict = scaler.inverse_transform(trainPredict)
trainy = scaler.inverse_transform([trainy])
testPredict = scaler.inverse_transform(testPredict)
testy = scaler.inverse_transform([testy])

import math
# calculate root mean squared error
trainScore = math.sqrt(mean_squared_error(trainy[0], trainPredict[:,0]))
print('Train Score: %.2f RMSE' % (trainScore))
testScore = math.sqrt(mean_squared_error(testy[0], testPredict[:,0]))
print('Test Score: %.2f RMSE' % (testScore))

# shifting train
trainPredictPlot = np.empty_like(dataset)
trainPredictPlot[:, :] = np.nan
trainPredictPlot[timestemp:len(trainPredict)+timestemp, :] = trainPredict
# shifting test predictions for plotting
testPredictPlot = np.empty_like(dataset)
testPredictPlot[:, :] = np.nan
testPredictPlot[len(trainPredict)+(timestemp*2)+1:len(dataset)-1, :] =
testPredict
```

```
# plot baseline and predictions
plt.plot(scaler.inverse_transform(dataset))
plt.plot(trainPredictPlot)
plt.plot(testPredictPlot)
plt.show()
```

7.9 Sequence-to-Sequence Models

The **seq2seq** models stand out for their ability to process and transform one sequence of data into another. This makes them invaluable for tasks like machine translation, text summarization, speech recognition, and chatbots, where understanding and generating sequences are crucial. There are two main important components of seq2seq model like Encoder-Decoder Architecture and attention mechanism. Encode-decoder architecture from seq2seq model consists of two main components:

- **Encoder:** Processes the input sequence, capturing its meaning and context. It can be an RNN like LSTM or GRU, or a transformer-based architecture.
- **Decoder:** Generates the output sequence, conditioned on the information encoded by the encoder. It also uses an RNN or transformer-based architecture, often with an attention mechanism to focus on relevant parts of the encoded sequence.

On the other hand attention mechanism is the key component that allows the decoder to selectively attend to different parts of the encoded sequence when generating each element of the output sequence. This helps capture long-range dependencies and improve the accuracy and coherence of the generated output. We can use it in Translating text from one language to another, considering the context and grammar of both languages and Generating a concise summary of a longer text document, capturing the main points and overall meaning.

The Seq2seq can be used in Converting spoken language into text, taking into account the nuances of pronunciation and context and Building conversational agents that can understand and respond to user queries in a natural way. It is very useful in Generating descriptions of images based on their visual content and Creating musical pieces based on specific styles or themes. The seq2seq architectures including transformer-based models like T5 and BART. It learns about advanced attention mechanisms like self-attention and masked attention and experiment with different loss functions and training techniques for seq2seq models. We can utilize libraries like TensorFlow and PyTorch for building and training seq2seq models. Let's have a look on the python implementation:

```python
import tensorflow as tf
from tensorflow.keras.layers import Embedding, LSTM, Dense
from tensorflow.keras.models import Model

# Define the Encoder
class Encoder(tf.keras.Model):
  def __init__(self, vocab_size, embedding_dim, enc_units):
    super(Encoder, self).__init__()
    self.embedding = Embedding(vocab_size, embedding_dim)
    self.lstm = LSTM(enc_units, return_sequences=True,
return_state=True)

  def call(self, x):
    x = self.embedding(x)
    output, state_h, state_c = self.lstm(x)
    return output, state_h, state_c

# Define the Decoder
class Decoder(tf.keras.Model):
  def __init__(self, vocab_size, embedding_dim, dec_units):
    super(Decoder, self).__init__()
    self.embedding = Embedding(vocab_size, embedding_dim)
    self.lstm = LSTM(dec_units, return_sequences=True,
return_state=True)
    self.dense = Dense(vocab_size, activation='softmax')

  def call(self, x, initial_state):
    x = self.embedding(x)
    output, _, _ = self.lstm(x, initial_state=initial_state)
    prediction = self.dense(output)
    return prediction

# Define the Seq2Seq Model
class Seq2SeqModel(tf.keras.Model):
  def __init__(self, encoder, decoder):
    super(Seq2SeqModel, self).__init__()
    self.encoder = encoder
    self.decoder = decoder

  def call(self, inputs):
    source, target = inputs
    enc_output, enc_state_h, enc_state_c = self.encoder(source)
```

```
    dec_output = self.decoder(target, initial_state=[enc_state_h,
enc_state_c])
    return dec_output


# Define the hyperparameters and instantiate the model
vocab_size = 10000 # Example vocabulary size
embedding_dim = 256
enc_units = 512
dec_units = 512


encoder = Encoder(vocab_size, embedding_dim, enc_units)
decoder = Decoder(vocab_size, embedding_dim, dec_units)
seq2seq_model = Seq2SeqModel(encoder, decoder)


# Compile the model (you may choose an appropriate optimizer and loss
function)
seq2seq_model.compile(optimizer='adam', loss='categorical_crossentropy',
metrics=['accuracy'])
```

7.10 Transfer Learning

The transfer learning emerges as a powerful technique for accelerating and enhancing the training process, especially for complex tasks and limited data. It involves
leveraging the knowledge gained from a pretrained model on one task (source task)
to improve performance on a related task (target task). Instead of training a model
from scratch on your specific dataset, you utilize a pretrained model that has already
learned valuable representations from a large dataset related to your task. This saves
time and computational resources.

Pretrained models often contain rich feature representations that can be adapted
to your target task, leading to faster convergence and potentially better performance
compared to training from scratch. When you have limited labeled data for your specific task, transfer learning allows you to leverage the knowledge from a larger dataset, mitigating the data scarcity issue. You don't simply copy the entire pretrained
model. Instead, you typically fine-tune its layers, adjusting the weights and biases toward your specific task using your limited data. This balances the benefits of pretrained knowledge with the need to adapt to your specific problem.

Transfer learning offers a valuable toolbox for deep learning practitioners, enabling faster training, improved performance, and efficient utilization of limited data.
By carefully selecting pretrained models, designing appropriate fine-tuning strategies,
and considering the limitations, you can leverage this technique to unlock the power

of deep learning for your specific tasks. Let's have a look on the following code that shows implementation:

```python
import numpy as np
import keras
from keras import layers
import tensorflow_datasets as tfds
import matplotlib.pyplot as plt


layer = keras.layers.Dense(3)
layer.build((None, 4)) # Create the weights

print("weights:", len(layer.weights))
print("trainable_weights:", len(layer.trainable_weights))
print("non_trainable_weights:", len(layer.non_trainable_weights))
layer = keras.layers.BatchNormalization()
layer.build((None, 4)) # Create the weights

print("weights:", len(layer.weights))
print("trainable_weights:", len(layer.trainable_weights))
print("non_trainable_weights:", len(layer.non_trainable_weights))


layer = keras.layers.Dense(3)
layer.build((None, 4)) # Create the weights
layer.trainable = False # Freeze the layer

print("weights:", len(layer.weights))
print("trainable_weights:", len(layer.trainable_weights))
print("non_trainable_weights:", len(layer.non_trainable_weights))

# Make a model with 2 layers
layer1 = keras.layers.Dense(3, activation="relu")
layer2 = keras.layers.Dense(3, activation="sigmoid")
model = keras.Sequential([keras.Input(shape=(3,)), layer1, layer2])

# Freeze the first layer
layer1.trainable = False

# Keep a copy of the weights of layer1 for later reference
initial_layer1_weights_values = layer1.get_weights()
```

```python
# Train the model
model.compile(optimizer="adam", loss="mse")
model.fit(np.random.random((2, 3)), np.random.random((2, 3)))

# Check that the weights of layer1 have not changed during training
final_layer1_weights_values = layer1.get_weights()
np.testing.assert_allclose(
    initial_layer1_weights_values[0], final_layer1_weights_values[0]
)
np.testing.assert_allclose(
    initial_layer1_weights_values[1], final_layer1_weights_values[1]
)
inner_model = keras.Sequential(
    [
        keras.Input(shape=(3,)),
        keras.layers.Dense(3, activation="relu"),
        keras.layers.Dense(3, activation="relu"),
    ]
)
model = keras.Sequential(
    [
        keras.Input(shape=(3,)),
        inner_model,
        keras.layers.Dense(3, activation="sigmoid"),
    ]
)

model.trainable = False # Freeze the outer model
assert inner_model.trainable == False # All layers in `model` are now
frozen assert inner_model.layers[0].trainable == False # `trainable` is
propagated recursively

base_model = keras.applications.Xception(
    weights='imagenet', # Load weights pre-trained on ImageNet.
    input_shape=(150, 150, 3),
    include_top=False) # Do not include the ImageNet classifier at the
top.
base_model.trainable = False

inputs = keras.Input(shape=(150, 150, 3))
# We make sure that the base_model is running in inference mode here, #
by passing `training=False`. This is important for fine-tuning, as you
```

```
will # learn in a few paragraphs.
x = base_model(inputs, training=False)
# Convert features of shape `base_model.output_shape[1:]` to vectors
x = keras.layers.GlobalAveragePooling2D()(x)
# A Dense classifier with a single unit (binary classification)
outputs = keras.layers.Dense(1)(x)
model = keras.Model(inputs, outputs)

model.compile(optimizer=keras.optimizers.Adam(),
        loss=keras.losses.BinaryCrossentropy(from_logits=True),
        metrics=[keras.metrics.BinaryAccuracy()])
# model.fit(new_dataset, epochs=20, callbacks=..., validation_data=...)

# Unfreeze the base model
base_model.trainable = True

# It's important to recompile your model after you make any changes
# to the `trainable` attribute of any inner layer, so that your changes
# are take into account
model.compile(optimizer=keras.optimizers.Adam(1e-5),
# Very low learning rate
        loss=keras.losses.BinaryCrossentropy(from_logits=True),
        metrics=[keras.metrics.BinaryAccuracy()])

# Train end-to-end. Be careful to stop before you overfit!
# model.fit(new_dataset, epochs=10, callbacks=..., validation_data=...)

tfds.disable_progress_bar()

train_ds, validation_ds, test_ds = tfds.load(
  "cats_vs_dogs",
  # Reserve 10% for validation and 10% for test
  split=["train[:40%]", "train[40%:50%]", "train[50%:60%]"],
  as_supervised=True, # Include labels
)
print(f"Number of training samples: {train_ds.cardinality()}")
print(f"Number of validation samples: {validation_ds.cardinality()}")
print(f"Number of test samples: {test_ds.cardinality()}")
plt.figure(figsize=(10, 10))
for i, (image, label) in enumerate(train_ds.take(9)):
  ax = plt.subplot(3, 3, i + 1)
```

```
    plt.imshow(image)
    plt.title(int(label))
    plt.axis("off")

resize_fn = keras.layers.Resizing(150, 150)

train_ds = train_ds.map(lambda x, y: (resize_fn(x), y))
validation_ds = validation_ds.map(lambda x, y: (resize_fn(x), y))
test_ds = test_ds.map(lambda x, y: (resize_fn(x), y))

augmentation_layers = [
  layers.RandomFlip("horizontal"),
  layers.RandomRotation(0.1),
]

def data_augmentation(x):
  for layer in augmentation_layers:
    x = layer(x)
  return x

train_ds = train_ds.map(lambda x, y: (data_augmentation(x), y))

from tensorflow import data as tf_data

batch_size = 64

train_ds = train_ds.batch(batch_size).prefetch(tf_data.AUTOTUNE).cache()
validation_ds = validation_ds.batch(batch_size).prefetch(tf_data.
AUTOTUNE).cache()
test_ds = test_ds.batch(batch_size).prefetch(tf_data.AUTOTUNE).cache()

for images, labels in train_ds.take(1):
  plt.figure(figsize=(10, 10))
  first_image = images[0]
  for i in range(9):
    ax = plt.subplot(3, 3, i + 1)
    augmented_image = data_augmentation(np.expand_dims(first_image, 0))
    plt.imshow(np.array(augmented_image[0]).astype("int32"))
    plt.title(int(labels[0]))
    plt.axis("off")

base_model = keras.applications.Xception(
```

```
  weights="imagenet", # Load weights pre-trained on ImageNet.
  input_shape=(150, 150, 3),
  include_top=False,
) # Do not include the ImageNet classifier at the top.

# Freeze the base_model
base_model.trainable = False

# Create new model on top
inputs = keras.Input(shape=(150, 150, 3))

# Pre-trained Xception weights requires that input be scaled
# from (0, 255) to a range of (-1., +1.), the rescaling layer
# outputs: `(inputs * scale) + offset`
scale_layer = keras.layers.Rescaling(scale=1 / 127.5, offset=-1)
x = scale_layer(inputs)

# The base model contains batchnorm layers. We want to keep them in
inference mode
# when we unfreeze the base model for fine-tuning, so we make sure that
the
# base_model is running in inference mode here.
x = base_model(x, training=False)
x = keras.layers.GlobalAveragePooling2D()(x)
x = keras.layers.Dropout(0.2)(x) # Regularize with dropout
outputs = keras.layers.Dense(1)(x)
model = keras.Model(inputs, outputs)

model.summary(show_trainable=True)

model.compile(
  optimizer=keras.optimizers.Adam(),
  loss=keras.losses.BinaryCrossentropy(from_logits=True),
  metrics=[keras.metrics.BinaryAccuracy()],
)

epochs = 2
print("Fitting the top layer of the model")
model.fit(train_ds, epochs=epochs, validation_data=validation_ds)

# Unfreeze the base_model. Note that it keeps running in inference mode
# since we passed `training=False` when calling it. This means that
```

```
# the batchnorm layers will not update their batch statistics.
# This prevents the batchnorm layers from undoing all the training
# we've done so far.
base_model.trainable = True
model.summary(show_trainable=True)
model.compile(
    optimizer=keras.optimizers.Adam(1e-5),  # Low learning rate
    loss=keras.losses.BinaryCrossentropy(from_logits=True),
    metrics=[keras.metrics.BinaryAccuracy()],
)

epochs = 1
print("Fitting the end-to-end model")
model.fit(train_ds, epochs=epochs, validation_data=validation_ds)

print("Test dataset evaluation")
model.evaluate(test_ds)
```

7.11 Using Pretrained Models

In the realm of deep learning, pretrained models stand as powerful allies, offering a significant head start for tackling new tasks. By leveraging their prelearned knowledge, you can accelerate training, enhance performance, and overcome data scarcity challenges. These are deep neural networks already trained on large, diverse datasets for general tasks like image recognition or NLP. They act as a foundation upon which you build further capabilities. This is the core technique where you utilize a pretrained model as a starting point for your specific task. It involves:

– **Feature extraction:** The pretrained model's earlier layers extract general features like edges in images or word embeddings in text.
– **Fine-tuning:** You adjust the final layers of the pretrained model using your own, task-specific data to adapt these features to your unique needs.

We can consider pretrained model to leverage the prelearned features, saving time and computational resources compared to training from scratch. Pretrained models often capture valuable representations, leading to better results on your task, especially with limited data. If you lack extensive labeled data for your specific task, pretrained models can bridge the gap, boosting your model's performance. Focus on building and fine-tuning the final layers, accelerating the development process.

7.12 Fine-Tuning and Feature Extraction

In the domain of transfer learning with pretrained models, both **fine-tuning** and **feature extraction** play crucial roles in adapting the pretrained knowledge to your specific task. This involves utilizing the pretrained model's earlier layers as a feature extractor. These layers, trained on a large, diverse dataset, have learned to capture general features like edges, textures, and word embeddings. Pass your own input data through the pretrained model up to a specific layer, typically before the final layers responsible for the original task (e.g., classification). These are the advantage flows:
– Efficiently extract meaningful features without training from scratch.
– Useful when your own data is limited, leveraging the pretrained model's knowledge.
– Can be combined with other feature engineering techniques for further enrichment

Fine-tuning involves adjusting the weights and biases of the pretrained model, typically in the **later layers**, using your own task-specific data. This adapts the general features extracted earlier to your specific problem. Train your model with your data, but only update the weights of the chosen layers (fine-tuning) while keeping the earlier layers (pretrained) frozen (not updating). Fine-tuning offers the following advantages:
– Adapts the pretrained features to your specific task, potentially improving performance.
– More flexible than feature extraction, allowing for more tailored adaptations.
– Requires more data for training compared to feature extraction.

7.12.1 Choosing the Right Approach to Fine-Tune

1. **Feature extraction:** Suitable when:
   1. You have limited data for your specific task.
   2. You need a quick and efficient way to extract features.
   3. Your task is closely related to the pretrained model's original task.
2. **Fine-tuning:** Suitable when:
   1. You have sufficient data for your specific task.
   2. You need to adapt the pretrained features significantly for your task.
   3. Your task is somewhat different from the pretrained model's original task.
3. **Additional considerations:**
   1. **Number of layers to fine-tune:** Depends on task complexity and data availability. Start with fewer layers and gradually increase if needed.
   2. **Learning rate:** Use a lower learning rate for fine-tuning compared to training from scratch to avoid disrupting the pretrained knowledge.
   3. **Data quality and quantity:** High-quality, well-labeled data is crucial for effective fine-tuning.

4. **Combining feature extraction and fine-tuning:**
   1. You can often combine these techniques. For example, you could extract features from earlier layers and fine-tune the later layers specifically.
   2. This can offer a balance between efficiency and performance, especially when you have moderate data and a task somewhat related to the pretrained model's original task.

7.13 Generative Adversarial Networks (GANs)

Generative adversarial networks (GANs) incorporate the strengths of the previous responses and address any mentioned shortcomings. GANs stand out for their ability to create realistic and diverse data, paving the way for exciting applications in image generation, text creation, and more. This response delves into their inner workings, explores their capabilities, and discusses key considerations for using them effectively. GANs are a powerful but complex tool. Understanding their core concepts, strengths, limitations, and best practices is crucial for successful implementation and achieving your desired generative outcomes.

7.13.1 Architecture of GANs

- **Two-player game:** A GAN comprises two competing neural networks:
- **Generator:** Aims to produce realistic and novel data samples, mimicking the target data distribution.
- **Discriminator:** Attempts to distinguish real data from the generator's outputs, acting as a critic.
- **Adversarial training:** Through a continuous game of "cat and mouse," the generator learns to improve its creations based on the discriminator's feedback, while the discriminator sharpens its ability to detect fake data.
- **Loss function:** Measures the success of both networks. The generator aims to minimize the discriminator's ability to correctly classify its outputs as fake, while the discriminator aims to maximize its accuracy in identifying both real and fake data. How accurately neural network is working, measured by cost function. The cost function is used to measure neural network. The hidden layers are processing the final output via neural network. The neural network forecast the output closer to the expected output. If the given neural network finds any errors during the hidden layers, then the cost function will penalize the network. The main goal of cost function is to increase forecasting accuracy and to minimize the errors. The least value of the cost function is the optimized output. The cost function can be defined with mean squared error then the function can be written as

$$\text{Mean squared error} = \frac{1}{N} \sum_{i=1}^{N} (y_2 - y_1)$$

7.13.2 Best Practices of GANs

1. **Choosing the right architecture:** Different GAN architectures like DCGAN, WGAN, and StyleGAN have specific strengths and weaknesses. Select one that aligns with your data type and desired level of control.
2. **Loss function and evaluation metrics:** Use appropriate loss functions and metrics to assess both the realism and diversity of generated data, avoiding overfitting to specific training examples.
3. **Training stability:** Employ techniques like gradient penalty, spectral normalization, or progressive growing to stabilize training and mitigate common issues like vanishing gradients.
4. **Data preprocessing and augmentation:** Prepare your training data carefully and consider data augmentation to improve the quality and diversity of generated samples.
5. **Monitoring and visualization:** Continuously monitor the training process and visualize generated outputs to identify potential issues and assess progress.

7.13.3 Application of GANs

1. **Image generation:** Creating realistic images of faces, objects, or scenes, useful for applications like product design, virtual reality, and art generation.
2. **Text generation:** Producing creative text formats like poems, code, or scripts, aiding in content creation, machine translation, and dialogue systems.
3. **Music generation:** Composing original musical pieces in various styles, valuable for music creation and personalized recommendations.
4. **Data augmentation:** Expanding datasets with synthetic data, enhancing the training of other machine learning models.

7.14 Regularization and Optimization in Deep Learning

The **regularization** and **optimization** play intertwined roles in steering the training process toward a successful outcome. Let's delve into the nuances of each and how they work together to create robust and effective models. Regularization is used in Preventing Overfitting and Generalizing Well. Imagine a neural network memorizing every training example perfectly. While this might seem ideal, such a model would likely fail miserably on unseen data – a phenomenon known as **overfitting**. Regularization techniques aim to prevent this by introducing constraints that penalize overly complex models and encourage them to learn generalizable patterns. The optimization is the techniques by Finding the Minimum loss in training model.

Think of the loss function as a landscape with valleys and peaks representing different model configurations. Optimization algorithms navigate this landscape, attempting to find the valley with the lowest loss – the optimal set of weights for your model. Some of the commonly used regularization techniques are given below:

1. **L1 and L2 regularization:** These methods add a penalty term to the loss function based on the sum of the absolute values (L1) or squares (L2) of the network's weights. This discourages large weights, promoting simpler models.
2. **Dropout:** During training, some neurons are randomly deactivated, forcing the network to learn robust features that don't rely on specific activations.
3. **Early stopping:** Training is stopped when the model's performance on a validation set starts to deteriorate, preventing further overfitting.
4. **Data augmentation:** Artificially increasing the size and diversity of your training data can improve model generalizability.

Regularization can make the optimization landscape smoother, with fewer local minima, making it easier for optimization algorithms to find the global minimum. Optimization algorithms can influence the effectiveness of regularization. For example, using a learning rate that is too high can negate the benefits of regularization. There's no one-size-fits-all approach. The best combination of regularization and optimization techniques depends on your specific problem, data, and computational resources. Experimentation is crucial. Let's have a look on the code with Linear Regression given below:

```python
import mglearn as ml
from sklearn.linear_model import LinearRegression
from sklearn.model_selection import train_test_split
from numpy import genfromtxt

dataset = genfromtxt('https://raw.githubusercontent.com/m-mehdi/tutori
als/main/boston_housing.csv', delimiter=',')
X = dataset[:, :-1]
y = dataset[:, -1]
X_train, X_test, y_train, y_test = train_test_split(X, y,
test_size=0.25, random_state=0)


lr = LinearRegression().fit(X_train, y_train)
print(f"Linear Regression-Training set score: {lr.score(X_train,
y_train):.2f}")
```

```
print(f"Linear Regression-Test set score: {lr.score(X_test,
y_test):.2f}")
```

```
================================Output================================
Linear Regression-Training set score: 0.95
Linear Regression-Test set score: 0.61
======================================================================
```

Try different techniques and combinations to find what works best for your task. Monitor your model's performance on both training and validation data to avoid overfitting. By understanding the roles of regularization and optimization, you can make informed decisions to train deep learning models that are both accurate and generalizable, performing well on unseen data and avoiding the pitfalls of overfitting. Remember, the journey to optimal performance often involves iterative experimentation and careful tuning of these essential elements. Some of the commonly used optimization algorithms are:

- **Gradient descent (GD):** A classic algorithm that iteratively updates weights in the direction that decreases the loss, taking small steps at each iteration. The gradient decent is an optimization algorithm. It is also known as slop of function. If the gradient is higher then the slope is steeper and the faster a model can learn. It is used to minimizing the cost and increasing accuracy of the model. For example, if we want to climb down the hill we should take small steps instead of jumping down at once. Like the same example if we starts from point 'a', we have to walk down slowly. i.e. we update the position to x timely and we continue the same until, we reach at the bottom. The bottom is considered as the lowest point of cost.
- **Momentum GD:** Similar to GD but incorporates momentum, accumulating past gradients to accelerate convergence toward the minimum.
- **Adam:** An adaptive learning rate optimization algorithm that automatically adjusts the learning rate for each weight based on its past updates, often leading to faster convergence.

Let's have a look on the Ridge Regression

```
import mglearn as ml
from sklearn.linear_model import LinearRegression
from sklearn.model_selection import train_test_split
from numpy import genfromtxt

dataset = genfromtxt('https://raw.githubusercontent.com/m-mehdi/tutori
```

```
als/main/boston_housing.csv', delimiter=',')
X = dataset[:, :-1]
y = dataset[:, -1]
X_train, X_test, y_train, y_test = train_test_split(X, y,
test_size=0.25, random_state=0)
from sklearn.linear_model import Ridge

ridge = Ridge(alpha=0.7).fit(X_train, y_train)
print(f"Ridge Regression-Training set score: {ridge.score(X_train,
y_train):.2f}")
print(f"Ridge Regression-Test set score: {ridge.score(X_test,
y_test):.2f}")
```

==================================Output===================================
Ridge Regression-Training set score: 0.90
Ridge Regression-Test set score: 0.76
===

```
import mglearn as ml
from sklearn.linear_model import LinearRegression
from sklearn.model_selection import train_test_split
from numpy import genfromtxt

dataset = genfromtxt('https://raw.githubusercontent.com/m-mehdi/tutori
als/main/boston_housing.csv', delimiter=',')
X = dataset[:, :-1]
y = dataset[:, -1]
X_train, X_test, y_train, y_test = train_test_split(X, y,
test_size=0.25, random_state=0)

from sklearn.linear_model import Lasso

lasso = Lasso(alpha=1.0).fit(X_train, y_train)
print(f"Lasso Regression-Training set score: {lasso.score(X_train,
y_train):.2f}")
print(f"Lasso Regression-Test set score: {lasso.score(X_test,
y_test):.2f}")
```

=============================Lasso Regression===============================
Lasso Regression-Training set score: 0.29
Lasso Regression-Test set score: 0.21
===

7.15 Batch Normalization

The batch normalization is a technique that stabilizes training and speeds up convergence, leading to better and faster-trained neural networks. BatchNorm introduces an additional normalization step within each layer of your deep neural network. It **normalizes the activations** (outputs) of each layer to have a mean of 0 and a standard deviation of 1 across the current batch of samples. Let's have a look in Fig. 7.10.

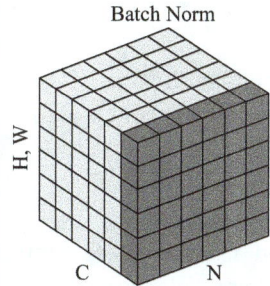

Fig. 7.10: Batch normalization.

The Fig. 7.10 shows the Batch normalization.

This simple yet powerful modification offers significant benefits:

1. **Faster convergence:** By normalizing activations, BatchNorm reduces the internal covariate shift that can occur during training, making the learning process more stable and allowing the network to learn faster.
2. **Improved performance:** The stabilized learning process often leads to better overall performance, achieving higher accuracy compared to models without BatchNorm.
3. **Less sensitivity to initialization:** BatchNorm makes neural networks less sensitive to the choice of initial weights, easing the training process and reducing the risk of getting stuck in bad local minima.
4. **Reduced gradient vanishing/exploding:** Normalization can help mitigate the issue of vanishing or exploding gradients, which can hinder training in deep networks. We apply a batch normalization layer as follows for a minibatch:

$$X_i = \frac{X_i - \text{Mean}_i}{\text{Std Dev}_i}$$

$$\mu_B = \frac{1}{m} \sum_{i=1}^{m} X_i$$

$$\sigma_B^2 = \frac{1}{m} \sum_{i=1}^{m} (x_i - \mu_B)^2$$

$$\hat{X_i} = \frac{x_i - \mu_B}{\sqrt{\sigma_B^2 + \epsilon}}$$

$$y_i = \gamma \hat{X_i} + \beta = BN_{\gamma, \beta}(x_i)$$

where γ and β are learnable parameters.

7.15.1 How BatchNorm Works?

BatchNorm is a valuable tool for training deep neural networks, offering faster convergence, improved performance, and reduced sensitivity to initialization. By understanding its core principles, benefits, and considerations, you can effectively leverage BatchNorm to achieve better results in your deep learning projects. The working mechanism of BatchNorm is given below:
– **Calculate mean and standard deviation:** For each layer and each batch of data, BatchNorm computes the mean and standard deviation of the activations across that batch.
– **Normalize activations:** Each activation in the batch is then subtracted by the mean and divided by the standard deviation.
– **Scale and shift:** To preserve information, the normalized activations are multiplied by learned scale and shift parameters (gamma and beta), allowing the network to adapt to the normalization step.

7.15.2 Best Practices of BatchNorm

1. **Batch size:** BatchNorm is typically used with small batch sizes, as it relies on accurate statistics within each batch.
2. **Hyperparameter tuning:** Tuning the learning rate and adjusting the scale and shift parameters can be crucial for optimal performance.
3. **Minibatch statistics:** BatchNorm uses statistics from the current minibatch, which can be an approximation of the population statistics. This might lead to slight inconsistencies during training and inference.
4. **Alternative normalization techniques:** Other normalization techniques like layer normalization and group normalization exist, offering different trade-offs and potentially better performance in specific scenarios.

7.16 Gradient Clipping

The **gradient clipping** emerges as a crucial technique to address a potential pitfall: **exploding gradients**. These excessive increases in gradient values can hinder training, causing the model to diverge and fail to converge. Gradient clipping, as the name suggests, acts as a safety net, preventing gradients from becoming too large and destabilizing the training process. Imagine training a deep neural network with many layers. As the error signal (gradient) propagates back through the layers during backpropagation, it can accumulate and become significantly larger at each layer. This can happen due to factors like vanishing gradients in shallower layers, leading to amplified gradients in deeper layers. Gradient clipping sets a **maximum threshold** for the magnitude of gradients. Any gradient value exceeding this threshold is "clipped" down to the threshold, effectively preventing it from growing further.

7.16.1 Advantages of Gradient Clipping

- **Maintain stability:** By keeping gradients under control, gradient clipping prevents the model from diverging and allows it to converge to a better solution.
- **Improve training:** Gradient clipping can sometimes help the model find a better solution faster by preventing it from getting stuck in local minima caused by excessively large gradients.
- **Reduce sensitivity to hyperparameters:** Gradient clipping can make the model less sensitive to hyperparameters like the learning rate, making training more robust.

Gradient clipping is a valuable tool for deep learning practitioners, providing a safety net against exploding gradients and aiding in stable and efficient training. By understanding its principles, benefits, and considerations, you can effectively implement gradient clipping to enhance the performance and robustness of your deep learning models. The three types of gradient clipping approaches available are:
1. **Global clipping:** Clips all gradients to a single maximum value.
2. **Layer-wise clipping:** Clips gradients independently for each layer, allowing for customization based on layer sensitivity.
3. **Norm-based clipping:** Clips gradients based on their norm (length), ensuring they stay within a specific radius.

Let's dive deeper into gradient clipping with following python code.

```python
import tensorflow as tf
from tensorflow.keras import Model, layers
import numpy as np
import tensorflow_datasets as tfds

# Hyperparameters
num_classes = 10 # total classes (0-9 digits).
num_features = 784 # data features (img shape: 28*28).

# Training Parameters
learning_rate = 0.001
```

```
training_steps = 1000
batch_size = 32
display_step = 100
# Network Parameters
# MNIST image shape is 28*28px, we will then handle 28 sequences of 28
timesteps for every sample.
num_input = 28 # number of sequences.
timesteps = 28 # timesteps.
num_units = 32 # number of neurons for the LSTM layer.


print(tf.__version__)


import neptune


run = neptune.init_run(project='common/tf-keras-integration',
api_token='ANONYMOUS')


from tensorflow.keras.datasets import mnist
(x_train, y_train), (x_test, y_test) = mnist.load_data()
# Convert to float32.
x_train, x_test = np.array(x_train, np.float32), np.array(x_test, np.
float32)
# Flatten images to 1-D vector of 784 features (28*28).
x_train, x_test = x_train.reshape([-1, 28, 28]), x_test.reshape([-1,
num_features])
# Normalize images value from [0, 255] to [0, 1].
x_train, x_test = x_train / 255., x_test / 255.


# Use tf.data API to shuffle and batch data.
train_data = tf.data.Dataset.from_tensor_slices((x_train, y_train))
train_data = train_data.repeat().shuffle(5000).batch(batch_size).
prefetch(1)


# Create LSTM Model. class Net(Model):
  # Set layers.
  def __init__(self):
    super(Net, self).__init__()
    # RNN (LSTM) hidden layer.
    self.lstm_layer = layers.LSTM(units=num_units)
    self.out = layers.Dense(num_classes)
```

```python
  # Set forward pass.
  def __call__(self, x, is_training=False):
    # LSTM layer.
    x = self.lstm_layer(x)
    # Output layer (num_classes).
    x = self.out(x)
    if not is_training:
      # tf cross entropy expect logits without softmax, so only
      # apply softmax when not training.
      x = tf.nn.softmax(x)
    return x

# Build LSTM model.
network = Net()

# Cross-Entropy Loss.
# Note that this will apply 'softmax' to the logits.
def cross_entropy_loss(x, y):
  # Convert labels to int 64 for tf cross-entropy function.
  y = tf.cast(y, tf.int64)
  # Apply softmax to logits and compute cross-entropy.
  loss = tf.nn.sparse_softmax_cross_entropy_with_logits(labels=y,
  logits=x)
  # Average loss across the batch.
  return tf.reduce_mean(loss)

# Accuracy metric.
def accuracy(y_pred, y_true):
  # Predicted class is the index of highest score in prediction vector
  (i.e. argmax).
  correct_prediction = tf.equal(tf.argmax(y_pred, 1), tf.cast(y_true,
  tf.int64))
  return tf.reduce_mean(tf.cast(correct_prediction, tf.float32), axis=-1)

# Adam optimizer.
optimizer = tf.optimizers.Adam(learning_rate)

# Optimization process. def run_optimization(x, y):
  # Wrap computation inside a GradientTape for automatic differentiation.
  with tf.GradientTape() as tape:
    # Forward pass.
    pred = network(x, is_training=True)
```

```
# Compute loss.
loss = cross_entropy_loss(pred, y)

# Variables to update, i.e. trainable variables.
trainable_variables = network.trainable_variables

# Compute gradients.
gradients = tape.gradient(loss, trainable_variables)

# Clip-by-value on all trainable gradients
gradients = [(tf.clip_by_value(grad, clip_value_min=-1.0,
clip_value_max=1.0)) for grad in gradients]

# Update weights following gradients.
optimizer.apply_gradients(zip(gradients, trainable_variables))

# Run training for the given number of steps. for step, (batch_x,
batch_y) in enumerate(train_data.take(training_steps), 1):
    # Run the optimization to update W and b values.
    run_optimization(batch_x, batch_y)

    if step % display_step == 0:
        pred = lstm_net(batch_x, is_training=True)
        loss = cross_entropy_loss(pred, batch_y)
        acc = accuracy(pred, batch_y)

        run['monitoring/logs/loss'].log(loss)
        run['monitoring/logs/acc'].log(acc)

        print("step: %i, loss: %f, accuracy: %f" % (step, loss, acc))
```

Some of the best practices of gradient clipping approaches are given below:

- **Clipping threshold:** Choosing the right clipping threshold is crucial. A too-high threshold might not be effective, while a too-low threshold might affect training speed.
- **Impact on performance:** While gradient clipping can be beneficial, it might slightly reduce the final accuracy of the model in some cases.
- **Experimentation and evaluation:** Experiment with different clipping approaches and thresholds to find what works best for your specific model and task.
- **Alternative techniques:** Other techniques like gradient normalization and adaptive learning rates can also help address exploding gradients.

Summary

The ANN is inspired by the human brain, and neural networks are **interconnected layers of artificial neurons** that process information. Each neuron performs a simple computation, and the connections between them determine the overall behavior of the network. These networks learn by adjusting the connections between neurons based on training data. The perceptrons and activation functions serve as fundamental elements in constructing neural networks, paving the way for complex learning and decision-making capabilities. Let's delve into their individual roles and how they work together. Imagine a perceptron as a simple neuron-like structure that receives input signals, processes them, and generates an output. It's the building block of neural networks, responsible for basic computations and information flow. TensorFlow is a powerful and versatile open-source software library, primarily used for **developing and deploying machine learning and deep learning models**. It provides a flexible and efficient platform for various tasks from image recognition and NLP to self-driving cars and scientific computing. Keras is a **high-level API for building and training deep learning models**, developed and maintained by Google. It sits on top of powerful libraries like TensorFlow and Theano, providing a simpler and more user-friendly interface for deep learning tasks. Here's what you need to know about Keras.

CNNs have emerged as champions in the field of image and video analysis. Their unique architecture, inspired by the human visual system, allows them to excel at tasks like image recognition, object detection, and video classification. Let's delve into the core concepts and capabilities of CNNs. **CNNs** play a crucial role in image processing, excelling in various tasks due to their unique architecture inspired by the human visual system. Let's delve deeper into how CNNs contribute to image processing and explore specific applications. In the fascinating world of image processing, **CNN architecture** serves as the blueprint for CNNs, dictating the flow of information and enabling them to excel at tasks like image classification, object detection, and image segmentation.

The **pooling and dropout layers** play distinct yet essential roles in boosting performance and preventing overfitting. Here's a breakdown of their individual functionalities and how they work together. **RNNs** emerge as a powerful tool for processing sequential data, where the order of elements matters. Unlike traditional neural networks that handle independent inputs, RNNs introduce a key difference compared to feedforward neural networks: **internal memory**. This memory allows them to retain information from previous inputs and use it to process the current input, enabling them to capture dependencies and context within sequential data. The **sequential data** emerges as a unique type of information where the **order of elements is crucial**. Unlike independent data points, understanding sequential data requires considering the past and anticipating the future within its inherent structure. Imagine a sentence, a song, a stock market timeline, or a video clip. These all represent sequential data, where each element (word, note, price point, frame) carries intrinsic meaning and influences those that follow. Processing sequential data effectively requires methods that capture these dependencies and context.

The **LSTM** and **GRU** networks stand out as powerful tools for handling **sequential data**, where order matters. Both are special types of **RNNs**, designed to overcome a major limitation of traditional RNNs: the vanishing gradient problem. This problem hinders their ability to learn long-term dependencies within sequences. The seq2seq stands for Bridging the Gap Between Different Sequences models. It emerges as a powerful and versatile tool for tasks involving the **transformation of one sequence of data into another**. From translating languages to generating captions for images, these models excel at capturing the relationships and context within sequences, enabling them to perform various impressive tasks. The transfer learning stands for Building on Existing Knowledge for Faster Progress. It emerges as a powerful technique that allows you to **leverage knowledge gained from one task to improve performance on a related one**. Imagine training a dog to fetch a specific toy; you wouldn't start from scratch each time it encounters a new object. Similarly, transfer learning enables models to "remember" what they've learned previously and adapt it to new situations, significantly accelerating the learning process and improving results. Fine-tuning involves **modifying the weights of a pretrained model** to adapt it to a new task. Typically, the lower layers of the model, which capture general features, are frozen, while the higher layers, responsible for more specific learning, are fine-tuned on your own dataset.

The **generative adversarial networks (GANs)** stand out as a powerful and fascinating technique for generating new data, like images, text, or music. Imagine creating realistic portraits of people who never existed, or composing music in the style of your favorite artist – that's the kind of magic GANs can achieve!

Vanilla GAN: The original GAN architecture, with separate generator and discriminator networks.

Deep convolutional GAN (DCGAN): Leverages convolutional layers in both the generator and discriminator, particularly effective for image generation.

Wasserstein GAN (WGAN): Improves training stability by using a different loss function and gradient penalty.

Generative adversarial networks with gradient penalty (GAN-GP): Combines aspects of DCGAN and WGAN for improved stability and performance.

StyleGAN: Utilizes style transfer techniques to generate highly diverse and realistic images.

The **regularization and optimization** are two fundamental techniques that work hand-in-hand to improve the performance and generalizability of your models. The **batch normalization (BatchNorm)** emerges as a powerful technique that **improves the training speed and stability** of neural networks. It acts like a **magic ingredient**, smoothing the training process and often leading to better performance. The **gradient clipping** emerges as a crucial technique for **preventing exploding gra-**

dients, a phenomenon that can hinder the training process and lead to unstable or even diverging models. Imagine training a dog: you wouldn't pull too hard on the leash, as it could make them resist or even run away. Similarly, gradient clipping helps you "control" the learning process by setting reasonable limits on the changes made to your model's weights.

Exercise (MCQs)

1. **In a convolutional neural network (CNN), what does the "pooling layer" do?**
   A) Normalizes activations in the previous layer
   B) Reduces the dimensionality of the feature maps
   C) Performs element-wise multiplication with a specific kernel
   D) Learns nonlinear relationships between features

2. **Which of the following is NOT a valid activation function for a neural network?**
   A) Sigmoid   B) ReLU   C) Softmax   D) Linear

3. **What is the main difference between gradient descent and Adam, two popular optimization algorithms for neural networks?**
   A) Adam uses adaptive learning rates, while gradient descent has a fixed rate.
   B) Adam is faster for large datasets, while gradient descent is better for small datasets.
   C) Adam requires less tuning of hyperparameters compared to gradient descent.
   D) Adam is more prone to overfitting than gradient descent.

4. **What is the purpose of dropout in neural networks?**
   A) To improve accuracy by reducing overfitting
   B) To speed up training by skipping some connections
   C) To prevent vanishing gradients in deep networks
   D) To learn more robust features by encouraging diversity

5. **What are the main challenges associated with training generative adversarial networks (GANs)?**
   A) Selecting the right architecture for both the generator and discriminator
   B) Ensuring stable training and avoiding mode collapse
   C) Evaluating the quality of generated data effectively
   D) All of the above

6. **Which of the following techniques is NOT typically used for regularization in deep learning?**
   A) L1 and L2 regularization
   B) Batch normalization

C) Early stopping

D) Data augmentation with label smoothing

7. **How can you interpret the weights of a trained neural network to understand what it has learned?**

A) By directly analyzing the weight values

B) Using visualization techniques like saliency maps

C) By performing feature inversion to reconstruct input data

D) All of the above

8. **What are the advantages of using pretrained models in deep learning?**

A) Faster training and improved performance on new tasks

B) Reduced need for large datasets and computational resources

C) Ability to fine-tune the model for specific applications

D) All of the above

9. **What are the ethical considerations involved in using deep learning models, especially those trained on large datasets?**

A) Bias and fairness in decision-making

B) Explainability and interpretability of model predictions

C) Privacy concerns and data security

D) All of the above

10. **What are the latest advancements and research directions in the field of deep learning?**

A) Explainable AI (XAI) for interpretable models

B) Continual learning for adapting to new data streams

C) Transformers for natural language processing and beyond

D) Neuromorphic computing for more efficient hardware

Answer Key

1. b) Reduces the dimensionality of the feature maps
2. d) Linear
3. a) Adam uses adaptive learning rates, while gradient descent has a fixed rate.
4. a) To improve accuracy by reducing overfitting
5. d) All of the above
6. d) Data augmentation with label smoothing
7. d) All of the above
8. d) All of the above
9. d) All of the above
10. c) Transformers for natural language processing and beyond

Some Basic Question

1. What is the difference between a neuron and a layer in a neural network?
2. What is the activation function used in the output layer of a neural network for binary classification
3. What is the purpose of backpropagation in training a neural network?
4. Which type of neural network is best suited for image recognition?
5. What are the key differences between convolutional neural networks (CNNs) and recurrent neural networks (RNNs)?
6. What is the role of attention mechanisms in transformers?
7. How are neural networks used in natural language processing (NLP)?
8. What are some applications of generative adversarial networks (GANs)?
9. How can neural networks be used for time series forecasting?
10. Explain the concept of backpropagation and its role in training neural networks.

Fill in the Blanks

1. _____ are a type of **artificial intelligence** inspired by the human brain.
2. _____ receive multiple inputs, representing features or attributes of the data.
3. _____reduces the dimensionality of the data, summarizing the information captured by the convolutional layer
4. _____ is a valuable tool for training deep neural networks, offering faster convergence, improved performance, and reduced sensitivity to initialization.
5. Gradient clipping sets a_____ for the magnitude of gradients.

Answers

1. Neural networks
2. Perceptrons
3. Pooling layer
4. BatchNorm
5. Maximum threshold

Chapter 8
Specialized Applications and Case Studies

8.1 Introduction to Natural Language Processing (NLP)

Natural language processing (NLP) is a field of artificial intelligence (AI) that deals with the interaction between computers and human language. Its goal is to enable computers to understand, interpret, and manipulate natural language in a way that is similar to how humans do. Its primary goal is to enable computers to understand, interpret, and generate human language in a manner that is both meaningful and useful. This includes written text, spoken language, and even sign language. NLP techniques often involve a combination of statistical models, machine learning algorithms, and linguistic rules to process and understand human language effectively. Recent advancements in deep learning, particularly with models like Transformers, have led to significant improvements in various NLP tasks, enabling more accurate and versatile language processing capabilities. Let's have a basic python code to download and install library NLTK along with some packages. We can install NLTK library using **pip install nltk** command on terminal and then you may execute the following code:

```python
import nltk

# downloading and installing required libraries
nltk.download('maxent_ne_chunker')
nltk.download('punkt')
nltk.download('words')
nltk.download('wordnet')
nltk.download('stopwords')
nltk.download('averaged_perceptron_tagger')


from nltk.tokenize import sent_tokenize, word_tokenize

text = """Natural Language Processing (NLP) is a field of artificial
intelligence (AI) that deals with the interaction between computers and
human language. Its goal is to enable computers to understand,
interpret, and manipulate natural language in a way that is similar to
how humans do. Its primary goal is to enable computers to understand,
interpret, and generate human language in a manner that is both
meaningful and useful. This includes written text, spoken language, and
even sign language."""
```

https://doi.org/10.1515/9783110697186-008

```
sentences = sent_tokenize(text)
print(sentences)
words = word_tokenize(text)
print(words)
```

```
================================Output=====================================
['Natural Language Processing (NLP) is a field of artificial intelligence (AI) that deals
\nwith the interaction between computers and human language.', 'Its goal is to enable
computers \nto understand, interpret, and manipulate natural language in a way that
is similar to how \nhumans do.', 'Its primary goal is to enable computers to under-
stand, interpret, and generate \nhuman language in a manner that is both meaningful
and useful.', 'This includes written text, \nspoken language, and even sign language.']
['Natural', 'Language', 'Processing', '(', 'NLP', ')', 'is', 'a', 'field', 'of', 'artificial', 'intelli-
gence', '(', 'AI', ')', 'that', 'deals', 'with', 'the', 'interaction', 'between', 'computers', 'and',
'human', 'language', '.', 'Its', 'goal', 'is', 'to', 'enable', 'computers', 'to', 'understand', ',', 'in-
terpret', ',', 'and', 'manipulate', 'natural', 'language', 'in', 'a', 'way', 'that', 'is', 'similar',
'to', 'how', 'humans', 'do', '.', 'Its', 'primary', 'goal', 'is', 'to', 'enable', 'computers', 'to', 'un-
derstand', ',', 'interpret', ',', 'and', 'generate', 'human', 'language', 'in', 'a', 'manner',
'that', 'is', 'both', 'meaningful', 'and', 'useful', '.', 'This', 'includes', 'written', 'text', ',', 'spo-
ken', 'language', ',', 'and', 'even', 'sign', 'language', '.']
===========================================================================
```

The above code will tokenize the words and sentences. It shows that NLP is a rapidly growing field with the potential to revolutionize the way we interact with computers and information. NLP techniques can analyze the structure and semantics of language to understand the intended meaning behind words and sentences. NLP can be used to create text, translate languages, and even write different kinds of creative content. We can use NLP in some of the fields below:

1. **Machine translation:** Translate text from one language to another. Automatically translating text from one language to another. This includes tasks like language translation, language detection, and multilingual text analysis. Improving the quality of machine translation systems by using word embeddings to encode source and target language words.

2. **Chatbots and virtual assistants:** Understand and respond to user queries in a natural way.

3. **Sentiment analysis:** Determining the sentiment or opinion expressed in a piece of text, whether it's positive, negative, or neutral. This is useful for analyzing customer feedback, social media sentiment, and product reviews. It is enhancing the performance of sentiment analysis models by representing words in a continuous vector space, capturing subtle semantic nuances.

4. **Text summarization and classification:** Summarize and classification on large amounts of text data into a concise and informative format. Generating concise

summaries of longer texts while preserving the key information and main points. This is useful for quickly extracting important information from large documents or articles.

5. **Automatic language identification:** Identify the language a piece of text is written in. Understanding the meaning and intent behind user queries or commands. This involves tasks like intent recognition, slot filling, and dialogue management in conversational systems.

6. **Speech recognition and text-to-speech:** Convert speech to text and vice versa. Converting spoken language into text. This is the technology behind virtual assistants like Siri, Alexa, and Google Assistant.

7. **Named entity recognition (NER):** Identifying and classifying named entities mentioned in text into predefined categories such as names of persons, organizations, and locations.

8. **Text generation:** Generating human-like text based on given input or prompts. This can be used for various applications such as chatbots, content generation, and dialogue systems.

9. **Question answering:** Automatically answering questions posed in natural language based on a given context or knowledge base. This includes tasks like reading comprehension and FAQ systems.

10. **Text mining:** Extracting useful insights and patterns from large volumes of text data. This includes techniques such as text clustering, topic modeling, and trend analysis.

11. **Part-of-speech (POS) tagging:** It helps into improving the performance of sequence labeling tasks by incorporating word embeddings as features in machine learning models. Let's have a look on the following code:

```python
from nltk.tokenize import word_tokenize
from nltk import pos_tag
text = """Natural Language Processing (NLP) is a field of artificial
intelligence (AI) that deals with the interaction between computers and
human language. Its goal is to enable computers to understand,
interpret, and manipulate natural language in a way that is similar to
how humans do. Its primary goal is to enable computers to understand,
interpret, and generate human language in a manner that is both
meaningful and useful. This includes written text, spoken language, and
even sign language."""
words = word_tokenize(text)
tagged_words = pos_tag(words)
print(tagged_words)
```

```
====================================Output====================================
[('Natural', 'JJ'), ('Language', 'NNP'), ('Processing', 'NNP'), ('(', '('), ('NLP', 'NNP'), (')', ')'), ('is',
'VBZ'), ('a', 'DT'), ('field', 'NN'), ('of', 'IN'), ('artificial', 'JJ'), ('intelligence', 'NN'), ('(', '('), ('AI',
'NNP'), (')', ')'), ('that', 'IN'), ('deals', 'NNS'), ('with', 'IN'), ('the', 'DT'), ('interaction', 'NN'), ('be-
tween', 'IN'), ('computers', 'NNS'), ('and', 'CC'), ('human', 'JJ'), ('language', 'NN'), ('.', '.'), ('Its',
'PRP$'), ('goal', 'NN'), ('is', 'VBZ'), ('to', 'TO'), ('enable', 'JJ'), ('computers', 'NNS'), ('to', 'TO'),
('understand', 'VB'), (',', ','), ('interpret', 'VB'), (',', ','), ('and', 'CC'), ('manipulate', 'VB'), ('natu-
ral', 'JJ'), ('language', 'NN'), ('in', 'IN'), ('a', 'DT'), ('way', 'NN'), ('that', 'WDT'), ('is', 'VBZ'), ('sim-
ilar', 'JJ'), ('to', 'TO'), ('how', 'WRB'), ('humans', 'NNS'), ('do', 'VBP'), ('.', '.'), ('Its', 'PRP$'),
('primary', 'JJ'), ('goal', 'NN'), ('is', 'VBZ'), ('to', 'TO'), ('enable', 'JJ'), ('computers', 'NNS'), ('to',
'TO'), ('understand', 'VB'), (',', ','), ('interpret', 'VB'), (',', ','), ('and', 'CC'), ('generate', 'VB'),
('human', 'JJ'), ('language', 'NN'), ('in', 'IN'), ('a', 'DT'), ('manner', 'NN'), ('that', 'WDT'), ('is',
'VBZ'), ('both', 'DT'), ('meaningful', 'JJ'), ('and', 'CC'), ('useful', 'JJ'), ('.', '.'), ('This', 'DT'), ('in-
cludes', 'VBZ'), ('written', 'VBN'), ('text', 'NN'), (',', ','), ('spoken', 'JJ'), ('language', 'NN'), (',', ','),
('and', 'CC'), ('even', 'RB'), ('sign', 'JJ'), ('language', 'NN'), ('.', '.')]
==============================================================================
```

12. **Semantic similarity:** Computing the similarity between words or phrases based on the similarity of their embeddings. This is useful for tasks such as information retrieval, recommendation systems, and question answering.

NLP uses various machine learning techniques, such as deep learning, to analyze and process language data. These methods are used to analyze the patterns and relationships between different elements of language. NLP incorporates knowledge of grammar, syntax, semantics, and pragmatics to understand the nuances of human language. NLP can help break down language barriers and facilitate communication between people and machines. NLP can automate tasks that currently require human intervention such as analyzing customer feedback or translating documents. NLP can help organizations make better decisions by providing insights from large amounts of textual data. Like every coin has two side one is head and tail, the same way by having the many positives with NLP still it is having few challenges as well, Some of them are given below:

1. **Language ambiguity:** Human language is often ambiguous and can be interpreted in different ways.
2. **Context dependency:** The meaning of a word or phrase can depend on the context in which it is used.
3. **Constant evolution of language:** Language is constantly evolving, which can pose challenges for NLP systems to keep up.

8.1.1 Tokenization

Tokenization is a fundamental task in NLP that involves breaking down a text into smaller units called tokens. These tokens could be words, subwords, characters, or even phrase s, depending on the specific requirements of the task at hand. The process of tokenization plays a crucial role in many NLP tasks because it forms the basis for further analysis and processing. These tokens can be individual words, characters, sentences, or even phrases, depending on the specific task and chosen technique. Computers cannot directly understand the meaning of continuous text. Tokenization transforms it into a format that machines can process and analyze. Tokenization lays the groundwork for various NLP tasks like sentiment analysis, machine translation, and text classification. We have some challenges to in the tokenization to, some of them are given below:

- **Handling contractions and special characters:** NLP systems need to decide whether to split contractions (e.g., "don't") and how to handle special characters like emojis or symbols.
- **Language-specific challenges:** Different languages have varying sentence structures and punctuation marks, requiring specific tokenization rules for each language.
- **Context-dependent words:** Words like "to" or "a" can have different meanings depending on the context, posing a challenge for tokenization algorithms.

By breaking down complex text structures, tokenization allows NLP models to focus on the essential information and perform these tasks more efficiently and accurately. Tokenization is typically one of the initial steps in the NLP pipeline, and it serves as the foundation for subsequent tasks such as part-of-speech tagging, named entity recognition, syntactic parsing, and semantic analysis. The choice of tokenization strategy depends on the specific requirements of the NLP task, the language being processed, and the characteristics of the text data. We can say that tokenization is a crucial first step in NLP tasks, preparing textual data for further processing and analysis by machines. We can categorize tokenization based upon its application and usage. Some of them are given below:

8.1.1.1 Types of Tokenization

1. **Word tokenization:** In word tokenization, the text is split into individual words based on space or punctuation boundaries. This is the most common type, and it splits the text into individual words based on whitespace or punctuation marks. For example, the sentence "The quick brown fox jumps over the lazy dog" would be tokenized into ["The", "quick", "brown", "fox", "jumps", "over", "the", "lazy", "dog"].
2. **Sentence tokenization:** Sentence tokenization involves splitting a paragraph or document into individual sentences. This is useful for tasks that require analyzing

text at the sentence level. For example, the paragraph "NLP is a fascinating field. It involves the interaction between computers and humans through natural language." would be tokenized into ["NLP is a fascinating field.", "It involves the interaction between computers and humans through natural language."]. This divides the text into individual sentences at full stops, exclamation marks, or question marks.

3. **Subword tokenization:** Subword tokenization breaks down words into smaller meaningful units called subwords or morphemes. This is particularly useful for handling out-of-vocabulary words and dealing with languages with complex morphology. Techniques like byte pair encoding and WordPiece are commonly used for subword tokenization.

4. **Character tokenization:** In character tokenization, each character in the text becomes a separate token. This approach is useful when analyzing text at a very fine-grained level or when dealing with languages with complex scripts. This breaks down the text into individual characters, which is useful for certain tasks like spelling correction or character-level language models.

5. **Phrasal tokenization:** Phrasal tokenization involves grouping consecutive words into phrases or chunks based on predefined rules or patterns. This can be useful for tasks like named entity recognition or chunking.

6. **N-gram tokenization:** This creates sequences of n consecutive words, useful for tasks like language modeling and machine translation.

8.1.2 Word Embeddings

Word embeddings are a type of word representation in NLP that aims to capture the semantic meaning of words in a continuous vector space. Traditional methods of representing words, such as one-hot encoding or bag-of-words, lack the ability to capture semantic relationships between words and often result in high-dimensional and sparse representations. Word embeddings address these limitations by representing words as dense vectors in a continuous vector space, where similar words are mapped to nearby points. These embeddings are learned from large corpora of text using unsupervised or semi-supervised techniques, such as neural network models. Word embeddings are a powerful technique for representing words as numerical vectors. These vectors capture the semantic meaning and relationships between words, allowing machines to understand language nuances beyond just the individual words themselves. Word embeddings are a fundamental building block for many NLP tasks. By encoding semantic meaning and relationships, they empower machines to understand and process language in a way that is closer to how humans do. There are two popular methods or algorithms for generating word embeddings such as

1. **Word2Vec:** Word2Vec is a popular algorithm that learns word embeddings by analyzing the co-occurrence of words in a sentence or surrounding context. Devel-

oped by researchers at Google, Word2Vec is a shallow neural network model that learns word embeddings by predicting the context of words within a window of text. It consists of two main architectures: Continuous Bag of Words (CBOW) and Skip-gram. CBOW predicts the target word based on its context words, while Skip-gram predicts context words given a target word.

2. **GloVe (global vectors for word representation):** GloVe is a method that uses global word co-occurrence statistics, capturing semantic relationships based on how often words appear together across the entire corpus. GloVe is an unsupervised learning algorithm for obtaining word embeddings by factorizing the co-occurrence matrix of words in a corpus. It leverages global statistical information about the entire corpus to learn word representations.

3. **FastText:** This algorithm was developed by Facebook AI Research, and FastText is an extension of Word2Vec that takes into account subword information. Instead of learning embeddings only for complete words, FastText constructs embeddings for character n-grams and averages them to obtain the representation for each word. This approach is particularly useful for handling out-of-vocabulary words and morphologically rich languages.

8.1.2.1 How Does Word Embedding Works?

– **Mapping words to vectors:** Each word in the vocabulary is assigned a unique vector, typically containing tens or hundreds of dimensions.
– **Learning word relationships:** These vector representations are learned automatically by analyzing large amounts of text data. The learning process considers the context in which words appear, allowing them to capture semantic similarities.
– **Similar words have similar vectors:** Words with similar meanings will have closer vector representations in the high-dimensional space. This means that simple mathematical operations on the vectors can reveal semantic relationships between words.

Word embedding is very helpful in some of the fields like:

1. **Capture semantic meaning:** Unlike traditional one-hot encoding, which simply represents words as unique identifiers, word embeddings capture the semantic meaning and relationships between words.
2. **Improve performance in NLP tasks:** By encoding semantic information, word embeddings significantly improve the performance of various NLP tasks like:
3. **Machine translation:** Translate text by understanding the meaning and relationships between words in different languages.
    1. **Sentiment analysis:** Analyze the sentiment of text data by understanding the emotions associated with words and their relationships.

2. **Text classification:** Categorize text data into specific groups based on the meaning encoded in the word embeddings.
3. **Question answering:** Answer questions accurately by understanding the context and relationships between words in the query and the text data.

8.1.3 Sequence Modeling for NLP

Sequence modeling is a fundamental technique in NLP that involves building models capable of understanding and generating sequences of data such as words, characters, or tokens. These models are designed to capture the temporal dependencies and contextual information present in sequential data, making them well-suited for tasks like language modeling, machine translation, sentiment analysis, and named entity recognition, among others. The sequence modeling techniques are continuously evolving, driven by advancements in neural network architectures, training methodologies, and the availability of large-scale datasets. By effectively capturing the sequential nature of natural language data, these models enable a wide range of NLP applications with improved accuracy and performance. In other words we can say, the sequence modeling refers to a group of techniques specifically designed to process and analyze sequential data like text, speech, and time-series data. This data inherently has an order and context that's crucial to understand its meaning. We can use sequence modeling techniques in the following algorithms:

1. **Recurrent neural networks (RNNs):** RNNs are a class of neural networks specifically designed to handle sequential data. They process input sequences one element at a time while maintaining an internal state or memory. This allows them to capture dependencies over time. However, traditional RNNs suffer from the vanishing gradient problem, which limits their ability to capture long-range dependencies. These models have internal loops that allow them to retain information from previous elements in the sequence and use it to process the current element.
2. **Long short-term memory (LSTM) networks:** LSTMs are a type of RNN architecture designed to address the vanishing gradient problem. They introduce specialized memory cells and gating mechanisms that allow them to selectively remember or forget information over long sequences. LSTMs have become a popular choice for various sequence modeling tasks in NLP due to their ability to capture long-range dependencies. LSTM is a special type of RNN designed to address the vanishing gradient problem, allowing them to learn long-term dependencies in sequences.
3. **Gated recurrent units (GRUs):** GRUs are another variant of RNNs that simplify the architecture compared to LSTMs by combining the input and forget gates into a single update gate. While they are conceptually similar to LSTMs, GRUs have

fewer parameters and are computationally more efficient, making them suitable for applications with limited computational resources.

4. **Transformer models:** Transformers are a recent advancement in sequence modeling that have gained widespread popularity in NLP. They rely on self-attention mechanisms to capture global dependencies between input and output sequences. Transformers consist of an encoder-decoder architecture, where the encoder processes the input sequence and the decoder generates the output sequence. Models like BERT (bidirectional encoder representations from transformers) and GPT (generative pretrained transformer) have achieved state-of-the-art performance on various NLP tasks by leveraging transformer architectures. These models use an attention mechanism to focus on the most relevant parts of the sequence when processing each element, overcoming limitations of RNNs in handling long sequences.

5. **Convolutional neural networks (CNNs):** While primarily used for image processing, CNNs can also be applied to sequence modeling tasks in NLP. CNNs operate on fixed-size input windows and learn hierarchical feature representations by applying convolutional filters across the input sequence. They are particularly effective for tasks like text classification and sentiment analysis.

Overall we can say that the sequence modeling plays a vital role in modern NLP. By considering the order and context of data points, these models enable machines to understand complex relationships and perform various NLP tasks with greater accuracy and effectiveness.

Why Does Sequence Modeling Important?

1. **Capturing dependencies:** Traditional NLP techniques often treat words or sentences independently, ignoring the crucial dependencies between them. Sequence models address this by considering the order and context of words or elements in a sequence.

2. **Understanding complex relationships:** Language involves intricate relationships between words, sentences, and paragraphs. Sequence models are adept at capturing these relationships, allowing them to perform tasks like:

    1. **Machine translation:** Understand the context of a sentence in one language and translate it accurately to another, preserving meaning and structure.
    2. **Sentiment analysis:** Analyze the sentiment of a text by considering not just individual words but also their sequence and how they influence each other's meaning.
    3. **Speech recognition:** Convert spoken language into text by understanding the sequence of sounds and their relationships.
    4. **Text summarization:** Identify and extract the main points from a piece of text by considering the flow and sequence of ideas.

8.2 Time-Series Forecasting

Time-series forecasting in NLP involves predicting future values or trends in text data based on historical patterns and sequences. While traditional time-series forecasting methods are often applied to numerical data, there are techniques and approaches that can be adapted for forecasting tasks in NLP. While NLP and time-series forecasting are distinct fields, they can be combined in certain applications to enhance the prediction of future events based on textual data. Time-series forecasting in NLP involves adapting existing methods and techniques from both fields to predict future trends and patterns in text data. By leveraging word embeddings, language models, neural network architectures, and attention mechanisms, it's possible to build accurate forecasting models for various NLP tasks. While still under development, the combination of NLP and time-series forecasting holds promise for enhancing the prediction of future events by leveraging valuable insights from textual data. We can use it in the following applications:

1. **Word embeddings for time series:** In NLP, words or tokens can be treated as time-series data, especially in tasks like sentiment analysis or topic modeling over time. Word embeddings, such as Word2Vec or GloVe, can capture semantic relationships between words in the context of time. By analyzing changes in word embeddings over time, it's possible to forecast future trends in language usage or sentiment.

2. **Language models:** Large pretrained language models like GPT or BERT have been used for time-series forecasting in NLP. By fine-tuning these models on historical text data, they can generate predictions about future text sequences. For example, they can predict the next word in a sentence or generate entire paragraphs of text based on past patterns.

3. **Temporal convolutional networks (TCNs):** TCNs are neural network architectures designed for sequential data processing, including time-series data. They use convolutional layers with causal padding to capture temporal dependencies in the input sequence. TCNs have been applied to text data for tasks like language modeling and text generation, making them suitable for time-series forecasting in NLP.

4. **Recurrent neural networks (RNNs) and long short-term memory (LSTM) networks:** RNNs and LSTMs are commonly used for sequential data processing including time-series forecasting. In NLP, these architectures can be adapted to model the temporal dynamics of text data and make predictions about future sequences. For example, they can be trained to predict the next word in a sentence or the sentiment of future text.

5. **Attention mechanisms:** Attention mechanisms, commonly used in transformer architectures like BERT and GPT, can be leveraged for time-series forecasting in NLP. These mechanisms allow the model to focus on relevant parts of the input sequence, which is useful for capturing temporal patterns in text data. By attending to historical text sequences, the model can make predictions about future trends or language usage.

There is no doubt that NLP is not a good algorithm but still we have some challenges into it in the model training such as:

Data integration: Integrating textual data with numerical time-series data can be challenging due to differences in format and structure.

Model complexity: Combining NLP and time-series forecasting techniques can lead to more complex models requiring larger datasets and computational resources.

Data quality and bias: The quality and potential biases within textual data sources can impact the accuracy and reliability of the overall forecasts.

8.2.1 Autoregressive Integrated Moving Average (ARIMA) Models

Autoregressive integrated moving average (ARIMA) models are a powerful statistical technique used for forecasting time-series data. They are widely used in various fields, including finance, economics, and business, to predict future values based on past data. They are particularly useful for capturing and predicting the temporal dependencies and patterns present in sequential data, making them applicable to various fields, including economics, finance, and epidemiology. While ARIMA models are primarily used for numerical time series, they can be adapted and applied to certain aspects of text data analysis, particularly when dealing with time-series trends in textual information. ARIMA is the combination of three components:

Autoregressive (AR): This component takes into account the impact of past values of the time series on the forecast. It considers how many past values (called lags) are statistically significant in influencing the current value or in the other words we can say. The AR component represents the relationship between the current value of the series and its past values. It models the dependency of the current observation on its lagged (past) values. The "p" parameter determines the number of lagged observations included in the model, where p, d, and q stands for:
- **p:** Number of autoregressive terms (lag order)
- **d:** Degree of differencing needed to achieve stationarity
- **q:** Number of moving average terms

Choosing the appropriate p, d, and q values is crucial for accurate forecasts. Various statistical tests and information criteria are used to identify the best fitting model.

Integrated (I): The I component represents the differencing of the time series to make it stationary. Stationarity is a key assumption in ARIMA modeling, as it ensures that the statistical properties of the series remain constant over time. The "d" parameter determines the order of differencing required to achieve stationarity. This component deals with nonstationary time series data where the mean, variance, or seasonality changes over time. Differencing is applied to the data to achieve stationarity, making it statistically stable for analysis and forecasting.

Moving average (MA): The MA component represents the dependency between the current observation and a linear combination of past error terms (residuals). It models the noise or random fluctuations in the time series. The "q" parameter determines the number of lagged residuals included in the model. This component considers the average of past errors (the difference between predicted and actual values) to improve the forecast by accounting for random fluctuations in the data.

ARIMA models are typically denoted by the notation ARIMA(p, d, q), where "p" represents the AR order, "d" represents the differencing order, and "q" represents the MA order.

While ARIMA models are primarily used for numerical data, they can be applied to certain aspects of text data analysis, particularly when dealing with time-series trends in textual information. For example, ARIMA models could be used to forecast the frequency of certain keywords or phrases in a text corpus over time. This could be useful for tasks such as analyzing trends in social media conversations, monitoring changes in public opinion, or forecasting demand for specific products or services based on textual data. We can use ARIMA model in Predicting future sales figures, Forecasting stock prices, Estimating customer demand, and Analyzing economic trends.

However, it's important to note that ARIMA models may not be directly applicable to all aspects of text data analysis, especially when dealing with unstructured textual information. In such cases, other techniques such as NLP and machine learning may be more appropriate for extracting insights and making predictions from text data.

ARIMA models are a valuable tool for time series forecasting, offering a robust and interpretable approach. However, it's important to be aware of their limitations and consider alternative methods for nonstationary or complex data or for long-term forecasting needs. ARIMA algorithm can't be used in some of the situation like:

1. **Assumption of stationarity:** ARIMA models require the data to be stationary, which may not be the case for all real-world time series data.
2. **Limited handling of nonlinear relationships:** ARIMA models primarily focus on linear relationships between past and future values and may not capture complex nonlinear patterns effectively.
3. **Challenges with long-term forecasting:** The accuracy of ARIMA models generally deteriorates with longer forecasting horizons.

8.2.2 Prophet and Neural Networks for Time Series

Prophet and neural networks are two different approaches used for time-series forecasting, each with its own strengths and applications. Both Prophet and Neural Networks are powerful tools for time-series forecasting, but they have their own strengths and weaknesses. Prophet and neural networks offer different approaches to time-series forecasting, each with its own strengths and weaknesses. Prophet provides a simple yet powerful framework for forecasting with strong seasonal patterns and special events, while neural networks offer flexibility and scalability for modeling complex dependencies in sequential data. The choice between these approaches depends on factors such as the nature of the data, the presence of seasonal patterns, and the computational resources available for model training and deployment.

Prophet: Prophet is an open-source forecasting tool developed by Facebook's Core Data Science team. It is designed to handle time-series data with strong seasonal patterns and multiple seasonalities. Prophet is particularly useful for forecasting tasks that involve trend changes, holidays, and special events. Some key features of Prophet include:

1. Automatic detection and handling of seasonality, including yearly, weekly, and daily seasonal patterns.
2. Flexibility in modeling various sources of uncertainty such as outliers and missing data
3. Intuitive model diagnostics and visualization tools for analyzing forecast results.
4. Built-in support for modeling holidays and special events that impact the time series.

Prophet is relatively easy to use and requires minimal data preprocessing, making it accessible to users with varying levels of expertise. It provides a powerful yet user-friendly interface for time-series forecasting, making it suitable for both beginners and experienced practitioners.

Neural network: Neural networks, particularly recurrent neural networks (RNNs) and their variants like long short-term memory (LSTM) networks, are a class of deep learning models capable of learning complex patterns and dependencies in sequential data. When applied to time-series forecasting, neural networks offer several advantages:

1. Ability to capture nonlinear relationships and complex patterns in the data.
2. Flexibility in modeling various types of time-series data, including both univariate and multivariate series.
3. Scalability to handle large-scale datasets and high-dimensional input features.
4. Capability to automatically extract relevant features from raw data, reducing the need for manual feature engineering.

However, training neural networks for time-series forecasting often requires a considerable amount of data and computational resources. Additionally, neural networks can be prone to overfitting, especially when dealing with small or noisy datasets. Proper model tuning and regularization techniques are essential to achieve good performance and generalization on unseen data. The Tab. 8.1 shows the Pros and cons of prophet.

Table 8.1: Pros and cons of prophet.

Pros	Cons
Simple and user-friendly: Easy to use and understand, requiring minimal data preprocessing and code.	**Limited flexibility:** Not as flexible as neural networks in capturing complex nonlinear relationships in data.
Interpretable model: Provides insights into the factors influencing the forecast such as trend, seasonality, and holidays.	**May struggle with nonstationary data:** May not perform well with data that exhibits significant trends or changes in variance over time.
Handles seasonality and holidays: Can automatically capture and model seasonal patterns and holiday effects.	**Limited feature engineering:** Offers limited options for incorporating additional features beyond the provided model components.
Fast and efficient: Requires less computational resources compared to neural networks.	

The Tab. 8.2 shows some of the Pros and cons of neural network.

Table 8.2: Pros and cons of neural network.

Pros	Cons
High flexibility: Capable of capturing complex non-linear relationships in data, making them suitable for diverse forecasting tasks.	**Complexity and difficulty of use:** Can be complex to set up, requiring more expertise in data science and machine learning.
Can handle nonstationary data: Able to learn from various types of data including nonstationary data.	**Interpretability:** Can be difficult to interpret the inner workings and reasoning behind the model's predictions.
Incorporation of additional features: Can be combined with other features beyond the time series data to improve accuracy.	**Computational cost:** Training neural networks can be computationally expensive and resource-intensive.
Data requirements: Often require less amounts of data to achieve optimal performance.	**Data requirements:** Often require larger amounts of data to achieve optimal performance.

When to Choose What?

The best choice between Prophet and neural networks depends on several factors:

1. **Data characteristics:**
   1. If your data exhibits seasonality, holidays, and limited non-linearity, Prophet might be a good choice for its simplicity and interpretability.
   2. If your data is complex, nonstationary, and requires capturing intricate patterns, a neural network might be more suitable due to its flexibility.
2. **Project requirements:**
   1. **Speed and ease of use** might be priorities if time constraints are tight and interpretability is crucial.
   2. **Focus on high accuracy and capturing intricate patterns** might outweigh complexity concerns if resources allow.
3. **Additional options:**
   1. **Hybrid approaches:** Combining Prophet with another algorithm like XGBoost can leverage the interpretability of Prophet while improving its ability to handle non-linearity.
   2. **Advanced neural network architectures:** Explore specific neural network architectures like LSTMs or Transformers designed for time-series forecasting and capable of handling complex patterns.

8.3 Recommender Systems

Recommender systems are a type of information filtering system that aim to predict user preferences or interests and recommend items (such as products, movies, music, and articles) that are likely to be of interest to them. These systems play a crucial role in various online platforms and services, helping users discover relevant content and improving user engagement and satisfaction. NLP offers a powerful toolkit for enhancing recommender systems by extracting meaningful insights from textual data, leading to more accurate, personalized, and insightful recommendations for users. Recommender systems are widely used in e-commerce platforms, streaming services, social media, news websites, and other online platforms to personalize user experiences, increase user engagement, and drive business revenue. The choice of a specific recommender system depends on factors such as the characteristics of the data, the available features, the scalability requirements, and the desired level of recommendation accuracy. There are several types of recommender systems, each employing different algorithms and techniques:

1. **Collaborative filtering:** Collaborative filtering (CF) methods analyze the interactions and preferences of users to generate recommendations. There are five main approaches within CF:

    1. **User-based collaborative filtering:** This approach recommends items to a user based on the preferences of users with similar tastes. It identifies users who have similar item ratings or interactions and recommends items that those similar users have liked or interacted with.
    2. **Item-based collaborative filtering:** In this approach, similarities between items are calculated based on the ratings or interactions of users. It recommends items that are similar to ones the user has already interacted with or liked.
    3. **Enriching user and item profiles:** Utilize NLP techniques to extract sentiment, topics, and themes from user reviews or feedback, enriching user profiles and leading to more nuanced recommendations.
    4. **Aspect-based sentiment analysis:** Analyze user reviews to understand opinions towards specific aspects (e.g., price and performance) of items, enabling recommendations that cater to user priorities.
    5. **Natural language understanding (NLU):** Utilize NLP models to understand the context and intent behind user queries, refining recommendations based on the user's specific needs expressed in natural language.

2. **Content-based filtering:** Content-based filtering methods recommend items to users based on the attributes or features of the items and the user's preferences. It analyzes the content of items (such as textual descriptions, metadata, or features) and recommends items that are similar in content to those the user has liked or interacted with in the past. The content based filtering can be divided into the several techniques.

    1. **Text similarity:** Analyze the similarity between user preferences (e.g., reviews and product descriptions) and available items based on keywords, topics, or semantic meaning extracted through NLP techniques like word embeddings.
    2. **Named entity recognition (NER):** Identify and extract relevant entities like products, locations, or people from text data, enabling recommendations based on specific user interests mentioned in past interactions. Let's have a look on the code below:

```
from nltk.tokenize import word_tokenize
from nltk import pos_tag, ne_chunk

text = """Natural Language Processing (NLP) is a field of
artificial intelligence (AI) that deals with the interaction
between computers and human language. Its goal is to enable
computers to understand, interpret, and manipulate natural
```

language in a way that is similar to how humans do. Its primary
goal is to enable computers to understand, interpret, and
generate human language in a manner that is both meaningful and
useful. This includes written text, spoken language, and even
sign language."""

```
words = word_tokenize(text)
tagged_words = pos_tag(words)
named_entities = ne_chunk(tagged_words)
print(named_entities)
```

=======================Output====================================
(S
Natural/JJ
Language/NNP
Processing/NNP
(/(
(ORGANIZATION NLP/NNP)
)/)
is/VBZ
a/DT
field/NN
of/IN
artificial/JJ
intelligence/NN
(/(
AI/NNP
)/)
that/IN
deals/NNS
with/IN
the/DT
interaction/NN
between/IN
computers/NNS
and/CC
human/JJ
language/NN
./.
Its/PRP$
goal/NN
is/VBZ
to/TO

enable/JJ
computers/NNS
to/TO
understand/VB
, /,
interpret/VB
, /,
and/CC
manipulate/VB
natural/JJ
language/NN
in/IN
a/DT
way/NN
that/WDT
is/VBZ
similar/JJ
to/TO
how/WRB
humans/NNS
do/VBP
./.
Its/PRP$
primary/JJ
goal/NN
is/VBZ
to/TO
enable/JJ
computers/NNS
to/TO
understand/VB
, /,
interpret/VB
, /,
and/CC
generate/VB
human/JJ
language/NN
in/IN
a/DT
manner/NN
that/WDT

is/VBZ
both/DT
meaningful/JJ
and/CC
useful/JJ
./.
This/DT
includes/VBZ
written/VBN
text/NN
, /,
spoken/JJ
language/NN
, /,
and/CC
even/RB
sign/JJ
language/NN
./.)

===

3. **Topic modeling:** Uncover hidden thematic structures within user reviews or product descriptions to categorize items and recommend ones within preferred topics.

4. **Keyword extraction:** Identify and extract key terms from user interactions or item descriptions to personalize recommendations based on user preferences or item characteristics.

3. **Hybrid recommender systems:** Hybrid recommender systems combine multiple recommendation techniques, such as CF and content-based filtering, to improve recommendation quality and address limitations of individual approaches. Hybrid systems can leverage the strengths of different methods to provide more accurate and diverse recommendations.

4. **Matrix factorization:** Matrix factorization techniques decompose user-item interaction matrices into lower-dimensional matrices representing user and item latent factors. These latent factors capture underlying patterns and preferences in the data and are used to generate recommendations. Matrix factorization methods are particularly effective for handling sparse and high-dimensional data.

5. **Deep learning-based recommender systems:** Deep learning models, such as neural networks, can be used to learn complex patterns and representations from user-item interaction data. Deep learning-based recommender systems can automatically extract features from raw data and capture intricate relationships between users and items, leading to more accurate recommendations.

NLP is very good in terms of performance and accuracy but still it has some challenges those are given below Table 8.3:

Table 8.3: Benefits vs challenges of NLP.

Benefits	Challenges
Improved accuracy and personalization: By incorporating nuanced insights from text data, NLP can enhance the accuracy and personalization of recommendations.	**Data quality and bias:** The quality and potential biases within textual data can impact the accuracy and fairness of recommendations.
Handling diverse textual data: NLP allows systems to understand various forms of user input, including reviews, social media posts, or search queries.	**Computational cost:** NLP techniques can be computationally expensive, requiring powerful hardware and efficient algorithms.
Discovery of hidden patterns: NLP techniques can unveil hidden patterns within text data, leading to unexpected and valuable recommendations for users.	**Semantic ambiguity:** Language can be ambiguous, and NLP models might misinterpret the meaning or intent of user-generated text.

8.4 Computer Vision Applications

Computer vision, a field of AI, focuses on enabling computers to interpret and understand visual information from the real world. It has numerous applications across various domains, revolutionizing industries and enhancing human capabilities. Computer vision has a wide range of applications across various industries. Here are some of the most common applications:

Here are some common applications of computer vision.

1. **Object detection and recognition:** Computer vision systems can detect and recognize objects within images or videos. This capability is used in various applications such as autonomous vehicles, surveillance systems, and augmented reality (AR). Object detection is also essential in retail for inventory management and in healthcare for identifying anatomical structures in medical imaging. Computer vision algorithms can detect and track objects in images and videos. This technology is used in various applications including security surveillance, traffic monitoring, and robotics.

2. **Image classification:** Image classification involves categorizing images into predefined classes or categories. This application is widely used in content moderation, where images are classified as safe or unsafe for certain audiences. Image classification is also employed in agriculture for identifying crop diseases, in manufacturing for quality control, and in e-commerce for visual search.

3. **Facial recognition:** Facial recognition technology identifies and verifies individuals based on their facial features. It has applications in security and law enforcement for identifying suspects or verifying identities. Facial recognition is also used in access control systems, user authentication in mobile devices, and personalized marketing. Facial recognition systems use computer vision to identify individuals from images or videos. This technology is used in various applications including security systems, social media platforms, and law enforcement.

4. **Medical image analysis:** Computer vision plays a crucial role in analyzing medical images such as X-rays, MRIs, and CT scans. It assists radiologists and healthcare professionals in diagnosing diseases, detecting abnormalities, and planning treatments. Medical image analysis techniques include image segmentation, tumor detection, and organ localization. Computer vision is used in medical imaging to analyze X-rays, CT scans, and MRIs to detect abnormalities and aid in diagnosis.

5. **Gesture recognition:** Gesture recognition systems interpret human gestures and movements from images or video sequences. These systems are used in human-computer interaction, sign language recognition, and virtual reality (VR) applications. Gesture recognition enables users to control devices, interact with virtual environments, and communicate nonverbally.

6. **Document analysis:** Document analysis techniques extract and interpret information from text documents, handwritten forms, and printed materials. Optical character recognition converts scanned documents into editable text. Document layout analysis identifies structural elements like headings, paragraphs, and tables. Document analysis is applied in document management systems, digital archives, and automated form processing.

7. **Autonomous vehicles:** Computer vision is a key technology in autonomous vehicles for perceiving the surrounding environment and making driving decisions. It enables vehicles to detect lane markings, traffic signs, pedestrians, and other vehicles. Computer vision algorithms process data from cameras, LiDAR, and radar sensors to navigate safely and autonomously.

8. **Visual inspection:** Visual inspection systems detect defects and anomalies in manufactured products during the production process. These systems inspect surfaces, textures, colors, and shapes to identify deviations from quality standards. Visual inspection is used in industries such as automotive manufacturing, electronics assembly, and pharmaceutical production.

9. **Self-driving car:** Computer vision is essential for self-driving cars to perceive their surroundings, identify objects like lanes, traffic signs, and pedestrians, and navigate safely.

10. **Augmented reality:** AR overlays digital information onto the real world. Computer vision is used in AR applications to track the user's environment and position digital elements accordingly.

11. **Virtual reality:** VR creates an immersive, computer-generated environment. Computer vision can be used in VR applications to track the user's movements and interact with the virtual world.
12. **Drone navigation:** Drones use computer vision to navigate their surroundings, avoid obstacles, and track targets.
13. **Robot vision:** Robots use computer vision to perceive their environment, interact with objects, and complete tasks.
14. **Quality control:** Computer vision is used in quality control applications to inspect products for defects
15. **Retail:** Computer vision is used in retail applications to track inventory, automate checkout processes, and provide personalized recommendations to customers.

8.4.1 Object Detection and Segmentation

Object detection and segmentation are two important tasks in computer vision, both involving the identification and localization of objects within images or videos. Object detection and segmentation are fundamental tasks in computer vision with numerous applications including autonomous driving, surveillance, medical imaging, and AR. These tasks enable machines to understand and interact with visual data, paving the way for a wide range of intelligent applications and services.

– **Object detection:** Object detection is the task of locating and classifying multiple objects within an image or video frame. It involves identifying the presence of objects in an image and determining their respective classes or categories. Object detection is typically performed using bounding boxes to outline the regions where objects are located. Common techniques for object detection include:
    – **Single shot multibox detector (SSD):** SSD is a popular real-time object detection method that predicts bounding boxes and class probabilities directly from feature maps at multiple scales. It achieves high speed and accuracy by efficiently processing images with a single feedforward pass through a CNN.
    – **Faster R-CNN:** Faster R-CNN is a two-stage object detection framework that uses a region proposal network to generate candidate object regions, followed by a detection network to refine the proposals and classify objects. It achieves high accuracy by jointly optimizing region proposals and object detection.
    – **YOLO (You Only Look Once):** YOLO is another real-time object detection method that divides the input image into a grid of cells and predicts bounding boxes and class probabilities for each grid cell. It processes the entire image in a single forward pass through a CNN, making it faster than two-stage methods like Faster R-CNN.
– **Object segmentation:** Object segmentation is the task of segmenting or partitioning an image into multiple regions, each corresponding to a distinct object or object instance. Unlike object detection, which identifies the presence of objects and

their bounding boxes, object segmentation provides pixel-level masks for each object in the image. Common techniques for object segmentation include:

- **Mask R-CNN:** Mask R-CNN extends faster R-CNN by adding a branch for predicting segmentation masks alongside bounding boxes and class probabilities. It generates pixel-wise masks for each object instance in the image, enabling precise segmentation of objects with complex shapes and overlapping instances.
- **U-Net:** U-Net is a fully convolutional network (FCN) architecture designed for biomedical image segmentation but widely used in other domains as well. It consists of an encoder-decoder structure with skip connections that preserve spatial information at different scales. U-Net is known for its effectiveness in segmenting objects from limited training data.
- **Semantic segmentation:** Semantic segmentation assigns a class label to each pixel in the image, without distinguishing between different instances of the same class. It provides a dense pixel-wise classification of the entire image, allowing for scene understanding and pixel-level analysis. Techniques such as FCNs and DeepLab are commonly used for semantic segmentation tasks. Let's have look on the code below:

```python
from nltk.corpus import wordnet

syn = wordnet.synsets('dog')[0]

# Get hyponyms for dog
hyponyms = syn.hyponyms()
print("Hyponyms of 'dog': ", [h.lemmas()[0].name() for h in
hyponyms])

syn = wordnet.synsets('poodle')[0]

# Get hypernyms for poodle
hypernyms = syn.hypernyms()
print("Hypernyms of 'dog': ", [h.lemmas()[0].name() for h in
hypernyms])

# Get Antonym
synsets = wordnet.synsets('good')
antonym = None

# Search for an antonym in all synsets/lemmas
for syn in synsets:
for lemma in syn.lemmas():
if lemma.antonyms():
```

```
antonym = lemma.antonyms()[0].name()
break
if antonym:
break
if antonym:
print("Antonym of 'good': ", antonym)
else:
print("No antonym found for 'good'")
```

```
================================Output============================
Hyponyms of 'dog': ['basenji', 'corgi', 'cur', 'dalmatian', 'Great_Pyrenees', 'grif-
fon', 'hunting_dog', 'lapdog', 'Leonberg', 'Mexican_hairless', 'Newfoundland',
'pooch', 'poodle', 'pug', 'puppy', 'spitz', 'toy_dog', 'working_dog']
Hypernyms of 'dog': ['dog']
Antonym of 'good': evil
==================================================================
```

8.5 Reinforcement Learning

Reinforcement learning (RL) is a powerful branch of machine learning concerned with training an agent to make optimal decisions in an interactive environment to maximize a cumulative reward. RL is a type of machine learning paradigm in which an agent learns to make decisions by interacting with an environment in order to maximize some notion of cumulative reward. Unlike supervised learning, where the model is trained on labeled input-output pairs, and unsupervised learning, where the model learns patterns in unlabeled data, RL learns through trial and error by receiving feedback from the environment. The RL offers a powerful approach to training agents to make optimal decisions in dynamic and interactive environments. With its potential to learn and adapt without explicit instructions, RL is transforming various fields and holds promise for even broader applications in the future. RL algorithms, such as Q-learning, deep Q-networks (DQN), policy gradient methods, and actor-critic methods, learn to optimize the agent's policy through iterative interactions with the environment. RL has applications in various domains, including robotics, game playing, autonomous systems, recommendation systems, and finance, among others. Here's a breakdown of key aspects:

8.5.1 Core Elements of Reinforcement Learning

1. **Agent:** The learning entity that interacts with the environment and makes decisions. The agent is the entity that interacts with the environment. It observes the state of the environment, selects actions, and receives rewards or penalties based

on its actions. The agent's goal is to learn a policy – a mapping from states to actions – that maximizes cumulative rewards over time.

2. **Environment:** The system or world the agent interacts with, providing feedback through rewards and penalties. The environment represents the external system or process with which the agent interacts. It is defined by a set of states, actions, and transition dynamics. The environment also provides feedback to the agent in the form of rewards or penalties based on its actions.

3. **Action:** The choices the agent can make within the environment. An action is a decision or choice made by the agent that affects the state of the environment. Actions can be discrete (e.g., selecting from a finite set of options) or continuous (e.g., specifying a value within a continuous range).

4. **Reward:** The feedback signal the environment provides to the agent, indicating the goodness or badness of its actions. A reward is a scalar feedback signal provided by the environment to the agent after each action. It indicates the immediate desirability or quality of the action taken by the agent. The agent's goal is to learn a policy that maximizes the cumulative reward over time.

5. **Policy:** The agent's strategy for choosing actions is based on the current state of the environment. A policy is a mapping from states to actions that defines the agent's behavior. It specifies the action the agent should take in each state to maximize expected cumulative rewards. Policies can be deterministic or stochastic, depending on whether they directly specify actions or provide a probability distribution over actions.

6. **State:** A state represents the current situation or configuration of the environment. It contains all the relevant information needed for the agent to make decisions. States can be discrete or continuous, depending on the nature of the environment.

7. **Value functions:** The value function estimates the expected cumulative reward that an agent can achieve from a given state or state-action pair. It quantifies the desirability of being in a particular state or taking a particular action and is used to guide the agent's decision-making process.

8. **Exploration and exploitation:** RL involves a trade-off between exploration (trying out new actions to discover potentially better strategies) and exploitation (selecting actions that are known to yield high rewards based on current knowledge). Balancing exploration and exploitation is crucial for effective learning.

8.5.2 Learning Process

1. **Trial and error:** Through interacting with the environment and receiving rewards, the agent learns by trial and error. It gradually improves its policy by selecting actions that lead to higher rewards over time.

2. **No explicit instructions:** Unlike supervised learning, RL agents don't receive explicit instructions on how to perform the task. They learn solely through the reward feedback mechanism.
3. **Delayed gratification:** RL agents need to consider the long-term consequences of their actions, not just the immediate reward, to achieve optimal results.

Let's have a look on the python code implementation:

```python
import gymnasium as gym
import math
import random
import matplotlib
import matplotlib.pyplot as plt
from collections import namedtuple, deque
from itertools import count

import torch
import torch.nn as nn
import torch.optim as optim
import torch.nn.functional as F

env = gym.make("CartPole-v1")

# set up matplotlib
is_ipython = 'inline' in matplotlib.get_backend()
if is_ipython:
    from IPython import display

plt.ion()

# if GPU is to be used
device = torch.device("cuda" if torch.cuda.is_available() else "cpu")
Transition = namedtuple('Transition',
                ('state', 'action', 'next_state', 'reward'))

class ReplayMemory(object):

    def __init__(self, capacity):
        self.memory = deque([], maxlen=capacity)

    def push(self, *args):
        """Save a transition"""
```

```python
        self.memory.append(Transition(*args))

    def sample(self, batch_size):
        return random.sample(self.memory, batch_size)

    def __len__(self):
        return len(self.memory)


class DQN(nn.Module):

    def __init__(self, n_observations, n_actions):
        super(DQN, self).__init__()
        self.layer1 = nn.Linear(n_observations, 128)
        self.layer2 = nn.Linear(128, 128)
        self.layer3 = nn.Linear(128, n_actions)

    # Called with either one element to determine next action, or a batch
    # during optimization. Returns tensor([[left0exp,right0exp]. . .]).
    def forward(self, x):
        x = F.relu(self.layer1(x))
        x = F.relu(self.layer2(x))
        return self.layer3(x)
# BATCH_SIZE is the number of transitions sampled from the replay buffer
# GAMMA is the discount factor as mentioned in the previous section
# EPS_START is the starting value of epsilon # EPS_END is the final
value of epsilon
# EPS_DECAY controls the rate of exponential decay of epsilon, higher
means a slower decay
# TAU is the update rate of the target network
# LR is the learning rate of the ``AdamW`` optimizer
BATCH_SIZE = 128
GAMMA = 0.99
EPS_START = 0.9
EPS_END = 0.05
EPS_DECAY = 1000
TAU = 0.005
LR = 1e-4


# Get number of actions from gym action space
n_actions = env.action_space.n
```

```python
# Get the number of state observations
state, info = env.reset()
n_observations = len(state)

policy_net = DQN(n_observations, n_actions).to(device)
target_net = DQN(n_observations, n_actions).to(device)
target_net.load_state_dict(policy_net.state_dict())

optimizer = optim.AdamW(policy_net.parameters(), lr=LR, amsgrad=True)
memory = ReplayMemory(10000)

steps_done = 0

def select_action(state):
    global steps_done
    sample = random.random()
    eps_threshold = EPS_END + (EPS_START - EPS_END) * \
                    math.exp(-1. * steps_done / EPS_DECAY)
    steps_done += 1
    if sample > eps_threshold:
        with torch.no_grad():
            # t.max(1) will return the largest column value of each row.
            # second column on max result is index of where max element was
            # found, so we pick action with the larger expected reward.
            return policy_net(state).max(1).indices.view(1, 1)
    else:
        return torch.tensor([[env.action_space.sample()]], device=device,
dtype=torch.long)

episode_durations = []

def plot_durations(show_result=False):
    plt.figure(1)
    durations_t = torch.tensor(episode_durations, dtype=torch.float)
    if show_result:
        plt.title('Result')
    else:
        plt.clf()
        plt.title('Training. . .')
    plt.xlabel('Episode')
    plt.ylabel('Duration')
    plt.plot(durations_t.numpy())
```

```
    # Take 100 episode averages and plot them too
    if len(durations_t) >= 100:
        means = durations_t.unfold(0, 100, 1).mean(1).view(-1)
        means = torch.cat((torch.zeros(99), means))
        plt.plot(means.numpy())

    plt.pause(0.001) # pause a bit so that plots are updated
    if is_ipython:
        if not show_result:
            display.display(plt.gcf())
            display.clear_output(wait=True)
        else:
            display.display(plt.gcf())

def optimize_model():
    if len(memory) < BATCH_SIZE:
        return
    transitions = memory.sample(BATCH_SIZE)
    # Transpose the batch (see https://stackoverflow.com/a/19343/3343043
for
    # detailed explanation). This converts batch-array of Transitions
    # to Transition of batch-arrays.
    batch = Transition(*zip(*transitions))

    # Compute a mask of non-final states and concatenate the batch
elements
    # (a final state would've been the one after which simulation ended)
    non_final_mask = torch.tensor(tuple(map(lambda s: s is not None,
                      batch.next_state)), device=device, dtype=torch.
bool)
    non_final_next_states = torch.cat([s for s in batch.next_state
                      if s is not None])
    state_batch = torch.cat(batch.state)
    action_batch = torch.cat(batch.action)
    reward_batch = torch.cat(batch.reward)

    # Compute Q(s_t, a) - the model computes Q(s_t), then we select the
    # columns of actions taken. These are the actions which would've been
taken
    # for each batch state according to policy_net
    state_action_values = policy_net(state_batch).gather(1, action_batch)
```

```python
    # Compute V(s_{t+1}) for all next states.
    # Expected values of actions for non_final_next_states are computed based
    # on the "older" target_net; selecting their best reward with max(1).values
    # This is merged based on the mask, such that we'll have either the expected
    # state value or 0 in case the state was final.
    next_state_values = torch.zeros(BATCH_SIZE, device=device)
    with torch.no_grad():
        next_state_values[non_final_mask] = target_net(non_final_next_states).max(1).values
    # Compute the expected Q values
    expected_state_action_values = (next_state_values * GAMMA) + reward_batch

    # Compute Huber loss
    criterion = nn.SmoothL1Loss()
    loss = criterion(state_action_values, expected_state_action_values.unsqueeze(1))

    # Optimize the model
    optimizer.zero_grad()
    loss.backward()
    # In-place gradient clipping
    torch.nn.utils.clip_grad_value_(policy_net.parameters(), 100)
    optimizer.step()

if torch.cuda.is_available():
    num_episodes = 600
else:
    num_episodes = 50

for i_episode in range(num_episodes):
    # Initialize the environment and get its state
    state, info = env.reset()
    state = torch.tensor(state, dtype=torch.float32, device=device).unsqueeze(0)
    for t in count():
        action = select_action(state)
        observation, reward, terminated, truncated, _ = env.step(action.item())
```

```
        reward = torch.tensor([reward], device=device)
        done = terminated or truncated

    if terminated:
        next_state = None
    else:
        next_state = torch.tensor(observation, dtype=torch.float32,
device=device).unsqueeze(0)

    # Store the transition in memory
    memory.push(state, action, next_state, reward)

    # Move to the next state
    state = next_state

    # Perform one step of the optimization (on the policy network)
    optimize_model()

    # Soft update of the target network's weights
    # θ′ ← τ θ + (1 − τ) θ′
    target_net_state_dict = target_net.state_dict()
    policy_net_state_dict = policy_net.state_dict()
    for key in policy_net_state_dict:
        target_net_state_dict[key] = policy_net_state_dict[key]*TAU +
target_net_state_dict[key]*(1-TAU)
        target_net.load_state_dict(target_net_state_dict)

    if done:
        episode_durations.append(t + 1)
        plot_durations()
        break

print('Complete')
plot_durations(show_result=True)
plt.ioff()
plt.show()
```

8.6 Application of Reinforcement Learning

1. **Robotics:** Training robots to navigate their environment, manipulate objects, and perform tasks effectively.
2. **Game playing:** Developing AI agents that can learn to play complex games like chess or Go at a superhuman level.
3. **Resource management:** Optimizing resource allocation in systems like traffic light control, energy grids, and network routing.
4. **Recommendation systems:** Recommending products or content to users based on their past interactions and preferences.
5. **Finance and trading:** Making investment decisions and managing portfolios in financial markets.

8.7 Challenges of Reinforcement Learning

Exploration vs. exploitation dilemma: The agent needs to balance exploring new actions to discover potential rewards with **exploiting** already learned successful actions.

High computational cost: Training RL agents can be computationally expensive, especially for complex environments.

Data scarcity: Learning effectively in RL often requires a large amount of data collected through interaction with the environment.

8.8 Q-learning

Q-learning is a popular RL algorithm used for learning optimal policies in Markov decision processes, particularly in settings where the agent has full knowledge of the environment. It is a model-free, value-based algorithm that learns an action-value function (Q-function) to determine the quality of taking a particular action in a given state. Q-learning is a specific model-free RL algorithm used to train an agent to make optimal decisions in an environment. It belongs to a family of algorithms known as value-based methods that learn by estimating the long-term value of taking specific actions in different states. Over time, as the agent explores the environment and receives feedback, the Q-values converge to the optimal action-values, indicating the expected cumulative rewards of taking each action in each state. The agent then follows the optimal policy by selecting actions with the highest Q-values in each state.

Q-learning is particularly well-suited for discrete and deterministic environments with finite state and action spaces. However, it can also be extended to handle continuous and stochastic environments through function approximation methods and experience replay techniques. Despite its simplicity, Q-learning has been successfully applied in various domains including robotics, game playing, and autonomous systems. Overall, Q-learning is a fundamental and versatile algorithm in the field of RL. Its simplicity and off-policy learning capabilities make it a popular choice for various applications. However, it's crucial to address the challenges of exploration, convergence, and dimensionality when implementing Q-learning in complex tasks. Some of the terminologies are used in Q-learning are:

1. **Q-value (Q(s, a)):** This represents the estimated future reward an agent expects to receive by taking action "a" in state "s."
2. **State (s):** The current situation or configuration the agent is in.
3. **Action (a):** The possible choices the agent can make in a given state.
4. **Reward (r):** The feedback signal the environment provides after the agent takes an action.

Any Q-learning-based model training requires the following steps

Initialization: Initialize the Q-function, $Q(s,a)$, where s is the state and a is the action, to arbitrary values. All Q-values are initially set to a chosen value (e.g., 0).

Exploration vs. exploitation: At each time step, the agent selects an action based on its current policy. The policy can be greedy (selecting the action with the highest Q-value) or exploratory (selecting a random action with some probability).

Action selection: Given the current state s, the agent selects an action **a** based on the policy.

Interaction: The agent takes an action (a) in the current state (s).

Observation and reward: The agent observes the next state s` and the reward **r** received as a result of taking action **a** in state **s**. The agent receives a reward (r) and observes the next state (s').

Update Q-value: The agent updates the Q-value for the current state-action pair (s, a) using the Bellman equation:

$$Q(s, a) = Q(s, a) + a\left[r + \gamma \max_a{}' Q(s', a') - Q(s, a)\right]$$

where a is the learning rate, controlling the step size of the updates. It controls the weight given to the new information (learning from the current experience)
- γ is the discount factor, determining the importance of future rewards (balancing immediate and long-term benefits)
- $r + \gamma \max_a{}' Q(s', a')$ is the target value, representing the expected cumulative reward of taking action **a** in state **s** and then following the optimal policy thereafter.

Termination: Repeat steps 3 (interaction)–5 (Termination) until the termination condition is met (e.g., a maximum number of iterations and convergence of Q-values). Next given table 8.4 shows the benefits of Q-learning and it challenges

Table 8.4: Benefits and challenges in Q-learning.

Benefits	Challenges
Model-free: Doesn't require a detailed model of the environment, making it applicable to various situations.	**Exploration vs. exploitation:** Balancing exploration of new actions with exploiting known good actions remains crucial.
Off-policy learning: Can learn from data collected using different policies, allowing for efficient exploration of the environment.	**Convergence:** In complex environments, convergence to an optimal policy can be slow or even impossible.
Simple and efficient: Easy to understand and implement, making it a popular choice for RL applications.	**Curse of dimensionality:** With large state and action spaces, the number of Q-values to learn can become very high, making learning inefficient.

8.9 Deep Q Networks

DQN, also known as deep Q-learning, is a powerful advancement in RL that combines the value-based approach of Q-learning with the function approximation capabilities of deep neural networks. DQN is a deep RL algorithm that combines Q-learning with deep neural networks to handle high-dimensional state spaces in RL problems. It was introduced by DeepMind in 2015 and has since become a cornerstone in the field of deep RL. DQN extends traditional Q-learning by approximating the Q-function using a deep neural network, allowing it to handle complex and continuous state spaces. DQN has been successfully applied to a wide range of RL tasks including playing Atari games from raw pixel inputs, continuous control tasks, and robotics. It has demonstrated strong performance and sample efficiency compared to traditional RL algorithms, paving the way for further advancements in deep RL. Here we gave given some steps to work with DQN:

– **Neural network architecture:** The core of DQN is a deep neural network that takes the state **s** as input and outputs **Q-values** for all possible actions. The neural network typically consists of several convolutional layers followed by fully connected layers. The use of convolutional layers allows DQN to handle high-dimensional input images efficiently.

– **Experience replay:** DQN employs experience replay to improve sample efficiency and stabilize training. During interaction with the environment, the agent stores transitions (s, a, r, s) (state, action, reward, next state) in a replay memory buffer. During training, minibatches of transitions are sampled uniformly from the replay memory and used to update the Q-network parameters. Experience replay helps decorrelate training samples and break temporal correlations in the data. Stores past experiences (state, action, reward, next state) in a replay memory. This allows the network to learn from a diverse set of experiences and overcome the limitations of learning from consecutive experiences alone.

– **Target network:** To stabilize training, DQN introduces a separate target network that is periodically updated to approximate the target Q-values. The target network is a copy of the Q-network with frozen parameters and is used to compute the target Q-values for updating the Q-network. Periodically updating the target network helps prevent oscillations and divergence during training. The target network introduces a separate target network that is periodically updated with the weights of the main Q-network. This helps stabilize the learning process by reducing the correlation between the target and action selection in the Q-learning update.

– **Loss function:** DQN uses the mean squared error (MSE) loss between the predicted Q-values and the target Q-values to update the Q-network parameters. The target Q-values are computed using the Bellman equation with the target network.

– **ε-Greedy exploration:** To balance exploration and exploitation, DQN employs **ε-greedy** exploration, where the agent selects a random action with probability ε and selects the action with the highest Q-value with probability $1 - \varepsilon$. The value of ε is annealed over time to gradually shift from exploration to exploitation.

– **Training procedure:** During training, the agent interacts with the environment, collects experiences, and updates the Q-network parameters using stochastic gradient descent based on the sampled minibatches of transitions. The target network is periodically updated to track the changes in the Q-network.

Challenges vs. benefits of Q-network are given in the table below:

Benefits	Challenges
Scalability: Handles large state and action spaces effectively due to function approximation with neural networks.	**Complexity:** Designing and training deep neural networks requires more expertise and computational resources.
Improved performance: Can achieve higher performance on complex tasks compared to traditional Q-learning.	**Exploration vs. exploitation:** Balancing exploration and exploitation remains crucial for optimal learning.
Sample efficiency: Learns effectively from a smaller amount of data due to experience replay.	**Hyperparameter tuning:** Tuning hyperparameters of the neural network and learning algorithm is crucial for achieving good performance.

8.10 Policy Gradient Methods

Policy gradient methods are a powerful class of RL algorithms that directly optimize the policy of an agent to maximize its long-term reward in an environment. Unlike value-based methods like Q-learning, which focus on learning the value of states and actions, policy gradient methods directly learn a policy that maps states to actions. The policy gradient methods directly learn a policy – a mapping from states to actions – by optimizing the expected cumulative reward. Unlike value-based methods like Q-learning, which estimate the value of state-action pairs, policy gradient methods directly parameterize the policy and update its parameters to maximize the expected return. Policy gradient methods offer several advantages including the ability to learn stochastic policies and handle continuous action spaces. Some terminology those are used in the policy gradient methods:

1. **Policy (π):** Represents the probability distribution over possible actions the agent can take in a given state.
2. **State (s):** The current situation or configuration the agent is in.
3. **Action (a):** The possible choices the agent can make in a given state.
4. **Reward (r):** The feedback signal the environment provides after the agent takes an action.

They have been successfully applied to a wide range of RL tasks including robotics, game playing, and NLP. Examples of policy gradient methods include REINFORCE, actor-critic methods, and proximal policy optimization (PPO). The policy gradient methods offer a powerful approach to RL, enabling agents to learn effective policies for complex tasks. However, addressing the challenges of variance, sample efficiency, and hyperparameter tuning is critical for successful application. Here are some steps that show how policy gradient method works:

Step 1. **Policy parameterization:** The agent interacts with the environment following its current policy and collects data (state-action-reward tuples). In policy gradient methods, the policy is typically parameterized by a neural network or another function approximator. The parameters of the policy network are denoted by θ, and the policy itself is denoted by π_θ (a | s), representing the probability of taking action **a** in state **s** given the parameters θ.

Step 2. **Objective function:** The objective of policy gradient methods is to maximize the expected cumulative reward, also known as the return. This can be formalized as maximizing the expected value of the cumulative reward under the policy:

$$J(\theta) = E_{\pi\theta}\left[\sum_{t=0}^{T} \gamma_t r_t\right]$$

where r_t is the reward received at time step t, T is the time horizon, and y is the discount factor that determines the importance of future rewards.

Step 3. **Gradient ascent:** Policy gradient methods use gradient ascent to update the policy parameters θ in the direction of the gradient of the objective function $J(\theta)$. The gradient of $J(\theta)$ with respect to the policy parameters is given by

$$\nabla_\theta J(\theta) = E_{\pi\theta}\left[\sum_{t=0}^{T} \nabla_\theta \log \pi\theta(a_t \vee s_t).G_t\right]$$

where G_t is the return from time step t onward, also known as the return or advantage.

Step 4. **Policy update:** The policy parameters are updated using stochastic gradient ascent:

$$\theta \leftarrow \theta + \alpha \nabla_\theta J(\theta)$$

where α is the learning rate.

Step 5. **Reward-to-go:** In practice, policy gradient methods often use the reward-to-go formulation, where the gradient is scaled by the return from the current time step onward rather than the total return. This helps reduce variance in the gradient estimates and improves training stability.

Challenges vs. benefits of policy gradient method is given in the table given below:

Benefit	Challenges
Direct policy optimization: They directly optimize the policy, which can be more efficient than learning state-action values, especially in large state spaces.	**High variance:** Estimating the policy gradient can be noisy and lead to unstable learning, requiring careful implementation and techniques like variance reduction.
Policy interpretability: In some cases, the learned policy can be interpreted, providing insights into the agent's decision-making process.	**Sample efficiency:** They can be sample-inefficient, meaning they may require a large amount of data to learn effectively.
Versatility: They can be applied to various tasks and environments including continuous action spaces.	**Hyperparameter tuning:** Tuning hyperparameters of the learning algorithm and policy network is crucial for achieving good performance.

There are a few types of popular policy gradient methods:
1. **REINFORCE:** This is a simple policy gradient method that directly uses the product of the reward and the gradient of the log-probability of the chosen action to update the policy.
2. **Actor-critic methods:** These methods combine an **actor** (policy network) that takes actions and a **critic** (value network) that estimates the value of the current state. The critic's feedback is then used to improve the actor's policy.

3. **Proximal policy optimization:** This advanced method addresses issues like the **policy gradient vanishing problem** and ensures that the updated policy remains close to the original one, leading to more stable learning.

Please have a look on the code given below:

```python
import gym

env = gym.make('CartPole-v1')
env.observation_space
env.action_space

import numpy as np

class LogisticPolicy:

    def __init__(self, θ , α , γ ):
        # Initialize paramters  θ , learning rate  α  and discount factor  γ

        self. θ  =  θ
        self. α  =  α
        self. γ  =  γ

    def logistic(self, y):
        # definition of logistic function

        return 1 / (1 + np.exp(-y))

    def probs(self, x):
        # returns probabilities of two actions

        y = x @ self. θ
        prob0 = self.logistic(y)

        return np.array([prob0, 1 - prob0])

    def act(self, x):
        # sample an action in proportion to probabilities

        probs = self.probs(x)
        action = np.random.choice([0, 1], p=probs)
        return action, probs[action]
```

```python
    def grad_log_p(self, x):
      # calculate grad-log-probs

      y = x @ self.θ
      grad_log_p0 = x - x * self.logistic(y)
      grad_log_p1 = - x * self.logistic(y)

      return grad_log_p0, grad_log_p1

    def grad_log_p_dot_rewards(self, grad_log_p, actions,
discounted_rewards):
      # dot grads with future rewards for each action in episode

      return grad_log_p.T @ discounted_rewards

    def discount_rewards(self, rewards):
      # calculate temporally adjusted, discounted rewards

      discounted_rewards = np.zeros(len(rewards))
      cumulative_rewards = 0
      for i in reversed(range(0, len(rewards))):
        cumulative_rewards = cumulative_rewards * self.γ + rewards[i]
        discounted_rewards[i] = cumulative_rewards

      return discounted_rewards

    def update(self, rewards, obs, actions):
      # calculate gradients for each action over all observations
      grad_log_p = np.array([self.grad_log_p(ob)[action] for ob, action in
zip(obs, actions)])

      assert grad_log_p.shape == (len(obs), 4)

      # calculate temporaly adjusted, discounted rewards
      discounted_rewards = self.discount_rewards(rewards)

      # gradients times rewards
      dot = self.grad_log_p_dot_rewards(grad_log_p, actions,
discounted_rewards)

      # gradient ascent on parameters
      self.θ += self.α * dot
```

```python
def run_episode(env, policy, render=False):
    observation = env.reset()
    totalreward = 0

    observations = []
    actions = []
    rewards = []
    probs = []

    done = False

    while not done:
      if render:
        env.render()

      observations.append(observation)

      action, prob = policy.act(observation)
      observation, reward, done, info = env.step(action)

      totalreward += reward
      rewards.append(reward)
      actions.append(action)
      probs.append(prob)

    return totalreward, np.array(rewards), np.array(observations), np.
array(actions), np.array(probs)

def train( θ , α , γ , Policy, MAX_EPISODES=1000, seed=None,
evaluate=False):
    # initialize environment and policy
    env = gym.make('CartPole-v0')
    if seed is not None:
      env.seed(seed)
    episode_rewards = []
    policy = Policy( θ , α , γ )

    # train until MAX_EPISODES
    for i in range(MAX_EPISODES):
      # run a single episode
      total_reward, rewards, observations, actions, probs = run_episode
(env, policy)
```

```
        # keep track of episode rewards
        episode_rewards.append(total_reward)

        # update policy
        policy.update(rewards, observations, actions)
        print("EP: " + str(i) + " Score: " + str(total_reward) + " ",
end="\r", flush=False)

    # evaluation call after training is finished - evaluate last trained
policy on 100 episodes
    if evaluate:
        env = Monitor(env, 'pg_cartpole/', video_callable=False, force=True)
        for _ in range(100):
            run_episode(env, policy, render=False)
        env.env.close()

    return episode_rewards, policy

#from gym.wrappers.monitoring.video_recorder import VideoRecorder from
gym.wrappers.monitoring.video_recorder import Monitor, load_results

# for reproducibility
GLOBAL_SEED = 0
np.random.seed(GLOBAL_SEED)

episode_rewards, policy = train( θ =np.random.rand(4),
                α =0.002,
                γ =0.99,
                Policy=LogisticPolicy,
                MAX_EPISODES=2000,
                seed=GLOBAL_SEED,
                evaluate=True)
import matplotlib.pyplot as plt

plt.plot(episode_rewards)
```

Summary

Natural language processing (NLP) is a subfield of artificial intelligence (AI) concerned with enabling computers to understand and process human language. It aims to bridge the gap between human communication and machine understanding, allowing computers to interact with us more naturally and perform tasks involving human language. Its primary goal is to enable computers to understand, interpret, and generate human language in a way that is both meaningful and contextually relevant. **Tokenization** and **word embeddings** are fundamental concepts in NLP that work together to enable machines to understand and process human language. Breaking down text into smaller units such as words or sentences is the process of tokenization. In NLP, **sequence modeling** plays a crucial role in tasks that involve analyzing and processing **sequential data** such as text, speech, and even protein sequences in bioinformatics. Unlike traditional machine learning methods that treat data points as independent, sequence models consider the **order and context** of elements within the sequence. ARIMA models are a class of statistical models commonly used for time series analysis and forecasting. They are particularly useful when dealing with data that exhibits non-stationarity, meaning the statistical properties of the data (such as mean and variance) change over time. They are particularly useful when the data exhibits **stationarity**, meaning the statistical properties (mean, variance, and autocorrelation) remain constant over time. Prophet is an open-source forecasting tool developed by Facebook's Core Data Science team. It is designed to handle time series data with strong seasonal effects and multiple seasonality. Prophet uses an additive model where different components of the time series (trend, seasonality, and holiday effects) are modeled separately and combined to make predictions. Both **Prophet** and **neural networks** are powerful tools for **time series forecasting**, but they differ in their approach, strengths, and weaknesses:

Collaborative filtering (CF) is a technique used in recommender systems to predict the preferences of a user based on the preferences of similar users or items. It's a powerful tool for personalizing recommendations across various domains like suggesting products, movies, music, or even news articles. The underlying idea is to leverage the collective wisdom of a group of users to infer preferences for individual users.

Exercise (MCQs)

1. **Which of the following is NOT a common task in NLP?**
   A) Machine translation
   B) Image recognition
   C) Text summarization
   D) Sentiment analysis

2. **What is the process of converting words into their base form called?**
   A) Tokenization   B) Lemmatization   C) Stemming   D) Normalization

3. **Which of the following is an example of a stop word?**
   A) Computer   B) The   C) Algorithm   D) Language

4. **What is the main purpose of a Bag-of-Words (BoW) model?**
   A) Identify named entities in text
   B) Capture the semantic relationships between words
   C) Represent text as a frequency distribution of words
   D) Generate new text based on existing data

5. **Which type of neural network architecture is commonly used in NLP tasks like sentiment analysis and machine translation?**
   A) Decision Tree
   B) K-nearest neighbors
   C) Recurrent neural network (RNN)
   D) Support vector machine (SVM)

6. **Which of the following is NOT a component of a time series?**
   A) Trend   B) Seasonality   C) Cyclicity   D) Random error

7. **What type of model uses past observations to predict future values without explicitly identifying trends or seasonality?**
   A) ARIMA model
   B) Exponential smoothing model
   C) Linear regression model
   D) Naïve forecast model

8. **The mean squared error (MSE) is a commonly used metric to evaluate the performance of a time series forecast. A lower MSE indicates:**
   A) A higher deviation between predicted and actual values.
   B) A better fit between predicted and actual values.
   C) No relationship between predicted and actual values.
   D) The forecast is always accurate.

9. **In which scenario would a seasonal ARIMA model be most appropriate?**
   A) Predicting monthly sales data with no clear trend.
   B) Forecasting stock prices with a daily frequency.
   C) Estimating annual economic growth rates.
   D) Predicting daily website traffic with a significant weekly pattern.

10. **Which of the following is NOT a common challenge in time series forecasting?**
   A) Missing data points
   B) Stationarity of the data
   C) Identifying the relevant factors influencing the series
   D) Overfitting the model to the training data

11. **Which of the following is NOT a type of recommender system?**
    A) Content-based filtering
    B) Collaborative filtering
    C) Hybrid recommender system
    D) Demographic filtering

12. **Collaborative filtering systems recommend items based on:**
    A) The user's demographics and purchase history
    B) The content and attributes of the items themselves
    C) Similarities between users based on their past interactions
    D) Explicit ratings or implicit feedback from users

13. **The "cold start problem" in recommender systems refers to:**
    A) Difficulty in recommending items to new users with limited interaction history
    B) Difficulty in recommending new items that haven't been rated by many users
    C) Both a and b
    D) Neither a nor b

14. **Matrix factorization is a technique used in:**
    A) Content-based filtering only
    B) Collaborative filtering only
    C) Both content-based and collaborative filtering
    D) Neither content-based nor collaborative filtering

15. **Which of the following is NOT an advantage of recommender systems?**
    A) Personalization: Providing relevant recommendations to individual users
    B) Increased sales and conversion rates
    C) Discovery of new items and products
    D) Eliminating the need for human intervention in product recommendations

Answers Key

1. b) Image recognition
2. c) Stemming
3. b) The
4. c) Represent text as a frequency distribution of words
5. c) Recurrent neural network (RNN)
6. c) Cyclicity (not a universal component, only present in some time series)
7. d) Naïve forecast model (assumes future values are equal to the last observed value)

8. b) A better fit between predicted and actual values (lower error means predictions are closer to actual values)
9. d) Predicting daily website traffic with a significant weekly pattern (ARIMA models can capture seasonality)
10. d) Overfitting the model to the training data (a challenge in all machine learning tasks, not specific to time series forecasting)
11. d) Demographic filtering (not a common type)
12. c) Similarities between users based on their past interactions
13. c) Both a and b (cold start affects both new users and new items)
14. b) Collaborative filtering only (used to reduce dimensionality in user-item matrix)
15. d) Eliminating the need for human intervention (not a complete replacement, humans still play a role in system design and optimization)

Some Basic Question

1. Explain how image segmentation is used in medical imaging analysis. What are some specific applications and the potential benefits for patients and healthcare professionals?
2. Explain the concept of ambiguity in natural language and discuss the challenges it poses for NLP tasks like machine translation and sentiment analysis. How do NLP algorithms handle these challenges?
3. Compare and contrast two different approaches to text summarization: abstractive summarization and extractive summarization. Discuss the advantages and disadvantages of each approach.
4. Explain the key components of a reinforcement learning system: agent, environment, states, actions, and rewards. How do these components interact with each other in the learning process?
5. Compare and contrast two different reinforcement learning algorithms such as Q-learning and DQN. Discuss their strengths and weaknesses in different scenarios.
6. Reinforcement learning is often used in situations where the environment is partially observable or dynamic. How do RL algorithms handle these complexities? What are some challenges and potential solutions for learning in such environments?
7. Explain the steps involved in the time-series forecasting process, starting with data collection and preprocessing to model selection, evaluation, and interpretation. What are some important considerations and challenges at each step?

Fill in the Blanks

1. Improving the quality of machine translation systems by using_____ to encode source and target language words.
2. Tokenization is a fundamental task in natural language processing (NLP) that involves_____ a text into smaller units called tokens.
3. _____ involves splitting a paragraph or document into individual sentences.
4. _____ is a method uses global word co-occurrence statistics, capturing semantic relationships based on how often words appear together across the entire corpus.
5. GRUs are another variant of_____ that simplify the architecture compared to LSTMs by combining the input and forget gates into a single update gate.

Answers

1. word embeddings
2. breaking down
3. Sentence tokenization
4. GloVe
5. RNNs

References

[1]   Raschka, S. & Mirjalili, V. (2019). Python Machine Learning: Machine Learning and Deep Learning with Python, Scikit-learn, and TensorFlow 2 (3rd ed.). Packt Publishing.

[2]   Géron, A. (2019). Hands-On Machine Learning with Scikit-Learn, Keras, and TensorFlow: Concepts, Tools, and Techniques to Build Intelligent Systems (2nd ed.). O'Reilly Media.

[3]   Barua, T., Doshi, R. & Hiran, K.K. (2020). Mobile Applications Development: With Python in Kivy Framework Walter de Gruyter GmbH & Co KG.

[4]   Müller, A.C. & Guido, S. (2016). Introduction to Machine Learning with Python: A Guide for Data Scientists O'Reilly Media.

[5]   Testas, A. (2023, November 27). Distributed Machine Learning with PySpark Apress.

[6]   Brownlee, J. (2016). Machine Learning Mastery with Python: Understand Your Data, Create Accurate Models, and Work Projects End-To-End Machine Learning Mastery.

[7]   Hiran, K.K., Doshi, R., Kant, K., Ruchi, H. & Lecturer, D.S. (2013). Robust & Secure Digital Image Watermarking Technique Using Concatenation Process Cloud Computing View Project Digital Image Processing View Project Robust & Secure Digital Image Watermarking Technique Using Concatenation Process. International Journal of ICT and Management, 117, https://www.research gate.net/publication/320404232

[8]   Harrington, P. (2012). Machine Learning in Action Manning Publications.

[9]   Patel, R. (2018). Python Deep Learning: Next Generation Techniques to Revolutionize Computer Vision, AI, and Deep Learning Packt Publishing.

[10] Pedregosa, F., Varoquaux, G., Gramfort, A., Michel, V., Thirion, B., Grisel, O., Blondel, M., Prettenhofer, P., Weiss, R., Dubourg, V., Vanderplas, J., Passos, A., Cournapeau, D., Brucher, M., Perrot, M. & Duchesnay, É. (2011). Scikit-learn: Machine Learning in Python. Journal of Machine Learning Research, 12, 2825–2830.

[11] Aggarwal, C.C. (2018). Python for Data Science: A Guide to Successful Python Tools for Data Science Springer.

[12] Jain, R.K. (2023, April 10). A Survey on Different Approach Used for Sign Language Recognition Using Machine Learning. Asian Journal of Computer Science and Technology, 12(1), 11–15. https://doi.org/10.51983/ajcst-2023.12.1.3554

[13] Vasques, X. (2024, March 6). Machine Learning Theory and Applications John Wiley & Sons.

[14] Wireko, J.K., Hiran, K.K. & Doshi, R. (2018). Culturally Based User Resistance to New Technologies in the Age of IoT in Developing Countries: Perspectives from Ethiopia. International Journal of Emerging Technology and Advanced Engineering, 8(4), 96–105.

[15] Heaton, J. (2018). Introduction to Deep Learning Using Python: A Guide for Data Scientists CreateSpace Independent Publishing Platform.

[16] Jain, R.K., Kant Hiran, K., Maheshwari, R. & Vaishali,. (2023, April 20). Lung Cancer Detection Using Machine Learning Algorithms. 2023 International Conference on Computational Intelligence, Communication Technology and Networking (CICTN), https://doi.org/10.1109/cictn57981.2023.10141467

[17] VanderPlas, J. (2016). Python Data Science Handbook: Essential Tools for Working with Data O'Reilly Media.

[18] LeCun, Y., Bengio, Y. & Hinton, G. (2015). Deep Learning. Nature, 521(7553), 436–444.

[19] Jain, R.K. & Agarwal, V. (2023, May 24). Comparative Analysis of Visual Positioning Techniques for Indoor Navigation Systems. Asian Journal of Engineering and Applied Technology, 12(1), 18–22. https://doi.org/10.51983/ajeat-2023.12.1.3596

[20] Bengio, Y. (2009). Learning Deep Architectures for AI. Foundations and Trends® in Machine Learning, 2(1), 1–127.

https://doi.org/10.1515/9783110697186-009

[21] Kingma, D.P. & Ba, J. (2014). Adam: A Method for Stochastic Optimization. arXiv preprint arXiv:1412.6980.

[22] Dadhich, M., Hiran, K.K. & Rao, S.S. (2021). Teaching–learning perception toward blended E-learning portals during pandemic lockdown. In Sharma, T., Ahn, Chang, Verma, O, Panigrahi, B, Soft Computing: Theories and Applications: Proceedings of SoCTA 2020, Volume Vol. 2 (pp. 119–129). Springer Singapore, Singapore.

[23] Hiran, K.K., Henten, A., Shrivas, M.K. & Doshi, R. (2018, August). Hybrid educloud model in higher education: The case of Sub-Saharan Africa, Ethiopia. In Quist-Aphetsi K., Kuada E., 2018 IEEE 7th International Conference on Adaptive Science & Technology (ICAST) (pp. 1–9). IEEE Ghana Section, IEEE.

[24] Mijwil, M.M., Aggarwal, K., Doshi, R., Hiran, K.K. & Sundaravadivazhagan, B. (2022). Deep Learning Techniques for COVID-19 Detection Based on Chest X-ray and CT-scan Images: A Short Review and Future Perspective. Asian Journal of Applied Sciences. 24: Volume 10, Issue 3 (Page. 224-231).

[25] Dadhich, M., Hiran, K.K., Rao, S.S. & Sharma, R. (2022). Factors Influencing Patient Adoption of the IoT for E-health Management Systems (E-hms) Using the UTAUT Model: A High Order SEM-ANN Approach. International Journal of Ambient Computing and Intelligence (IJACI), 13(1), 1–18.

[26] Srivastava, N., Hinton, G., Krizhevsky, A., Sutskever, I. & Salakhutdinov, R. (2014). Dropout: A Simple Way to Prevent Neural Networks from Overfitting. Journal of Machine Learning Research, 15(1), 1929–1958.

[27] Hiran, K.K., Khazanchi, D., Vyas, A.K. & Padmanaban, S. (2021). Machine Learning for Sustainable Development. Machine Learning for Sustainable Development, https://doi.org/10.1515/9783110702514

[28] Saini, H.K., Jain, K.L., Hiran, K.K. & Bhati, A. (2021). Paradigms to Make Smart City Using Blockchain. Blockchain 3.0 For Sustainable Development. 10, p.21.

[29] Tyagi, S.K.S., Mukherjee, A., Pokhrel, S.R. & Hiran, K. (2020a). An Intelligent and Optimal Resource Allocation Approach in Sensor Networks for Smart Agri-IoT. Smart Agri-IoT. I E E E Sensors Journal, 21(16), 17439–17446. https://doi.org/10.1109/JSEN.2020.3020889

[30] Jain, R.K. & Rathi, S.K. (2021). A review paper on sign language recognition using machine learning techniques. In Emerging Trends in Data Driven Computing and Communications (Ed. Mathur, R. et al.) Springer. Page No. 91–98.

[31] Abadi, M., Agarwal, A., Barham, P., Brevdo, E., Chen, Z., Citro, C., Corrado, G.S., Davis, A., Dean, J., Devin, M., Ghemawat, S., Goodfellow, I., Harp, A., Irving, G., Isard, M., Jia, Y., Jozefowicz, R., Kaiser, L., Kudlur, M. & Zheng, X. (2016). TensorFlow: Large-scale Machine Learning on Heterogeneous Systems. Software available from tensorflow.org.

[32] Zeiler, M.D. & Fergus, R. (2014). Visualizing and understanding convolutional networks. In Fleet, D, Pajdla, Schiele, B, Tuytelaars, T European Conference on Computer Vision (pp. 818–833). Springer, Cham.

[33] Prajapati, R.K., Bhardwaj, Y., Jain, R.K. & Kamal Kant Hiran, D. (2023, April 20). A review paper on automatic number plate recognition using machine learning : An in-depth analysis of machine learning techniques in automatic number plate recognition: Opportunities and limitations. In 2023 International Conference on Computational Intelligence, Communication Technology and Networking (CICTN). https://doi.org/10.1109/cictn57981.2023.10141318

[34] Wong, K.K.L. (2023, October 31). Cybernetical Intelligence John Wiley & Sons.

[35] Jain, R. & Hiran, K.K. (2024). BIONET. Advances in Systems Analysis, Software Engineering, and High Performance Computing Book Series. https://doi.org/10.4018/979-8-3693-1131-8.ch004

[36] Simonyan, K. & Zisserman, A. (2014). Very Deep Convolutional Networks for Large-scale Image Recognition. arXiv preprint arXiv:1409.1556.

[37] Acharya, S., Jain, U., Kumar, R., Prajapat, S., Suthar, S. & Jain, R.K. JARVIS: A Virtual Assistant for Smart Communication. ijaem, 3(6), pp. 460–465.

[38] Pajankar, A., & Joshi, A. (2022). Hands-on Machine Learning with Python: Implement Neural Network Solutions with Scikit-learn and PyTorch. apress.

[39] Hochreiter, S. & Schmidhuber, J. (1997). Long Short-term Memory. Neural Computation, 9(8), 1735–1780.

[40] Goodfellow, I., Bengio, Y., Courville, A. & Bengio, Y. (2016). Deep Learning (Adaptive Computation and Machine Learning Series) The MIT Press.

[41] Jain, R.K., Hiran, K. & Paliwal, G. (2012). Quantum Cryptography: A New Generation Of Information Security System. Proceedings of International Journal of Computers and Distributed Systems, ISSN, 2278–5183, 2(1), Page No. 42–45.

[42] Kuhn, M. & Johnson, K. (2013). Applied Predictive Modeling Springer.

[43] Marsland, S. (2015). Machine Learning: An Algorithmic Perspective Chapman and Hall/CRC.

[44] McKinney, W. (2017). Python for Data Analysis: Data Wrangling with Pandas, NumPy, and IPython (2nd ed.). O'Reilly Media.

[45] Hossain, E. (2023, December 26). Machine Learning Crash Course for Engineers Springer Nature.

[46] Russakovsky, O., Deng, J., Su, H., Krause, J., Satheesh, S., Ma, S. & Fei-Fei, L. (2015). ImageNet Large Scale Visual Recognition Challenge. International Journal of Computer Vision, 115(3), 211–252.

[47] Szegedy, C., Liu, W., Jia, Y., Sermanet, P., Reed, S., Anguelov, D. & Rabinovich, A. (2015). Going deeper with convolutions. In Proceedings of the IEEE Conference on Computer Vision and Pattern Recognition IEEE Xplore, USA (pp. 1–9).

[48] Abadi, M., Barham, P., Chen, J., Chen, Z., Davis, A., Dean, J. . . . Kudlur, M. (2016). TensorFlow: A system for large-scale machine learning. In 12th USENIX Symposium on Operating Systems Design and Implementation, USENIX ASSOCIATION, (OSDI 16) (pp. 265–283).

[49] Goodfellow, I., Pouget-Abadie, J., Mirza, M., Xu, B., Warde-Farley, D., Ozair, S. & Bengio, Y. (2014). Generative Adversarial Nets. Advances in Neural Information Processing Systems, 3(11), 2672–2680.

[50] Oliphant, T.E. (2007). Python for Scientific Computing. Computing in Science & Engineering, 9(3), 10–20.

[51] Hiran, K.K. & Doshi, R. (2013). An Artificial Neural Network Approach for Brain Tumor Detection Using Digital Image Segmentation. Brain, 2(5), 227–231.

[52] Hiran, K.K. & Henten, A. (2020). An Integrated TOE–DoI Framework for Cloud Computing Adoption in the Higher Education Sector: Case Study of Sub-Saharan Africa, Ethiopia. International Journal of System Assurance Engineering and Management, 11, 441–449.

[53] Mahrishi, M., Hiran, K.K., Meena, G. & Sharma, P. (Eds.) (2020). Machine Learning and Deep Learning in Real-time Applications IGI global.

[54] Hiran, K.K., Jain, R.K., Lakhwani, K. & Doshi, R. (2021). Machine Learning: Master Supervised and Unsupervised Learning Algorithms with Real Examples (English Edition) BPB Publications.

[55] Chollet, F. (2017). Deep Learning with Python Manning Publications.

[56] Hiran, K.K., Jain, R.K., Lakhwani, K. & Doshi, R. (2021). Machine Learning: Master Supervised and Unsupervised Learning Algorithms with Real Examples BPB Publications.

[57] Bisong, E. (2019, September 27). Building Machine Learning and Deep Learning Models on Google Cloud Platform.

[58] Khazanchi, D., Vyas, A.K., Hiran, K.K. & Padmanaban, S. (Eds.) (2021). Blockchain 3.0 For Sustainable Development Vol. 10 Walter de Gruyter GmbH & Co KG.

[59] Ye, A. & Wang, Z. (2022, December 27). Modern Deep Learning for Tabular Data Apress.

[60] Lakhwani, K., Gianey, H.K., Wireko, J.K. & Hiran, K.K. (2020). Internet of Things (IoT): Principles, Paradigms and Applications of IoT (English Edition).

[61] Hiran, K.K., Doshi, R., Fagbola, T. & Mahrishi, M. (2019). Cloud Computing: Master the Concepts, Architecture and Applications with Real-world Examples and Case Studies Bpb Publications.

[62]   Hiran, K.K. & Doshi, R. (2013). Robust & Secure Digital Image Watermarking Technique Using Concatenation Process. International Journal of ICT and Management. Vol- I, Issue - 2, Page no. 117–121.

[63]   Müller, A.C. (2016). Advanced Machine Learning with Python: Explore the Most Sophisticated Algorithms and Techniques for Building Intelligent Systems Packt Publishing.

[64]   Acharya, R. (2019). Python Data Science Cookbook: Discover the Latest Python Tools and Techniques to Help You Tackle the World of Data Acquisition and Analysis Packt Publishing.

[65]   Priyadarshi, N., Padmanaban, S., Hiran, K.K., Holm-Nielson, J.B. & Bansal, R.C. (Eds.) (2021). Artificial Intelligence and Internet of Things for Renewable Energy Systems Vol. 12 Walter de Gruyter GmbH & Co KG.

[66]   Doshi, R. & Hiran, K.K. (2024). Explainable artificial intelligence as a cybersecurity aid. In Ghonge, M. M., Pradeep, N., Jhanjhi, N., & Kulkarni, P. Advances in Explainable AI Applications for Smart Cities (pp. 98–113). IGI Global.

[67]   Lakhwani, K., Bhargava, S., Somwanshi, D., Doshi, R. & Hiran, K.K. (2020, December). An enhanced approach to infer potential host of coronavirus by analyzing its spike genes using multilayer artificial neural network. In 2020 5th IEEE International Conference on Recent Advances and Innovations in Engineering (ICRAIE) (pp. 1–5). IEEE Delhi Section, India.

[68]   Hardas, M., Mathur, S., Dadhich, M., Bhaskar, A. & Hiran, K.K. (2023, August). Multi-class classification of retinal fundus images in diabetic retinopathy using probabilistic neural network. In 2023 International Conference on Emerging Trends in Networks and Computer Communications (ETNCC) (pp. 275–282). IEEE South Africa Section.

[69]   Narkhede, N., Mathur, S., Bhaskar, A.A., Hiran, K.K., Dadhich, M. & Kalla, M. (2023, August). A new methodical perspective for classification and recognition of music genre using machine learning classifiers. In 2023 International Conference on Emerging Trends in Networks and Computer Communications (ETNCC) (pp. 94–99). IEEE South Africa Section.

[70]   Mijwil, M.M., Hiran, K.K., Doshi, R., Dadhich, M., Al-Mistarehi, A.H. & Bala, I. (2023). ChatGPT and the Future of Academic Integrity in the Artificial Intelligence Era: A New Frontier. *Al-Salam*. Journal for Engineering and Technology, 2(2), 116–127.

[71]   Prajapati, R.K., Bhardwaj, Y., Jain, R.K. & Hiran, K.K. (2023, April). A review paper on automatic number plate recognition using machine learning: An in-depth analysis of machine learning techniques in automatic number plate recognition: Opportunities and limitations. In 2023 International Conference on Computational Intelligence, Communication Technology and Networking (CICTN) (pp. 527–532). IEEE UP section, India.

Index

www.ingramcontent.com/pod-product-compliance
Lightning Source LLC
Chambersburg PA
CBHW080125220326
41598CB00032B/4954